Over But Not Out

Also by Richie Benaud

Over But Not Out

My Life So Far

RICHIE
BENAUD

HODDER

First published in Great Britain in 2010 by Hodder & Stoughton
An Hachette UK company

First published in paperback in 2011

1

ISBN 978 1 444 70593 5
Ebook ISBN 978 1 444 71121 9

Typeset in Sabon by Hewer Text UK Ltd, Edinburgh
Printed and bound by Clays Ltd, St Ives plc

Hodder & Stoughton policy is to use papers that are natural,
renewable and recyclable products and made from wood grown
in sustainable forests. The logging and manufacturing processes are expected
to conform to the environmental regulations of the country of origin.

Hodder & Stoughton Ltd
338 Euston Road
London NW1 3BH

www.hodder.co.uk

DEDICATION

Much of life is unplanned. You might set out determined to pursue a particular course and suddenly it all unravels. At other times what might have started out as lack of planning will be right at the close of a day or even the close of play on a cricket field.

Over the years many people have had a beneficial influence on cricket and the manner in which it is played. Two of those were Ted Dexter and Colin Cowdrey, who conceived the idea of the Spirit of Cricket, which is now written as the Preamble to the Laws of Cricket. It is so good that, as each year passes, it underlines for me that it should be no hardship to embrace the Spirit of Cricket, as well as the winning of the game, for anyone in any way connected with it. In the most subtle fashion possible, Cowdrey and Dexter asked of cricketers whether it is impossible to win a match without what, in these modern times, is known as sledging.

One thing in life you cannot do is choose your parents, but my brother John and I could not have been luckier to have Lou and Rene, who were pioneers in every sense of the word and lived their lives in the way the Spirit of Cricket suggests can be done with the game. Whether it was around the meal table or on any sporting field, they were pioneers in the very best sense of the word; straightforward people, honest, loving and dedicated to bringing up a family and, at the same time, to having a beneficial influence on youngsters they met in classrooms or in life.

They passed on their advice in this way: 'Do your best, never give up and don't take yourselves too seriously.'

ACKNOWLEDGEMENTS

W HEN I mentioned to Daphne in 1998, after *Anything but . . . an Autobiography* was published, that this would be the last time we would write a book she was pleasantly surprised. However, so many things happened in the next six years that *My Spin on Cricket* was written in order to bring things up to date in 2005. Five years on from there, *Over But Not Out* provides a different-style book in that it retains some of the more pertinent aspects of *Anything but . . .* and at the same time introduces different slants on the modern game of cricket.

We have been very lucky over the years that many of the same people have been involved with the books and that the organisation is handled by Vivienne Schuster and Jacquie Drewe of Curtis Brown.

John Benaud again has used his great cricket knowledge and discerning journalistic eye to help commit the pages of transcript to paper, Clare Oldridge in London is our personal assistant and good friend and I still raise a glass with Bob Gray for accidentally coming up with the title of *Anything but . . .* That book was also worked on by our secretary of the time, Margaret Roseland, sadly no longer with us, but missed by all who came into contact with her.

In Australia, our secretary Cathy Mycock is a tower of strength in the office, a delightful friend, a fine golfer and lover of all sport. Daphne, with her knowledge of cricket and of television, her discerning eye with people from all areas and her ability to remain calm is a delight to be with.

Just think of all the fun I've had since walking on to a cricket field to play my first Sheffield Shield match in 1948 and into a television commentary box in 1963 for the BBC.

CONTENTS

Photographic Acknowledgements

The author and publisher would like to thank the following for permission to reproduce photographs:

Philip Brown/Reuters/Action Images, Tim Clayton/Action Images, Gareth Copley/Press Association Images, Nigel French/Empics Sport, Eranga Jayawardena/AP/Press Association Images, Getty Images, Jason O'Brien/ Action Images, Michael Regan/Livepic/Action Images, Clive Rose/Getty Images, Lakruwan Wanniarachchi/AFP/Getty Images, Tim Wimborne/ Reuters/Action Images, Greg Wood/AFP/Getty Images.

All other photographs are from private collections. Illustration by Rodney Paull.

INTRODUCTION

WHAT luck, what good fortune to have meandered through many years working in the television world and the print media in all cricket-playing countries. Writing has always been something special for me, though I know no one should get carried away by working at a job; it is trying to improve that provides the fun. Improvement can be achieved in different ways. Never discard listening as a source of learning. It could be the most important decision you ever make.

Book titles can sometimes be a problem. When *Anything but . . .* went on sale in 1998 very few people thought it a good title. The favourite, before a word was actually written, was *Richie Benaud: My Autobiography*. Mentioned briefly in the Acknowledgements is Robert Gray. Originally we were competitors in the sense that he was the cricket writer for the Sydney *Daily Mirror*; I was the cricket writer for the Sydney *Sun*. We both enjoyed horseracing and having a small bet or two, small being the operative word because we were both on the impecunious side of hard up, but we managed a few winners here and there.

It was Gray who said at Odin's restaurant in London, on 7 July 1997, 'Not an autobiography, Benaud . . . anything but an autobiography.' Out of small paragraphs sometimes are born splendid ideas. And, the title made it through the various meetings at Hodder where Roddy Bloomfield held sway; he also holds sway thirteen years later as the consummate editor. This time he has with him Tim Waller, a younger editor who has done a brilliant job.

One of the lucky things was in 1956 when the rest of the

Australian team went for three weeks' holiday to the Continent. This was because the Australian Board of Control had decreed that on the way home the Australian team would play one Test on the matting in Pakistan and then three other Tests in India. Instead of taking the holiday, I asked Tom Sloan, Head of BBC light entertainment, to construct for me a three-week TV course, 11 a.m. to midnight every day, and, having completed that, I flew to Italy to join the team and on to Pakistan. Television had started that year in Australia, but I never used what I had learned in England over those three weeks until seven years later when I was asked to join the BBC. On returning to Australia in November 1956, Lindsay Clinch, the editor of the *Sun* newspaper, moved me from the counting house to the editorial section to work under Police Roundsman Noel Bailey. It was the most wonderful experience.

There are four men, themselves Test cricketers, who were my mentors. Without their guidance I would never have made the grade. I was lucky enough to play with Arthur Morris, Keith Miller and Ray Lindwall at Sheffield Shield and Test level. Bill O'Reilly was the fourth when, in 1953, he gave up a dinner with his great mate Lindsay Hassett to have dinner with me and explain where I was going wrong with my bowling and how I could put it right. He added, correctly, it would take me four years to achieve. It was a privilege to have been associated with all four of them.

One of my favourite quotes remains: '*In the thirty-five years over which my memory sweeps, cricket has undergone many changes. The game we play today is scarcely like the game of my boyhood. There have been silent revolutions transforming cricket in many directions, improving it in some ways and in others robbing it of some elements of its charm.*' No, it is not the work of some genial and talented journalist wordsmith but the thoughts of W. G. Grace in 1899, the same year that Australian Victor Trumper first toured England. He also wrote about past champions like Alfred Mynn. He said of Mynn that '*he would, I doubt not, stand amazed at the metamorphosis fifty years have effected in cricket. The very ground itself would bewilder him. He played on open*

*commons with rude tents as dressing rooms and the vast enclosure
and palatial pavilion would dazzle his senses.'*

Cricket never ceases to evolve and, as was the case 112 years ago,
it is vital that it continues and it is up to the modern administrators
to make certain that happens. Even more important is that the
administrators are aware of the importance of the traditional part
of the game as well as all the new things that have happened in
recent years.

TWO IMAGES OF CRICKET:
CHEATING . . . AND BRILLIANCE

Match-fixing

It is my belief that when it comes to handing out awards to
those who have done outstanding things for the game of cricket,
the names of two Indian policemen should be noted. They are
not well known. One is Ishwar Singh Redhu, a Delhi-based
crime branch detective, and the other is K. K. Paul, a Joint-
Commissioner of Police. Detective Redhu was investigating
extortion in the Indian business world and, in listening to taped
telephone conversations, he suddenly heard a voice discussing
cricket matches, money and winners and losers of games. He
reported this to K. K. Paul.

Mr Paul was an outstanding investigator, always calm and
dedicated, and on 7 April 2000 he and his team of detectives
charged South African cricket captain Hansie Cronje and three of
his team-mates with being involved in the match-fixing of cricket.
Cronje vehemently denied the accusation. Mr Paul was subjected
to intensive ridicule for twenty-four hours until he released details
of a tape recording of Cronje, on his mobile telephone, speaking in Afrikaans to a punter or bookmaker in South Africa about
match-fixing.

There was no shortage of drama and, on 11 April 2000, Cronje
said he had not been entirely honest in his denials and, in fact, he
had accepted thousands of dollars from a London-based bookmaker for 'forecasting' results.

Then came the King Commission in Johannesburg, at which Cronje pleaded guilty, and the setting up of the ICC's Anti-Corruption and Security Unit under Lord Condon. Lord Condon retired in mid-2010 and was succeeded by Sir Ronnie Flanagan, a former police Chief Constable in Northern Ireland. Sir Ronnie nominated as 'zero tolerance' his approach to match-fixing. This was a timely statement because his taking-over coincided with a blaze of publicity in the United Kingdom about new match-fixing claims.

This was to do with 'spot-fixing', an insidious way of manufacturing an incident which can then be used to wager money with the bookmakers, the advantage being that the punter knows, in advance, what is going to happen. The three Pakistan cricketers alleged to have engaged in spot-fixing were found guilty by the ICC Commission, chaired by Michael Beloff, QC, and the trio have appealed to the Court of Arbitration for Sport in Lausanne, Switzerland. The court will make a decision on whether or not the appeal will be upheld.

My view about those who tarnish the game in this way is that it must be a grim life where you glance in the mirror each morning and are quite uncaring if, despite careful polishing, the reflection still looks grubby.

And I agree with people like Tim May, the Chief Executive of FICA, and David Morgan, who early in 2010 retired as President of the ICC, that everyone needs to be alert because cricket is again under massive threat because of match-fixing.

T20
In the evolution of cricket, nothing has been more important than day-night cricket and T20 matches. In Australia for T20 there have been wonderful crowds of up to 30,000 and Channel 9's research shows clearly that children take their parents to T20 and the reverse is true of Test matches, where parents take their children to the games.

Although techniques are different in the two forms of the game, those adept at 20 overs maximum for an innings can adjust their techniques for first-class and Test cricket. It can, however, be a much more difficult task for a Test cricketer to adapt his game to T20.

1

THE BENAUDS AND THE SAVILLES: PIONEERS

PENRITH in the 21st century is a thriving centre, thirty-four miles to the west of Sydney in New South Wales. At high noon on Monday, 6 October 1930, it was a small and serene town close to the Nepean River, with High Street as its main thoroughfare and several other streets running off what was a friendly hive of activity. There were the usual businesses, an hotel, a newsagent, some general food and produce stores, eating places including Mrs Tipping's popular 'Star' Refreshment Room, and some shops listed as 'Baker and Pastrycook', a saddler's noted as a 'Practical Saddle, Harness and Collar Maker', two cinemas, four shops selling meat and ham, and the business premises of a watchmaker and jeweller, Richard Benaud, full name Richard Grainger Napoleon Benaud, who lived in the flat above with his wife, Nellie. Their daughter-in-law, Irene (*née* Saville), was staying with them because she and her husband, Lou, were about to become parents.

Rene had travelled by train a week earlier from Koorawatha, where there was no resident doctor, and within hours was to have a baby. However, her husband Lou was still in Koorawatha, two hundred miles south-west of Sydney, in the tiny local town of Warrandale where he was the only schoolteacher for a small number of children. School holidays would not start for another six weeks, so there was no chance of modern-day paternity leave for him. Lou received the news the following day that his son Richard had been born, but that it might be some time before we set eyes on one another. During October and November 1930 I stayed in Penrith with my mother, who had been strictly forbidden to take me back to Koorawatha because I was looking, as they say nowadays, 'not too crash-hot', having gone down with a severe bout of gastroenteritis. When eventually, six weeks later, my mother and Lou's sister, Gladys, were allowed to take me back to Koorawatha on the steam train and in a severe heatwave, the medico wished my mother well, but was said to have voiced the private opinion to friends of my grandparents that, sad as it may be, and though he had done his best, he wasn't holding his breath about seeing me again.

It was both an exciting and an unhappy time in Australia; unhappy because of the Great Depression which saw businessmen ruined, families split, and the picture for the future was very gloomy and problematical. Country areas were particularly hard hit, but with many of the residents descended from pioneer stock, they were very resourceful. Living off the land was never better exemplified than in those years in Australia when the Great Depression didn't merely hover over everyone, it wrapped itself around the country, and for a time the continent was all but smothered. Money was scarce, and employment of any kind, along with reasonable health, was the greatest thing that could happen. A two-year drought had turned country areas to a mixture of burnt grass and dust.

It was an exciting time because Australian sporting heroes and aviation pioneers took people's minds off their problems, and the year I was born a youngster named Donald Bradman captivated the country with his batting exploits on the 1930 cricket tour of England.

Around the time that Bradman and others enjoyed the nervous excitement of their first air flights, Major Charles Kingsford Smith was making headlines by flying from England to Australia in an Avro Avian sports plane, and three other British pilots, C. W. Hill, C. J. Chabot and C. E. Pickthorne, were attempting the same journey: Hill, in a Moth, hoping to beat the fifteen days set as a record by Bert Hinkler; the other pair in a two-seater trying to do it in seven days.

The endeavour to conquer the skies reached a climax on the

evening of Monday, 6 October 1930, with the numbing news of the crash and explosion of the R101, the world's largest airship, which came to grief near the French village of Beauvais. Buffeted by high winds and heavy rain it was flying at 55 mph at an altitude of only 300 feet when it hit a hill, forty miles north of Paris. Of the fifty-four on board, forty-six perished in the flames and huge explosions.

On the day I was born this was front-page news around the world in newspapers large and small, one of the latter variety a pink newspaper, pink in colour that is, not politics, the conservative *Richmond River Herald*. It was published in Coraki and had been established by my great-uncle, Louis Ferdinand Branxton Benaud, in 1886. The first issue was a test of nerve and willpower, because the office and the newspaper plant went up in smoke and flames a few hours before the presses were due to run. He set his jaw and pinned on the wall the phrase 'do your best and never give up'.

Louis Ferdinand was the brother of my grandfather, Richard Grainger Napoleon Benaud, and the son of Captain Jean Benaud, who had named his children so his original French heritage would be maintained.

My ancestors the Benauds and the Savilles had come to Australia at roughly the same time. James and Martha Saville had seventeen children in the sixty-nine years they were married before James passed away aged ninety-four. Martha died three years later aged ninety-two. Ten children survived James and there were seventy-eight grandchildren and seventy-six great-grandchildren. The eleventh of the seventeen children was George Saville, born on 28 January 1872, and he married Lillian White; they were my mother's parents.

The Savilles journeyed on the SS *Euphrates* in 1855, after emigrating from England where the family farmed in Langley and Ely in Essex. At Langley, in the mid-1800s, living conditions were said to be mediocre and wages poor, and in the case of the Saville family, there were now too many children to farm the same amount of land. Their new life in Australia must have been something of a shock to them, and despite their determination and acceptance of the obvious challenges, they knew what they were undertaking would be far from easy.

The Savilles were pioneers, in the sense that almost immediately following their arrival in Sydney they joined a bullock wagon-train and made their way 500 miles to the north. James Saville worked for five years for a farmer, Mr Ogilvie, as stockman, blacksmith and general factotum at 'The Ten Mile' station. James's wages were 25 shillings a week and a double ration of flour, tea, meat and jam. They then moved to Gordonbrook station, which was owned by Mr Frank Bundock, for another ten years, where James continued his work.

There was nothing fancy about the food in those early days in Australia. It was said the outback was under the yoke of a 'muttonous' diet, and the Savilles and other newcomers quickly became used to its chewy qualities. I particularly like the name given to one such dish: they called it 'The Old Thing', and it consisted only of mutton and damper, a light, flat bread about two inches thick and eighteen inches wide, which if poorly cooked in the campfire was heavy enough to be known as 'buggers on the coals'. As a schoolboy, I had a liking for damper, but it has gone out of fashion now with the arrival of some very good hot bread shops, such as Baker's Delight, the one we use in Coogee Bay Road.

In September 1861, six years after the Savilles arrived in the area, Casino's first representative cricket match was played, a return game for one played in Grafton in July that year; the matches were between two teams from the districts of the Clarence River and the Richmond River. To travel to Casino from Grafton, the Clarence team had to ford rapid-flowing creeks, boggy roads and rest jaded horses. On arrival all the problems were forgotten in the euphoria of the contest and the festivities which were held in their honour at the Durham Ox hostelry opposite the ground.

The cricket ground with the pub alongside was a reminder of their English village life, something jealously guarded by writers of the time. Four years before the Savilles' arrival in Australia, the Rev. James Pycroft, BA, wrote in *The Cricket Field* in high praise of the English heritage, but with scant regard for the enthusiastic and ambitious Associate and Affiliate European Members of the modern-day ICC, 'No single cricket club have we ever heard dieted either with frogs, sour crout or macaroni.'

1861 was an important year in Australia: the first Melbourne Cup had already been won in November by Archer, but sadly, 1861 also marked the deaths of the two explorers, Burke and Wills, who perished trying to cross the continent so others would eventually know the extent of the vast land.

In cricket, that first representative match in the Northern Rivers area preceded by only 116 days the first game of cricket ever played between an English team and one from an Australian colony. It was in late 1861 that Spiers & Pond, the British catering firm with a branch office in Melbourne, decided to sponsor a team to visit Australia. The players departed England on the steamship *Great Britain* on 18 October 1861, arrived in Melbourne to a tumultuous welcome on Christmas Eve, were magnificently fêted during most of the hours between then and the start of their match, and still managed to win! They were 116 years in advance of World Series Cricket, for they played in coloured clothing with different coloured hatbands and sashes so they could be identified by spectators.

After their ten-year stint was up at Gordonbrook, the Savilles applied, with a mixture of trepidation and excitement, to select, or to be allowed to purchase a lease on, a block of farming land at One Tree in the Richmond River area. It was as it sounded, land with one proper tree, a solitary and large gum on an open flat, and much frequented by the cattle for the shade it afforded. In 1870 they moved on to the bare land at One Tree Farm seven miles from Casino, and it was thirty-two years before they actually owned the selection.

The Savilles eventually moved into dairy farming, which was all done by hand, and James Saville's six horses and flat dray were a familiar sight as he took his cases of butter and cheese into the co-op or to private sale. All travel was by spring-cart, horse and dray, horseback, or by Shanks's pony. The production of the cheese was a good example of pioneering and innovation: it was made in the stump of a hollow tree, with a block of wood at the cool base on which the cheese vat was placed. A bag of stones was then lowered on to the vat by use of a long pole and pressure was exerted. They were able to make only one cheese a day using that innovative method, although no one in the family now seems certain if that was because there was only one suitable hollow tree stump or that the volume of available curds was insufficient for something more grandiose.

Life was interesting for my mother's antecedents the Savilles: James, a tall, sinewy character with a built-in refusal to be beaten at anything, and Martha, hard-working and supportive, and, judging from a glance at the family tree, keen to start some kind of minor dynasty in the new country. Life was also tough.

Captain Jean Arthur Albert Benaud, born in Bordeaux, became a naturalised citizen of Australia in 1849, nine years after he arrived on the vessel *Ville de Bordeaux*. For many years Captain Benaud traded between Sydney and the Richmond and Manning rivers in his ketch *Lightning* and was one of the characters of the Northern Rivers. His son Louis Ferdinand was only three when Jean died, but Louis made sure twenty years later that the shipping section of the *Richmond River Herald* was outstanding and interesting reading, although that always sounded a complete contradiction in terms to me, until I read E. Annie Proulx's *The Shipping News*.

Jean Benaud loved horses and was a keen horseracing man. As soon as any ship of which he was captain reached Taree on his trips up and down the coast, he would rent a horse and go for long rides in the bush. He was killed in an accident when thrown from a horse in Pulteney Street, Taree, after returning from a race meeting in nearby Wingham on 3 July 1866. He was in a coma for three days before the effects of the fractured skull proved too much. Two of his children were Louis Ferdinand the newspaper founder and Richard Grainger Napoleon the jeweller and watch-maker, my grandfather.

On 18 July 1925, in Sydney, there was some laughter and chiack-ing when the assembled Teachers' College graduates heard the first announcement of their initial postings and that their co-graduate Lou Benaud would be going to what sounded a remote spot, One Tree. In fact, they had forgotten he was born down the road from what was to be his first teaching school. Coraki might have been a very small place, but it made up in warmth and care what it might have lacked in numbers and my father often told me of what a wonderful childhood he was given there by his parents and his friends. Perhaps that was one of the reasons he and my mother tried to make the same thing happen for me and for John in later years. Lou was one of a number of kids in the town who played cricket on the grassy area between the main street and the river. The south arm of the Richmond river was joined at Coraki by the north arm and then it was used by ships and river boats as a way to reach Lismore. 'Coraki' itself is an aboriginal name which means 'meeting of the water'.

Richard and Nellie Benaud, and their children Jack, Gladys and Lou, lived on the western bank of the river in a weatherboard home with a surrounding verandah, with the front facing in such a way that the sun burst on them early in the morning. In the account left by my father, *The Kid From Coraki*, the children never seemed to have a moment to spare in any day. They were always *doing* something, making their own fun. Cricket was played using bats home-made from carefully cut packing case material, knotty river-bank willow or lantana roots. Stumps were kerosene tins, and tennis balls were used.

Richard Grainger Napoleon Benaud, my grandfather the watchmaker, made Lou and his brother Jack a clockwork boat each, which they started sailing in a large bathtub before graduat-ing to the river, where they always made certain they had strong, light thread attached to the tiny vessels so they could be retrieved in case of sinking in some rough water. Sugarcane was shipped downstream on the south arm of the river and pieces were thrown on to the bank for the congregating children to sample, and every weekend picnics were organised by the Benauds and their friends the McCallums to go up the South Arm. The two large rowing boats went up the river past the goannas lying along the tree limbs, past the masses of redbills, water hens and shags, and the clever thing was to spot the mopokes high in the trees, the birds' feathers blending perfectly with the foliage.

Richmond Terrace was the hub of Coraki and Lou's favourite shop was the one owned and run by his mother Nellie. Many of the items in the shop were still brought by ship from Sydney, in the same way as many years earlier, Captain Jean Benaud had brought goods up the coast. In 1910 there was Turkish Delight, Bulgarian rock, marshmallows, Tobler's Swiss chocolates, diamond jubes and liquorice belts and pipes. The most popular items, and the best sellers, were Nellie Benaud's home-made meat pies, plus her special vanilla ices, which were churned by whichever member of the family might be available – these were regarded by customers on the river as outstanding.

Aged sixteen, older brother Jack left school wanting to be a postmaster and accepted a job in the post office at Bangalow, a town near Byron Bay north of Casino.

Richard Grainger Napoleon Benaud accepted the position of manager of a jewellery and watchmaking business at Grafton, a hundred miles to the south on the Clarence River. Nellie, Glad and Lou went to Penrith on holiday to have a look, for the future, at a town my grandmother knew well, as she had been born not far away on the other side of the Blue Mountains, at Lithgow. Lou thought he could never feel sadder than when Jack went to Bangalow, but the day the family left Coraki for ever, he felt, aged thirteen, his heart would break. He had to say goodbye to his schoolboy friends, farewell to the place he loved and to the newsagent's little fox terrier called Toby who, for most of both their lives, had followed Lou all around Coraki every day.

Just as twilight was settling, the three Benauds went to

Government Wharf and the drogher took them to Oakland where the steamer was already loading cargo. Nellie, Glad and Lou boarded the ship and went to their cabins.

'That night, as the ship steamed down the Richmond, I lay on my bunk and wept quietly in the realisation that it was farewell to Coraki and all it meant to me – a beautiful place where two streams met, inhabited by wonderful, happy and friendly folk who had made my boyhood a time to cherish.'

Eight years later, in 1925, he was to return, not as a boy, but a man, and was to start a new, exciting and, at the same time, frustrating period of his life.

2

LOU BENAUD: CRICKET AND OTHER THINGS

L OU travelled for thirty-three hours by ship from Sydney to Byron Bay after being informed of his teaching posting to One Tree, then had a further train journey to Casino. Having been born in that part of the world my father knew the area well, and despite the absence of the bright lights and brighter living of Sydney, he loved it as a young man and soon came to like it very much as a workplace. The reason for that was the people. Country people in Australia have great character and have always enjoyed welcoming strangers into their midst and making them feel part of the family. Life became a mixture of teaching the thirty-four children in the eighteen-foot-square schoolhouse and mixing socially in the sports events and community activities which made living in the country such a pleasure.

In all the stories my father told me of the cricketers of that time on the northern coast, one of the names which kept cropping up was Sam Anderson, and another, slightly less prominent, Alex James. Sam Anderson and Alex James were aboriginals. James died aged seventy-two and Anderson was seventy-nine when he passed away and, in a poignant farewell poem, Keith Barker wrote in part:

> . . . They found him dead in a drover's shack,
> on a lonely road, off the beaten track . . .
> . . . They buried him down at Coraki
> and few were there, to grieve and cry . . .
> . . . They won't care if his skin was black,

Or that he came to them from a drover's shack,
For they judge men, up there, by their deeds they say
and Sam was a champion in his day.

My father was sure Sam Anderson was good enough to play Sheffield Shield cricket, and possibly for Australia, but one of the main problems he faced was homesickness. Anderson was in his forties when my father played against him, although he had watched him play many times before that. Anderson went to Sydney at one stage to play cricket but soon returned to the north of NSW because of loneliness and a thorough dislike of the city life compared to the countryside. My father said, 'Given a chance, he could have been a champion.'

By coincidence Bradman, in those days a New South Wales player, several times found himself in the north of the state around the Casino, Lismore area. In May 1929, on a short coaching tour after the cricket season had ended, he listened to entreaties from the locals and was kind enough to rearrange an extremely tight schedule to play for the Railway team against the Butter Factory side; he made a duck off the 'trial ball' bowled by 'Snakey' Marshall, a medium-pace bowler of off-cutters. After that reprieve he then made a stylish 31 and, with his leg-breaks, took 7–4 when the Butter Factory batted. The crowds were large and appreciative when Bradman toured England in 1930, but the *real* old-timers on the north coast still talk about that Railway versus Butter Factory game the previous year as more of a highlight than the 1930 Australian tour of England.

Charlie Macartney was one of Bradman's favourite cricketers and my father's as well. Separately each had seen Macartney bat during the final Test at the SCG (Sydney Cricket Ground) in 1921 when he made 170: Bradman taken from Bowral to the SCG by his father George, Lou given the trip as a seventeenth-birthday present by Richard Grainger and Nellie. Macartney was in wonderful form when my father watched him late on the first day and, with 33,000 others, for almost four hours on the second. Whenever I asked my father about the great players, he would name Bill O'Reilly as the finest bowler he saw or occasionally played against, and Don Bradman as the greatest batsman he ever watched. And he would always add, as if not to do so would be disloyal to the 'Governor-General' he had seen on his birthday trip, 'But Charlie Macartney, when I watched him, was wonderful. It's difficult to believe anyone could be a better batsman.'

While he was at One Tree Farm on his teaching duties Lou also played for the Combined Casino side against a Combined New South Wales team on the Recreation Ground at Lismore. Captained by Australian Test cricketer Alan Kippax, the NSW side won, though not by much, 224 to 212. My father took 3–65 and made 39*, a good performance. At the end of the game Kippax called him into the opposition dressing-room and congratulated him on what he had done, adding that if Lou were thinking of coming to Sydney he could arrange for him to play with a Sydney club. This led to a variety of invitations to attend bowling talent quests in the city, but not only did the NSW education department decline to send him anywhere near Sydney, they flatly refused him permission even to have leave to bowl at the SCG in front of the NSW state selectors. It was very much a case of, 'Benaud, your application for leave is refused and if you don't like it, there are plenty of others ready to do your school-teaching job!'

In some ways things haven't changed a great deal. Half a century later when there was a fracas between the Australian Cricket Board and the players, a prominent Australian cricket administrator said to Rodney Marsh, 'Rodney, if you don't like the present payscale, there are plenty of others ready to do it for nothing.'

After Bradman's wonderful tour of England the year I was born, he noted in his book *My Cricketing Life* that no Australian cricketer can give reasonable service to his employer during those touring months. 'In view of the terrific strain on modern players, amidst the fierce glare of publicity, this is a subject which will become of increasing importance as time goes on for there are fewer players each year who can afford the luxury of Test cricket,' he added.

There was no better example of the financial gulf between players and administrators than in one of the best attended Test series in the history of Australian cricket, the Ashes battle in 1936–37 with Bradman captaining Australia. The eighteen Australian players who took part in the five Tests received, between them, £1,800. Gate takings were £90,000.

It is hardly surprising I recall nothing of Koorawatha or of Warrandale, having left there before I turned two years of age, but I do remember Jugiong on the Murrumbidgee River quite well, although the memory is typical of a youngster approaching the age of seven. Seen through the eyes of a boy, things always appear bigger than is actually the case. I always had the impression the Jugiong schoolhouse was vast, but as a hollyhock in the garden was taller than I was, that is understandable. I went back to have a look at the schoolhouse in 1965 and it seemed tiny, although in fact it was, if anything, a little larger than in 1938, when we had departed; the peppercorn tree in the playground was massive and the extension to the verandah at the front was small.

We used to play cricket and rounders and vigoro, an Australian game not dissimilar to cricket though the pitch is only nineteen yards long instead of twenty-two. There are stumps and bails at each end, but the players bowl from only one end.

The temperatures were extreme in Jugiong. In the winter one of the delightful things for a little boy was to make a glass of milk with vanilla and sugar before going to bed, and then to put it, with a saucer on top, outside the back door. In the morning the milk would be frozen into an ice block.

In the summer there was no shortage of snakes. Occasionally one could be seen from the back window and there was one day when my father had to go up to the back paddock at the top of the hill to check on where our dog had gone. Nipper in fact was up there with a snake and either he had the snake bailed up, or the reverse applied. My father had taken a spade with him and in the end he accounted for the snake and carried it on the spade, down the hill and past the kitchen window. It was one of the most menacing sights I have seen, even though it was dead!

My memories of Jugiong are good, possibly because one of the things my parents did was empty a small room of pieces of furniture and knick-knacks and encourage me to throw a ball against one of the walls and hit it when it came back at me. In that room my father showed me how to hold the bat correctly and how I should bowl, and he kept an eye on me to make sure I was doing it roughly along proper lines. At the weekends when the Jugiong team played cricket, I would have a ball tossed underarm to me, although I found it more difficult with a bat which came up to my chest, rather than the smaller one Dad had made for storeroom use.

The teams I made up at that stage were taken from a book my father kept called *The Australian Team in England, 1934*, produced by the Australian Broadcasting Commission in Sydney. It had about fifty pages with drawings and some blank scoring pages on which my father had written out the names of the Australian and English players in large capital letters.

My first memory of participation in any kind of sports event was when Jugiong played against Bookham School at cricket and tennis and, aged six, I partnered May Purtell, who was eight, in a mixed doubles event. We played against two twelve-year-olds and beat them six–love. Shortly after that I played cricket for Jugiong School and made 12 runs, but that was the extent of my competitive sport before we made our way to the big metropolis.

At our home in Jugiong we had a massive Kreisler radio, on which we listened to the ABC Radio broadcasts of the Sheffield Shield and Test matches. My father had heard some Test matches from England in 1934 when the ABC had provided simulated broadcasts organised by Charles Moses. We also heard some of the 1936–37 Test matches in Australia, when Bradman's team, after being two down in the series, came back to win the last three. Aged six, and having made 12 runs in the match at Jugiong School, I knew I was listening to something good on the radio, but how good I only really found out in later years. Alan McGilvray's voice was one I heard at Sheffield Shield matches, although that didn't really strike a chord with me at the time; later I was to regard him as one of the finest of all radio broadcasters. A voice which stayed more in my memory then was that of Mel Morris, a Victorian with a deep-voiced delivery, fascinating listening for a six-year-old.

From 1932 to 1936 the Jugiong team played regular competition matches against Berremangra, Murrumburrah, Harden, Binalong, Gundagai, Cooney's Creek, Cunningham Creek, Muttama, Yass and Bookham, all of them captivating names. At the end of each season, Jugiong played a match against Manly, a team from the Sydney club competition. They called themselves the Manly Ramblers, though were not to be confused in Jugiong with the Harden Ramblers, who were not nearly as convivial a bunch. Those Manly Ramblers, under the leadership of Len Ray, were an outstanding group of city slickers, combining the playing and socialising in perfect fashion. They played the game hard, but in a happy frame of mind and it was competitive, but great fun.

One of the occasional players for Manly, and an enthusiast from Sydney, was 'Banna' Edwards, who was from the Central Cumberland Club and was headmaster of Burnside Public School. He knew my father because of Lou's previous association with Parramatta High School where Lou was a pupil in the 1923–24 season and had taken all 20 wickets in a match in the Penrith area when playing for Penrith Waratah against St Mary's in a club competition. This was a remarkable achievement, and the ensuing publicity resulted in Dad playing for the Central Cumberland first-grade side in the last match of that season. Having spotted my father's talent and great enthusiasm for cricket, Edwards was instrumental in August 1937 in having us move from Jugiong to North Parramatta. This was a double benefit for my father, who was able to teach at Burnside and also play for Cumberland again, although no one at that stage thought of representative honours.

*   *   *

My father was good enough to play first grade at the start of the season in October, then played two matches in the seconds, where he took 11 wickets and was back to the firsts, finishing with 26 wickets for the season in the premier grade. One of the things my father talked about during and outside mealtimes, which were some of the many occasions cricket was discussed in our home, was the quality of the pitches, better than anything he had previously encountered. Cumberland's home pitches were at Parramatta and Lidcombe and their preparation was in the hands of Phil Connolly and Bert Drew, two outstanding groundsmen, so good that other clubs around Sydney looked forward to their matches at either ground, both in that summer and in 1938–39.

I have never forgotten one Cumberland match of those times, because it involved Bradman. He was taking part in a Sheffield Shield match in Brisbane the same day as Cumberland played Randwick at Kensington Oval, rather than Coogee, normally Randwick's home ground. Cumberland bowled out Randwick for a moderate score and then the news came through that a bowler named Jack Stackpoole, making his Sheffield Shield debut, had dismissed Bradman in Brisbane, caught at short-leg first ball. My father said this was very unusual, but it was bad news for a nine-year-old, because Bradman was my hero. Worse was to come. My hero in the Cumberland side, Jack Fitzpatrick, was also out for a duck, bowled late in the day by Randwick fast bowler Charlie McLaughlin. It was a miserable trip home.

Those first two summers gave my father a good grounding in Sydney club cricket, and the following summer, in 1939–40, he did very well, falling only four wickets short of the first-grade club record of 56 wickets established in 1913–14 by Rupert Coogan. In the *Cumberland Annual Report* it was mentioned of Lou that 'he achieved a marvellous feat to obtain 52 wickets, and although one of the club's most successful bowlers, he is also one of the most unfortunate as numerous catches were dropped off him.'

I was only nine at the time, but was already playing backyard cricket and back verandah Test matches at Sutherland Road, using the 1938 *NSW Cricket Association Yearbook* for my teams. That yearbook contained all the scoreboards from the 1936–37 Test series in Australia. I had an *Unrivalled Pocket Cricket Scoring Book* and used to take it to the matches with my father and, in the same way as you see some of the youngsters doing on television these days, I would score throughout the match.

Nine-year-olds had a good time in those days, not understanding what people were talking about when they mentioned a World War was about to start. Life was all about playing sport: non-stop cricket in the summer, and football in the winter in the paddocks across the way from Sutherland Road. Cricket was always a real challenge. Sometimes we would play on the pitch we had manufactured in the paddock, using a shovel as a leveller and occasionally we were allowed to borrow a tennis court roller to flatten down a few of the bumps. We also played down at Belmore Park, a few hundred yards away from my parents' home where now there is the sign 'Belmore Park and Richie Benaud Oval'.

For children like me, everything was geared to sport, to listening to the radio, mystery stories on the airwaves, comedies like *Yes What?* where the pupils were allowed to be cheeky to the teachers, but then invariably were caned for being so. It was the radio, in those days called the wireless, which kept us all in touch with the world. There was a lot of sport on the radio throughout the week, and in the winter Andy Flanagan gave a wonderful rendition of the game of rugby league he had watched that day, referees' whistles and all. The cinema was popular in Parramatta. There were three of them, the Roxy, which was the high-class one, the Astra and the Civic. I secretly wanted to go to the Civic because it might be showing something like *Dracula's Sister Meets Frankenstein's Brother*, but my parents only allowed me to go to the Roxy, or sometimes the Astra, where, as though by magic, the electric organ and organist would appear from the area below the stage, and play tunes.

It was during the 1939–40 season that I saw my first Sheffield Shield match. It was between New South Wales and South Australia and it was played at the Sydney Cricket Ground, a place up to that moment I had never seen. The game had a profound effect on me. It was played early in January 1940 and the participation of Bradman and other stars like McCabe and O'Reilly produced the second 75,000 match crowd that summer for a Shield game. That was the day when I first felt the urge to bowl leg-breaks, after watching Clarrie Grimmett bowl out NSW, taking 6–118 from 22 overs. The NSW spinners, O'Reilly and Pepper, took ten and six wickets respectively in the match and NSW won by 237 runs, after Grimmett had bowled them out in their first innings for 270.

The NSW victory gave them the Sheffield Shield, though that didn't mean a great deal to me then; nor did I know that the NSW opening batsman, Mort Cohen, who was making his debut and joined a select group of cricketers by making the two highest individual scores in the match, was later to be my accountant and a very good friend. I didn't see much of Bradman on the first day because NSW won the toss and batted, although he did come in late in the day and was 24 not out at the close of play. Bill O'Reilly took his ten wickets in wonderful attacking style, but it was Grimmett who caught my imagination because I actually watched him do it in the first innings, bowling from the Sheridan End where we were seated on the stairway of the stand of the same name. It was a delightful day, very much a wide-eyed nine-year-old's day, and when we arrived back at Sutherland Road I had wondrous stories to tell my mother. I can still remember the names of the players in that match and the twelfth men; for many years they held pride of place in my little scorebook.

In those days there were no club games for Cumberland when there were top-line Sheffield Shield matches, so we were able to go to the SCG again when Victoria were the visitors a fortnight later. I watched Doug Ring take four wickets, without dreaming for a moment that I would tour England with him and Lindsay Hassett thirteen years later. This was the match where Hassett made 122 in each innings. Because of the war, this was the last such competition until 1946–47. In retrospect, one of the interesting things about the match was that Keith Miller didn't bowl at all. In fact, he didn't bowl in any first-class match up to the war. It was with the Services team in the UK in 1945 that he first began bowling and *Wisden* said of him, 'As an opening bowler he was the liveliest seen in England during the summer.' The Almanack added, with an eye to the future, 'He is destined to become one of the great men of Australian cricket.'

During my penultimate year at Burnside School, where my father was still teaching, we won our own little competition. I was hoping to do well enough scholastically at Burnside the following year to be able to gain a place at Parramatta High School, which my father had attended. The Burnside team had some great games at different grounds and against different schools. Generally the outfields were of paspalum, sometimes mown, sometimes not, and the pitches were always concrete, which was an interesting exercise because there was a great deal of bounce from the surface. The match was usually played with a ball made of cork and some rubber. I was bowling offspin and slow medium pace at this stage – my father wouldn't allow me to bowl leg-breaks because of the damage I might do to my muscles, ligaments and tendons at such a young age. That was some of the best parental control I ever had, although, like all youngsters, I occasionally sneaked a leg-break in the garden cricket at Sutherland Road.

Two of the players in the Burnside team were brothers, Harold and Laurence Barnes, both good cricketers. In 1997–98, when ACT made their debut in the Mercantile Mutual Cup in Australia, the match was played at the beautiful Manuka Oval in Canberra. Before the match started, a chap came to the commentary box and said, 'You won't remember me. My brother and I played with you at Burnside.'

'Then you must be a Barnes,' I said. 'But which one?'

'Harold,' was the answer, and he lived at Eugowra, eighty-five miles north of Jugiong. It was fifty-six years since I had seen him.

3

BIG SCHOOL FOR
A LITTLE BOY

I N 1941, my last year at Burnside, I sat for the entrance examination, found I had passed, and was able to attend Parramatta
High School, although it was said I might be considered too young
because I had only turned eleven on 6 October 1941. Early in 1942
I caught the bus from Sutherland Road to the railway station, and
walked up to Parramatta High School with my entrance papers.
With a great deal of trepidation, I joined something like another
hundred students, all of us hoping this would be the start of a
splendid learning process. I also hoped there would be plenty of
sport to play. My father made sure I was able to play tennis and
football, as well as cricket, although my footballing was generally
restricted to soccer, rather than rugby, because of a hernia problem I had as a youngster.

On my first day at high school, smallest person of the intake, I
was sitting on a two-foot high wall feeling lonely, eating the sandwiches my mother had packed in my small Globite suitcase, when
another student sat down next to me and said, 'Hello, my name's
Doug Milner, I'd like to be friends with you.' I could hardly have
been more pleased at the time, and in later years as well.

Doug was a very good friend and we played cricket together,
soccer against one another and visited each other's homes in
Parramatta and Lidcombe, where Doug lived. His family was of
Scottish descent and his mother and father were delightful people,
warm and welcoming. He turned out to be a *much* better student
than I was, but we had five very good years at Parramatta High.

Both of us played soccer at the weekends, and our clubs were in the Churches' competition, which, year after year, produced some excellent players. I played with St Andrew's Parramatta. Doug's team, Lidcombe Presbyterian, was strong and it used to be the highlight of the season when we met in a sort of 'local derby'. The matches were tough and generally Lidcombe beat us, although we did have one or two successes. They had a couple of players who went on to far greater things in the football world. One Parramatta High School student who started in 1941 also went on to greater things – Rod Taylor became a very successful actor in Hollywood, starring in several prominent films and series.

The war was now coming closer as far as Australians were concerned, although at that stage Japan hadn't entered the battle in the Pacific. At Sutherland Road we had built an air-raid shelter and made notes of the air-raid precautions. Then, in December 1941, the Japanese bombed Pearl Harbor, which meant the Americans came into the war as well. It was a good thing they did, because without America's assistance, Australia would have been quickly over-run and we would now be under Japanese dominance.

Sport and schoolwork kept us busy, and our history and geography lessons were now partly geared to wars and how world maps had changed over the centuries. We were suddenly aware of the awful possibilities if Singapore fell to the Japanese, and this was underlined by the first bombing of Darwin in February 1942, and then on fifty more occasions. New Guinea was invaded a month after the first Japanese bombs fell on Darwin. It was three long years before Japan surrendered on 2 September 1945, one of the most momentous and celebratory days I have known.

The cricket in Sydney in 1940–41 and 1941–42 consisted of two-day club matches, but 1942–43 saw the advent of one-day cricket, or, as it was called then, one-afternoon cricket. It was exciting, too, although the traditionalists disliked it. My father preferred two-day matches but enjoyed the one-dayers and was very successful at this shortened version of the game, taking 78 wickets for the season at 11.6; he took 32 wickets in first grade and 46 in the seconds when the selectors for some extraordinary reason decided they would play an extra medium-pacer in first grade instead of the spinner. Record club attendances were the rule, and spectators, paying their sixpence at the gate, were guaranteed a result and watched a lot of exciting cricket. There were twenty-three matches in the season and Bill O'Reilly's club, St George, were first grade, second grade and Club Championship winners.

In the 1942–43 season, which spanned my first year at high school and the start of the second, I scored for Cumberland second-grade team, a jump up from the *Unrivalled Pocket Cricket Scoring Book* to the *Unrivalled Scoring Book, Full Size*. I had a wonderful season, because in addition to the scoring I was allowed to field if any of the players either turned up late or hadn't been able to get leave from the Services; once I was able to field throughout the match, which meant someone else scoring, but it was heaven.

Sometimes I went to the matches with Jack O'Donoghue, the second-grade captain. I always dressed carefully in white shirt, light fawn or white shorts, white socks and sandshoes so that I could have some fielding practice with the team before the start, and if it happened someone had been unable to turn up on time, I was dressed properly to go on the field.

Better than heaven was when the team was one short and, aged twelve, I was allowed to bat for Cumberland against Petersham in 1942, at Petersham Oval. I took quite a good catch off my father's bowling when they batted and then, with nine wickets down, I went out to bat. We needed four runs and I had one ball to play in the over. Everyone was crouched around, I played forward and dropped the ball at my feet. Milton Jarrett, the big hitter and medium-pace bowler, took strike at the other end, smashed the first ball for six and the game was over. It was like playing in a Test match, or so it seemed at the time. When I walked off the field Milton Jarrett looked ten feet tall. I felt the same, and there was no happier twelve-year-old in Sydney.

The season commencing October 1943 was a great one for me. I was in second year at Parramatta High School, had just turned thirteen years of age, was captain of the fourth-grade cricket team at school, played again for a schools' representative team and was told by my parents I was about to have a brother or sister. This was excellent news, even though, if the former, it would be a few years before we were able to play cricket with one another, but it all sounded good. Certainly it did nothing but good for my fitness because apart from playing cricket in the daylight, there were long walks to be undertaken every evening as part of my mother's fitness regime.

My mother and father were approaching forty at this time, and John's birth in May of 1944 was great for both of them. We didn't know it at the time, but JB was to go to Parramatta High School eleven years later, play cricket for NSW and Australia and become one of the most respected journalists and editors in NSW newspapers.

The schools' representative match was played at Chatswood Oval between a Combined High Schools' team and the premiers, North Sydney Boys' High, managed by Arthur Henry, a prominent rugby and cricket figure. I returned home only half happy, having made a few runs but having 40 smashed off 10 overs. At the other end, Phil Tresidder, later to become a close friend of Daphne's and mine, took 8–32 from 15 overs of excellent pace bowling.

I scored again for Cumberland seconds that summer, and Doug Milner and I had a wonderful day at North Sydney Oval No. 2 when the side was two men short and we had to go in to bat at a crucial time, with wicketkeeper Joe Anderson the last of the recognised batsmen at the crease. Doug made ten and I made five, more off the edge than the centre of the bat, but it didn't matter at all to us, nor to the skipper Phil Bowmer who had a 'well done' and a pat on the back for us.

For Doug and me it was a marvellous afternoon. At the end of the summer it was very sad to realise there would be no more cricket for several months, though there was always football, and Doug and I went off to play for our respective clubs, and against one another when that local derby came along.

The first two years at high school had been wonderful: I thoroughly enjoyed the schoolwork, and every other available moment was taken up either playing and practising cricket, or, in the football season, having long practice sessions with a very good friend, Lloyd Blain. Lloyd played for St Andrew's at right-half as it was known in those days, and we would ride our bikes a few miles down into Parramatta Park where the soccer goalposts had been set up by the Parramatta Council, and practise taking penalties and dribbling the ball.

The following summer, 1944–45, was a little different. It was decided I would play cricket at school as usual, and rather than score at weekends for Cumberland seconds, I would play in the local junior competition on the matting pitches, where instead of bowling spin, I would bowl with the new ball, something I thoroughly enjoyed. I also liked batting on coir matting, the aim of this being to improve my back-foot play, because the ball lifted relatively sharply off the mat. As the usual flat and grassless turf pitches meant front-foot play was the norm, particularly early in the summer, this matting cricket was to provide a different type of challenge.

It was a successful summer, and, aged fourteen, I played Green Shield (Under-16) matches as well, making 177 runs at 25 and taking 20 wickets at 17 apiece from 57 overs, but with most of our team only fourteen years old, we weren't a real contest for the other clubs.

In the holidays we went to the SCG to watch matches between Combined teams and a Services side, and two of our Cumberland players, Bert Alderson and Brian Bowman, were chosen to play. It was a slightly sobering experience watching from the Sheridan Stand as I suddenly realised there were some really fast bowlers in the world. One bowler named Ray Lindwall took the new ball against Bert and gave him a torrid time. Lindwall took four wickets and could have had more and they said he was likely to go on to greater things in cricket.

During these summers I went with my father to the weekly practices at the Cumberland Oval in Parramatta; I was allowed to field all afternoon, which was a real treat. Doug Kennedy, a Cumberland first-grader and great friend of our family, would keep a running total of the runs I had saved, and this stiff examination at practice every Thursday afternoon was, more than anything else, the reason I fielded so well when I moved into the higher level of cricket.

The following summer, 1945–46, I went to Cumberland's preliminary practices at Lidcombe Oval, this time as someone trying out for selection, and I made it into third grade. It was a good place to start and my father stressed that at fifteen years of age and in the fourth year at high school it was time to find out a few things about my cricket. It was excellent experience, we played on some *very* bad pitches when we were away from Parramatta and Lidcombe Ovals. *The Cumberland Annual Report* of the pitch for the final match, at St Paul's University, described it as 'a natural grass pitch, innocent of any treatment from the roller', but it gave me the chance to be competitive against higher-class players.

I was promoted to second grade for the last match of the summer against Gordon, and before I left for the game my father gave me a piece of good advice. 'Jack Prowse,' he said, 'is a very good bowler and I've played against him for many years. He is a legspinner, but hardly turns the ball at all, it's his topspinner you must watch, it hurries off the pitch like lightning. You must play forward at him even if the ball is short.'

When I went out to bat at number seven, Jack was bowling. The first ball *was* short, I played forward and it hit my bat as I was still bringing it forward. He stood there mid-pitch, hands on hips, and said, 'Your father's been telling you about me.'

My father had again topped the club's first-grade bowling, most wickets, best average and best strike-rate, where he was averaging a wicket every twenty-five balls – not bad for someone who turned forty-two years of age just before the end of the summer!

4

UP A LEVEL, BUT CAN I HANDLE IT?

NINETEEN forty-six to forty-seven was the season when everything seemed to be happening as far as I was concerned. I was in my last year at high school and studying for my Leaving Certificate, as it was called in those days, and I was selected for first grade with Cumberland, playing in the same team as my father. In addition, I was the captain of the Green Shield team and captained the Combined Sydney Green Shield team against Newcastle, as I had done the previous summer. When a New South Wales Second XI team visited Newcastle in the Christmas vacation, I was named twelfth man when the team was announced. Soon afterwards came the news that I had passed the Leaving Certificate. Not by much, mind you – it was known as the sportsman's pass, with four Bs. Even so, it was a relief to have made it, a feeling reciprocated in heartfelt fashion by my parents, who had agonised through every moment of the last few weeks of cramming.

Although the ultimate personal ambition of every cricketer is to play for his country, Australian cricketers share an ambition only a little short of this, in that they are desperate to play for their state and to win the Sheffield Shield. When I first played Sheffield Shield there were five teams in the competition; Western Australia and Tasmania were admitted in 1947 and 1977. Gaining a place in a team was a cut-throat business, and holding your place in the side was dependent on a combination of skill, potential, some law changes, and on whether or not there was a youth policy in the state in which you lived. As it happened, I was extremely fortunate that all four things applied after I left Parramatta High

School, and the NSW selectors were constantly on the lookout for young players.

In 1946, the year I left school, aged sixteen, the NSW selectors named me in a strong team of youngsters to tour Forbes, Dubbo and Wellington, three country towns in NSW, to see how the players shaped up in a team environment. Although I didn't realise it then, the state selectors were way ahead of their time in their policy decisions. The MCC team were about to arrive in Australia for the first Ashes battle after the war, and while NSW and the other states had plenty of experienced cricketers, the youngsters were very much an unknown quantity. The selectors decided to find out about them.

It was a wonderful experience for a sixteen-year-old, the cricket was very good and very competitive, and the selectors saw enough of the youngsters in the team to get a good idea of which players might be put into a 'possible' category for the State Colts' XI Interstate matches when they resumed.

I started the 1946–47 cricket season in third grade and had two very good matches, one second-grade game against Western Suburbs, and then was rapidly promoted to the firsts. We were well beaten by Glebe in my debut match, but the second game provided some happier moments. Cumberland had lost 4–34 when I walked out to bat to join allrounder Gordon Clark. We added 111, and by the time I was close to the nineties my father was in with me batting number nine. I missed the century by two runs, being stumped off NSW Sheffield Shield offspin bowler Vince Collins. My father was disappointed, as I was, but he took 4–22 the next Saturday, bowling out Marrickville to give us the victory in what was a good family effort.

At Parramatta Oval that summer I shared in one of my most enjoyable partnerships. I was in with Arthur Clues, and it was his final innings before boarding the ship for England where he was going to play rugby league for Leeds. Arthur was one of the greatest rugby league footballers produced by Australia and I had watched him as a youngster. When I started going to the Cumberland practices in 1939, Arthur was always in the practising group.

Arthur looked a good cricketer and he also had a flow of language that brought either envy or the raised eyebrow, whichever way you looked at it, or listened to it. It was fascinating to a youngster to hear Arthur's penetrating voice ringing out across the Oval with one of his milder entreaties: '"Bowie", you stupid bastard, catch the bloody thing . . .' 'Bowie' was Brian Bowman, a mate of Arthur's. Jack Jeffery, our family doctor and Central Cumberland offspinner, had a slightly disapproving look, and my father would cast one eye at Arthur and keep the other on me, trying to judge whether or not I was within hearing distance. I promise you, the stationmaster at Parramatta railway station was in fact within hearing distance, but each time I caught my father's eye I kept a perfectly straight face. No chance of me providing a reason not to be at the practice.

This day at Parramatta Oval, Cumberland had to follow on against a strong Manly bowling attack, and Arthur and I shared a century partnership. Arthur made 115 not out in 89 minutes, and I watched, slightly bemused and in admiration at the other end, and made 40 not out. It was one of the best exhibitions of strokeplay I had seen, and that after he had also top-scored in the first innings. It was some farewell to Cumberland.

The Cumberland Club and its practices, and the manner in which it embraced the players, was an example to all. I'm sure there were other clubs in the Sydney metropolitan area which were also good, although even fifty-eight years later, it is quite impossible to conceive that anything could have been better. There had been three Test players at that stage, of whom W. P. (Bill) Howell was the most famous. He was born at Penrith, NSW, in 1869, and was an apiarist, and played eighteen times for Australia. In his first match in England, against Surrey at The Oval in 1899, he took all ten Surrey first-innings wickets for 28. The other Test players were Gerry Hazlitt, who toured England in 1912 after playing against them in Australia in 1911–12, and Frank Iredale who played in 1894–95 in Australia and then in 1896 in England.

Cumberland had been one of the founder members of the district cricket competition in Sydney, beginning in 1893 with seven other teams. As far back as 1840, the year Captain Jean Benaud arrived in Australia from France on the *Ville de Bordeaux*, cricket was played and the event recorded at Parramatta; it was a match 'for 25 pounds and a supper at mine hosts of the Royal Exchange'. Five years later teams were complaining the opposition used unfair tactics, including having recourse to their own umpires. There is a delightful account of a match between the Currency Club and the Parramatta Club in 1845 where the Currency team won by 112 runs, but were upbraided for the fact that the ball they used had been deliberately soaked in linseed oil for a long time so that it was *completely non-elastic*. Tough times.

At the beginning of December 1887 Mr Vernon's touring England team played against Eighteen of Parramatta at the Parramatta ground, and in 1891–92 W. G. Grace captained Lord Sheffield's team to Australia. Their fourth match was against Twenty of Cumberland at Parramatta. It got away to a bad start when the local captain, Kirby, and 'WG' went out to toss. Kirby called and Grace picked up the coin, pocketed it and told Kirby Cumberland were to bat on a wet pitch. Kirby protested that he had called correctly, but Grace said, according to the *Parramatta Argus* report of 12 December 1891, 'That sort of thing won't suit me, I won't stand it from anyone!' When Grace was bowled for a duck by the Parramatta man 'Joe' Wilson, the England captain was cheered off the ground in lively fashion by more than 1,000 spectators.

My father told me a lot about the rich tradition of the club and talked about those three Test players and the others who had played in some representative cricket. When MCC beat NSW by four wickets during the Bodyline tour, Cumberland player Ray Rowe, making his debut, had double-figure scores, 70 and 11, in the two low-scoring innings. There were only four other double-figure efforts, from Bill Brown, Don Bradman and Jack Fingleton, all Test batsmen then or later.

Ray Rowe was my first captain when I made it into Cumberland's first-grade side in 1946. He was also captain seven years earlier in a match which will always stick in my mind as a spectator, Cumberland v Northern District at Waitara Oval.

A Sheffield Shield match between NSW and South Australia was played in blistering heat that same weekend at the SCG, and it was the game when Don Bradman, playing for SA, equalled C. B. Fry's feat of making six successive centuries in first-class matches. This Cumberland match was on 14 January 1939, the time of appalling bushfires in Sydney, which destroyed homes all around the metropolitan area and turned the tinder-dry bushland to ash. My father said he had never played cricket on a hotter day. Cumberland's bowlers were thrashed for 420–5 at Waitara in front of seventeen spectators.

Seven thousand turned up to see Bradman fourteen miles down the road, but with Charlie Walker nursing a broken finger, Bradman kept wicket and then was twenty-two not out at stumps. He eventually made his century to equal Fry's record, but not until the fourth day of the match because the second and third were washed out with wonderful, delightful, glorious and so badly needed rain, which thankfully put out every one of the awful bushfires.

1947–8 was a very heavy season and a most successful one for the Benaud family. I finished second in the club batting averages and aggregate, but again my problem was with my bowling. I had a strike-rate of a wicket every 72 balls, which was poor, and took only nine wickets in the season.

I was in my second year of employment at the time, in Alan Savage's chartered accountant's office in Pitt Street, Sydney, having started there under the watchful care of John Maloney and Mr Savage. I was never sure I was cut out for accountancy, but at Parramatta High School, in keeping with all other secondary schools, they provided tests for pupils to see for what they would be best suited. I loved English but the testers said I was outstanding at mental arithmetic, so accountancy it was.

My father and I started cricket practice in July 1948 out at Bert Alderson's home at Northmead and by the time the official practices began at Lidcombe Oval on the first Saturday in September, we were all in reasonable form, though mine was more in the batting department than bowling. I was hitting the ball very well, but my legspinners weren't coming out right at that stage, in retrospect possibly because I was trying to bowl several different types of ball each over.

I made 20 against Gordon in the first match of the summer which Cumberland won, then 86 against St George, 57 against Manly and 69 against Western Suburbs and was chosen for the NSW Colts team for the match to be played against Queensland. This was a wonderful adventure. I had just turned eighteen, had been out of Sydney only when on holidays and visiting relatives in the country, or with NSWCA teams on their country visits when staying in an hotel was an adventure in itself.

After I had arranged leave from Mr Savage's accountancy firm, the team assembled at Central railway station and we travelled by train to Queensland. That NSW v Queensland game was a triumph for Alan Walker, the fast left-arm bowler who later was to play Sheffield Shield cricket and tour South Africa with the Australian team in 1949–50, and also for Ron Briggs and Jim Burke, who made centuries; both later played Sheffield Shield and 'Burkie' played for Australia.

I batted and bowled well enough to be satisfied with the week. NSW won the match with ease, and for many of the young players it was the start of careers at a level above grade or club cricket in Sydney. It was exciting and I wanted to continue to be part of it.

Don Bradman's all-conquering team had returned to Australia, and at the conclusion of the season Bradman played his last match for South Australia in a game which was designated as a testimonial for former Test player Arthur Richardson. Bradman fell and twisted his ankle on the second day of the match and took no further part in the game.

I once said to Keith Miller how disappointed I was to have made my debut in the same year as Bradman finished. How wonderful it would have been to have watched him play at the SCG in 1940 and then been able to bowl at him on the same ground. Nugget looked at me and remarked drily that everyone has one lucky break in a lifetime and that may well have been mine!

Bradman had announced he intended to retire from the game which he had graced for such a long period and a testimonial match was arranged for 3–7 December at the Melbourne Cricket Ground. It drew 94,000 spectators and it was a batsman's match, with 1,672 runs coming in the four days' play and the game itself finishing in a tie.

Television wasn't to hit Australia for another eight years, so I listened to the match on the radio, although my main interest was in the Sheffield Shield; NSW were playing Queensland on the same ground where I had recently played in the Colts match. Their performances in that Colts game had earned Alan Walker a place in the Shield team and Jim Burke the position of twelfth man. It was significant that the Colts match was being seen as a genuine path to first-class cricket in NSW. While the NSW v Queensland Shield game was being played in Brisbane, I made a good 69 in a grade match against Western Suburbs at Parramatta in front of state selector Selby Burt.

The traditional New Year fixture at the SCG in those days was always NSW v Queensland. I was walking back to the office after my lunch break when I saw in the Sydney *Sun* the story of my selection for the NSW Sheffield Shield team. It wasn't your normal run-of-the-mill match either because the ground was hit by a cloudburst the night before the scheduled start and then more heavy rain in the early morning meant the abandonment of the opening day. The curator started work at 4 a.m. on the second day and had the very grassy surface rolled hard enough by the start of play, but Arthur Morris had no hesitation in putting Queensland in when he won the toss and I was happy not to be in the centre, batting. It was really difficult and Ray Lindwall and Alan Walker were very fast and dangerous. I failed with the bat in the first innings but I wasn't required to bat again, nor was any batsman in the NSW side other than Morris and Burke, and I never looked like being called to the bowling crease.

Arthur later said, 'Sorry about that, son, but I didn't think the pitch would suit you all that much.' Even at that young age, and keen as I was to bowl for the first time in a Sheffield Shield game, I realised the batsmen's eyes would have lit up had they seen a debutant legspinner coming on to bowl instead of Lindwall, Walker or Miller. I was happy enough for the reprieve.

5

A CHANGE OF FORTUNE, BUT NOT FOR THE BETTER

IF luck had played a part in my selection for the state team, it then immediately turned the other way because I had at the same time been chosen in the NSW Second XI team to play Victoria in Melbourne. This was slightly unusual, but because I was only eighteen at the time, and a rather immature eighteen at that, the selectors had decided I needed as much experience as possible. I suppose you could say I was one of the NSW Second XI's more experienced players, having played one Sheffield Shield match, albeit without having had the slightest success. I was soon to realise cricket was a much more punishing and painful game than it might have appeared in the backyard at Parramatta or when playing for Central Cumberland.

In the *Sydney Morning Herald* and the Sydney *Sun* over the previous ten days there were minor reports and abbreviated scores of matches between Victoria and Tasmania. The name Jack Daniel cropped up twice, once when he took 6–37 to rout the Tasmanians for 132 on Christmas Day and then, six days later, when he took 6–20 and bowled them out for 65. Born in Yorkshire and brought to Australia as a youngster, he was classed as 'fast bowler J. Daniel'. The Victorian wicketkeeper was I. H. McDonald. I had no cause at that stage to know about either of them, but I was to know them much better within a few days!

We arrived in Melbourne by train on the morning of 10 November 1949, a team full of hope for victory and future selection after what our dreams told us might be a series of splendid performances over the three days of the big game. These were two strong teams, with future Test players in Colin McDonald and Jack Hill in the Victorian side, plus nine other Sheffield Shield players of the future. NSW had Graeme Hole, Jim de Courcy and me as future Test players, though we weren't to know this at the time, and there were five others who would play Sheffield Shield. It was always likely to be a tough contest and, even in those days, a Victoria–NSW game stirred the players' blood whether it was at Sheffield Shield level or just below that exalted position.

NSW bowled Victoria out for 276 and again I didn't reach the bowling crease. Ron Briggs and Graeme Hole opened the innings with less than an hour to play and Brian Dwyer asked me to pad up as nightwatchman. I was very happy to do it, otherwise I might have been down at six or even seven. When the first wicket fell at 35 that evening, I went out through the gate to an atmosphere I had never before encountered on a cricket field. It was sheer aggro which, some time later, was transformed to friendliness when we were back in the dressing-room and the day's play was over. It was the first really good lesson which showed me that on the field the game should be fair but very hard, and off the field it should provide the chance to meet people and to sit down and chat over a drink.

The following morning, Jack Daniel bowled a bouncer before I had added to my overnight score and I was carried off the field on a stretcher. Ian McDonald, who had been behind the stumps at the time, had seen exactly what had happened and described it to me some years later. The ball was thumped in short and I went for the hook shot, but didn't move far enough inside the line. My memory of it was that I was trying to pull the ball, which I thought would arrive at about chest height, but that it lifted more than I expected and left me stranded. I saw a blur of ball, and then there was a very nasty thud against my forehead, just above the right eye. In that, I was lucky: two inches lower and I might well have lost an eye, or worse. McDonald later said he had never heard a worse sound on the cricket field than that ball hitting and splintering bone.

As might be imagined, everything was a bit hazy after that, although I can clearly recall two things to this day. The first was the sight of Jimmy de Courcy, the next man in for NSW, standing impassively at the gate as I was carried past him. He gave me a slight nod and then I was on my way into the dressing-room. The other was that once I had been put on the massage table, what I wanted most in life was to take my boots and socks off as I had pins and needles in my feet. What my team-mates thought about all this scarcely bears imagining. This was the guy who, a few minutes earlier, had walked out of the dressing-room full of confidence, hoping to make a packet of runs and a name for himself, and now here he was, stretched out with his legs kicking, asking people to take off his boots and socks. In addition, he had a hole in his forehead exactly the size of half a cricket ball.

They took me off to hospital, where doctors and nurses gave the impression that in a matter of minutes they would have X-rays which would show the extent of the damage, although it was nothing like as simple as that.

There is a true story of a cricketer hit by a ball who went to the hospital for X-rays and the media bulletin handed out in the press box a couple of hours later said the X-rays of his head showed absolutely nothing! That brought a deal of hilarity at the time, and the first part was repeated this day in Melbourne. The X-rays showed nothing. Twenty-eight X-rays and there was still nothing on film, although the doctors, who by now were a little perplexed, did say there had to be something there, you couldn't have a hole that deep in a forehead without something being fractured.

Ian McDonald was very concerned and Brian Dwyer made me promise to go to my own GP, Jack Jeffery, the Cumberland cricketer, and to make sure more X-rays were taken. Like all young people I took note of the advice, though not straight away and not until I had been home to see Mum and Dad, or rather Mum first as she was the one who opened the door to me. I can't recall exactly what she said, but she told me later she needed all her pioneering instincts to keep a level tone in her voice. I'm not surprised. In the space of a couple of days the injury had bled internally, and my face was a mixture of black and yellow, and the colours had run down into the neck area. It wasn't a pretty sight. Late in the afternoon I went down to Parramatta town to see Jack Jeffery, who took one look and phoned the hospital, then took me there himself for further X-rays.

The next day Cumberland's first-grade team were playing at Lidcombe Oval, so, as I couldn't play, I did the next best thing and cadged a lift down to see the match. While I was there Jack Jeffery arrived at my parents' home in Sutherland Road with the new X-rays and the information that I had a badly shattered frontal bone in my forehead. When told where I was, he organised a very quick phone call to officials at Lidcombe Oval to tell me not to do anything to jar my head and under no circumstances to get anywhere near a cricket ball.

I had been only moderately worried up to that moment; at my stage of life youthful optimism told me it was little more than a medical quirk that I had a hole in my forehead, but no fracture had shown. Now it was very different and the urgency in the various voices sent a little tremor up my spine, because of the implication that another blow in the same spot could be fatal. When I got home to Sutherland Road I went into my room and had a look in the mirror. What previously had been merely multi-coloured, now had about it a menacing and ugly touch, and although it was only fear of the unknown, the mirror showed that fear.

Jack Jeffery lined up the best man in Sydney, surgeon George Halliday, to perform the necessary operation, and without going into too many gory details, it all worked, even down to what the surgeon told me about scarring. He said, 'After we've opened you up from outside your left eye across to outside your right eye and sorted out the bits of bone, within a couple of years the operation scar will be nothing more than a thin line across your nose. People will assume it is a mark left by your spectacles. Just say, "Yes, of course!"'

After a two-week stint at the Royal Prince Alfred Hospital in Sydney, I discovered very quickly I was allergic to penicillin. Two weeks of penicillin shots in the backside whilst in hospital hadn't been a problem, but no one had completely prepared me for arriving back at Sutherland Road and waking up the following morning, having not had a shot for the first time in fourteen days, and being unable to open my eyes properly. There was a very good reason for this. When I took a glance in the bathroom mirror I looked like a Michelin tyre advertisement with great folds of swelling. The only difference was, unlike the ad, I wasn't smiling. That lasted just a week, but it was enough to have me carry a note from then on and an instruction on a medallion that says 'NO Penicillin'.

Musing about these medical matters later, it did cross my mind to ask the doctors what might happen, when I started playing cricket again, if I collected on the same spot another blow from a cricket ball. I decided it might be better not to know.

At the start of the next summer I found myself facing a character-building split second at the crease. By the time we had gone through four Sundays of practice at the Aldersons, I was hitting the ball really well and was very much looking forward to the first match of 1949–50, which was to be a tough one against Western Suburbs at Pratten Park. Their bowling was opened by Russ Hill, a tall and versatile pace bowler who could also bowl quickish offspin on responsive pitches. Wests, with two NSW state selectors present, had made 148–5 declared, we lost a couple of quick wickets and I went out to face Hill, whose first ball was a perfectly pitched bumper. I hooked it past square-leg for four, and the question hanging in the air was answered, for the moment anyway! There had never been any suggestion I should give away the pull shot or the hook – why in fact consider that when it had, with the exception of the game at the MCG, always been one of my most productive strokes?

When January 1950 arrived my salary at the accountancy

firm moved up to the princely sum of three pounds a week and I was promptly put off. Although I was disappointed at the time, it turned out to be a good and thoroughly sensible thing for both employer and me. From my employer's point of view, he could put on another youngster at a pound a week as an articled clerk, and be guaranteed far more regular attendance, with no cricket practices and matches intervening. It was hardly a workable proposition to have someone putting green ticks on a page and then being away from the office for a week. From my point of view, I was about to experience the delights or otherwise of being on the open employment market, so the first thing I did was look through the jobs vacant section of the newspapers.

Sometimes luck plays a part in life, and I had a stroke of good fortune which had a wonderful effect on my cricket career. One advertisement to catch my eye was for a position at the *Sun* newspaper, in the counting house, acting as a clerk, no grading necessary with a starting salary listed at six pounds a week. Six pounds a week! I had just finished one job at three pounds a week and now there was a chance that, aged twenty, I might be able to double that figure if only I could obtain the job.

I was interviewed by the head accountant, a Mr Scotford, a cricket fan who had heard of me, which did me no harm at all. It was agreed I would be given time off for cricket practice as long as I tried to make up the lost hours by various rostering methods. Bert Scotford was one of the finest men I have met. He died a few years ago, and in all the time I knew him he never changed, a gentle but firm man, married to a delightful lady, Jessie, and with two children, Tony and Narelle. Bert was one of the reasons I was able to perform as well as I did in the early days of my cricket career.

Jack Fearnside was in charge of the section to which I was first allocated at the *Sun*; I made good friends in the six years I worked in various sections of the accounts department of what was a splendid newspaper. It was produced in the morning, with the first edition coming out to hit the streets around eleven o'clock. I was able to obtain the late final extra when dashing for the train to Parramatta late in the day. When I started I was vaguely aware that Keith Miller worked in the building on a publication called *Sporting Life*, having transferred from Melbourne at the start of the 1947–48 season. Dick Whitington worked there as well, as did Johnnie Moyes, a fine attacking batsman and a highly respected commentator, and 'Ginty' Lush, who had played in the first Sheffield Shield match I ever watched.

It was a wonderful privilege to be able to slip up to the *Sporting Life* offices occasionally and listen to some of the opinions on the game and its various players. Miller was as forthright in his conversation as he was on the field, and there seemed little that was defensive about his attitude to life, which was hardly surprising I suppose when you consider the things he and others had gone through during the war. Ginty Lush was a wonderful, swashbuckling character and a fine cricketer who had played for Sir Julien Cahn's team in England. As captain of the Gordon club in Sydney, he was always one to champion the cause of young cricketers.

Johnnie Moyes, the editor of *Sporting Life*, was a good enough cricketer to be chosen for the Australian tour of South Africa in 1914, the tour cancelled because of the First World War. He wrote one biography and called it *Bradman*; he wrote another in 1962, a year before his death, and titled it *Benaud*. In it he said of my Melbourne head injury:

> When years later I watched Benaud hooking Tyson and Wesley Hall I marvelled at his courage. That tremendous blow, received at the beginning of his career, might well have caused him to flinch when the ball was dropped short – or at least it could have ended any desire he had to play the hook stroke. It didn't. He continued to hook – Tyson, Trueman, Hall and others – and to hit the ball with tremendous power. A man who will do that has a fighting heart, real personal courage, and indeed, audacity.

It never occurred to me there was anything more brave in *my* doing it, or attempting to do it, against fast bowlers than would be the case with a batsman who hadn't had his skull badly fractured. The most important thing was that I had a lot of fun with it and I like to think the spectators did as well.

It was very important I should have a good season with Cumberland, and I managed that, heading the batting aggregates and average with 460 runs at 51.1 and taking 21 wickets at 17.8 to be on top of the bowling figures as well. My father, now aged forty-five, was second to me in the first-grade bowling figures and in third position in the second grade.

Having been picked twice as twelfth man for NSW at the SCG that season, I was chosen to play for the NSW Second XI at the SCG No. 2 in a midweek match against Victoria. I was to do battle again with the same state against which I had sustained my head injury, though not against the same bowler, Jack Daniel, whose success in club matches had placed him on the short list for their Sheffield Shield side.

In this, my comeback game, I made a duck. Having seen Jack Hill bowl at the MCG, my instinct told me to push forward to his topspinners; my feet had me playing back and plumb lbw, one of Hill's eight victims for 34 in 11 overs. In the second innings Ron James and I added an unbeaten 32 for the fifth wicket to produce a very hard-fought victory against a state with which I was destined to have many battles over the years.

Ten days later I was chosen for the NSW team to go on the Southern Tour, playing against South Australia and Victoria in successive weeks, the game against Victoria to be played over Christmas weekend, followed by a match against Queensland in Sydney at New Year. A lot could happen before that match. Keith Miller had been flown to South Africa after an injury to Bill Johnston, and Ron James had been given a young NSW team to captain, though there was experience in the bowling attack with Tom Brooks and Fred Johnston, the latter a fine legspin bowler, very accurate and with the ability to trouble batsmen if there happened to be anything at all in the pitch by way of spin.

The first match of the Southern Tour didn't start too well when we lost the toss, but Alan Davidson, making his debut in Sheffield Shield, began brilliantly by having Bob McLean lbw in his first over. Tom Brooks cleaned up six more, Davo collected three others and we were back at the hotel that evening at 39–0 after SA had mustered only 181. I did little with the bat, being lbw to Kevin O'Neill for 10, and then Phil Ridings played a magnificent innings of 131 to restrict us to first-innings points.

In the match against Victoria, where we met Jack Iverson for the first time, Jim Burke made a magnificent 162 and he and I shared a good partnership. Fred Johnston suffered very badly from dropped chances in this match, as had been the case in Adelaide, but it was still a big shock when he was left out of the side for Sydney, where we were to meet Queensland at New Year.

Even then, I knew enough about selection to be aware that this was not a good decision, as I was the one now chosen to play as the sole spinner. However, an injury to Ernie Toshack brought Fred back into the side and justice was done, because he took 6–85 in an exciting encounter where NSW won by one wicket, with much drama at the end. I took one wicket in the second innings, that of Test player Bill Brown, and it was from a ball which I am confidently able to say is the worst I ever bowled.

There was an amusing aftermath to this when Mick Raymer, who was seriously deaf, came out to bat at the fall of Brown's wicket and, passing his skipper, received instructions to bat quietly. 'Possum' Raymer had nodded but had not properly heard the order, not unusual when you consider that once on a Queensland Southern Tour he listened to a joke told by a team-mate, laughed uproariously, and then straight away told the identical joke, this time to even greater laughter. He did indeed bat carefully, other than for the umpire calling 'no ball' when Tom Brooks was bowling. Tom, later a Test match umpire, was a tall fast bowler who emitted a very loud grunt with each delivery. In fact Tom did bowl two no-balls, but he didn't bowl fifteen, which was the number Mick thought he heard called and to which he played the most wonderfully extravagant hook and pull shots. Raymer made 57 in an hour of mayhem, with Don Tallon and Len Johnson his bemused partners at the other end and, in the course of his brilliant innings, he broke Jim Burke's finger when the latter tried to catch a fierce pull at midwicket. He was eventually bowled by legspinner Wally Yeates, who didn't grunt at all.

The last two matches of the season were very important for me. I made 93 and shared a 129-run stand with Ron James and we beat South Australia by an innings and 41 and then accounted for Victoria by 196 runs. That win came despite Iverson bowling us out for 142 in the second innings, taking 6–30 in 10 overs. Graeme Hole made his first-class debut in this game against Victoria but that was the only time he ever represented his home state. In both these games Davidson bowled magnificently, picking up 13 wickets in all and gaining selection in the Australian side to New Zealand, as did Iverson.

Davo had a splendid tour, Iverson was even better and the New Zealanders could hardly lay a bat on him. The following season, however, the NSW batsmen got to Iverson in the match in Sydney and ankle injuries then restricted his cricket. I have no doubt that, had Iverson been fit and available and keen for the 1953 tour of England, there would have been no celebrations for the home side that year. It needed Lindsay Hassett to be with him to set the fields and tell him, perhaps, to shift his line another three inches towards middle stump, something he would then do. He was as accurate as that; I had never seen anything like it. He was basically an offspinner, but one who gained a tremendous amount of bounce from the pitch and he bowled, as well, a topspinner and leg-break without a discernible change of action.

Iverson had made his debut the previous summer when the Australian team were touring South Africa and had taken 46 wickets at 16 apiece, not quite unheard-of figures but certainly something to have the Australian cricket world buzzing. He also had the attention of the three Australian selectors, Sir Donald Bradman, Jack Ryder and 'Chappie' Dwyer who, a week later, were to choose the Australian team to play England in Brisbane. Jack's grip of the ball was unique in cricket. He held it firmly between the thumb and first two fingers of his right hand and *flicked* it outwards and upwards with his second finger as he brought over his arm – unorthodox but wonderfully effective.

6
PROMISING MUCH BUT DELIVERING LITTLE

B Y the time the 1950–51 summer began I was in good heart, had practised well and was looking forward to challenging for a place in the state team, but 'challenging' was very much the operative word. This was likely to be a most difficult year, as the touring team had returned from South Africa and all the players from that extremely successful side were available for selection for Sheffield Shield. A fast start was essential and I took 6–28 in the opening club match against Northern District at Waitara, but then indifferent weather meant chances were limited for everyone.

Having been twelfth man for the opening games of the season, I gained a place in the side against MCC led by Denis Compton because Freddie Brown was injured. I took Trevor Bailey's wicket, which was more than I managed on a regular basis in later years, and then made 20 not out before the declaration which led to a draw with rain washing out the final hour and a half of the match.

I was feeling more confident now and it was a boost to be chosen in the next Sheffield Shield match, against Victoria in Melbourne, which provided a good opportunity to have a close-up look at Lindsay Hassett in action. As a boy I had watched him from the grandstand as he made centuries, so to bowl against him was an education. Now in Melbourne, he made 179 in four hours against Lindwall, Miller, Walker, Fred Johnston and me, and I bowled 7 overs for 47 and didn't manage to get a ball past his bat.

We needed 375 to take first-innings points. I was listed to bat at seven. My turn came around quickly and things were look-ing very bad when I joined Ron James and we added 109 for the sixth wicket. Then Lindwall and James made 33 before James was out to Bill Johnston bowling his slower orthodox left-arm. It was Iverson who dismissed me that day in Melbourne, caught down the legside by Ian McDonald for 55, but I was happy enough with the innings. I had struggled at the start, but had batted for over two hours in all and towards the end was hitting the ball well.

In the second innings I took three wickets, including Hassett lbw, and I'd like to be able to say it was an absolute ripper that had him playing down one line while the topspinner fizzed through on another and trapped him. In fact it was a topspinner, but as often happened in those days at the MCG, the pitch had masses of cracks in it by the final day and the ball hit the edge of one of those and shot through and hit him on the foot.

The runs and wickets, and two useful catches in that Melbourne match, wouldn't have done my prospects of staying in the NSW team any harm, and the following game in Adelaide, the week before the Brisbane Test, was also a bonus. I made 48 and took five wickets in the match, four of them in the first innings, but I had five chances dropped and, in a slightly bizarre happening, three of them, all difficult and from successive balls, were missed by wicketkeeper Stan Sismey. Stan was a very reliable 'keeper, recently returned from a most successful tour of New Zealand with the Australian second team, and he had been the wicket-keeper for the Services team captained by Hassett. The hat-trick non-victims were Geff Noblet and twice 'Chucker' Wilson, the latter with whom I was later to tour in the 1956 Australian side.

Everything had been going well, but there was a rude awakening for me in the next Sheffield Shield match in Perth: a duck in the first innings and only four overs with the ball in a match which was played at the same time as the extraordinary First Test in Brisbane. However, after the Perth match it was a pleasant shock when I was named in the twelve players for the Australian XI side to play MCC in Sydney ten days later on 15 December. It was a wonderful moment to see my name there, the most exciting thing to happen to me to that point in my career.

A small piece of advice: assume nothing and never become

too wrapped up in success or pleasure, because there is always something around the corner to cut you down to size. Six days before the MCC game, Cumberland had a one-day match to play against Paddington at Cumberland Oval. Off the last ball of the day the batsman pushed the ball out into the covers where I was fielding and I moved across to cut it off. The ball wasn't travelling very fast at all, but it bounced awkwardly and hit me on the right thumb, only a glancing blow but enough. I sensed there was a problem but didn't realise how bad it was. I knew an hour later: by the time I had walked the mile home to Sutherland Road, I was certain there was a break. The glancing blow had actually chipped off a piece of bone, and I still have the scar of it all these years later, though the mental scar disappeared much faster.

In fact, it was an even worse break than I had feared, and because it was on my bowling hand, I had to be absolutely certain it had completely recovered before attempting to play. It was torment, and I was reduced to training rather than playing, going through all the training schedules without actually doing anything with a bat or a ball.

I came back in the club match against Balmain and took 4–66 and made 66, knowing that I had to show the selectors that not only had the injury healed, but I was in decent form. They played me in the Sheffield Shield side to take on South Australia at the end of the season, but there had been a gap of nine weeks from the time I had played in Perth to the moment when I stepped on to a first-class cricket field once again. Torment is an understatement! I made 37 and took two wickets in the match, and NSW won the Sheffield Shield again by a clear margin.

In 1951–52 the West Indians who had toured England in 1950 were scheduled to visit Australia, and there was a lot of anticipation, but the schedule prepared for the tourists by Australia's administrators seemed, even to my inexperienced eyes, extraordinary.

Hassett's team were regarded as world champions at the time, and this tour was billed as the world championship of Test cricket. They started the West Indians in Sydney with a one-day game, which gave them only the match against Queensland on 3 November as a lead-up to the opening Test.

West Indies came to Sydney to play NSW immediately after the Test in Brisbane, which Australia had won narrowly, and they were presented with a very green pitch which prompted John Goddard, justifiably, to put us in to bat. At 96–7 I went out to bat at number nine to join Ray Flockton and we hit 100 in an hour to pull things around. The Windies were bowled out for 134 on the second day in front of 23,000 spectators and then just failed to make the 380 they needed to win.

When the Second Test of that series began on 1 December at the SCG, NSW were playing South Australia in Adelaide. In reply to South Australia's 217 we lost our first four wickets for 90 and I walked in to join the skipper, Sid Barnes. Left-arm spinner Jack Wilson had Barnes caught and bowled off a leading edge trying to push the ball to the legside and, at 106–5 and needing 112 for first-innings points, we had a problem.

It was against this background that I hit my first century in Sheffield Shield. As an innings it was something of a mixture, with a lot of good shots and a few streaky ones. There was a touch of luck about it as well because Jack Wilson dropped me off his own bowling when I had made 44 and then I was dropped at 93. Ron Kissell and I shared a 75-run partnership and I reached my century during the last over of the day. What I had done was totally eclipsed by ex-NSW player Les Favell in the South Australian second innings – what a debut! Eighty-six at his first attempt and then 164 in four hours at his second, with some glorious strokeplay in the 280 made while he was at the crease. It was a brilliant performance and it was the type of batting Les was to produce over many years at Shield level.

Phil Ridings made an excellent declaration, setting us 281 to make in just over four hours. We fell 14 runs short in what was a wonderful last day's cricket, with more than 300 runs made and 10 wickets going down in all.

Two things happened towards the end of this summer which had a big influence on my future. Firstly, the Australian selectors, right out of the blue, chose me to make my Test debut in the final Test of the series against the West Indies at the SCG. Secondly, when Sid Barnes captained NSW in the final Shield game of the season, he put me in to bat at number three.

With 3 and 19, the run-out of Frank Worrell and 1–14 with the ball, I didn't do much in the Test, which was an unusual game where the pitch was the same colour and texture as the rest of the square and pace bowling dominated. Hassett won the toss against Stollmeyer, who had taken over the captaincy from Goddard, Australia batted and 19 wickets fell for 180 on the opening day. The game lasted less than four days in all.

Lindwall and Miller bowled very fast in both innings, the West Indian batsmen, other than for a brave effort from Stollmeyer, were unable to cope and Australia won by 202 runs. When Hassett took the second new ball, seven wickets fell for 24 and he brought me on to bowl against Everton Weekes and Alf Valentine right at the end of the innings. I started bowling to Weekes and Gil Langley dropped him at the wicket in my first over. It would have been a good start to collect the wicket of one of the great batsmen, but I settled for Alfred in my fifth over to end the match. When asked in later years, I've always listed Valentine as the finest number eleven I have seen.

Two weeks later, and with a weakened side, we were to play our final Shield game of the summer against South Australia. Keith Miller was playing for a specially convened Commonwealth side in Colombo but that loss was partly balanced by the fact that Graeme Hole of South Australia was with him for that match. Arthur Morris had a thigh strain and Sid Barnes was captain. We were unbeaten to this stage in the Sheffield Shield that summer and, with Victoria the closest to us but 12 points in arrears, we were certain to be premiers.

It was here that Sid Barnes gave me my great chance. He won the toss, pinned the batting order on the wall and I was listed at three to go in after Jim Burke and Jack Moroney. I was delighted at the promotion. In matches when the Test stars had been present earlier in the summer, I had often batted at seven and once at eight, so to be promoted in this way was a real opportunity, if I happened to be good enough to take it.

Tom Brooks, Alan Walker and Ray Lindwall bowled South Australia out for only 159. Bruce Bowley, the South Australian opening batsman and allrounder, was hit on the head by an Alan Walker bumper, and had to be taken to hospital where, fortunately, X-rays showed no fracture. This injury upset me, as I was on the spot as he reeled away from the crease and fell, and I instantly thought of my own close shave at Melbourne.

Late in the day I took Jack Manning's wicket to end their innings and then, suddenly, I was padded up as Jim Burke and Jack Moroney walked to the centre; no rest for a number three batsman. Moroney and I put on 60 to the close of play and then he was out almost immediately the next morning to an outswinger from Bowley, now recovered and back from hospital, and sixteen-year-old Ian Craig was on his way to join me. Craig was making his first-class debut in this match. He had been playing brilliantly in club cricket and many of the 9,000 crowd had come specifically to see his first innings, such had been the positive publicity for his recent performances.

I wandered across to greet him, a twenty-one-year-old youth trying to instil confidence into someone five years his junior, but I needn't have worried. I've no doubt he was nervous, but he didn't show it at all and right from the start he played with perfect poise against Noblet, Burton and Bowley. We put on 118 in even time before Noblet took the second new ball and almost immediately removed me from the game. Three short of a century was disappointing, and just when we were starting to will Ian along to his century he was lbw to Jack Wilson, the left-arm spinner, for 91.

Jim de Courcy made a century and, with a first-innings lead of 269, we were right in the box seat. Phil Ridings was the hero of the South Australian second innings; he was the skipper and an absolutely fearless cricketer. When Jack Manning was run out and Bruce Bowley came back out to bat at number seven, his head still bandaged, Ridings was in full cry, dominating the bowlers and hooking and pulling everything even a fraction short of a good length.

'Pancho' Ridings had been a splendid cricketer with South Australia for a long time, having started with the state side aged twenty in a match against Western Australia in the 1936–37 season. His brother, Ken, later tragically lost in action over the Bay of Biscay, followed him into the team the next season, making his debut against NSW, with Phil twelfth man. He was to be twelfth man on many occasions in that very strong cricket state; his brilliant fielding was no handicap to the selectors when they were deciding the twelve before the drinks carrier was nominated.

The summer following this match at the SCG, Ridings was to be one of the Australian selectors to choose the teams to play against South Africa and then the party to tour England. He was one of the more experienced cricketers in Australia, and in 1949–50, he had been vice-captain to Bill Brown in the Australian team which toured New Zealand. Good cricketer, tough performer.

When Bowley came out to join him at the SCG, Ridings met him halfway from the pavilion and they chatted. Walker was the bowler although he had already been dealt with harshly. The first ball he now bowled to Bowley was a bumper which whistled past his nose, and Bowley and Ridings received a succession of bouncers during a fiery interlude. When another flyer seared Bowley's lint headgear – no helmets in those days – Pancho Ridings meandered across and, purely by accident, happened to be at a spot on the pitch where 'Wakky' Walker was also arriving at the identical moment. The conversation, out of the side of Pancho's lips, was along the lines that if A. K. Walker managed to hit Bowley, as seemed to be his aim, he, Pancho, would pursue him around the SCG and perform the extraordinary feat of placing his bat handle into Wakky's mouth and extracting it from his nether regions. This seemed to have the desired effect of lightening the red mist that so often clouds a fast bowler's common sense, although it had an effect on 'Panch' too. I came on to bowl in place of Walker, rolled over my arm and Phil pushed a perfectly normal, half rat-power leg-break back to me for the softest caught and bowled you have ever seen.

This was five years before television began in Australia, and while the writers in the press box knew something slightly off-beat had happened on the field, they didn't know what. It was the match about which respected writer, Tom Goodman, said the next day in the *Sydney Morning Herald* that 'late in the day there appeared to be a minor altercation between the NSW left-arm fast bowler, A. K. Walker, and the South Australian captain, P. L. Ridings.' Such is life, or rather such was life, in what many call the 'old days' when, everyone now claims, there was very little short-pitched bowling and even less sledging!

We won the match in only three days, and we won the Sheffield Shield again. It had been a very interesting summer: a Test debut, some reasonably good performances in Sheffield Shield and other matches, and the chance to look forward to the arrival of the South Africans in November.

7

'BAGGER' BARNES AND
THE SPRINGBOKS

I N Australian cricket there has always been an extra touch of excitement about the end of a summer which brings selection of the team to tour England to battle for the Ashes. The South Africans were also due to tour Australia: we didn't know a great deal about them but our returning team in 1950 had seemed to think they were able to play.

One of the problems with grade cricket in Sydney is that if you are playing representative matches as well, your club doesn't see much of you, and that was the case this summer, when I played only five innings, topped the averages but not the aggregate, and took just 11 wickets in 90 overs.

In what for me was a short season with the club and for my father a longer one, there was an extraordinary coincidence in that in first grade, aged twenty-two, I made 196 runs at an average of 49.00 to head the batting averages. In second grade, where at the age of forty-eight Lou Benaud was captain, *he* headed the batting averages with 196 runs at 49.00! At the same time, in Central Cumberland's fifty-four-year history, I became the fifteenth player to take the field with them and achieve the double of 1,000 runs and 100 wickets in first grade.

Prior to the start of the tour by South Africa, the Australian Cricket Board had been in touch with their South African counterparts expressing their grave disquiet about the potential financial horrors of the tour. In South Africa there had been conjecture about sending the team, and the South African players were hardly given an overwhelming vote of confidence by administrators around

Australia. The South African Cricket Board, after the Australian
Cricket Board had repeated their disquiet in yet another letter to
South Africa, had secretly agreed to stand losses on the tour up to
a figure of £10,000.

Disquiet is probably a low-key word, because the Australian
administrators actually feared, and said, that the tour would be a
complete failure, among them Sydney Smith, who was President
of the NSWCA and had been charged with the task of proposing
the *welcoming* toast to the South Africans at a function in Sydney
prior to the match between South Africa and NSW. There was
nothing comforting, either, about the behind-the-scenes administration in Australia at that time.

The name Sid Barnes was prominent in this season because he
was seeking a place in the Australian team against South Africa
and then for the tour of England. Barnes's selection for the Third
Test, at Adelaide, against West Indies the previous year had been
secretly vetoed by the Board. Two weeks earlier Barnes had made
107 against Victoria and shared a 210-run partnership with
Arthur Morris and so the national selectors had chosen him for
the Adelaide game.

Gilbert and Sullivan at their very best could hardly have done
better than the Board with the ensuing events. They had started by
vetoing Barnes's selection, but then refused to say anything about
it. When it had come to the vote it had been ten–three in favour
of excluding Barnes, with Aub Oxlade, Sir Donald Bradman
and Frank Cush voting against the motion put to the meeting.
Bradman had been captain of the 1948 side which included Barnes
as a player, Oxlade and Cush were two of the three NSW delegates. Oxlade later lost his place as Chairman of the Australian
Cricket Board, and Chappie Dwyer, also of NSW, his position as
Australian selector. It was very much, in Australian cricket administration, the night, week and year of the long knives, and the
NSWCA members were the sufferers.

Furthermore the Board, incredibly, fiddled the minutes of a
meeting in the most extraordinary fashion, producing a document which bore no relation to what actually happened, and

pretended there had been no discussion concerning Barnes and his exclusion.

Barnes subsequently instigated a court case in Sydney and there were some very unusual happenings in the course of the legal skirmishes and after the event. One of the strangest was that following the axing of Oxlade and Dwyer, Keith Johnson the 1948 team manager and NSW Board representative actually retained his Board place. He had voted against Barnes, had been party to the doctored minutes of the particular meeting and then, in court, agreed that in his end-of-tour review to the Board after the 1948 tour he had given every player, including Barnes, what was termed 'a glowing report'.

Chappie Dwyer, as honest a man as you would find in or out of cricket circles, said of Barnes in the witness box, 'I have a high opinion of Barnes as a cricketer and no objection to him as a man.'

The defendant in the case was a Mr Jacob Raith, someone who suddenly appeared as a letter writer to a Sydney newspaper, castigating Barnes and casting aspersions on his character and supporting the Board. *Raith's* Counsel made a statement to the judge when the defence had disintegrated and the defending Counsel's words should have reverberated around the walls of Cricket House, and every other administrative room in the land, but I doubt they did so. He said, speaking of the Board's actions and words, 'Seldom in the history of libel actions has such a plea failed so completely and utterly. The Board has presented an awful image of the chaos and bigotry under which Australian cricket is administered.'

No such reverberating happened. If anything, the whole issue strengthened the power of the Board in that it could clearly be seen that anyone who had the hide to have a dissenting voice, or even a dissenting thought, may not be absolutely sure of a continuing career in the game.

You can take it for granted that, aged twenty-two and trying desperately again to play for Australia, I had no intention of sticking my neck out in any way which might have given anyone the

slightest excuse to ask: 'That young Benaud in NSW, good cricketer but does he have some kind of problem?'

When, in December 1951, that Australian team to play West
Indies in Adelaide had assembled without Barnes, the twelve
consisted of Lindsay Hassett (captain), Arthur Morris (vice-
captain), Jim Burke, Neil Harvey, Keith Miller, Graeme Hole, Ray
Lindwall, Ian Johnson, Doug Ring, Gil Langley, Bill Johnston and
Geff Noblet – a good team with a balanced look about it. That
idyllic state of balance lasted only until the practice the day before
the game was due to start when Lindsay Hassett slightly strained
a muscle in his hip and pulled out of the side.

The selectors chose Phil Ridings, a fine cricketer, as his replacement. However, not every single Board member around Australia
was able to be contacted by telephone that Saturday morning, so
what did they do? You may think they would have had in place
a method whereby a small committee, say an executive committee, would have been empowered to ratify any selection changes
needed; or the Chairman of the Board invested with some powers.
What, for example, if three players had been injured in a car
accident?

As it was, so lacking in foresight were the Board, that precisely
the same twelve players as originally named *had* to represent
Australia with what was now a very unbalanced line-up. It was a
crass piece of administration. The players knew it and the public
knew it, but it made no difference.

Some years later, when writing about my own and other young
players' thoughts at the time, I said of the Board, 'Those were
the days when you spoke with a touch of reverence and a certain
amount of humility to cricket officials in their navy blue suits,
white shirts and strong leather shoes. Jack might have been as
good as his mate in the outback of Australia in the 1800s but it
took a while for the idea to permeate through to the various state
Associations and the Australian Cricket Board.'

For me, every match would count this summer, no doubt failure would be lurking somewhere nearby, but success might also
not be far away. Having played a Test at the end of the previous

summer and batted many times at seven and once at eight, I was hoping for permanent batting-order promotion this year, particularly in the light of the 97 batting at number three against South Australia in the last Sheffield Shield match.

Although Barnes had led the side in that final game, Arthur Morris was the NSW captain the previous summer. A bombshell came in the second week of October in this 1952–53 season when Morris was sacked by the state selectors and Keith Miller was named as skipper. No one ever told Morris why he was sacked. An apocryphal story went the rounds that his hand-made suede shoes with their crêpe rubber soles were regarded as far too flamboyant for NSW cricket, but the real reason probably was that the state administrators wanted to be seen to be taking action in the light of falling attendances, something they were at a loss to explain. Perhaps the Bradman factor and his retirement may have been an explanation, or it could have been that the habits of the public were changing. Many people now owned motor cars, and instead of going to the cricket they probably went on picnics or similar jaunts.

There was nothing wrong with the cricket Morris and NSW had played, and NSW had been successful the previous season, easily winning the Sheffield Shield, with Arthur, as captain, making 700 runs in fast time at an average of over 50 an innings. Difficult to find anything more attacking than that. No one bothered to tell Morris of his sacking, even though NSWCA officials were well aware he was in Hong Kong on a cricket tour to celebrate the centenary of the Hong Kong Cricket League. It was unfeeling administration, though not in any way unique.

The advent of Miller as skipper made no difference to the batting order at this stage, and after he won the toss in the first Shield match at the 'Gabba, we made 499 against Queensland. I made a brisk 63 at number eight and did a lot of bowling, taking five wickets in the match. In Queensland's second knock, Colin McCool added to his first-innings 100* with a delightful 88 in two hours and looked a classy player.

Colin was a tough character, but a very good player, who was beset throughout his career with spinning-finger problems. He gave the ball a tremendous tweak and it was no wonder he ripped away some of the skin from his spinning fingers, which was extremely painful. How do I know that? Well, I suffered from exactly the same thing and there were times when it was agonising.

At the end of this match I was sitting in the dressing-room looking at my bowling hand when Colin came over and asked to have a look at my fingers. 'Son,' he said, 'find some bloody way to fix those or you'll have an extremely short career.'

That wasn't exactly what I wanted to hear. I knew he had a very good point, but when I asked him how to fix them he said he didn't know. Apparently he'd always had the problem and it had cost him a place in the final Test at The Oval in 1948 when he had the bad luck at breakfast to sit near Bradman who saw the damage.

My only method of coping with my finger problems at that stage was simply to bear the pain. Grit your teeth and keep bowling. I would come back to the dressing-room from some bowling stints with blood either running from my two spinning fingers or caked on them. I tried Friars' Balsam, methylated spirits, every known skin hardener and softener, and even a type of plastic glue which was said to form some sort of coating over the skin and wouldn't come off. It lasted two overs at best. Nothing worked, nothing even looked remotely like working.

McCool told me that if I were not prepared to bear the pain I might just as well stop playing. He was a realist, and he was certainly a help, because he added that he never, even for one hour in any one day, stopped trying to find a remedy, and that's what I must do. I listened hard, and, from October 1952, I never stopped trying to find the answer to this painful and career-threatening problem.

8

WELCOME SPRINGBOKS

WHEN the South African team to tour Australia was announced after a washed-out trial match in Cape Town, Jackie McGlew of Natal and Jack Cheetham of Western Province were named as vice-captain and captain. They were two fine cricketers of very different types. The manager of the team was Ken Viljoen, who had been in the 1931–32 South African team, and he and Cheetham set about turning the players into a well-drilled unit and one of the finest fielding teams to tour any country. They succeeded, I suspect beyond even their wildest dreams, but there was nothing accidental about it. I liked the way Cheetham, formerly a fitness instructor, organised his special fielding drills and exercises, many of which we had never seen before. In modern times, coaches, who abound at every turn, are of the opinion they have produced something new in cricket. They may not know it, some of them may even not know the name Cheetham, but they are merely copying the South African captain of 1952 and, despite the time warp, sometimes not doing it as well.

The South African tourists were officially welcomed at a reception at a function room in the old State Theatre complex in Market Street. I was keen to meet up with the South Africans, and when I first saw them, they seemed very happy, courteous, well mannered and calm. They needed to be during this evening!

Sydney Smith, who had previously aired his fears for the success of the tour, started on the congratulatory note that no South African team had done anything in Australia, which was why there had been so few tours. Percy Sherwell's team, he reminded the packed room, had not only been very fortunate to win a Test in 1910–11, but they shouldn't actually have been in the country at all. Syd would have known all about that because he was secretary of the Australian Board between 1911 and 1926, having been appointed to the position by W. P. McElhone. It had been agreed that the Australians would play in the 1912 Triangular series in England, only on condition that the South Africans toured Australia the previous summer. When I later decided to look back on their record for that tour, they seemed a talented side, and won the Adelaide Test by 38 runs despite Victor Trumper making 214 against them in an Australian first innings of 465. There was much more along critical lines from Mr Smith during that speech and it seemed as though it would never end, but fortunately it did.

Jack Cheetham was a quietly spoken man and he thanked Mr Smith for his hospitable welcome, coupling Mr Smith's name with that of the NSWCA . . . together with all others present. There was an embarrassed hush at this, and a certain amount of shuffling of feet, and I could have sworn there were some present who would have preferred their names not to be linked with what was supposed to be a welcome, and an hospitable one at that.

Cheetham tied in his very short reply with the sheep and cattle industries of both countries, finishing with the thought that after the welcome afforded his team tonight, he knew Australia to be ahead in some things, notably in the area of exporting stud cattle or, as it was known in South Africa, *bull-shipping*! I've rarely heard such applause, and all of it had come in response to a perfectly laid-back, straight-faced delivery.

I was twelfth man for the First Test against South Africa in Brisbane. It was a tough game in which the Australian selectors were booed as they took their seats because Gil Langley was in the side instead of local hero Don Tallon. Gilbert was a fine 'keeper, not the tidiest of custodians as regards dress, but very good with the gloves. When Gil missed stumping John Watkins off Ian Johnson on the second day of this Brisbane Test, the crowd didn't miss him. Fortunately for him there were only 10,000 there that day, although they made enough noise for 30,000. Keith Miller developed a throat infection and had to fly back to Sydney so he was unable to bowl in South Africa's second innings. It gave me the chance to do plenty of fielding but it wasn't the way I'd have liked it to happen.

The match was played on a very slow pitch and Ray Lindwall turned in one of his finest performances. With no Miller at the other end, Doug Ring, after taking six wickets and bowling superbly in the first innings, was unable to get anything out of the pitch in the second, and some of the fielding bore little relation to what you would normally see from an Australian side. It was, to put it mildly, sloppy, and there were questions asked even at this early stage of the summer about the mobility of some of the players who had served Australia so well over the previous six years since the end of the War. There were also comparisons with the South Africans' athleticism. Ian Johnson bowled very well, and his combination with Lindwall, and the latter's five wickets, proved too much in the end for the South African batsmen.

We flew back from Brisbane to Sydney the day after the match, happy to have won what was in fact a much tighter contest than it appeared on paper. I went to practise my batting and bowling at the SCG the following day, and particularly my fielding. When watching my father play for Cumberland I had always been mortified at the number of catches dropped from his bowling and the sometimes poor ground fielding. Two of the things he had always stressed to me were that if I couldn't be a good cricketer, at least I should try to look like one, and that I should try to make myself into one of the best fieldsmen in the country. My father had listened to as much of the Test as possible on the radio and said that while the remarks from the commentators had been very positive about my fielding, the general tone had been critical of Australia's out-cricket. 'Make sure you field well,' he said again.

The Australian selectors named a young team for the Australian XI side to meet South Africa at the SCG, something of a trial match for those chosen, and there was a clear indication here that selectors were looking towards youth for the forthcoming tour of England. At least, I hoped they were! Phil Ridings was captain and he was one of the best fieldsmen I had seen. He was also an

Australian selector. I set myself to do whatever I could in emphasising the value I put on good fielding and, from a slightly selfish point of view, thereby impressing one of the three important men of the summer.

Rain on the third day of this Australian XI encounter with South Africa meant we were unlikely to achieve a result, although there was no doubt we had the best of the match. I made 60 and 37, and although I took only one wicket, aged twenty-two, I was in the twelve for the Melbourne Test to be played over the Christmas break. This match was the turning point for the South Africans, who were still being patronised around Australia. As it happened, it took only forty-seven days for Syd Smith's speech to become *really* humorous, because South Africa beat Australia by 82 runs at the MCG in this Second Test of the series. The feature of the second day was the South African fielding, and if ever there were to be a lesson about the value of great fielding, it was here. They saved runs in the field by diving and sliding, took magnificent catches and generally looked like a wonderfully athletic and talented side.

It was during this game I first experienced the full special field-setting employed by the South African offspinner Hughie Tayfield: often three men, or even four, in positions loosely described at the time as silly or short mid-on and mid-off, although they weren't really in those spots at all, rather they were back for the lofted drive and positioned a yard or two down the pitch from the batting crease at the non-striker's end. 'Toey' Tayfield was a great flight bowler who could spin the ball as well.

It was with the flight and the unusual field-settings that Tayfield caused most problems, and one of the catches taken to dismiss Arthur Morris, via Cheetham on the offside of the wicket, was magnificent, the ball having bounced off Cheetham's hands and shoulder after the fierce drive, before Tayfield performed an acrobatic dive to complete the dismissal. Miller was caught by Russell Endean, a wonderful effort out on the boundary which brought 25,000 spectators to their feet, cheering Endean for a full minute. I had never heard anything to match it for an outfield catch.

These days in Australia we have on Channel 9 Television Classic Catches, which are very popular both for watching and as a competition. Endean's effort this day at the MCG would have been a winner, remarkably similar to Steve Waugh catching Roger Harper at the MCG some years ago to win a Classic Catches sequence.

We needed 373 to win the Second Test and were beaten by 82 runs. This win by South Africa was a boost to the tour but an embarrassment to those who had written off the touring party. It did little for the confidence of the beaten players, I can tell you. Suddenly the situation had changed dramatically. When I had set out from Sydney to play in the Test, I was full of confidence; now it was a different matter, with the Test series all square and still three matches to go and a team to be chosen to tour England at the end of the summer.

Two days after this setback, NSW were to play South Africa in the New Year match at the SCG, a match which turned out to be completely dominated by Ian Craig. Miller won the toss and put South Africa in to bat and we bowled them out for 196; I took 3–37 and Sid Barnes 3–24. When we batted we had as much trouble as the South Africans. I had never seen the ball swing more, and Anton Murray and Michael Melle in particular were very difficult to play. We lost Carroll, Morris and de Courcy for 80, and Craig and I had added 32 when he played a ball to the right of Gerald Innes. Craig called for a single and I responded. Innes dived away to his right, gathered in the ball just as 'Craigie' shouted 'No' and 'Sorry', the two words you never want to hear when running between the wickets. We met in the middle of the pitch looking very woebegone. Innes had plenty of time to make his choice and he decided to return the ball to 'keeper Johnny Waite. I said to Ian, 'Come on,' and ran past him. There was no need for any third umpire.

I didn't even mention to Craig that in the light of his 'call' he should make a hundred, but he did anyway, and then went on to a double century. It was wonderful to watch. His 213 not out thrust him into the forefront of players under scrutiny for the tour of England.

The cricket writers went absolutely berserk. 'The New Bradman' was the theme. 'A blind man can see he is another Bradman.' Bill O'Reilly led the chorus in a campaign that could only have done harm to Ian. It was the kiss of death for a young batsman in Australia to be so tagged, and the sad thing was that the critics were well aware of what they were doing, as still happens today. The search for a catchy intro to a story and a blazing headline was an invitation too glittering to ignore, or even refuse. There will never be another Bradman, no one will be a good enough batsman and they knew it, but still wrote on that angle.

This was a busy time. My fiancée and I were rushing around making arrangements to be married between the Third and Fourth Test matches in Sydney and Adelaide. We had met when we worked together in Alan Savage's accountancy office, had been engaged for two years and, like so many other young people at the time, were looking forward to a happy life. The events of the next few days put a slight dampener on proceedings and required more mumbling than clear answering, having made it to the church on time.

9

SEEING THE INSIDE OF ANOTHER HOSPITAL

THE Third Test at the SCG was the one where Australia needed to make a big comeback and the selectors chose an unchanged side. There was considerable interest in the match now that the South Africans had squared the series. The pitch was green and slightly moist, and Lindwall, Miller and Bill Johnston bowled magnificently on the first morning, or so I'm told. I know they bowled very well in the first hour because I was on the field rather than in hospital. Hassett had cleverly brought on Bill Johnston at the Paddington End after Lindwall had finished six magnificent overs. With the moisture in the surface there was some turn for Bill in his slower style, which was left-arm over-the-wicket spin. Twice he found the outside edge of the bat and I edged closer and closer to the bat at short gully waiting for the possibility of a catch. Then suddenly Bill let go a faster ball – he was most of the time a very lively fast-medium bowler – and Johnny Waite connected with a fierce square cut.

The ball hit me flush in the mouth and, as I was helped off the ground, the player standing at the gate ready to come on as the twelfth man and substitute fieldsman was Jim de Courcy – again. Only four years earlier he had stood at the gate of the MCG when I had been stretchered off with that head injury in the Second XI match. He was still a man of very few words; he nodded to me as I went past him. Jim and I seemed to be making a habit of this kind of thing.

Although Waite's shot had been hit with all his power, and although it hit me absolutely straight on the mouth, it was also one of the luckiest things which ever happened to me. You may wish to query that with a raised eyebrow, even two raised eyebrows, but yes, it was very lucky. After I had been carted off in the ambulance to nearby St Vincent's Hospital, the doctors made it clear in their examination that if the ball, struck with such force, had hit me two inches to the right or left it would have shattered my cheekbone. Had it hit me in the eye I may well have lost an eye; an appallingly broken nose would have been the result with a square-on hit; a broken jaw a little further down. Had it struck me on that previous fracture, the one sustained in the Second XI game in Melbourne in 1949, I may not have walked anywhere, let alone back on to a cricket field. They explained, in high good humour, that this was a lucky break for me, not only because it hit me on the soft tissue of my mouth but also because I had dentures which I'd worn from the age of fifteen after a shortage of body calcium had resulted in teeth and bone problems. The dentures had shattered into twenty-seven pieces, which I'd had the foresight instinctively to spit into a handkerchief. In effect, said the doctors, all I now needed to do was pull myself together but, above all, be very wary indeed of the possible shock, which could come within twenty-four hours. When I asked if I might make it back on to the field in this match, the doctors wouldn't discount the thought but they kept stressing I needed to be careful of the post-impact shock. They were right.

There was quite a shock to the system the following day, but it didn't last all that long. I went to see Alf Hall, a dental mechanic, and he put the twenty-seven denture pieces back together again. Alf was my first captain at Cumberland, a tall, soldierly man, a fine leader of young cricketers, a thoroughly genuine player and person, and as a bonus, a very good dental man. I stuck some plaster over a very badly cut top lip and went back to the SCG on the third day, when I was stupid enough to make a duck, lbw playing forward to Michael Melle. The most disappointing thing of all after the medical men had given me the clearance and I had been able to walk out on to the SCG again, was not to have been able to make the most of it.

Neil Harvey was one who did make the most of the batting conditions, playing a superb innings of 190 which gave Australia a 270-run lead and plenty of time in which once more to take the lead in the series. Lindwall, Miller and Bill Johnston did it again and although Hassett didn't *have* to bowl me he kindly gave me six overs at the end and I picked up the wickets of Percy Mansell and Anton Murray. It was good to be back in the game, I can tell you, and as I also took a really good catch, diving at leg-slip to dismiss Roy McLean off Lindwall to end a century stand with John Watkins, I finished the game a little happier than I had started, even if it had been of less than four days' duration, part of which I had spent in hospital.

If the Australian selectors, Messrs Ryder, Brown and Ridings, were seen to be testing and encouraging the cricketing youth of the country, and at the same time were keen on fostering young players for the future, the same could be said for the NSW selectors. Starting back in 1946 with those tours to country areas inside NSW, this encouragement had continued with the NSW Colts games against Queensland, and Second XI matches against Victoria. A variety of selections such as Ian Craig and others emphasised that this was the beginning of a new era. After the Third Test against the South Africans, the NSW selectors produced another young player for the game against Victoria in sixteen-year-old Bob Simpson, who had been making a name for himself in Sydney club cricket. NSW won the match on the first innings and Simpson made 44* and 8*, a very good debut against a Victorian side which not only played well but was not lacking at all in determination and the desire to let the opposition know they were in for a tough game.

In the break between the Third and Fourth Test matches Marcia and I were married, although my vows were mumbled because of the mouth injury. We had a brief honeymoon at Jervis Bay and in Sydney and then we flew to Adelaide for the Fourth Test.

The Australian selectors underlined their interest in youth throughout the summer, and they extended that, in a sense, by bringing in seventeen-year-old Ian Craig as twelfth man for the Test to be played in the City of Churches, in an otherwise unchanged team. Australia took most of the honours in Adelaide, making 530 and then bowling out South Africa for 387, and this despite losing Ray Lindwall and Keith Miller with leg and back problems. These injuries were very disturbing for Lindsay Hassett, who would be captain for the tour of England, and for me too, since both Miller and Lindwall played with NSW and the Sheffield Shield would be affected. The bowling attack in Adelaide looked thin without them, something that would have exercised Hassett's mind.

It did, however, allow me to take another step towards England, because Bill Johnston and I did most of the bowling. I finished with 4–118 in 44 overs. One very significant aspect of the match was that Colin McDonald made 154 and shared an excellent partnership with Hassett. Graeme Hole continued his solid form with 59. The selectors were seeing something from those two, and from me, although my performances were steady rather than sensational, and there was still one Test to go in the series.

I was confident enough to believe I would be chosen for the Melbourne Test after having taken 4–118 in Adelaide and this proved to be so. However, there were some surprises in the selectors' nominations for the final game; Australia couldn't lose the series but it could be drawn if the South Africans won. Exactly what people like Syd Smith and the other administrators who had knocked the South Africans were now thinking was never made public, but the Australian players had never been in any doubt about the difficulty of beating the Springboks. What happened next turned the tour into a real fairy story for Jack Cheetham's South Africans, and if not a horror story for those who had rubbished them, then not far short of it.

Ian Craig came into the XI in Melbourne and did very well and Ron Archer and Geff Noblet were chosen to replace Lindwall and Miller who were being rested. It was a rather strange-looking Australian side, but the accent once again was on youth. From my point of view, I needed a decent game if I were to secure a place in the touring side which was to be announced on the last day of the final Test in Melbourne.

In the event Australia lost, after being in charge for much of the time, and I had an ordinary match, making 20 and 30 and taking 0–55 and 1–41. It's not often a team loses a Test after making more than 500 in their own first innings, and not often a team wins one at the MCG batting last and needing almost 300 for victory.

There was no excitement to be had in losing, only trepidation that the loss may well have persuaded the selectors that I needed more experience before being chosen for an overseas tour.

When the team was announced it was more of a relief than anything when I found my name among the touring party of seventeen. There were others who were unhappy at their exclusion. An hour after the announcement excitement took over, but it was definitely tempered by the knowledge that there would be very few accolades flying about in the media for the players about to undertake the trip. That was certainly shown to be correct by the sports pages in the newspapers the following morning, but perhaps they knew best because we did leave the Ashes behind in England.

The team was: Lindsay Hassett (captain), Arthur Morris (vice-captain), Ron Archer, Richie Benaud, Ian Craig, Alan Davidson, Jim de Courcy, Neil Harvey, Jack Hill, Graeme Hole, Bill Johnston, Gil Langley, Ray Lindwall, Colin McDonald, Keith Miller, Doug Ring, Don Tallon.

There was plenty happening in Australian cricket at this time. Although Jimmy Burke, my very good mate from Sydney, had missed the trip to England, he was enthusiastic about an invitation he had received to go on a short cricket tour to India. In addition to Burke, other NSW players were invited on the Indian tour – Jack Moroney, Geoff Trueman, Ray Flockton and Alan Walker – along with prominent players from other states. The organiser was a former Australian umpire, Andy Barlow, a highly respected character in Australian cricket.

The Board gave Barlow's tour very short shrift, something they have tended to do over the years with anyone who has ideas of organising anything to do with what is termed 'other cricket'. One of the sticking points for the Board was that each player was to be paid £750 plus all expenses, remuneration that, pro rata, could have put the Board's own payments for Test matches and tours in a poor light.

A Commonwealth team did eventually tour India that year but it was organised by Ben Barnett the former Australian wicket-keeper. The tour was to celebrate twenty-five years of the Indian Board of Control and it produced one intriguing happening when Jack Iverson, unavailable for the tour of England, was flown in as a replacement for 'Sonny' Ramadhin who had to return to the West Indies for a Test series. Iverson did well, which only underlined my thinking then and later that had he been with us in England, the Ashes would have returned to Australia.

On the domestic front, I was newly married, was working at the *Sun* newspaper and there was not much money around. My wife continued working as a secretary, which was unlikely to be a great deal of fun for her as a newly-wed. The Australian Board policy was clear on the question of wives being allowed to see husbands on tour, or even to be in the same country as a touring team. Looking back, it seems extraordinary that such rules could exist and there is no doubt it put considerable strain on marriages and had done so since cricket teams had begun touring.

The tour of England was going to be a little less than eight months in length and the payments were small, although no one in the side would have thought of mentioning it. The Board claimed that they had no money available to pay more to the players, and made a point of the fact that the Sheffield Shield was losing money, though they admitted grudgingly that Australian cricket overall was in quite good shape.

Between the end of the last Test match on 12 February and stepping on to the *Orcades* in Sydney on 4 March, there was a lot of packing to be done, injections and inoculations to be arranged, private life to be sorted out, having been married only a few weeks, and a non-stop series of functions to attend. These functions were sometimes financially beneficial and I was grateful to the friends who privately set them up, realising what problems there would be for my wife at home having to manage on the fee paid to players.

I had been given an inkling of the feelings of Board of Control members on matters fiscal on the afternoon the team was announced. I was on the steps of the Windsor Hotel, having just returned from the MCG, when Board member Frank Cush, a very pleasant chap from NSW, hailed me and kindly offered his congratulations. He then took me aside and said very quietly, 'Never let money interfere with your cricket, Richie, never think of money, only play for the love of the game.'

I saw what he meant when he walked down the steps and got into what looked like a very large Pontiac which had apparently recently been imported from America. Judging by the scale of pay I had seen listed that afternoon for the tour of England, money was most unlikely to be a distraction for any of the players.

10

ENGLAND FOR THE FIRST TIME

THE arrangement in those days, before Tasmania became a Sheffield Shield team, was that the touring side played two games in the Apple Isle, one against Tassie and the other a Combined XI against an Australian XI. The games were first class, and competitive. I didn't play in the first one but made 167* and took 5–87 and 2–50 in the second match, which was played on a beautiful batting pitch at Launceston. It was the first occasion when, as an Australian XI player, I shared in some good things on the field with Alan Davidson. Davo made 90 and we put on 167 in 86 minutes. He also took 3–45 and it was the start of a useful ten-year partnership between us in Australian cricket. It was a quirk of the game that the brilliant left-arm over-the-wrist spinner of schooldays was now the great all-round hope of Australian cricket as a left-arm pace bowler.

We flew back to Melbourne and boarded another plane for Perth where we were to play a match against Western Australia before rejoining the *Orcades* which was steaming around the Bight and on its way to Fremantle.

As often happens to people travelling overseas for the first time, I had some reaction to the typhoid and cholera injections but, oddly, after seven days in Tasmania I had no reaction at all to the vaccination for smallpox. The yellow form said that if there was no reaction after a week it hadn't 'taken' and to seek medical advice and have it done again. This I did, in Launceston, and the full reaction hit me in Perth the day and night before the match against WA. I was sweating and experiencing all the symptoms of a mild case of smallpox, but I didn't want to miss the match because it was being played on the Thursday, Friday and Saturday and I knew Hassett, Miller, Bill Johnston and a couple of the other players had planned a social Saturday in the committee room at the Ascot races, and I certainly didn't want one of them to have to miss out.

There was an interesting aftermath. I had specified my left arm for the vaccination, because I wanted to be able to bowl with minimum discomfort, but what I hadn't realised was that there would be such a severe reaction and that my left arm would be very stiff. Arthur Morris was captain, he lost the toss and we bowled out WA for 179. When I went out to join Craig we added 148 in 106 minutes, I reached my hundred in almost even time and I did it with the very sore left arm, which was something of a lesson for me. It was much more comfortable for me to keep my arm bent, in a position similar to some of the coaching photographs where batsmen are exhorted to 'keep your left elbow up'. I found I automatically played in more correct fashion, something everyone had been telling me to do over a period of many years. Perhaps I needed more smallpox vaccinations.

The match finished in a draw, and it gave me a chance to take stock of the summer and see what I had achieved, apart from the obvious thing of making it into the Australian team to tour England. My chances of selection had been done no harm by being in the right place at the right time, as well as by the aftermath of the ridiculous new-ball legislation – 55 overs in England and 40 overs in Australia when it began – and the fact that a new selection committee was looking to youth for the future. I finished seventh in the Australian first-class batting averages for the whole season and seventh in the aggregate runs (734 at 43.17). I was eighth in the wickets taken with 38 but, at 32 runs per wicket, they had been expensive. I was ahead of most, but behind some other good players. The thing to do now was work very hard and learn what I could from this tour.

We had a day in Perth after the game against Western Australia for some last-minute shopping and then it was down to Fremantle to join the ship as the last passengers for what was going to be a fast and, in the end, record-breaking trip by sea to Tilbury.

My room-mate for the tour was Graeme Hole. 'Olley' was a fine cricketer, at the time playing with South Australia but originally from NSW, and a good chap, generous and quiet and very keen indeed on his cricket. We didn't know it at the time, you never do when faced with having a room-mate for months on end, but we were to become good friends in a short space of time, a friendship that would remain for many years until his untimely death, aged fifty-nine, in 1990.

Shipboard life might not suit a lot of people, I suppose, but after a hectic summer I very much appreciated the drop in tension, and the chance to have myself really fit for the start of the tour.

There are a lot of things you can't do on a ship because of the rolling motion; even with very good stabilisers on board you must be careful you don't suffer an injury. Neil Harvey, with his experience of the 1948 tour, was the one who was able to explain to us what we might be able to do, and he and I developed a very good fitness regime on that tour and later in 1956 and 1961. The days might sound boring to some, but for a cricket team they worked out very well. Some of the players wanted nothing more than complete relaxation, and I could understand that, particularly the pace bowlers like Miller and Lindwall who had gone through a gruelling summer. Others like Neil and I wanted relaxation plus some specific exercise during the twenty-one days on board, and that in itself needed careful planning. We also had 15,000 autograph sheets to sign, all of which had to be accounted for to George Davies, the manager of the team.

George's sense of humour had already appealed to us on our way from Essendon Airport to the Windsor Hotel in Melbourne. Suddenly the bus stopped, not long after we had left the airport, and George got out.

'Where are you going, George?' we enquired.

'Well, home of course,' was the reply. 'I live in the next street. No point in going to stay with you jokers. You know the Windsor Hotel, it's in Spring Street.' Not what you would call Plan A in the managerial stakes, and George's sense of humour was looked on with a slightly wary eye for some time.

The relaxation and exercise programme I worked out with Neil Harvey involved taking second-sitting breakfast before moving to the private lounge where the whole team assembled to sign the autographs, something like 750 a day. Then we went up on deck for a relaxing hour before a game of over-the-net deck tennis with the circular quoits. This game resembled a combination of squash, tennis and badminton with its constant but careful turning and twisting, bending and jumping. We would enjoy a quiet hour on deck after lunch, then another two hours of deck tennis, again to our own rules, where we caught everything and used it as a fitness tool. A hot shower or a sea bath was followed by dinner, more relaxing on deck and bed. This meant plenty of relaxation but also three hours of solid fitness training every day. When we arrived at Tilbury on 13 April I had never been fitter, even though it was not in keeping with my previous personal strictures about training for cricket almost exclusively with cricket exercises.

I couldn't sleep the last night out of port and I was up early looking at the land as it appeared through fog and filmy mist. I was a long way from Parramatta, and a long way too from Jugiong and the little store room, a considerable distance for a Parramatta boy who had played in the paddock across the road, had hit a ball through Mrs Vidler's window and had scored for Cumberland seconds during the war years, hoping all the while there might be a chance of fielding for ten minutes if one of the soldiers or airmen didn't turn up. A lot of people might think of it as a dream come true, but it was more than that. It was almost beyond belief that in two days' time I would be walking into Lord's, referred to in all those wonderful books I had read as 'The Home of Cricket'.

'Jeezzz, Harv, it's not even level, *it slopes*!' It wasn't something that would have bothered Thomas Lord had he heard me say it, because the man who had created the ground would have been well aware of this. Neil and I, with Alan Davidson and Ron

Archer, had stepped out of our car at the Grace gates at Lord's and walked inside. Neil told us to turn slightly right so we were looking at the ground from the area of the Old Tavern. Neil had been there in 1948 and he stood back as we, the newcomers, saw it for the first time.

'Not level, eh,' he said. 'And it slopes. So would you if you were 139 years old!' The slope in fact is eight feet from west to east, left to right if you are looking from the Members' Pavilion, a fall of 1 in 56. It works out at something like a two-inch slope in one pitch, and generally it means that pace bowlers at the Pavilion End would be wise to have, as their line, six inches outside off stump, rather than directly at it.

That morning and the following two weeks of practice confirmed for me it was a delightful old place. In the ensuing 57 years it has changed a great deal, with a new-style Grand Stand, changes to the Mound Stand, an excellent new Media Centre and the installation of lights for day-night fixtures. There are more changes to come with the Compton-Edrich stands; splendid modern-day thinking, but still retaining the wonderful atmosphere.

After one indoor practice session at the Television Centre at Alexandra Palace, an arrangement with BBC Television which was excellent publicity for the team, we had a fortnight of practices at Lord's, as well as lunches, dinners and receptions. The evening functions were mostly black tie and some of the speeches were magnificent. Sir Norman Birkett, who later became Lord Birkett, first Baron Birkett of Ulverstone, was said to have one of the world's greatest legal minds. I can't vouch for that, but he was the best after-dinner speaker I ever heard. He spoke at Skinners' Hall at the Cricket Writers' dinner.

The Cricket Writers' Club was the brainchild of E. W. Swanton who came up with the idea when he was covering the MCC tour of Australia in 1946–47. Wally Hammond was captain of that team, and it was a brave move by MCC to undertake the tour so soon after the end of the war. Jim Swanton was a fine writer. Concentrating more on cricket than anything else, he worked first for the London *Evening Standard* from 1927 to 1938 and then painted word pictures of cricket for more than fifty years in the *Daily Telegraph*. He was with BBC Radio from 1934 onwards and with BBC Television from 1946 through to the 1980s, and also on *Test Match Special*. The Cricket Writers' Club began as a loosely woven group of cricket writers, most of them skilful as wordsmiths and in their command of the English language, and they wrote for conservative broadsheets or for English newspapers of massive circulation.

Sir Alan Herbert, MP and *Punch* columnist, was in fine form at the British Sportsman's Club lunch at the Savoy, and I heard him speak on later tours as well. He was able to remind Lindwall and Miller, 'When you rub the ball on your groin or belly . . . remember how it looks on telly!'

The opening of the Lord's Imperial Cricket Memorial Gallery was an exciting event, and in those days there was nothing anachronistic about the Royal Empire Society giving a cocktail party for the team. None of the cocktail party circuit worried me: as a responsible twenty-two-year-old playing for his country, I wouldn't dream of allowing alcohol to pass my lips, because in a couple of weeks I had a cricket match or two to play and I didn't want to do anything that might in any way have an effect on my performance. Rather prissy!

The practices went well and the practice pitches were excellent, though not covered, which was a good idea because in those days match pitches in England weren't covered. We needed all the practice we could manage on what was for most of us, a new type of surface. I still think it is a great pity that there is total covering of pitches now in England, and I believe the reliance on covering has affected some areas of English batting skills. Harvey told me I would find it quite an experience playing against top-line bowlers on slightly grassy pitches and then finding rain had completely changed the character of those surfaces. Hassett spent a lot of time with the younger players making certain we knew what we should be doing and how we should be practising, even if we couldn't always manage it as he suggested.

The younger players tended to stick together in this early part of the tour. If we were teetotallers we weren't to be found in the bar having a beer, although this was no different from the Sheffield Shield matches in Australia, where after the game Jimmy Burke and Ian Craig and I might go to the cinema and afterwards have a glass of orange juice. In London we stayed at the Park Lane Hotel in Piccadilly, and the first night we were there Neil Harvey said he knew of a little sandwich bar at Piccadilly Circus where five years earlier he had found outstanding sandwiches made to order. We walked up past Eros and a few yards into Shaftesbury Avenue, and he was right. Iced coffee and a roast beef and English mustard or chutney sandwich, or any other variety, turned out to be a delightful and inexpensive meal, the latter of some importance as money was scarce for me in England and for my wife in Australia for the eight months I was away from home. One thing we never lost sight of, though, was the fact that in some areas in England at that time, rationing and coupons still applied, better than in 1948 Neil said, but still something to be borne in mind.

It was at the Park Lane during our first week that Lindsay, having ordered a double ice-cream for dessert, was unfortunate enough to have the waiter drop it in his lap; they looked at one another and he sensibly declined the waiter's offer to retrieve it with a metal scoop. Instead, he stood up, removed his trousers, handed them to the waiter and asked, poker-faced, to have them cleaned and returned in time for coffee. Oh, and could he please have another double ice-cream? Wouldn't get away with it these days, would he?

Our first match, only a one-day game, was against East Molesey, and Bill Johnston and the team had the most appalling luck when he damaged his right knee so badly he wasn't able to play for a considerable time and even then could only show a glimpse of his former skills.

Our first trip out of London was to Worcester, the ground about which I had heard so much, and where Bradman had made 236, 206, 258 and 107 in his four appearances. There were good cricketers in the opposition and we knew we would need to be in good form. Worcestershire made 333 in icy and wet conditions.

I fielded in four sweaters and bowled in two and if I could have fielded in six I would have done so. It was impossible to get warm, and had they been around at the time, I would have worn a couple of T-shirts underneath my cricket shirt. I took 2–66 in 29 overs but found it difficult to grip the ball, let alone spin it. We started in abysmal fashion, losing McDonald, Morris and Hassett for 28 before Miller began to dominate and made 220. I made 44 and thoroughly enjoyed it. Miller was down to talk to me at the end of every over and his main advice was to 'Get forward, son, this is a slow low pitch, get forward.' Ron Archer heeded his advice a little better than I did and he made a dashing 108 including 18 boundaries.

Our match against Yorkshire was played at Bradford where, unbelievably, it was colder than Worcester. Fortunately, in the dressing-room was a wonderful, glorious, log fire. We didn't actually huddle around it, but we sat there in wicker chairs, keeping warm and keeping the blood circulating.

We were away to a reasonable start, and I again shared a partnership with Miller. 'Different pitch, son, you still need to be forward because the ball's moving off the seam but you'll need some back-foot play here as well.' Keith and I put together 152 in two hours. I made the most of Miller's advice and was three short of a century when Norman Yardley came on and had me caught behind by Don Brennan.

We closed at 453–6, and shortly afterwards I saw one of the finest sights of my life and heard one of the strangest sounds. The sight was Len Hutton's stump cartwheeling towards Gil Langley and the sound was silence. I'd never experienced this before: normally a wicket would bring a roar from a crowd, but this one brought a hush, matched only by what happened up the road at Headingley eleven weeks later when Lindwall bowled Hutton with his second ball in the Test match. I followed Lindwall at the Pavilion End at Bradford this day and took 7–46 in the Yorkshire first innings, and up to this time I had every cause to be happy with my form.

At The Oval in the game against Surrey we were all superfluous to the short but exciting battle between Ray Lindwall and Peter May. It was important, Lindsay told us, to dent Peter's confidence after his successes against South Africa and India. Ray was given the job and completed it successfully with one of the greatest overs I have seen. It was a maiden for starters and it consisted of five outswingers which went past the outside edge and one inswinger which came back between bat and pad and missed the off stump by a whisker. Ray had him caught behind for 0 by Don Tallon in his next over. It was wonderful bowling and was the main reason Peter played only two Tests that summer.

I made my first appearance at Lord's against MCC with a big crowd present. It was a wonderful moment to walk on to the ground as a player representing Australia. I top-scored with 35 in a low-scoring game, and then took 1–20.

Our match against Nottinghamshire was reduced to two days due to the Coronation.

We were told that unfortunately there was no chance at such a late stage of being able to see the procession 'live', but then Ronnie Cornwell was able to organise seating for us in a building still to be completed. Ronnie was the father of David who, as John le Carré, was later to become one of the outstanding mystery and spy writers of our time. The elder Cornwell was a business entre-preneur who had thrown a lunch party for us earlier in the tour. He was a businessman in the millionaire class, although when things went wrong he was a little below that, but it was a very interesting day, made more so by our manager George Davies.

At that country-house lunch, George and I decided we needed to go to the loo but there was only one available and, when we arrived, there was a queue around eighty yards long. Eventually, after what seemed hours, George and I arrived at the point where the queue turned at right angles and ten yards further on was the prize. I glanced at George and thought I detected a desperate look in his eyes, perhaps partly brought on by the tight crossing of his legs. Around the corner, with what *definitely* seemed a desperate look in his eyes, came a peer of the realm, hopping. He was a very nice chap and a very important peer, but like George, he was also wearing an intense look, in his bid to arrive at the right place at the right time.

Being very important is only relative at times like that: out snaked George's arm and it landed on the shoulder of the peer and turned him around face to face with our manager. George muttered to him through gritted teeth, 'Down the back of the queue . . .'

From the playing point of view, I was starting to find some difficulty in the non-stop on-field action and travel, although I had said to Lindsay Hassett at the start of the tour that I would be quite happy to play in every game. He had nodded and given a half-smile. He knew better. As a team we were struggling with our batting, Bill Johnston's injury was a real problem and I was in trouble with both batting and bowling.

When we came to the First Test at Trent Bridge it could hardly be said I was in form and full of confidence. The match was a disappointment because of the rain, but from a personal point of view, it was worse. Alec Bedser was too good for most of us except the experienced players, and the remainder of our batting disintegrated. I was caught behind glancing Trevor Bailey in the first innings and then Bedser got me in the second innings with a leg-cutter, which almost did, pitching on leg stump and hitting middle. The match finished in a draw, with rain intervening, and the only worthwhile thing I did was to take two very good catches.

Perhaps that's not quite right about the catches being the only good thing to happen to me that week, because Lindsay Hassett gave me a very good lesson in loosening up – 'taught me a lesson' might be more accurate. It wasn't a lesson to compare with Bill O'Reilly's bowling advice at the end of the tour, or with Harvey's advice in the nets about the best way to bat on English pitches.

Whilst in Nottingham we went to the home of Bert Edwards of Nottingham Lace. Chatting with Lindsay at the function, I mentioned, 'I couldn't possibly have a drink, thanks, we're on a cricket tour.' Even more prissy than earlier on the tour!

Lindsay nodded sympathetically at the youngster offering him a stricture on how to play cricket, before I compounded things by agreeing to try a sip of his proffered Scotch and venturing the opinion that anyway it was tasteless stuff. His poker-faced answer was to ask the perfectly dressed barman to give Mr Benaud a Scotch his high-class taste buds may be able to savour. I began to like the taste after half a dozen doubles, the disappointment of the batting failures faded and I had six more from my new very best friend, the generous bartender.

It proved to be a painful experience, as the next day I suffered my first ever hangover. I still don't drink Scotch these days, although I am partial to a glass or two of high-quality white Burgundy, Chardonnay or Shiraz, a gin and tonic with ice and lemon, or a beer from a green bottle. And, I think I'm able to say that Hassett's poker-faced lesson made me a little less prissy!

On the Saturday night of the Second Test at Lord's we had an official function with a difference, as Prime Minister Menzies threw a dinner for the team in the River Room at the Savoy. Douglas Jardine was one of the guests and it was a most convivial evening with splendid speeches from Menzies and Hassett.

The match was the scene of the epic draw when Trevor Bailey and Willie Watson played so well and we couldn't separate them until too late. Watson for Peter May turned out to be an inspired selection. I did little with the bat or the ball and was dropped for the Old Trafford Test, which was marred by rain and in which we reached only 35–8 in our second innings.

I made 52 against Middlesex and was back in the side for the Headingley Test, during which Trevor Bailey distinguished himself again, on this occasion, however, for deliberately wasting as much time as possible and bowling to a packed legside field. Bill Johnston, almost recovered from injury, took 6–63 against Glamorgan after this Test and was selected for the final Test at The Oval ahead of Doug Ring and me.

With the final Test, England regained the Ashes after a break of nineteen years, and, understandably, there was great jubilation around the country. We even had a drink or two ourselves, but it was more in disappointment than anything else after we had congratulated the England players on what was a splendid victory.

Out of a loss sometimes comes a gain, and that was the case, from a personal point of view, after we were beaten at The Oval. A few of us met Gillian Morley, as she was to become, that evening, and three years later at the start of the 1956 tour, renewed that acquaintance and met her husband-to-be, John. They were two of the greatest characters I have met, John known only as 'Morley', Gillian as 'Dumpy'. Their daughter Georgina attended Madame de Brissac's Garden House School for young ladies. In all the years they lived in London, their flat in William Street, Knightsbridge, was a warm, welcoming place.

During the 1953 tour Neil Harvey suggested to me one night that we queue for tickets to see Margot Fonteyn dance in *Swan Lake* at Covent Garden. Fonteyn was simply magnificent, and, although we were in the second back row of the 'gods', it was one of the experiences of my life. Three years later we met Dame Margot at the Morleys, along with many of the other Royal Ballet stars, including Sir Frederick Ashton, Sir Anthony Dowell and, a frequent visitor, the Mistress of the Ballet, Gerd Larsen, a delightful person and also a wonderful character.

Motor cars mean different things to different people. In the Morleys' garage in 1956 was the most striking car I had seen – a black, front-wheel drive Citroën with mudguards and running boards, the type of car you used to see in French detective films, where policemen would hang on to the side in an exciting chase. Morley in his younger days, in 1928, had breezed around Brooklands in a Bentley in excess of 100 mph, not a track record, which was held by Sir Tim Birkin, but fast in those days.

The Morleys also had a 12/50 Beetleback 1930 Alvis, a wonderful car which was later to have an association with Australia. When Morley 'popped his clogs', to use Dumpy's phrase, she presented a cup to the Alvis Register Club for annual competition and, in 1997, it was won by L. D. Donnan and taken to Palmwoods in Queensland, Australia. The Morleys' Alvis was host to many well-known passengers over the years, one of whom, pictured in Scarborough, is the slow driver but fast bowler, Frederick Sewards Trueman, who is chatting to a friend of ours and the Morleys, John Robson.

The Nawab of Pataudi Jr was a frequent visitor to Morley and Dumpy's home over the years, and generously once brought two blue Indian silk shirts as presents and handed one to me. I had to tell him that it might be the right size for him, but unfortunately it was three sizes too small for me. He always had a dry sense of humour, 'Don't worry about that,' he murmured. 'Just give it to Oxfam and I'll have it back inside the month!'

John O'Reilly Cicconi and 'Sparrow' Harrison were two who lived in the same building in William Street, Knightsbridge. 'Chic', a young man about town, and 'Sparrow', a Welshman and President of the Stutterers' Association of the United Kingdom, each had a hand in running a cricket team based on village stand-ards of play and wonderful hospitality. I had said rather vaguely that in retirement I would be happy to turn out for them, so there we were, a quarter of a century, in a second-class carriage on the train to Lewes, en route to Ripe and Chalvington. At the country manor, it was very much a social affair, with white Burgundy and delicious ham, poached salmon and chicken sandwiches, and this set the scene for the contest of the day.

Our captain was 'Jumping Joe' Bean, much experienced in the vagaries of village cricket over the past fifty years. Sparrow was team manager and Chic an elegant, modern-day version of William Hickey. They all stressed to us that the fixture against Rottingdean was very much a grudge match.

At starting time there was disquiet in our group. We were there, but where were they? An hour later telephone contact was made and our messenger returned grim-faced and asking to see the fixture list again. Sparrow pointed triumphantly to the entry: Ripe and Chalvington v Rottingdean. The messenger replied, 'Quite so, but their fixture list says they should be playing thirty miles away, which is where they are, having a very enjoyable match.'

Our return journey was highlighted by Sparrow, the club's financial organiser, announcing on the Lewes station platform he had saved some money for the impecunious club by purchas-ing more second-class rail tickets. We then had a stroke of luck. The West Indian ticket collector on the train said 'Tickets, please,' looked at me and said, 'Mr Benaud, you can't possibly travel in here. I will unlock the next-door first-class compartment for you. Just wait a moment.' He returned very quickly and said, 'Come this way, Mr Benaud, mmm . . . and I suppose your friends had better come too!'

11

'TIGER' O'REILLY

WE had other games to play to finish the 1953 tour. They went off without incident and with mixed success, until we arrived at Scarborough for the Festival game against T. N. Pearce's XI and I hit 29 in the first innings. It was on the second evening of this match that Bill O'Reilly gave up a convivial night with Hassett to have dinner with me, something organised by Tom Goodman, who was with the *Sydney Morning Herald* as their cricket correspondent. Tom was a real gentleman and a fine cricket writer, constructive and thoughtful. He knew a lot about the game and was able to translate that into print for his readers. He told me Bill O'Reilly had become increasingly frustrated watching the methods I was using in my bowling, and if it was OK, he would like to have a talk to me. The only problem I had was Bill giving up an evening with Hassett, but I grabbed the chance of being offered some advice by the greatest bowler the world has seen. We had a meal in the hotel dining-room at Scarborough and then repaired to Bill's room for an after-dinner beer or two and a bowling lesson.

It remains one of the most beneficial events in my cricketing life. We talked, or rather Bill talked and I listened. The upshot was that I needed to take stock of what I was trying to do and how I could relate that to whomever was captaining me and others. Bill was a mate of Hassett's but he made the point, and forcibly too, that Hassett was such a wonderful player of spin bowling that he had no proper respect for it. I went away and summed up the advice and pointers I had heard during the fascinating two hours.

- Give the batsmen absolutely nothing!
- Develop one ball as your stock ball and perfect it. Spend a year, even two years, doing that and don't be swayed by anyone – friends, captains, selectors, hangers-on, do-gooders, ear-bashers – into doing anything else.
- That ball should be your leg-break, and from your point of view it should be both an attacking and defensive weapon; attacking because, if you are pitching it as you want, you will be giving yourself a chance of taking a wicket; defensive because, if a batsman is in full flow, you have the chance of stopping him if you have complete control over your bowling and your own mind.
- Don't try to take a wicket every ball.
- On the surface that may seem poor advice, but it's not. If you are bowling six different balls an over, as you are at the moment, or eight different balls, as you were in Australia last summer, you will bowl one loose one in the over, and by the time you have bowled a spell of eight overs, you could have none for 32. Yet, at the same time, you might have bowled forty very good balls. The captain will take you off.
- Never forget, even for one moment, that the batsman is an enemy on the field. You might have a beer with him at the end of the day, and that's good. On the field, attack him, but above all, give him nothing, absolutely nothing.
- Bear in mind that almost every captain under whom you will play will be a batsman. Batsmen know a lot about many things, including batting. With very few exceptions they know nothing whatsoever about the technique of spin bowling.
- They often have a good or very good idea of how to bat against it, but about the technique, the field-placings needed for particular batsmen and the best methods and the thought processes of a spin bowler, they know very little.

If you read that at normal speed you are able to finish it in seventy seconds. That's the way good advice should be – brief and simple – and that is precisely the way Bill conveyed it to me that evening. It was to form the basis of my bowling for the next ten years and, allied to my father's advice, it was one of the reasons why, for a time, I became Australia's leading wicket-taker in Test cricket and was able to reach the bowling part of the statistic of being the first Test cricketer ever to do the double of 2,000 runs and 200 wickets.

Because I believe in apportioning credit where due, I always said publicly what Bill had done for me. When Bill was asked about it by journalists, he was inclined to gloss it over with a wave of the hand and say, 'Anyway, advice isn't worth anything if the person can't use it properly.'

The final part of that Scarborough match provided me with a great finish to the tour: I opened the Australian second innings with Arthur Morris and we put on 163 for the first wicket. I finished with 135 including eleven sixes to equal the then record and we won the match.

When I returned to Australia and told Lou about the chat with his fellow schoolteacher 'Tiger' O'Reilly, he was delighted. 'Greatest bowler of all time and a good bloke,' he said. 'You won't be given any better advice than that.'

Whether or not I would be able to carry it out was another matter, because I did need to turn in better figures. Although the tour had been very much a learning process, I had had a disastrous time in the Tests, and even though I had managed some decent performances in other matches they were spasmodic rather than consistent. I had started out as a promising allrounder and that was where I had finished the tour, though I had tried to learn as much as possible. My spinning fingers were still raw after every day's play. As yet there was no good news to impart to McCool.

12

THE SELECTORS' FAITH
REWARDED, BUT NOT
AGAINST ENGLAND

I T was very good to be back home again after such a long
tour: from start to finish it had taken eight months, and I had
gone away from home after being married for only seven weeks.
Playing cricket continuously for most of the time had provided
plenty of interest for me and both high and low spots, but it was
quite different for my wife and the other players' wives who were
not permitted to travel with the tour, to visit or to be anywhere
near their husbands in that time.

The situation in those days was that administrators considered
the success of a tour the only thing that mattered. It was just a
fact of life that, almost half a century ago, there would be long
absences brought about by ship travel and a programme that took
in pre-tour games and five months of non-stop cricket in England.
It mattered to the players also that we should do well and that
Australia should win, but looking back on it, the strictures of the
Board provided a very strange background, one that was sometimes compared to wartime absences of husbands.

On the domestic cricket front, the Australian Cricket Board
members were busy declining the chance to tour South Africa and
New Zealand. The New Zealand application was given a very
frosty reception, owing to the fact that for many years the Board
considered them a second-rate cricketing country and unwor-
thy of Australian administrative attention. They did, however,
permit the New Zealand team returning from South Africa to play

matches in Perth, Adelaide and Melbourne at the conclusion of this 1953–54 summer. There were problems, too, for India, who had asked for an Australian team to tour and had been given very short shrift, despite the fact that the two countries had not met since 1947–48.

The New Zealanders had some fine cricketers around this time including Bert Sutcliffe with his brilliant footwork, one of the best left-handers I saw over the years, and John Reid, a top-class allrounder who made 1,000 runs and took 50 wickets on the South African tour. Australian cricket audiences were never permitted to see them play in Test matches against our best cricketers, and that at a time when no vast number of tours were organised, compared with now.

It was during this 1953–54 year with Cumberland I had my first experience as captain of the first-grade team, and I found it not only a challenge but extremely interesting as well. I was now twenty-three years old and it was said that it would be a good thing for me to take some responsibility as one of the more experienced players in the side. Ron James, who had captained Cumberland for the previous five years, told the club committee that he would do so again but wanted them to know he would prefer to stand down in my favour once I had returned from England. I was very grateful to him, not only for this but also for the manner in which he had captained the side and had been prepared to pass on various tips to me over those five years. As it was, I played only seven innings for the club in the whole season because of representative commitments.

I was in good form throughout the club season, and in even better form at first-class level. There was a good reason for this. I had recently come through the experience of a tour of England and, with the very necessary help of the older players on that tour, had improved my technique with both bat and ball. It was all due to the fact that the older players in the side were, in turn, willing to impart their experience and I was willing to learn.

Competition for places in the NSW side was intense. There was a lot of talent around at the time, and this season was to see the start of nine unbroken years of Sheffield Shield victories for NSW. Many young cricketers in the state never had the chance to show how good they were because their opportunities were so restricted.

One aspect of the season was disquieting, in that my fingers were raw at the finish of several games and nothing I tried by way of a remedy was in the least successful.

Following Lindsay Hassett's retirement there was a lot of media hype about who would take over the captaincy of Australia; it seemed clear that either Ian Johnson of Victoria or Keith Miller, ex-Victoria and now NSW, would be skipper when England toured Australia the following season. Johnson had missed selection for the team which recently had toured England, and Miller was the best cricketer in Australia, as well as the finest allrounder in the world. It was forty-four years later that another little piece of Australia's cricketing jigsaw fell into place when Gideon Haigh, in his outstanding book *The Summer Game*, recounted a conversation between Hassett and Johnson at a party on New Year's Eve, 1953. The conversation was said to be at 3 a.m. on New Year's Day, which only shows that Hassett, at a party, hadn't lost his touch, even though he was in retirement. The gist of it was that Johnno should 'get stuck in' with his bowling, and if he did, he might captain Australia the following summer. Hassett's information, I assume, would have floated from a Board member because they were the ones who chose the captains in those days. It was good advice from a very good friend and it certainly had Johnno moving – he took eight wickets in the match which began eight hours later.

Johnson did indeed captain Australia, against England in Australia, then in the Caribbean and after that in England. Up to the time Hassett chatted to him, he had taken 1–119 from 31 overs and he finished the summer with 45 wickets at 22.75. Victoria, under his captaincy, beat NSW, skippered by Miller, in a tight match at the SCG and by then the media were having a field day on the question of the captaincy.

Once the domestic part of the summer was over, the New Zealanders played their three games, beating Western Australia and South Australia and playing an honourable draw with Victoria. It was actually a good performance, but it seemed to make little impression on the Australian Board.

Over the whole season, players from the tour of England showed improvement. Colin McDonald, with a brilliant century and double century in two crucial matches at the end, finished with most runs, 857 at 57.13, Graeme Hole had 851 at 47.27 and I was third in the aggregate with 811 at 62.38. I also finished third in the wickets taken, with 35 at 30.54 behind Ian Johnson and Jack Hill. It was all a very good lesson for me that there is no real substitute for experience and hard work. The fact that I had been lucky enough to tour England and had listened and wanted to learn was the main reason I'd had such a good season.

An Ashes battle always has something extra about it. England's arrival brought anticipation but, in the end, no joy at Test level for any Australians during the 1954–55 season. There was plenty of controversy at times, but no regaining of the Ashes, despite the fact that we won the opening Test of the series. For a number of reasons we were no match for England: the main one was that England's general bowling attack, led by the two fast bowlers, Frank Tyson and Brian Statham, was simply too good for us.

It was a strange summer in many ways. The Australian Cricket Board decided in their wisdom, if that isn't a contradiction in terms, that there would be a restricted programme of Sheffield Shield matches, so, in theory anyway, I should have been able to play more club cricket with Cumberland. In fact, I managed only six innings with the club in the whole of the summer, topped the batting averages and finished second in the aggregates, and headed the bowling averages.

Another to do well on the club scene was Lou Benaud. My father, aged forty-nine, was playing third grade for Cumberland at this time. He was known within the club as 'The Colt' and he took 30 wickets at 15.37 apiece with a strike-rate of one every 28 balls. He was said in the annual report to have been sorely let down by a spate of missed chances. John Benaud, my brother, was now showing signs of real ability and it was looking as though something might be made of his cricket. He had one advantage that had also come my way: he had a very good mentor.

The rest and recreation had done me good in the off season and I started with 67 in the opening round against Northern District, then 104 and 146 against Gordon and Waverley, and took wickets as well, so I was in form for the arrival of the England side captained by Len Hutton.

Len had been captain in 1953 when England regained the Ashes at The Oval; now he had what looked, on paper anyway, to be a very strong combination with an accent on fast bowling. No luck for Fred Trueman, who took 114 wickets for Yorkshire but wasn't chosen in any of the four Tests against Pakistan and was left out of the touring party for Australia, the first of several disappointments for him and possibly related to the 1953–54 England tour of the West Indies. Fred during his career played 67 Tests out of a possible 121 for England. Contrast that with the fact that I played 63 Tests out of a possible 70 for Australia.

One who *was* chosen was Frank Tyson, the bowler I had seen at Northampton in 1953 who had taken the first two wickets on the opening day of our match and then watched Neil Harvey hit a century before lunch. Neil had said at the time he was 'decidedly quick'. Tyson took 70 wickets in this 1954 summer in England, which was good without being sensational, but he did something else that impressed the England selectors when he played for Northants against Middlesex at Lord's: he bowled out the home side with a blistering exhibition of pace, laid out Bill Edrich with a bumper and had him in hospital for observation overnight. When Edrich came back to bat on the last day, Tyson gave him another bumper straight away and continued to bowl at searing pace against a man known for his courage and ability against fast bowling. That performance gained Frank a Test cap in the last game against Pakistan at The Oval, where he had match figures of 5–57 in a losing side. The selectors were very impressed, and he was inked in for the tour of Australia.

It was twenty-six years since Australia had found themselves in the position of trying to regain the Ashes in Australia, and we weren't assisted at all by the decision to play the Sheffield Shield on a restricted basis. The idea had come from administrators in NSW and was typical of cricket controllers who hadn't thought things through. It was shown to be ridiculous enough to be permanently discarded at the end of the summer. In the first Shield match of the season Queensland made 405 against us at the 'Gabba, and it was on this Northern Tour that my spinning fingers had 'gone', to the extent that the tour selectors, Miller and Morris, decided to call for an additional player and Jack Treanor, my Cumberland team-mate, was given his chance.

The following week I went to Melbourne to play for an Australian XI side against MCC and had my first taste of batting against Brian Statham, who was fast. I made 47, but a few of those runs came off a thick inside edge when I was a little late with the stroke. I had three wickets and Ian Johnson six, but it was a rain-marred match which didn't show much to anyone, other than the fact that England would be tough competitors.

Every English journalist was interested in only one thing – when I batted against Lindwall the previous week and made a century, was he still fast? I left them in no doubt: 'A yard quicker than last year.'

Nothing really went right for England in the First Test, from the moment Godfrey Evans had to pull out on the morning of the match with sunstroke. Len put us in to bat and watched gloomily as we made 601–8 and won the match by an innings and 154. Worse still, Denis Compton broke a bone in his hand trying to save a boundary when he grabbed at the fence, and he couldn't play again until the Third Test in Melbourne. The series was squared at the SCG, with England winning by 38 runs in a low-scoring game. I had been made vice-captain to Arthur Morris as Ian Johnson and Keith Miller were both out of the team with knee injuries. Why I was given that job with Ray Lindwall and Neil Harvey in the side was quite beyond me and, I suspect, many other people as well. Arthur said he would chat to me on the field, but he hoped I wouldn't take offence if he had a word with Ray and Neil. I certainly wouldn't, because I found it all quite embarrassing.

The Third Test in Melbourne was a sensation.

Having won the First Test in Brisbane and then lost the Second in Sydney, there was considerable interest in the team over what type of pitch would be provided for the Third in Melbourne, particularly as there was a new curator-groundsman at the MCG, Jack House, who was at the Albert Ground in a similar capacity. Bill Vanthoff was normally the full-time curator and was at the ground when the Australian XI played MCC at the beginning of November. There had been plenty of life in the pitch and a bit of turn for the spinners back then, but it did look as though, but for rain forcing the last two days to be abandoned, there might have been some bad cracking in the surface. That game had been played in cool, damp conditions, but there seemed no real problems with the pitch when we played our traditional Sheffield Shield match with Victoria in pleasant weather the week prior to the Test. There were no centuries made but there were eight half-centuries, which indicated some stability in the surface.

When we arrived in Melbourne, according to the weather forecasters, the Test was likely to be played in very hot conditions, and the temperature was approaching 90 on the old scale when the captains went out to toss on the first morning. The pitch was damp. The groundsman had left a lot of water under the surface because he had checked on the long-range weather forecast which said hot, and hotter for New Year's Eve and New Year's Day, and then really hot on the Sunday which was the rest day of the match. They said it would be *a scorcher*. The forecasters had it right for 1 January: there was a strong northerly blowing, the worst wind in Melbourne, and the temperature was well over the 100 mark; out in the centre of the ground it was 120. Harv had said to me at the end of the second day, and moving into the rest day, that he didn't like the look of it at all: 'It might be unplayable.'

When we arrived at the ground after the rest day, the pitch, which at the end of the second day's play had been a mass of cracks with the edges of some pieces turning slightly upwards, had suddenly turned into a perfect strip. Unfortunately, though, it was a little damp from the watering it had been given by the new curator.

Percy Beames, a former Sheffield Shield cricketer and cricket writer for *The Age* newspaper, broke the story on the morning of the last day of the game, after the Melbourne Cricket Club had denied any watering and suggested an underground spring might have sprung up. Percy was always thought to have seen the watering as he jogged along outside the ground on the Sunday – there was a gap between stands in those days before the Melbourne Olympics of 1956. Percy never confirmed or denied that when we taxed him, but there was always a knowing smile on his face. I'm not surprised he gave us a bit of a grin. Percy had actually had a phone call from Bill Vanthoff on the rest day evening, the Sunday, telling him the pitch square had been watered!

England won by 128 runs with several hours to spare, assisted by the watering because they were able to bat on a good pitch in their second innings. Because it was surface watering just to close the cracks, the latter soon opened up again in the heat and it became a very poor batting surface. Frank Tyson took 7–27 and to this day no one will confirm the rumour that the Australian authorities would have had the game played again if the Australians had won!

England won the Fourth Test in Adelaide by five wickets. We were in with a chance on several occasions during the game, but simply weren't good enough against Tyson and Statham to clinch a win, even when Miller came at them with a tremendous burst at the start of their second innings. With Johnson off the field, Miller was acting captain and he dismissed Hutton, Edrich and Cowdrey and caught May off Bill Johnston, a brilliant diving effort at cover, but then Compton and Evans saw them through; not, however, before Len had said to Denis when he was on his way out of the dressing-room, 'Boogers have done us, Denis.'

'Steady on, Len,' Denis said over his shoulder, 'I'm just on my way out.' Denis made 34 not out and then poured Len a celebratory drink.

The rain-marred final Test at the SCG was the last match of the summer at the end of February, appalling programming. It was also a dismal affair for Australia as we had to follow on but managed to escape with a draw, and that after beating MCC by 45 runs in Sydney a week earlier.

It was a very odd summer, and to put into perspective the way ball dominated bat, I finished seventh in the national aggregates with only 530 runs at 29.44, and the only two Australians who made more runs than I did were Neil Harvey, with 1,009, and Les Favell, 663. The other five batsmen were all English!

Six years of first-class cricket and no Test series victory over England wasn't what I had in mind. It was a miserable situation.

13

THE CARIBBEAN CAPERS OF WEST INDIAN CRICKET

FAILING to regain the Ashes was a low point of the year, and although I had been chosen to go to the West Indies with the Australian side and had set my sights on then being in the team to go to England in 1956, there was no pleasure at all in having been beaten again by England. Despite being in first-class cricket for seven years I had been in only one Australian team which had beaten England in a Test and I had played in two series where the Ashes had gone to England. It was not a good feeling. In fact, it was a lousy feeling, having previously spent my youth reading about how Bradman's team had demolished them in 1946–47 and in 1948.

Because of currency restrictions the Australian touring team had to fly to the Caribbean via a number of scattered places, including Tahiti, Mexico, then Vancouver in Canada, Calgary, Regina, Winnipeg and Toronto. We finally landed in Jamaica after a forty-nine-hour flight.

There had been one or two minor incidents on the way, including a landing in a snowstorm at Calgary, and missing an aeroplane which was landing at Winnipeg by all of twenty yards as we were taking off, someone apparently having made a minor error in the flight controllers' schedule.

We received a tumultuous welcome from 3,000 Jamaican cricket fans who crowded the small airport terminal, and its surrounds. Had there been trees growing in the area, the fans would have climbed them to seek a better view. They were wonderful.

There was no shortage of rum punch in Jamaica and, because

we were not yet in strict training and the drink was new to us, we had a little dash at it and very pleasant too.

One of the more extraordinary and impressive things at our airport reception was the steel band which played welcoming songs for us, classics and popular music played on oil drums with funny markings on the top of the metal. It made the most wonderful sound to young ears. These days steel bands are commonplace because, in the intervening years, people like Harry Belafonte, Bob Marley and many others have made West Indian music and reggae famous around the world. Steel bands hadn't been seen a great deal in Australia up to 1955, though Belafonte was very well known with 'Jamaica Farewell' and other songs. To see it happening, rather than merely hear it, was new and wonderfully enjoyable.

We were fresh from the series against England in which pace had been our undoing in the shape of Tyson and Statham, both of whom had left their mark. The West Indies had prepared for our tour with a number of trial matches between the islands and we were quick to note that a Barbadian, Frank King, had been most impressive as a fast bowler, taking 15 wickets at 10 apiece, and apparently bowling with considerable pace.

Luckily there seemed to be only one of him, whereas there had been two of the Englishmen, plus good supporting bowlers, and this could make a considerable difference.

The previous year the West Indies had hosted the England side, and the general impression we had been given in conversation with them was that their sojourn in the Caribbean had been anything but happy. For my part, however, I was keen to see the West Indies and glad to be in the Caribbean. It always had a nice ring to it when people talked of the culture and the tropical nature of the place, and it was to be a new experience. I had settled on making up my own mind about the West Indies, deciding not to worry about what I had been told by others.

During the England tour, there had been crowd disturbances in Georgetown and Trinidad over umpiring decisions and other matters. Georgetown apparently had been particularly difficult, to the extent that the British Governor had been thinking seriously of calling out the Guard, or whatever passed for the Guard at that time.

We knew, by reputation, the West Indian crowds could be volatile but there was no reason for them to be volatile with us. We had nothing to do with the West Indies' background, or their cricket for that matter, other than having played two series against them, and I didn't intend to become involved in any internal matters of island rivalry or colour. We were there to play what we hoped would be enjoyable and serious cricket and, in the meantime, until the matches started, have a look around, meet some cricket fans and followers, and have a few rum punches off the field.

We also knew the West Indians were brilliant cricketers. The three 'Ws' had been in form against England, Ramadhin and Valentine were still playing, and doing well, and there was a challenge in front of us.

We hadn't realised it when we arrived, but we were to become involved in a very strange controversy about the West Indian captaincy. You may well ask what the hell that had to do with a bunch of Australian cricketers. The short answer is nothing, but we were the people on the spot, at the wrong time, or the right time, whichever way you look at it. There was clearly a great deal of pressure being applied by various people to have Frank Worrell made captain, and we wondered mildly from time to time in the first couple of weeks of the tour why, on the other hand, Worrell appeared to be so much out of favour with West Indian administrators. We were to find out a bit more about it over the next few months.

Jeff Stollmeyer was listed to be skipper in the First Test, but the West Indian Board had thrown a wild card into the ring when, right out of the blue, they named Denis Atkinson as captain of the next West Indian team to tour New Zealand in a year's time. Having done that, and said also that Bruce Pairaudeau would be his vice-captain in the land of the long white cloud, the West Indies Board *then* said Atkinson would be vice-captain to Stollmeyer in the series about to take place in the Caribbean against the Australians.

Now what would you make of that? What would you call it? Shrewd? Clever? Calculating? Brave? We looked at it and, even to eyes inexperienced in the ways of West Indian cricket administration, it seemed more a recipe for trouble if, that is, anyone wished to stir it and there appeared to be no shortage of people in the latter category. Although it was none of our business as visitors to another country, there was a scenario to contemplate.

The West Indies tour of New Zealand was twelve months off, five Tests were to be played between Australia and the West Indies and, for reasons known only to them, West Indies had gone through an intriguing process of naming Atkinson and Pairaudeau for New Zealand, and then, immediately naming Stollmeyer and Atkinson as captain and vice-captain for our series, with Worrell, Weekes and Walcott all playing in the side. Worrell had been vice-captain of the West Indies team when England had been in the Caribbean the previous year. All very strange!

C. L. R. James, a West Indian journalist and a good writer on cricketing and social matters, was Frank's strongest advocate, and bear in mind this was way back in 1955, five years before Frank eventually brought the West Indian side to Australia for what turned out to be the Tied Test series. The West Indian media might have been full of good publicity and some wonderful overtones about the five-Test series, but it was also full of many undertones. As visitors, we may not have understood it all, but we did understand the guts of it, mainly the fierce and bitter rivalry between islands which were supposed to make up one nation; it merely underlined that every island was very much a separate country.

Getting to and around Kingston was an interesting exercise at this early stage of the tour, and also when we came back for the final Test of the series. In Kingston we always travelled as a team, in a red bus. It was well named the Red Terror, and called a few other things as well, but our driver's given name is now long forgotten. His sobriquet was 'Pontius' and he seemed always to believe he was in charge of a low-flying aircraft. We invariably arrived at our destinations in the shortest possible time, and Pontius never stopped chuckling at the athletic tactics of pedestrians, some of whom, by remarkable reflex actions, actually made it to the safety of the grass verge. This was character-building for a young cricketer who had spent most of his time in a circumspect, but thoroughly reliable, Morris Minor.

Tennis matches, practice and a lot of bowling in the nets had me ready for the first game against West Indies. That warm-up match against Jamaica finished badly for Alan Davidson, who went over on his right ankle in delivering a ball to Allie Binns and ligaments were so badly torn that he was unable to play either in the Test or the following game against Trinidad.

If Jeff Stollmeyer thought he had problems agonising over what he could say to Frank Worrell after it was announced Denis Atkinson would be vice-captain in the series and Frank, in turn, would merely be a number on the card, it was nothing to the problems around the corner at Sabina Park. The West Indian side had been practising just down the road at the Wembley Club, and as Jeff was walking off the ground, someone hit a ball towards the stand. Seeing that it might hit one of the spectators, he stepped across and casually put up his right hand, the ball hit it and, although no bone was broken, his right forefinger was so badly sprained he was unable to play the following day.

Denis Atkinson was now captain.

I had met Denis in Australia in 1951–52 and liked him. He was a very good cricketer, a tough one too, and I found him one of the most approachable and dedicated players I came across in the twelve years I played Test cricket. I knew he was on a hiding to nothing in this Test in Jamaica, and also in the remainder of the series as regards the captaincy. It was as though those holding the power in West Indian cricket had gone searching for a difficult solution and, somehow, had managed to find it. Making Denis captain of West Indies in 1955 was roughly the equivalent of the Australian Board making me captain of Australia at that time. No matter what he did, there would be islands and critics who would tear him apart if they could possibly find a reason for so doing; or, if they couldn't find one, invent one.

West Indies could hardly have been a settled team at the time with all this going on, which could be to our advantage, so our prime object was to jump in there and seize them by the throats. After all, we were hardly in the first flush of success ourselves, having been on the receiving end of defeats for the past three years!

As it happened, the West Indies in their first innings of this opening Test made only 259, and struggled as well in the second for 275 against our 515–9. After we had won the toss and batted first the ball started to keep low late on the second day on a pitch which started out so shiny you could see your reflection when you looked down. I took two wickets in the first innings, none in the second, but was very happy with my bowling form.

I don't know if the West Indies Board and selectors had a death wish, but as a lead-up to the Second Test in Trinidad, the selectors brought back Stollmeyer as captain, which was normal, but left out Denis Atkinson, the vice-captain, on the basis of island selection, 'Bunny' Butler of Trinidad being chosen instead to make a Test debut after his six-wicket haul against us in the island match. It was, to say the least, a little bemusing and also rather amusing, though I doubt if Denis thought so at the time.

The pitch for the Trinidad Test at Queen's Park Oval had no grass visible on the cut portion, and it produced 1,255 runs for 23 wickets. It was tough to be a bowler at that ground, though we did have some good moments, and at one point it looked as though we might even be able to force a win. Clyde Walcott put a stop to that with a century in the second innings to go with the one he had made in the first, Everton Weekes made 87 not out to balance his first-innings 139, and McDonald, Morris and Harvey made centuries for us. Collie Smith had a taste of the vagaries of cricket; he made a pair to follow his debut century.

More problems for the Windies prior to the Guiana Test, in the country then known as British Guiana. Rumours abounded in the West Indian camp, Walcott threw a scare into them with more back problems and Sobers was also a worry with what they said was a hint of appendix trouble.

The West Indian selectors again excelled themselves. In the lead-up to Georgetown, they dropped Collie Smith, but almost as unbelievable was their dropping of Ramadhin and Valentine for a match where the ball, according to all reports, would certainly turn. When those selectors eventually had a glimpse of the surface, they panicked, found 'Ram' and instructed him to get himself on to the first plane for Georgetown. If they had been able to contact 'Val', he would have been there as well. Val, however, had gone missing. Sensible chap.

In the event, nothing went right for the West Indies in the Third Test on what turned out to be a poor pitch and a low-scoring match. To make it total doom and gloom, they lost Stollmeyer with what at the time was thought to be a dislocated shoulder after he tried, with his foot, to stop a ball near the boundary edge. He trod on the ball and fell on the point of his shoulder; X-rays and further medical examination showed he had badly torn ligaments, and he played no more in the series. I took 4–15 in their 182-run first innings including three in four balls, Weekes, Marshall and Ramadhin. Then, when we had lost 4–161, I made 68, although no one was very fit on that second day and I was one of a number who had gone down with dysentery. Ian Johnson bowled beautifully to take 7–44 in the second innings and we won easily by eight wickets to take a two-nil lead in the series – not bad so far, but the team we were playing against had a problem, in that they weren't merely playing against our touring team but lots of their own as well.

For the Barbados Test, with Stollmeyer now unable to play, the campaign for Worrell to be captain instead of Atkinson intensified everywhere but in Barbados, and the West Indian administrators came under a lot of pressure. In the end they were all stuffed out of sight by Atkinson, who stayed as captain and proceeded to share in a world-record stand of 347 with Clairemonte Depeiza. Atkinson's was, considering the circumstances, one of the finest and most courageous exhibitions of batting and character I had seen, and have seen to this day. I liked Denis, as a cricketer and as a person. He was completely straight and honest, a tough competitor and someone who improved his cricket all the way through the season in the face of personal attacks. The match finished in a draw; we had six of them out in the second innings when stumps were drawn, but we couldn't make the final breakthrough.

Leading two-nil in the series and with one match to go, at Sabina Park Jamaica, we won a handsome victory, but there was a real sadness when Bill Johnston damaged his right knee so badly he never played cricket again. He was trying to take a catch at square-leg when Walcott miscued a hook off Lindwall. Bill fell awkwardly and tore the cartilage which had been damaged at East Molesey in the 1953 tour of England.

Clyde Walcott made a century in each innings of a Test twice in this series, the first player ever to do so, and he showed what a great batsman he was. He also was part of a slightly bizarre incident on the fifth day of the final Test when he had made 17 of his eventual 110. Miller bowled him a bumper, and in hooking down to deep fine-leg, he trod on his leg stump and his off bail was dislodged, but the umpire said he was unsighted and gave him not out.

The two young West Indian players, Sobers and Smith, had looked very good for the future. Neither averaged 40 with the bat and both were expensive with the ball but you could tell, looking at them, they were going to be stars.

In the last Test I hit the fastest Test century in fifty-two years. I can't actually say I came in at a tough time with my team-mates on the edge of their seats, because when I approached the centre of the ground the score was 597–6.

I had a considerable amount of difficulty in concentrating after receiving news that back in Sydney my wife was ill. Our first son, Greg, had been born only a week before the team left for the West Indies, and having a newborn child and a husband who was thousands of miles away made life very difficult, more so with the arrangements for the return trip to Australia. This, again because of the Government currency restrictions and to save money for the Board, was an unusual piece of organisation, as we returned by ship and via New Zealand. We left Kingston on 23 June on the *Rangitane* sailing to Wellington and then went by ferry to Christchurch and it took three weeks to arrive back in Sydney, making five months in all away from home. It was a long tour following on the Ashes battle and I know I wasn't alone in feeling weary.

Australians subsequently had little to do with West Indian cricket in the five years to the 1960–61 tour when Frank Worrell finally *was* captain and we played the first tie in Test cricket history.

14

ENGLAND AGAIN, AND WE STILL CAN'T WIN

T HE prize at the end of this summer was the tour to England, and the chance to be in a team which, at long last, would beat England in a series. I had come out of the West Indies tour happy with my bowling against some of the best stroke-players in the world. In Australia it was purely a domestic summer with some very competitive games. A Test trial was scheduled in early January at the SCG between two teams at that stage to be captained by Ian Johnson and Keith Miller.

I had a very good summer with bat and ball and at the end of it I was chosen to go to England. The first part of the journey was to go by ship to Melbourne and, from there, to go on to play the usual two matches in Tasmania and one in Perth while the SS *Himalaya* continued to Fremantle.

Pat Crawford was one of our players, and his pregnant wife, Sheila, travelled with us from Sydney to Melbourne. There the Australian Cricket Board tossed her off the ship, not literally, but they instructed Crawford to remove her. Sheila had to board another ship, the *Strathaird*, and the two ships passed one another, on the same route in the Mediterranean. The Crawfords, by courtesy of the captains of the ships, were able to send a message to each other through the wireless rooms. No wives were allowed to be with husbands and, from the moment the team arrived in England, if a wife had the hide to be in the same country, she wasn't allowed to stay in the same house, flat or hotel. Husbands and wives were permitted to talk on the telephone, but not much else!

The control was extended at the end of the tour when Pat, who had played Lancashire League cricket where he had met his wife, decided to try to play for a county. He hadn't read the fine print of his Board contract which said he wasn't allowed to play first-class cricket anywhere in the world, other than Australia, for eighteen months after the tour ended.

Interestingly, had an Australian Board member decided to go to England to watch the Test series, he could have taken his wife with him, and would have done so.

On board ship, in the same way as in 1953, we relaxed and exercised and made certain we were as fit as we could possibly be by the time we arrived in England and headed to Lord's for the first net practice after doing the rounds of the official functions.

We played a one-day match against the Duke of Norfolk's XI at Arundel, one of the most beautiful cricket grounds in the world. The Duke, a real cricket lover who was later to manage the 1962–63 MCC team to Australia, had chosen some promising cricketers in his XI as well as one or two from years past. It was simply an enjoyable and festive occasion.

We then headed for Worcester for the traditional start of the tour proper and made a great start by bowling out Worcestershire for only 90. We were 137–1 at one point then lost four for 29 and, with the gates closed, the capacity crowd were in high delight.

It would have been nice to say that my first half-hour was exactly as I had planned but, in fact, I played and missed at Jack Flavell on four occasions in quick succession and he didn't fail to let me know I was a lucky young sod. I thought this was a bit much because although I was only 25, Jack was still two weeks away from turning 26. As we had never met before this day it seemed also in his conversation that he was taking a few liberties with my parents' attitude towards a number of things in life, so when Len Maddocks and I met in mid-pitch I mentioned I had had enough of this joker. I picked him up off leg stump and hit him for six over square-leg, then through the covers and when he came back later after Maddocks' dismissal, I hit him straight down the ground for six, over the BBC box and into New Road. This was part of 38 from two of Flavell's overs, then he injured his hand trying to field a fierce drive I hit off Bob Berry. He had the last laugh, though, as he came back on to the field and bowled me for 160, but I thoroughly enjoyed the stoush!

I enjoyed playing against Nottinghamshire in early May just as much. Bruce Dooland, the former Australian legspinner now playing with the county, offered to turn up early on the Monday to show me how to bowl the 'flipper'. It was one of the most valuable lessons I was ever given and made a wonderful difference to my bowling after I had carried out his advice, which was to practise the ball in the nets until I perfected it and to try very hard not to bowl it in a match until I had done that.

The First Test was something of a fizzer. It was marred by rain, produced fewer than 700 runs and the pitch looked odd, with a real reddish look about it until rain changed its colour. England had played Laker, Lock and Appleyard but, in the end, although the ball turned sharply, the rain and lack of time, plus some excellent batting from Jim Burke and Peter Burge, saw us through.

In that game we had suffered a dreadful double blow as regards injury, with Ray Lindwall straining a muscle early in the first innings and Davidson slipping in a bowler's footmark and chipping his ankle. He was carried off, the ankle was put in plaster and we were in real trouble, with the Second Test at Lord's starting only nine days after the completion of the one at Trent Bridge. Davo couldn't play again until the match against Surrey in August, and then, with a combination of solid batting and left-arm orthodox spin bowling, forced his way into the team for the Fifth Test at The Oval.

The Second Test at Lord's produced a great win for Australia, and although it was everyone's victory, it was really Miller's match. Keith made 28 and 30 at critical times, and took ten wickets in his 70 overs, all in the knowledge that Lindwall, Crawford and Davidson would not be at the other end. England had changed their side for the firm, well-grassed Lord's pitch, bringing in Brian Statham and Johnny Wardle for Bob Appleyard and Tony Lock; Alan Moss was also omitted from the team which had taken the field at Trent Bridge.

We knew this was to be Miller's last tour and that he planned to retire from the game on his return to Australia, where he would continue writing and would be the Channel 9 sports correspondent with television about to start in Australia. This then was his last major appearance at Lord's, which he had first seen as a competitor when he walked out to play in the Services game in 1945. He was the greatest allrounder I played with or against, bearing in mind Garry Sobers had started his career just two years earlier and I was destined to play only one further Test series against him.

They say about life that luck's a fortune. So it is. I had lots of good luck balancing a few moments of misfortune, and the very best of luck was to have started my career with three particular players: Miller, Arthur Morris and Ray Lindwall. Morris was my first captain, Lindwall and Miller were also in the team the day I made my debut at the SCG and they all remained mentors until they retired and beyond. Mentors can be anything, but these three were top class. They were prepared to take the trouble and spend the time, not too much, but enough to let you know they were keeping an eye on you and were prepared to help.

Ray continued in the game after 1956 and then played under my captaincy. He was a champion and his fast-bowling combination with Miller was one of the most outstanding things in Australian cricket history, equalled only by Ted McDonald and Jack Gregory, in the time after the First World War, and Dennis Lillee and Jeff Thomson, who started in 1974–75. As a team-mate, one of the best sounds I have heard was Lindwall warming up in the 'Gabba dressing-room, the old one that is, where the home team and the visitors were separated only by a thin wall, and a corrugated iron roof sheltered them from the heat or the rain. 'Lindy' would do his warming-up exercises and running-on-the-spot on the heavy wooden floor, and while the opposition opening batsmen would be unable to see him, they could certainly hear what was going on, with the boots hitting the floor and the sound bouncing off the metal roof.

Nugget Miller wouldn't bother with anything like that: he would be relaxing prior to exploding on the field with some of the fastest bowling anyone was likely to see or, if the fancy took him, a few off-cutters and offspinners and an occasional leg-break.

These days with videotapes and a variety of coaching methods, including coaches, it may seem a trifle gauche to be enthusiastic about experienced players in a team sitting at a table and moving salt and pepper shakers, and matches and spoons, into various positions to illustrate a point about bowling or field-placing; even about batting when a young batsman had been pulled into an error situation by a clever bowler.

Miller was the best captain I played under, and he was the best captain never to lead Australia. In those days it was of vital importance to the Australian Cricket Board that what they perceived as their own image should be perpetuated, and it was unlikely someone with Miller's personality and extrovert nature, and his popularity with the public, would have been chosen by the Board to captain Australia. The things I saw and learned from Miller may not have been apparent all the time to those watching from the outside. A move in the field might have come with a slight nod, or an even slighter head-shake.

This victory at Lord's was a tremendous confidence boost for the remainder of the Test series, and we reckoned that, given decent pitches, we were in with a big chance of regaining the Ashes. There were many complimentary notes in the media about the part I played in the unfolding events of the five days, including the Colin Cowdrey catch, the innings of 97 and the bowling in both innings despite my fingers being a mess.

So, if Miller was the greatest, what kind of rating do I give Ken 'Slasher' Mackay? Well, a champion is generally regarded as a cut above the rest of the field, so it is a matter of taking care in the world of hyperbole when one talks of a cricketer being a champion. Slasher Mackay in his own way was a champion, though not for the generally accepted reasons. He may have been a better player had I not interfered with his career when I was his captain. I turned him from a high-scoring batsman into an allrounder because it suited me to do so. When he retired it was with 1,507 Test runs and 50 Test wickets, something that makes good reading, as alongside him in 133 years of Test cricket the only Australians to have achieved that double are Warwick Armstrong, Ray Lindwall, Greg Matthews, Keith Miller, Monty Noble, Bob Simpson, Steve Waugh, Mark Waugh, Shane Warne and Richie Benaud.

Ken Mackay was a number of things to me: he was a good tough cricketer, and in all the years I played and watched the game, he remained one of the finest of men and proudest Australians ever to walk on to a cricket field. He died of a heart attack on the rest day, the Sunday, of the Lord's Test in 1982 when England were playing India, the same ground where, a little more than quarter of a century earlier, he had played such a staunch part in 'Miller's match', one of Australia's greatest Test victories.

It was in that Lord's game in 1956 that Slasher and I started our partnership, although at that stage I had no idea I might one day be captaining him. The wicket he took in England's first innings was that of Colin Cowdrey and I was the man who took the catch with England's score at 60. It is the one often shown in later years, depicting the ball in my left hand as I am knocked over with the force of the blow. In fact, I caught it in both hands right in front of my nose and was knocked backwards.

'Slash' seemed to be pleased with the effort, although he never used to say a lot. When he walked up to me and said, 'Caught, "Benords",' it was the equivalent of a politician's speech, and there was even a half smile on his weather-beaten countenance.

On the Monday morning of that match and not out over the weekend, I was caught with many others in an awful jam around Marble Arch on my way to the ground, eventually arriving at Lord's with no time for a spell of batting practice. On the way out to the centre I said to him, 'Slash, if ever I've needed a hundred it's today.'

He looked straight ahead and said, 'Don't let's get run out . . .' Several indifferent strokes later he came up to me and said, 'Benords, you don't have to hit everything out of the ground, let's just take our time . . .'

One thing I did know about Slash was that he would upset the

England players with his skill at leaving the ball alone, sometimes when it was only a matter of a couple of inches outside the off stump, but I didn't know until later how much he was upsetting them.

Peter May, without smiling, said very quietly to him at the end of one over during which he had allowed three to pass by an inch, 'You must really enjoy batting, Slasher.'

Slash looked at him and said just as quietly, but with the hint of a smile, 'I enjoy it so much, Peter, I'm going to try to be here all day.' It didn't work out like that but when he was out his innings had taken up four hours and twenty-five minutes and he had outlasted me.

The runs I made that day provided the single most important happening in my Test career to that time, far more so than the century I had made under no cricket pressure at Sabina Park the previous year against the West Indies, or, for that matter, any other innings I had ever played. The game was critically balanced, we were hampered by injuries and desperately needed to make enough second-innings runs so the target was difficult for England. To make 97 at Lord's was good enough, but it was the way I made them which mattered most to me after the most indifferent start imaginable to the innings.

Keith Miller had taken me to John Arlott's home the previous Sunday when our team were playing against Kent at Canterbury and the two of us were being rested. It was a convivial day and Neville Cardus was present. I had met him before, but only briefly, and it was interesting to listen to him, and even more interesting to hear him discussing classical music with Miller. The following Wednesday, the day before the Lord's Test began, Cardus wrote an article in the *Manchester Guardian* concerning some of the Australian players – Harvey, Miller, Archer, Burke and Benaud.

In general terms he said:

A great cricketer, once he has known greatness, if only momentarily, can again be visited by greatness as long as he remains capable of reasonably healthy physical motions and responses. No team can be taken for granted as beaten before the match begins if it contains Harvey, Miller, Archer, Burke and Benaud.

A slight raising of the eyebrow may well be caused by the mention of Benaud's name in this context; for this young cricketer's performances in Test matches against England have not been, in Mr Attlee's terminology, outstanding.

I doubt if any English player would be trusted by our selection committee so far and for so long, with no more practical or visible contribution to the cause than Benaud's. Yet, he is plainly gifted.

When he first came to England in 1953, Benaud in the third match of the tour against Yorkshire at Bradford scored 97 in two hours, then took seven wickets for 46. Now it is not possible for mediocrity ever to rise to the level of this kind of mastery. And what a man has done once he can do again.

I thought I was able to play, but it was certainly true that what I had promised so far had not been translated into deeds.

I had practised hard at the nets at Lord's on the Tuesday and had hit the ball well. Cardus had been there and he finished his preview of the game with the theme that it wouldn't surprise him if I did something quite reasonable: 'I saw him at the nets at Lord's on Tuesday, defending seriously, scrupulously behind the ball; and his strokes, when he liberated them, were clean, true, strong. His reactions were swift and natural. Benaud is twenty-five and looks every inch a cricketer. It will be no matter for wonder if at any moment he confounds those of his critics who have more or less written him off.'

That Cardus article and what I did to live up to it is one of the reasons I have always considered the Lord's match in 1956 a turning point for me. In the following Tests, played on some strange pitches, I didn't bat too badly and I was prepared to try a few things I might not have had the confidence to try without Lord's.

After Lord's, pitches occupied most of our waking hours. The defeat by Surrey earlier in the tour on a pitch where the ball spun sharply, was in our minds, so we were interested to see what was being provided at Headingley for the Third Test. It was a very dry pitch and looked to be a surface where 'solid' was almost the last word to be used to describe it. 'Grassy' was definitely the last one.

We didn't start well by losing the toss, but we made up for that by having the first three wickets for 17 and Cyril Washbrook walked out to join Peter May. The pair put on 187 and, with Bailey and Evans batting very well, we eventually had them out for 325. It was not what we had in mind because the ball was starting to do some very strange things, divots were being taken from the surface and it was a good thing the rain came to cover up the pitch deficiencies.

I finished with 3–89, including the wicket of Washbrook, who was out for 98 going for the boundary which would have given him his century. As a team we regarded Cyril very highly: he was a fine player and we knew he deserved a century here. The method of dismissing him was what pleased me, though obviously it would have been better had I been able to do it earlier. I asked Ian Johnson, as ostentatiously as he liked, to bring in the man from deep midwicket and I would try to set Cyril up – a couple of leg-breaks to have him defending and then the shorter topspinner for him to pull. It worked with an lbw decision.

Trevor Bailey's first over in our innings produced one that pitched middle then took off past Colin McDonald and was taken in front of slip by Godfrey Evans. We had a fair idea then that the pitch was not what might be termed ideal. Fortunately for everyone it rained, not that anyone likes to bat on a damp pitch, particularly if the sun then comes out, but it's preferable to batting on one where the top has gone. It became merely a rain-affected pitch. If Miller and I had been able to save the follow-on from being enforced, we may well have been OK, but they were too good for us.

I had gone in at 69–6 the previous evening in the doom and gloom, mostly the latter, and had survived with Miller until the close of play. There was one delightful moment when it was close to pitch black out in the centre, the lights were gleaming on the scoreboards and in the committee room, but umpires Dai Davies and Syd Buller declined to give us our light appeal. Jim Laker was bowling from the Football Ground End, and after our third light appeal, I jumped down the pitch and drove Laker with plenty of power along the ground, straight past mid-off and into the crowd. It was a good shot, beautifully executed! However, as I walked past Miller on my way back to the striker's end, a sixth sense told me not to catch his eye. It was no good.

'What the bloody hell do you think you're up to?' he said, and it wasn't a happy question. 'I'd just about talked them into giving us the light, but we've no chance now.'

The next day every ball took a divot from the soft pitch, I holed out to Oakman on the square-leg boundary and then four wickets fell for 1. In the dressing-room Ian Johnson was putting the best possible face on it: 'We'll make 500 and we've still got a chance!'

Miller put down *Sporting Life* and added, 'Six to four we don't.'

We made only 140 in the second innings although we batted an hour longer than in our first effort, but were still beaten by an innings and 42.

England played very well at Old Trafford after they won the toss on a pitch that, in colour and texture, looked very similar to the one at Headingley: likely to be good for batting the first day and then taking a lot of spin.

There is no doubt they completely outplayed us. Richardson and David Sheppard both made centuries, Peter May made 43 and Godfrey Evans 47. In reply we made 84 and Jim Laker took only nine wickets. He did better than that in the second innings where we batted through 150 overs and, with the assistance of rain, weren't far off saving the match.

In the second innings I batted a long time for 18 before being bowled by a quicker change of pace by Jim who already had dismissed four players. The crowd cheered Laker off the ground, and so they should have done. He was cheered all over England, not only by cricket supporters but by the man in the street, and through it all he remained perfectly calm and happy, which he should have been and had every right to be, and modest and realistic, which he always was.

There was no such euphoria in Australia where our performance was regarded as being on the poor side of mediocre, and that of Bert Flack the groundsman, possibly more so. I heard later that my own minor protest, in taking a long time patting down the pitch and not being quite ready for the bowler as he turned to run in, wasn't totally appreciated by one leading English official: 'Should never have any position of responsibility in an Australian team,' he exploded to an Australian counterpart seated alongside him.

David Sheppard, later Bishop of Liverpool, had a more liberal sense of humour. When the pitch-patting resulted in a ball whistling past my left ear on the full into Godfrey Evans's glove, and brought the exhortation 'Pat that one down, you little bastard' from bowler Tony Lock, David was quickly into our dressing-room to apologise at the tea interval. I chuckled and hastily said I'd forgotten about it, no apology was necessary but thanks very much anyway. My captain wasn't disturbed by it either. He even appealed to the umpires against the sawdust blowing in the wind.

There were some on the spot at Old Trafford who considered the pitch to be far from ideal. Bill O'Reilly's report for the *Sydney Morning Herald* said this at the conclusion of the first day's play:

> Let's have it straight, this pitch is a complete disgrace. What lies in store for Test cricket if groundsmen are allowed to play the fool like this? Regardless of who wins the toss and which country wins the Ashes, the simple fact remains that no groundsman, no sub-committee anywhere, has the slightest right to turn on such a tragic pitch as this. Steps must be taken without delay to safeguard Test cricket against the continuance of this state of affairs which already has ruined two Tests in this present series.

Neil Harvey and I weren't drinking champagne at the close of play, but we did sit out on the balcony having a beer when almost all the spectators had drifted away after cheering Jim Laker and wondering if they would again see the like. The answer to that is 'probably not' and the answer to the question Harv and I were asking ourselves was 'possibly yes'. Our question: 'If we work and try very hard, can we regain the Ashes in two years' time in Australia?'

Laker finished the job on us in the final Test at The Oval where the match was drawn, I was third top score with 32 in our innings of 202 and only bowled one over.

In the Test series I finished second in the batting averages and had three ahead of me in the aggregates, not that this was anything to write home about, but all these things are relative. In all first-class matches I was sixth in the batting, second in the number of wickets taken to Ron Archer and fourth in the averages. I had learnt a lot and been taught even more, not only in playing but also in teamwork and in what can happen on a cricket tour. The real downer was that my spinning fingers, if anything, were in worse shape than at the start of the Test series. I had gleaned plenty of information about pitches, and about people.

There were still a few matches to be played, end-of-the-tour games against festival teams and up in Scotland as well.

Our game against Scotland at Glasgow produced a lovely short contest between Keith Miller and the Rev. Jimmy Aitchison, who was the leading batsman in the Scotland team. Keith came on first change and, for fun, bowled a bumper to the Reverend, who ducked and then fell over. This produced hilarity around the packed ground, so Keith, again for fun, gave him another. It whistled into the shrubbery at deep square-leg and this brought a roar from the crowd and shouts to give him another. That one hit the seats at deep square-leg and bounced back on to the field. Nugget had had enough of this little game so he fired a few more in and the 'Rev. J' hooked them, either well or off the top edge, and raced to 100 out of 196. It was a delightful innings and was tremendously appreciated by the crowd.

Our second match was in Aberdeen and was memorable to me for a different reason involving a short but lively encounter with my skipper.

I bowled 13 overs and took 2–24 and again badly ripped open my fingers. Nothing unusual about that, it had been happening all the time, but because it was a second-class match with nothing at all hanging to it, and it was the last match of the tour, I went to Johnno in the dressing-room and showed him my hand and asked if it would be all right if I bowled offspinners in the second innings to give my fingers a bit of respite. I can only think that I asked at the wrong moment and I've no idea what his reasoning was but he gave me a long, hard look and told me that I would bowl leg-breaks and, furthermore, I was to get stuck in to it. Jack Wilson who was standing next to us walked away shaking his head.

I was less than happy with the reply I'd received, but when I came on third change, I bowled 17 overs straight and took 6–34. It was of little consequence against Scotland, but I was seething enough to grab the ball at the end of every over and return to my mark without looking at the captain.

Coming off the field at the end of their second innings, Johnno said to Jack Wilson, 'See, "Chucker", I got him steamed up and you see how well he bowled.'

Chucker was more direct, especially since he didn't want a long conversation when there was a beer waiting for him in the dressing-room. He merely said, rather throatily, 'The bastard's mad.'

When we arrived back in the room Johnno called out to me, 'Do you want to say anything to me?'

'No,' I said, 'not one word.'

'Good,' was the only other word we had on that, but I doubt it would have been noted favourably in the little black books of the manager or, for that matter, of the captain.

15
IVAN JAMES

THERE is something slightly off-beat, even bizarre, about battling for the Ashes in England, going through a hectic three-week television course, flying to Rome to have dinner, then from Ciampano airport to Pakistan and India to play four Test matches. All the boys were in good spirits on 8 October when I met them after their three-week break, and so was I. I had been working so hard on a BBC TV course, I hadn't had time to think much about cricket. The course had been arranged for me by Tom Sloan, BBC's Head of Light Entertainment at that time. I worked from 11 a.m. to midnight almost every day of the three weeks. It was wonderful! The purpose was to try to find out something about television, other than in watching it, because this was the year the medium began in Australia.

Channel 9 was first on the air in Australia, and I had no idea at the time that twenty years later I would be working for them and would continue to do so for another thirty years; nor did I have plans at that stage to work for the BBC for almost forty years, but I suppose the course was just one of those things that seemed a good idea at the time. I wasn't trying to learn about the finer points of production and directing, but to give myself a general knowledge of what happened each time a television programme went to air, from everyone's point of view. It would be accurate to say that my main desire was to look at it more from the commentator's point of view than anything else.

In retrospect I suppose all the production assistants, and the producers as well, slumped their shoulders a little when the news came through that this guy Benaud was coming along as an observer, just to have a look and to try to learn something for Australian television. Whatever they might have thought, however, they were all great; nothing was too much trouble; particularly as I seem to recall the occasional question about what I was doing in television in Australia, and I replied each time that I didn't do anything!

I sat with producers, in directors' vans, with the audience on some occasions, at the side of a stage, talked with Denis Monger the producer and trailed behind Peter O'Sullevan at Newbury races and watched how he prepared so meticulously for his job. I watched what Alec Weeks did at the speedway races at Wembley and how the commentators reacted to everything that went right and wrong.

We might not have done all that well with the cricket, but 1956 was very much a year for Australia in other sports which had an influence on my career in television.

While the Tests were being played, Wimbledon was on as well, and I watched and listened to Dan Maskell as he commentated in his inimitable style on Hoad beating Rosewall in four sets in the men's singles final, and when Peter Thomson won the 1956 Open Championship at Hoylake, Henry Longhurst was the commentator who caught my ear. I didn't meet either of them for many years, but what I saw and heard from those two, and O'Sullevan, has stayed with me over the years, not in the same way as O'Reilly's advice or Dooland and the flipper, but in a more abstract way. I had the privilege of being able to learn from what I saw and heard them doing, and confirm the way they went about it.

Having caught up with the team after the television course, we all stepped on to the plane in Rome and arrived in Karachi in time to have a day's practice before we started the match against Pakistan on 11 October. It would be gilding things a little to say it was anything by way of a success. We were totally, conclusively and absolutely thrashed, and I can't say, hand on heart, that I enjoyed my first experience of Pakistan. Ten days of illness, injury and a beating on the field is not actually the formula designed to have you jumping up and down with pleasure.

We stepped on to the plane the night the match finished to fly to Madras for the opening Test against India, arrived late in the evening and then had the following day in the nets as practice, readying ourselves for a five-day Test on turf. I had been impressed by Jim Laker's bowling style in recent months – his relaxed manner and his run-up and delivery, which seemed to be both methodical and economical – and it was here I took another step forward in my bowling career by putting into practice what I had been toying with for some time.

I worked on shortening my run-up to the crease, making myself more balanced in delivery stride and, hopefully, becoming more settled in my overall bowling method. I worked at it in the Madras nets for an hour and I had Neil Harvey to help me. He watched first of all from behind me, then moved to the side and finally went down to see what it looked like from the crease. His verdict was that in delivery it looked almost the same as before, although for some reason it appeared considerably smoother, possibly because I was running in over a shorter distance, the six paces. It may also have been because I was running in a little slower.

It felt better but I was nervous about the whole thing: although I had thought about it for a month, I had done it in a day. I was now looking forward to the blowtorch treatment of using it for the first time in a match. What I needed was a good performance to act as a confidence-booster. What I didn't need was to hear that Ron Archer's leg was too bad for him to play, or that Keith Miller's knee was playing up and that Alan Davidson had a muscle problem.

This was unfortunate, although, depending on my form and on the new action, I might have plenty of work on what looked as though it would be a very batsman-friendly pitch.

Our bowling attack was Lindwall and Crawford with the new ball, Mackay, Johnson and me. The pace bowlers weren't able to break through and I came on with the score at 40–0, hoping nothing tangle-footed would happen to me with the first ball and that it would land on the cut portion. I immediately had Pankaj Roy caught by Harvey, then Vinoo Mankad, attempting to drive, lofted a slower ball to Colin McDonald at mid-off. Vijay Manjrekar, a great exponent of the cut shot, made 41 and we bowled them out for 161. I finished with 7–72, which remained the best figures I ever produced in a Test innings, and I never for one instant thought again about a longer run.

We finished up winning the match by an innings and five runs, with Ray Lindwall, out of a sick bed, taking 7–43 in the second innings, one of the more extraordinary efforts I saw from him, and this on a grassless pitch not at all in favour of the faster bowlers.

For the Second Test in Bombay, Ian Johnson was ill, so too Craig and Langley, and Miller, Archer and McDonald were injured. I managed 45 overs in the second innings but lacked a certain amount of zip, having come down with something diagnosed as dengue fever. As well as the profuse sweating, according to my room-mate Jimmy Burke there was also plenty of moaning, groaning and yelling while he was trying to sleep.

As happens with something like dengue, there are recurring bouts, but I was OK for the final Test of the three, in Calcutta, to the extent that, on an unusual-looking pitch, I took 11–105 from 53 overs. As a confidence boost, this could hardly have been better: taking all these wickets with a new run-up, things were looking good.

Before the Calcutta match, I had been sent for an anti-tetanus injection because of the rough and bloody nature of my fingers and the risk of infection from the soil from which the pitch was made. That might seem cautious, but I can assure you it was a wise precaution. I was understanding more every match what McCool had meant when he said that bowling and pain would always go together: 'and if you don't want to face up to it, son, go and do some other bloody job.'

We arrived back in Australia on the evening of 7 November 1956, and were met by the TV cameras, television having now started in Australia. Keith Miller with his new job at Channel 9 did some interviews with the captain and the other players. All of this was very interesting to me, having only a month earlier spent the worthwhile time on the BBC course.

On the way back in the plane I had been musing on various aspects of the tour. The real downside was that we had failed to regain the Ashes, that no player had made a century in the Tests against England, that the bowling sometimes had been very good, at other times ordinary. I had learnt a lot on the tour, had turned in some good efforts with the bat and ball and my fielding had stood up very well to the high standards I had set myself.

However, demerit marks would have been clashes with authority in the Aberdeen match, and I had no way of knowing how that would be interpreted in any reports going in to the Board. There had been other times where my idea of what I wanted to do with my bowling and Johnno's ideas of what he wanted me to do were not as one. I was still working hard on O'Reilly's words and advice, though I wasn't trying to bowl like O'Reilly; that would have been ridiculous. Tiger's ideas, though, happened to coincide with my father's ideas on legspinning. Ian, on the other hand, wanted me to do it in another fashion and that brought a difference of opinion. He was trying to be helpful, to do the right thing as he saw it as a captain and a spin bowler. I was trying to pursue legspin bowling as a planned campaign. I felt it was working, he didn't, and it's difficult even now to know who was right at the time, although for various reasons it worked out for me. He regarded me as a stubborn young bugger who wouldn't take his excellent advice on tossing the ball up and constantly giving it more air.

I regarded Ian as well meaning, but with ideas which might have been good for him, and for other spinners who were primarily flight bowlers, but were useless for me if I wanted to become a slow bowler who could take wickets and against whom batsmen would have difficulty in scoring runs.

After the 1956 tour I went in to see Lindsay Clinch, the Editor of the *Sun* newspaper, to pursue our earlier conversation that I should talk to him after the tour about a transfer to the editorial department. At the time there was no better or tougher editor in Australian newspapers, and I haven't heard of anyone better since then. He said he had decided to approve a transfer for me and that he wanted me to write a sports column, which someone could ghost for me if necessary. That wasn't what I wanted at all and I said to him I wanted to work on News and Police Rounds if possible, to learn about newspapers and how to write for them.

'OK, go and see Jack Toohey the news editor,' he said. When I was at the door his quiet voice came from behind me, 'He's expecting you!'

Jack Toohey greeted me with, 'Good to see you, Richie. Lindsay told me you'd be in and we've organised that you'll be working under Noel Bailey in Police Rounds.'

This was a very lucky break for me: Bailey was a magnificent journalist who had some legendary battles with another very good Police Roundsman, Bill Jenkings of the *Daily Mirror*. In those days the afternoon newspapers in Sydney and other states had police rounds as the hub of the news section.

These days motor-car accidents, murders and assaults are so commonplace that they may not be reported, or they could be lumped together on a page where a running total is kept. Back in 1956, whilst not rare they were certainly newsworthy, and cases like the one involving the murder of a prison warder and the subsequent manhunt for two chaps called Simmonds and Newcombe kept us all on our toes.

Building up contacts in the police force was quite important for a young reporter, but the finest training of all was to trail on the coat-tails of Noel Bailey. It was wonderful to see and hear him in action, phoning stories to catch an edition. There were no mobile phones in those days: you needed to find a public telephone, and sometimes this would happen, with your pocket stuffed with shorthand notes, about five minutes before the edition was due to run. If it were a big story and they were holding the front page with say twenty-five paragraphs, about 600 words for Bailey, it was an education to see the way he went about it. He adlibbed everything. His eyes would flick to the relevant notes, some in shorthand, some scribbled, and he would always remain perfectly calm, no matter what the pressure of the clock ticking down, or the editor back in the office grabbing the copytaker's headset and barking in his ear.

I was never able to do any of this as well as Bailey, nor would I expect to, but it taught me how to dictate my own stories against time and against space. I didn't know it at the time, but there has been nothing I have done in life which has proved more valuable in presentation on television. Because of Bailey's training I have been able to teach myself to finish on zero when the count is being made in my ear at the end of a cricket telecast, a very valuable attribute when you know that if you over-run by five or ten seconds, that has to be made up in some manner in the studio if the six o'clock news is to start on time.

It was a varied life on the *Sun*. Being in the Police Rounds section meant there was plenty of excitement, and not always to do with police matters. Once, when a USA fly-by-night promoter was trying to sign the great Australian athlete Herb Elliott to run professionally, I had a successful but also hilarious night tracking down the American, who had flown secretly into Sydney on a cargo plane. Lindsay Clinch also called me in one day to say the directors, particularly Vincent Fairfax, wanted me to cover the Billy Graham Crusade when it came to Sydney. One of the more interesting aspects of this assignment was when I arranged, through his PR people, to play golf with him at Royal Sydney. It was a success and a front-page story.

The assignment came to an end when, after writing along the same lines most days about people making their way to the stage and to Billy Graham, my final paragraph mentioned the 'sound of the wind soughing in the trees'. Lindsay Clinch called me in and said, 'Nice final paragraph – I think we understand you're all written out. Take a day off and we'll find someone else!'

It was an Australian summer during which, because of the finger problems, I had awful trouble practising. Trying to conserve my fingers was a full-time job, though I still finished on top of the NSW bowling with 32 wickets, and with 38 wickets was second in the Australian first-class figures to Lindsay Kline. My batting fell away completely, with a top score for the season of only 63 and I had a considerable setback in general physical fitness because of the dengue fever.

A week later, before the start of the season, another dimension had been added to my game when the announcement was made that Ian Craig would be captain of the NSW team. It was a disappointment to me but not totally unexpected. The NSW delegates to the Australian Board had the clear inference that if I were to captain NSW the state might be unlikely to have an Australian captain. They did the pragmatic thing on this occasion, something they were also to do in various areas in later times.

There were all kinds of little nuances during this 1956–57 season. Neil Harvey and I were very good friends, and with Ian Johnson retired, Neil was captaining Victoria and was the frontrunner for the Australian captaincy, having been a member of Bradman's 1948 team and played in forty-eight Tests to this time. He was an outstanding batsman and was correctly regarded as having the finest cricket brain of any of the players in Australia.

The touring team had arrived back so late after England, India and Pakistan that we missed the opening Sheffield Shield game against Queensland in Brisbane. We were there for the next one, when NSW played Western Australia at the SCG, and I took three wickets in the first innings and 5–59 in the second and we won by 80 runs. My fingers had healed after the tour but they broke open again after a couple of overs in this game.

Our traditional Christmas match against Victoria, normally at the MCG, had to be transferred to St Kilda Oval. The pitch for this game looked, and turned out to be, very ordinary indeed. This was my first sighting of William Morris Lawry, later to become one of the great batsmen of Australian cricket; here, though, he made only 1 and 7. This wasn't the foremost feature of the game, however: instead it was that we played the first tie in the history of Sheffield Shield cricket. Three of the Ashes touring team, McDonald, Harvey and Burke, made runs in the game; Burke scored 132 but fractured a finger at the start of our second innings.

We had a multitude of problems. Craig had gone down with tonsillitis and was so ill he had been ordered to take no further part in the game. We visited him in hospital and he looked appalling.

I was acting captain while Craig was laid up, with Harvey my opposite number, and NSW had to make 161 to win by the time we had bowled the Victorians out for 197. That looked a difficult enough proposition, but by the time we were 70–7 and they were clambering all over us, it looked close to impossible. At 63–5 a message had come out to me that Craig had arrived at the ground and was padding up.

I was having plenty of trouble with Ian Meckiff and Lindsay Kline at this time, as well as with Harv's bowling changes and field-placings, and I was both heartened and aghast when Ian walked out on to the field – heartened because it was good to see him, but aghast because he looked absolutely awful. It seemed there was no way he would be able to do anything. He confirmed that he felt the way he looked when I asked him, but said he would do his best. In fact, he did plenty. It was a very brave effort considering he could hardly stand up, let alone run between the wickets, and we put on 75 for the eighth wicket. Then, trying to drive Kline, I didn't pick the wrong'un and John Shaw caught me at slip for 63. Jim Burke batted at 10 after retiring hurt and he was finally caught at the wicket with the scores tied after adding 12 with Alan Wyatt.

When we played the return at the SCG there was also plenty of excitement, though of a slightly different kind. The Australian team for New Zealand had been announced that day, with Ian as captain and Neil vice-captain; I was included in what was a very young side. Colin McDonald, in the nets as the toss was being made, swept at a ball and it flew into his face and broke his nose. Bill Lawry had been announced and confirmed as Victoria's twelfth man at the toss. Craig put Victoria in to bat, and Neil, after returning to the dressing-room and hearing the bad news about McDonald, asked Ian if he could alter his side to bring in Lawry. The answer was 'No'. We had to take a point from this match to keep Queensland from winning their first Sheffield Shield.

There was considerable interest in the match in Sydney. In Victoria interest was heightened by Harvey being passed over

The village of Benaud in France, from which the first Benaud journeyed to Australia on the *Ville de Bordeaux* in 1838. Daphne and I scanned the archives in Clermont-Ferrand and Vic-le-Comte in the Auvergne and found some fascinating Benaud history around Revolution time.

A delightful few minutes in 2005, a celebratory glass of good-quality white with Daphne at the conclusion of 42 years of television commentating and writing in the United Kingdom.

Left A favourite photograph of my father Lou, at Sutherland Road in North Parramatta. He and Rene lived there for almost fifty years and brought up two very happy and grateful children, John (J.B.) and me.

Below Skill and determination from the Benaud Trio. *From right to left:* Richie, Gregory and Jeffery when we were all a little younger; now all have passed the half-century mark.

I watched my first Test match in December 1946 at the SCG; Don Bradman and Sid Barnes each made 234. Bradman played every shot, none better than the sweep depicted here.

Keith Miller was a great allrounder, Australia's best. He was a magnificent pace bowler partnering Ray Lindwall and, as a batsman, he was a splendid striker of the ball with a perfect set-up as he awaited the bowler.

The photograph above was taken by Daphne in 1991 at English Harbour, Antigua. I was in my 14th year of commentary with Channel Nine Australia and we have now completed 33 years as sports consultants for the Nine Network.

No pace bowler from any country had a better bowling method than Fred Trueman. He had a classic action, pace, swing and determination that no batsman would ever get the better of him. He was also one of the great characters of cricket.

Old Trafford 1956 and Jim Laker. When I was making some changes to my bowling run-up and action, it was this photograph I studied and I then put it into practice for the first time 80 days later in Madras. Did it work? Well, I took 7-72, my best-ever bowling figures in Test cricket!

In 1956, the Lord's Test was 'Miller's match'. Lindwall and Davidson couldn't play because of injury; Crawford broke down in the first session. Miller, who had graced Lord's over the years, was playing his last match at the ground. His bowling figures were 34.1-9-72-5 and 36-12-80-5. The photograph is one I prize very much, acknowledging generous applause from the packed Lord's crowd at lunch on the second last day when I was 90 not out.

I am often asked by youngsters if I ever played cricket, an understandable question because they have only ever seen me on the television screen. That tour in 1956 started well for me, this straight drive to the boundary off Jack Flavell was part of a score of 160. Plenty of bat handle showing.

With Neil Harvey on arrival in England in 1961, the last tour when Australian teams travelled to England by ship. 'Harv' was my vice-captain and we took the mythical Ashes back to Australia in September of that year.

Ted Dexter, one of the best batsmen and greatest entertainers I played against. He always played in the best spirit and, with Colin Cowdrey, was responsible for the Spirit of Cricket Preamble to the Laws of Cricket.

Colin Cowdrey, a typical neat cut to the third man boundary.

Peter May, a wonderful batsman, smashing Keith Miller straight down the ground in the final Test at The Oval in 1956.

Fortunately Ted Dexter wasn't playing against Australia at this moment when he has deposited the bowler over the long-on boundary.

to me another man in a white coat, this time dispensing
nes rather than decisions out in the centre of the ground.
at's the matter with your fingers?' he asked.

, it's from the way they get ripped about from bowling, it's
he seam of the ball cuts through the skin.'

at do you use on them?'

 tried everything – hardening them, softening, everything –
e just got to live with it, I'm afraid.'

ve something that might be a help. I've found it very benefi-
r the treatment of leg ulcers for ex-servicemen, particularly
 are suffering the after-effects of being gassed.'

d to him, 'I think I've tried everything, but I'll try anything
nything at all. A fellow named Colin McCool once told me
o let a day go past without trying to find a remedy.'

handed me the sulpha tablets, which I put in my pocket,
en gave me a small wide-mouthed bottle, plus a container
hite powder and a piece of paper with his suggested remedy
 on it. It said:

OILY CALAMINE LOTION BPC '54
BORACIC ACID POWDER

 the lotion into the wound and then dab off the oil which
es to the surface.

 in the boracic acid powder so that it forms a waxy filling in
wound.

 doing this as much as possible and definitely whenever there
recurrence of the skin tearing. Make sure you keep the waxy
tance filling the hole all the time.

added that I should carry with me a piece of fine sandpaper
 before using the remedy I could sand off any bits of dead
 skin.

ked at this with a very wary eye, but as he had taken
uble to ask me about my fingers and then make up his
 and write out the details and instructions, I thanked him

On slow-motion film Jeff Thomson had the
most perfect bowling action you could envisage.
He was also the fastest bowler I ever saw other
than Frank Tyson.

No one loved bowling fast and playing for
Australia more than Dennis Lillee. When injury
threatened to end his career he returned from
four months in a back plaster to play again for
his country and regain the Ashes.

If I wanted someone to bat for my life it would
be Ian Chappell. He was a splendid batsman
for Australia and a great captain.

Three of the greats of fast bowling. *Left to
right*, Fred Trueman, Ray Lindwall and Dennis
Lillee, the latter having formed a partnership
with wicketkeeper Rod Marsh unequalled in
Test history.

Daphne somehow secretly organised a *This is Your Life* appearance in 1976, but she has been forgiven thirty-four years later. Ted Dexter, on the left of picture, alongside him Ivan James, the spinning finger-remedy genius from Timaru, New Zealand, who saved my bowling career in 1957. My mother Rene and father Lou are on the right of the middle row, brother John back centre right.

A splendid team! BBC commentators watching a replay. Tom Graveney and Jim Laker on my right, Peter West in the front row with John Edrich, scorer Michael Fordham behind Peter and a youngster in front of me hoping that one day he might play for England.

for the captaincy; in Brisbane it was inter captained by Ray Lindwall, might make his

Tension rose a little when Harv, who was to deal with on things like this, stormed back after the refusal and, as he grabbed for his ow Maddocks to do the same. He proceeded, w of anger, to play one of the best innings I h Shield, making 209 and ensuring Victoria ma good news, but we managed, in the end, to and retained the Sheffield Shield by a point.

There were two things I wasn't to know ab the following six months, the first of which wa is quite a nasty ailment: suddenly I would star to find my way to the nearest resting place. S dengue fever and its treatment of those days, w was, purely by accident, to be the saving of my s and the end of the McCool pain barrier.

We flew out to New Zealand two weeks l captain and Harvey as vice-captain. The oper Christchurch and I had all my normal cricketin of the tablets I had been taking from the mom been diagnosed back in November. In my wa tion written by Dr Jack Jeffery to purchase t of sulpha tablets. Our fourth match on the against the Combined Minor Associations. It a two-day game but the first day was totally

That evening, checking through my gea decided, for no particular reason, I would ta wander off to the chemist shop I had seen do him make up the next lot of sulpha tablets.

I was cranky and frustrated, my fingers ha few days earlier bowling in Dunedin, and a them up a little they were painful. They pretty sight when I handed the prescription chap who recognised me and asked how I His name as it turned out was Ivan James, courteously, paid the bill and walked out of the shop and back to the hotel. It seemed a long shot and much too simple, but I'd give it a go.

The word genius is much over-used in our society.

Mr Ivan James turned out to be a genius.

16

SOUTH AFRICA: A WHOLE NEW CRICKET BALL GAME

I T is difficult to convey what a difference it can make to a bowler used to bowling with raw fingers suddenly to be free of that pain and inconvenience. It was like beginning a new bowling career. The treatment instantly worked and the skin was toughened so that even prolonged bowling spells didn't produce cracking, which was easily the worst part of the problems I had been going through. I was always careful to have the containers in my cricket bag wherever I travelled. Meeting Ivan James was a remarkable piece of luck and there has never been one moment of doubt in my mind that walking into that chemist's shop in Timaru saved my bowling career and was one of the key reasons why from that moment I moved into top gear as an important allrounder in Australian cricket.

I don't know enough about medicine to understand why it should have been so successful, only that it was. Others who asked for the remedy were given it with the greatest of pleasure: for some it worked, for others it didn't, although I suspect some were nowhere near as dedicated in its use as I was. My dedication might have seemed a bit boring to others, but never to me. 'Jeez, Benords, you're not using that stuff *again*!'

From the time the next match came along, titled a representative fixture, the first of the three games so quaintly named against New Zealand, I was suddenly in a new world, not completely pain- and hassle-free, but veering in that direction.

My pain threshold might have changed, but nothing had changed in regard to the Australian Cricket Board's attitude to

New Zealand cricket. It had been with reluctance they had agreed to the tour, and they had refused requests that there should be any kind of fancy names attached to the matches. They were representative games; nothing more flamboyant than that. It was to be another sixteen years until the Australian Board deigned to send a Test side, or indeed to have one from New Zealand in Australia.

In the three representative games played I bowled 53, 38 and 67 overs. I took 15 wickets too, but the best thing for me was that I bowled the overs and only in the second game in Wellington did I have any slight finger problems. As soon as I came off the field I would work away with the Ivan James' formula, and in the end, even the other players became a little interested. Ian Craig, being a pharmacist, took note and although he couldn't offer too many explanations as to why it should be working, he was of the opinion that, if it had a beneficial effect on leg ulcers for ex-servicemen, then there was no reason why it shouldn't do a toughening job on a bowler's ripped fingers.

By the time the short tour was completed I was in good form, my fingers were OK and I had a few months with my family before going to South Africa. Greg was two years old and we were expecting another child, who, if a boy, would be named Jeffery after our family doctor Jack Jeffery.

The selectors had chosen a young side for New Zealand, they now followed that up by choosing a young team for South Africa, with Ian Craig captain, Neil Harvey vice-captain and Peter Burge as the third selector. The third selector on tour sat in with the captain and vice-captain at meetings; their role began as soon as the team left Australia and they had in effect taken over from the national selection committee.

There was nothing to be read into Peter's appointment although, as more experienced players, Colin McDonald or I might normally have been thought of as possible candidates. It wasn't a continuing matter of any 1956 tour report to the Board, but this time merely the Board being cautious. It was well known that, although Ian and I were team-mates and good friends, Harv and I were also good friends, and the Board's thinking was that if I had been third selector it could have meant an intriguing situation with Harvey and Craig if things weren't going well.

The team flew direct from Sydney by Super-Constellation on 5 October, but sadly without our original manager, Jack Jantke of South Australia, who had a heart attack shortly before the side were due to leave Sydney. Jack Norton was appointed in his place, having recently been our manager in New Zealand. Jack Norton, thrust into the job perhaps because he had the experience of New Zealand, was ambitious and zealous. The ambition was good and we were delighted to see it. We were all ambitious, full marks for that. At Christchurch on the New Zealand tour, during the first of the three main matches, he had suddenly instituted a curfew, everyone in their rooms by 10 p.m. and to stay there. I had to point out gently that I tried never to be asleep before midnight during a match, so I could sleep soundly for eight hours, then have breakfast and get ready to go to the ground. Furthermore, I had already arranged to have dinner on the Sunday night with a New Zealand family and it would depend when the dinner finished.

Neil Harvey and Peter Burge were in a similar situation and said so. Ian Craig held out his hand and said very quietly to Norton, 'I'm out to dinner, too, Jack, we'll need the keys of the team car, please.' Ten out of ten for the new captain who then made 123, with Harvey making 84 and Burge 45 not out.

That incident was something to think about once we knew Jack was to be our manager for the next six months. Curfews were one thing with a group of youngsters, but it was something else having a manager trying to impose his own ideas of fitness on Test players who knew precisely what muscles they would be using on the field and wanted to stay at peak fitness in their own way. In New Zealand the Board, through Norton, had issued their own fitness schedule. What I for one wanted to do now, and had done in New Zealand, was train for bowling and batting, and my own personal exercises did that perfectly when allied to net practice. No one in cricket trained harder than I did, and I did it with common sense and the knowledge gained on three overseas tours prior to the current summer.

Norton had been disappointed in New Zealand that players, including me, preferred to keep doing those exercises which they had designed particularly for their individual requirements. Having reported that information to the Board, he now had the backing of the ACB and issued his own very firm instructions. Another curfew was brought in, again 10 p.m., and a list of exercises was handed to each player. What the Board and Norton wanted was warming-up and warming-down; in fact, we did our own warming-up and down as a matter of course and simple common sense. There was a lot of other stuff as well, but I made up my mind to do my own thing as regards the exercises and my fitness for batting and bowling.

I had already set myself the most arduous of practice schedules to lead up to the time the first ball was bowled in a match on the tour, and I didn't really want some ageing administrator, sitting in a leather armchair in Australia, underlining that a little knowledge of fitness was an extremely dangerous thing; nor did I want a manager endeavouring to do a similar thing whilst trying to impress the ACB.

My practice schedule in Australia was always to arrive at the SCG at 3 p.m. and bowl until 6 p.m., breaking off most days for a twenty-minute batting spell. In South Africa my schedule was to be based on the same premise, and it would be geared to practical matters, not theory.

The venue for me to pursue this, from the day after our arrival in Johannesburg on 6 October until we flew to Northern Rhodesia, as it was then known, was the nets at the Wanderers ground. We always practised in the mornings, the afternoons were free. After the morning practice, the players would lunch, play golf, go to race meetings, relax at the hotel, sleep, do whatever they wanted. I would stay at the Wanderers to practise along the lines of my SCG sessions. I bowled something like twenty overs in the morning, then after lunch, on my own other than for a couple of youngsters to throw the balls back to me, I would bowl another ten to fifteen overs, which I spun as fiercely as I could, all aimed at a spot I had marked on the pitch. About 95 per cent were leg-breaks, some of the others were flippers. It was the best bowling fitness campaign I had undertaken and there wasn't an Australian Cricket Board member or fitness authority jogging into view. And, Ivan James's finger remedy was working perfectly.

I had practised my flipper assiduously in the nets in Australia, and I had worked as hard on it in the nets at the Wanderers but had so far not bowled it in a match. It was very difficult to perfect. I had some assistance from the rest of the team, in that the batsmen gave me a running commentary on how difficult it was to see that it involved a ball delivered with a slightly different action. This assistance was very important, and although there was some surprise expressed outside the team at what we were doing, to me it was perfectly normal.

People asked questions like, 'Yes, but what about when you're back in Australia and you're bowling to all the chaps who are your team-mates here?'

My answer was, 'So what? They're team-mates here and it will be up to me to find some other way of concealment when I move into another area. At the moment they're my mates and they're helping me all they can.'

It wasn't the same as happened at the 'Gabba in Brisbane, in 1950, when Lindsay Hassett wouldn't allow any batsmen from states other than Victoria to bat against freak spinner Jack Iverson in the nets, in case they managed to learn something about him in matches later to involve Victoria in the Sheffield Shield. You might think I'm having you on, but it's true.

This, although I didn't know it at the time, was approximately the halfway point of my Test career. I had played twenty-seven Tests in six years and with moderate success; I was to play sixty-three in all, the last period with considerable success. Miller, Lindwall, Bill Johnston, Ron Archer and Ian Johnson had gone from the bowling attack and now I was the main spinner; Alan Davidson was to be the main pace bowler. We were ready to do a job and we did it from that day. My career and that of Alan Davidson were to be linked for the next five years of Australian cricket triumphs.

The desperately bad news was that Neil Harvey had broken a finger in the practice sessions at the Wanderers, trying to take a high outfield catch, and we had to go to Rhodesia without him while he remained in Johannesburg for treatment in a bid to have him ready for the opening Test two weeks later. As bad was the fact that we were without Colin McDonald, whose jaw was broken while batting in the nets when he was hit by a short-pitched delivery.

Kitwe, Northern Rhodesia, is an unlikely place to start a new career phase but that was where it happened for me with almost instant success for my new ball, the flipper. Ten overs, 9–16, was a good start, and I could hardly have asked for a better way to begin what was likely to be an arduous tour. Seven of the batsmen were lbw or bowled playing back to the flipper, deliberately pitched short of a good length, and there was no doubt the ball hustled off the pitch throughout the bowling spell.

The Kitwe ground was a small oasis, reasonably pretty for a cricket ground in a copper mining area, and the pitch was good for batting. The bowling figures were enough to remember, but to have bowled from the Smelting End was an added memory jog in later years. To add to the pleasure, I had no problems with my spinning fingers and, despite the intense heat, I felt really fit, a direct reflection of the fact that I had prepared for the tour in my own way, with sheer hard work of the practical kind I would be undertaking during the tour. The work in the nets had allowed me to drop half a stone in weight.

In Salisbury we had a good look at Paul Winslow because he made 81 and 139 against us. He was an interesting character and looked a very dangerous batsman. Ian Craig made a delight-ful century in the first match at Salisbury and I turned in a good double there, with 117 not out and 6–93 in the second innings. Alan Davidson had 100*, and bowled well within himself in both innings in Salisbury but stretched himself a little when he arrived in Bulawayo, taking 5–36 from 14 overs in Rhodesia's first innings and then 2–22 from 14 overs in the second. He looked good, so did Ian Craig who hit another century at Bulawayo.

We moved on to Johannesburg to play Transvaal and had our first sighting of Neil Adcock and Peter Heine, together with Hugh Tayfield. They were a very strong team but we demolished them by nine wickets. Davo bowled beautifully, picking up 2–36 and 2–26 and, as he also made 100 against a strong bowling attack, he could be said to be hitting his straps even at this early stage of the tour. We were already having some fitness worries: Ian Meckiff had a muscle strain, John Drennan was struggling with a slight hamstring problem and there were also the injuries to Harvey and McDonald. We set out to damage Paul Winslow's Test chances in the game in Pretoria when he made 12 and 22 and intense pressure was applied to him all the way through; nothing verbal mind you, only silent pressure. We had reasoned he could be a danger, with his clean striking of the ball and fast scoring, so we were happy he had missed out: we would much prefer a defensive-style batsman who might make the same runs against us but take three times as long.

Just to make certain the South African selectors would be unsure of whether or not to choose him, we kept praising his batting to the skies every time we were asked about him.

The lead-up to the first match in a Test series is always a tense affair, particularly if there are selection problems, and both teams definitely had those. For South Africa Clive van Ryneveld had split webbing between his fingers in the field, and Jackie McGlew had been made captain. We had our own problems, with Neil Harvey injured again and unable to play. Hardly believable, but he broke the same finger again fielding off his own bowling in the light-hearted match at Benoni. John Drennan was also out with a recurrence of his hamstring trouble, a crushing blow on the eve of the Test, and the injuries meant Ken Mackay would have to bat at three.

We lost the toss on the first morning of the First Test and South Africa batted very well, although we were hampered for a time on the opening day by light rain and a slippery ball. In the light of what had happened so far on the tour and to underline the vagaries of cricket, the two least impressive performers were Benaud and Davidson. Astonishingly we returned identical figures, 1–115, and both simply failed to perform on the day.

When they closed their innings at 470–9 in front of a crowd of 30,000, we needed 321 to save the follow-on, and the ball was starting to turn for Tayfield. When I made it to the crease at number seven, we were 151–5. At the close of play we were 307–7, I was 80 not out and we were within 14 of saving the follow-on. The key period had been when Trevor Goddard was brought on from the Wanderers End to tie things down.

Trevor was left-arm over-the-wicket and extraordinarily accurate, but, apart from his pinpoint accuracy, he moved the ball in the air and off the pitch as well. He was as close to Australia's Ernie Toshack as you are likely to see. It was very much a case of having a dash at him this day, otherwise, if we were pegged down, saving the follow-on would be out of the question and we were unlikely to escape from the match with a draw. I hit him for four fours in the first over he bowled to me, two of them straight down the ground, one over midwicket and the other through the covers. We lifted his figures from 0–19 from 13 overs to 0–57 in 16 overs, and that did the trick, for a time anyway.

We had only Ian Meckiff and Lindsay Kline to come the following morning, and when Wally Grout was brilliantly caught by Endean off Tayfield, we had a real problem. I solved that with a couple of hook shots and a back cut and now it was a case of get what I could and then perhaps we might even think about a win. Meckiff and I put on 42 in 27 minutes and we finished with 368 in what was a good recovery.

By lunch we had South Africa 19–4, with Davidson taking 3–11 and Meckiff 1–7, but they managed to escape. I had 15 hit from two rather stiff overs and then never saw the bowling crease again, not what I had in mind although I could partly appreciate Ian Craig's point of view, in his first Test match as captain, not wanting to sacrifice the fightback we had achieved. In the end they made 201, with Davo taking 6–34 and Meckiff 3–52. Russell Endean had a very good match for South Africa, with 50 and 77, Johnny Waite made 115 and 59.

We needed 304 to win, but had no chance of doing that in the available time, and 162–3 gave us the draw. Our rating by the slightly one-eyed South African scribes, who claimed we were the weakest team to visit South Africa, had been dented.

We had been given the finger-in-the-chest treatment on many occasions and been told we had no chance of beating South Africa. We were, in fact, 4–1 outsiders. When we had suggested it would be a good idea if they put their money in the same place as their big mouths, at £100 to £25, one of them accepted. That bet was now looking better. Harv had also met two Australian businessmen at the races, 'Blue' Schwarer and George Thompson, who were not only very nice people and avid racegoers but also good betting men. Before I had hit the hundred in the First Test we had dinner with them both, and during a discussion on horse-racing, they tipped us the eventual winner of the biggest handicap in Durban, which we backed antepost. Schwarer asked me if I thought we could win the Test series, because he wanted to have a character-building bet at the 4–1 with a few of his bookmaking friends. I said, 'Yes, go for it. We're all in good form.' There was an interesting follow-up later in the series.

The toss was all-important in the Second Test in Cape Town. We made 449, then finished the game off with time to spare, bowling South Africa out for 209 at their first attempt and then for 99 when they had to follow on. It was a very good team effort. Lindsay Kline, the left-arm over-the-wrist spinner, took a hat-trick, to finish off the match. I had nine wickets in the match and our fielding, this time, was outstanding. We had problems with fitness, though: Ian Meckiff broke down with a shoulder injury, Davidson was in trouble with various muscles, particularly in his right leg and right ankle, which was the one taking the strain of landing on the batting crease in delivery.

Alan was showing many signs of the greatness to come, but the injury problems, most of them real and only a few imaginary, provided plenty of humour in the dressing-room. At the end of this game we made him a presentation of a beautifully engraved plaque which said: 'The A. K. Davidson Autograph Massage Table'. The message on the card which went with it was: 'For Services To Physiotherapy and the Massage Profession'. He took it in good part and raised a glass to the team as we started celebrating.

Alan had bowled magnificently, and one of his second-innings victims, Johnny Waite, merely appears as J. H. B. Waite c Benaud b Davidson 8. Davo was bowling left-arm but at reduced pace, I was in the gully and Waite had played at a couple of balls which had come off the outside edge but had dropped short of me. In between overs I asked Ian if I could come up three yards because it didn't look as though a 'nick' would carry.

'Fine,' he said, 'do what you want.'

I went up three yards, Davo bowled the one he pushed away from the right-handers, Waite played a glorious square drive, hit it off the meat of the bat and I threw myself to the right and caught what was a red blur.

Circumstances play a big part in publicity. A year earlier I had caught Cowdrey at Lord's with one that was rated in various ways; Catch of the Century is one name given it. More relevant might have been Photograph of the Century. No photographer took a proper shot of the one at Newlands, but you can take my word for it that, as catches go, it was considerably better than the one at Lord's because I had dived and caught it rather than managing a form of self-preservation. As I rolled over twice, Davo, hamstring and ankle problems and all, was alongside me shouting, 'Great catch, Rich, it was the old trap, you know . . .'

We had two matches to play before the Third Test in Durban, one in Transvaal and the other in Natal, at Pietermaritzburg. Davidson and I played both and we had a good Test practice in the latter game. Davo made 123 and took three wickets, I made 187 and had six for 88 in the match.

The Durban Test itself was one of the most boring games of cricket in which I have played at paddock, school, club, first-class or Test level. We were bowled out for 163 on a greenish pitch, Craig made a very good 52, playing with composure against the fast bowling, then South Africa batted for thirteen hours five minutes in making 384. At that point we had no chance of victory and needed 221 to make them bat again. We had to battle to avoid defeat rather than look at any chance of a win, but managed it with excellent batting efforts from Harvey, who made 68, Burke 83, McDonald 33 and Slasher Mackay, just the man for a pressure situation, making 52 not out and defying Adcock, Tayfield and Goddard in a splendid innings. When I went out we were 18 runs ahead with six wickets in hand at tea but the ball was turning square. I made 20 in 71 minutes of defence and the game eventually petered out into a draw.

The one thing we did know was that the South Africans would be formidable in Jo'burg. Heine and Adcock gave it everything after we had won the toss and batted: there was no lack of short-pitched deliveries, nor of fire in the verbal exchanges, which actually were all one-way traffic.

Colin McDonald and Jim Burke remained silent and weathered it but the morning was tough going in front of a big and understandably partisan crowd. McDonald was out at 43, lbw trying to sweep Tayfield, and the *'Slegs vers Spielers'* (Players Only) sign on the gate was never the same again as 'CC' came through it, seething and bat swinging.

Craig came to me as Harvey and Burke walked out after lunch and told me to pad up and bat at four. It was an inspired decision as it turned out, his instructions were to take the initiative away from the Springboks. Good captaincy. We still finished with only 217–4 at the end of the day from 60 overs, but considering the state of the series, it was a good performance. I hit an even 100 before trying to hook Heine and skying to midwicket.

I had one stroke of luck, as did the team, when Adcock, who was suffering from a heavy cold, left the field and was forced to return to his hotel after bowling 21 overs. It meant some hostility was gone from the attack late in the day and also from the verbals. In that respect Peter Heine managed to make up for the loss of his partner. Each bumper was followed by a verbal barrage but one thing I had quickly found was that Peter loved eye contact.

I don't mind a bit of eye contact, but you need to judge your opponent, and my judgement this day was that I would see what effect it would have if I declined to catch his eye. It was hilarious, though without television you missed the best of it. Bumper, hook, verbal would be the sequence. I would turn my back on Peter in the batting crease, which would infuriate him, and he would try to ease himself into my eye line. There we would be, shuffling around the batting crease like a pair of ballet dancers seeking perfection in the *pas-de-deux*, and it looked, I'm told, very amusing to the naked eye. Stump microphones would have been handy, too, then viewers could have judged that some of the suggestions he was making to me would, if successfully concluded, have had me a finalist in the next sexual Olympic Games.

We made 401 and forced them to follow on, bowling them out for 203, and they made only 198 at their second attempt. I finished with 4–70 and 5–84 and we won by ten wickets, McDonald scoring the one run needed from Roy McLean's bowling.

The last South African wicket to go was that of Neil Adcock. Obviously we couldn't hear the radio commentary on the incident, but when later I listened to a recording, it was an hilarious little interlude between Charles Fortune and Eric Rowan, the former Test cricketer who had become a radio summariser. Ken Funston was batting against me, and in trying to keep the strike, he tapped me to backward point and ran. Adcock tripped in mid-pitch and was flat on his face when Meckiff at point picked up and threw wildly past Grout. Adcock looked up, saw he had a chance, tried to scramble to his feet and fell down again. Burke, who had backed up well at midwicket, gathered the ball and threw underarm to Grout for the dismissal. In the commentary box Eric shouted to a million listeners, 'Get up, you stupid bastard, Adcock,' something 'Addie' was totally unable to do, and the rest of us were also help-less with laughter.

The victory meant we had clinched the series two-nil, not bad for the worst team ever to leave Australian shores. My individual effort meant I was the first Australian in a Test to make a century and take five wickets in an innings and, as well, nine wickets in the game.

There were not many Australian supporters to cheer us to

victory, but we did have some backing in South Africa from the black and coloured and other minority groups. In every Test match centre they packed the special enclosures as they weren't permitted to sit outside and mix with the whites. They barracked for us, they were right on our side, and in Jo'burg, when we left the field at the end of the South African first innings, they gave me a memorable ovation as I returned to the dressing-room enclosure. In smaller numbers they did the same when we had won the match, a gesture very much appreciated, as were the calls of 'Bwana Benaud'. All our players found that a bow to their assembly, and a grin and a wave at all the grounds around the country, did no harm to our cause. Wherever we were playing, the whole team took opportunities to talk to the occupiers of those stands whenever we were down on the fence and close to them. They responded by adopting us, as apparently they did with other teams.

During the 1997 Test match in Hobart, the Australian Cricket Writers' Association tendered a farewell to respected NZ journalist Don Cameron, and Bert Sutcliffe told me the story of the moving reception given to him and Bob Blair at Ellis Park in Johannesburg in 1953 in terribly sad circumstances.

It was the Second Test and Sutcliffe had been hit by an Adcock bumper and taken to hospital where he twice fainted before being allowed to return to the ground. Against the instructions, wishes and advice of his skipper, Geoff Rabone, he donned his creams and went back in at the fall of the next wicket. He told Rabone, 'Have a look at the scoreboard. We're too many gone, for not enough.'

Bert told me that while he was waiting to go out to bat, a South African friend came into the dressing-room, said he had something for him which would fix his headache and handed him a *very* stiff Scotch, which he downed, and immediately was in a far more positive frame of mind.

Bert was swathed in bandages when he walked down the steps past the '*Slegs vers Spielers*' sign and out on to the ground to an ovation from the capacity crowd, more particularly from the black stand. He reached his half-century with a third six off Hughie

Tayfield, and then, when the ninth wicket fell and the players were starting to leave the field, there was a sudden silence.

Bert said, 'I looked up and there was Bob Blair coming down the steps. I hadn't even known he was at the ground, because we had left him at the hotel trying to cope with the news of the Tangiwai rail disaster in New Zealand which had killed 150, including his fiancée, Nerrissa Love. I didn't want him out there, he shouldn't have been there and I walked over and put my arm around him. I had difficulty getting any words out because I was crying. So was he. When we met, there was hushed applause. I said to him, "Bob, you've got no right to be on the ground, let's just throw the bat at everything and get the hell out of here."'

Between them Sutcliffe and Blair hit four more sixes and then Blair was stumped trying to hit another and walked off to a tremendous ovation. Bert said, 'I've never heard anything like it from one section of a crowd, the black area. Their cheers and deafening shouts were extraordinary when Bob and I walked up the steps arm in arm.'

The morning after our Fourth Test victory against South Africa at the Wanderers, the phone rang in my room. It was Blue Schwarer. 'If you're free, come down to my office at ten, I want to talk to you,' he said. When I arrived there he produced a little white packet full of a lot of things that looked like glass. They were diamonds.

'Choose one,' he said. 'I had a very good win on the Test series with Australia having been offered 4–1 and I mightn't have backed them without you assuring me you were certain to win.'

I knew as much about a diamond as I would about the qualities of reflective glass so he chose one for me and it was gratefully received. I thought it wiser not to go into the business of young cricketers being full of bravado, always feeling they are going to win, and offering grandiose, puffed-up opinions, particularly if they've had a few Lion lagers at a convivial dinner. Blue was so happy it would have been a shame to spoil the illusion of Benaud the soothsayer!

When my wife had the gem set in a ring, it looked very nice and added to the pleasure of us becoming parents again, our second son Jeffery having been born thirty-eight days before I was handed the diamond in Johannesburg.

In the match against Western Province at Newlands I took 5–41 and 2–91 to reach 96 wickets on the tour and go past the previous best figures by Australians Clarrie Grimmett and Bill O'Reilly. Way back in 1913–14 the great English bowler, Sydney Barnes, had taken 104 wickets on MCC's tour of South Africa.

When we arrived in Port Elizabeth to practise for the final Test we noted carefully that the pitch was as well grassed as any we had come across during the tour. It stayed that way for the match, with the mower blades high enough not to bruise the grass in the final 'cut' before the game began.

Adcock and Heine were said to be very fit and keen to see us. The 'poke-the-finger-in-the-chest brigade', this time at the Port Elizabeth pre-Test reception, were happy to let us know that if we thought we had *earlier* problems, we wouldn't know what the word meant until we walked out on to the ground the following day, on a 'green-top', against that pair.

It was quite a match and a magnificent finale, but not for South Africa. Instead it was a triumph for Craig as captain, Harvey as his deputy and for the team labelled as the worst to leave Australian shores. It was also a delightful end to the series for Alan Davidson and for me, with good performances as allrounders. We bowled them out in their first innings for 214 and the fielding of the team was magnificent. We then made 291 and Heine and Adcock were fast and dangerous, producing a bumper barrage far more dangerous and consistent than any short-pitched bowling I had previously seen. In their second innings they could manage only 144. Davidson, 5–38, was close to unplayable and, at the other end, I took 5–82.

It was a good way to end the Test series with the ball, the boys from Lisarow and Parramatta sharing the bowling ends and all 10 wickets. We needed 67 to win and such was the degree of short-pitched bowling in seven overs from Adcock and Heine, that Clive van Ryneveld, their skipper, had to step in and say that enough was plenty. He was right. Fifty-three bumpers in fifty-six balls was slightly close to the line! I was in the centre, 6 not out, with Wally Grout 35, when the match was won. It was a good feeling.

It was also the day we started a South African fast-bowling dynasty. One of the room attendants was a lad from Grey College and he was thoroughly impressed by the searing pace at which Adcock and Heine bowled, also by the fact that Australian batsmen seemed discomfited by the short-pitched delivery; even more so by the fact that when one of our batsmen arrived back in the dressing-room his bat had preceded him, landing against the metal lockers and making one hell of a din. The young room attendant's name was Peter Pollock. So inspired was he by what he saw and heard that day that he went on to take 116 Test wickets for South Africa, and his son Shaun very successfully continued the pace-bowling dynasty.

In this, my thirty-second Test, I joined a very select band of cricketers in reaching the Test double of 1,000 runs and 100 wickets, took my 100th wicket for the tour and it was the 500th first-class wicket of my career. When we returned to Cape Town for our last game we beat the Combined Universities easily and I took four wickets to become the highest wicket-taker on a South African tour.

It was a very successful tour in many ways. When challenged in another area, we beat the Western Province baseball team four-one and then beat South Africa in Johannesburg one-nil, something they said set South African baseball back many years. When we arrived home in Australia, a baseball game was arranged against a representative side of Claxton Shield quality at Petersham Oval in Sydney and we beat them four-one. We had a good team.

17

AN EXTRAORDINARY
SEASON: THE CAPTAINCY
AND THE RETURN
OF THE URN

THERE was still conjecture over the Australian captaincy: Ian Craig had encountered problems with the bat, so had Neil Harvey and the finger injuries had set him back badly. Two of my former captains, Lindsay Hassett and Ian Johnson, had interesting views. Hassett said Craig needed early form in the new season to gain him inclusion in the side. He added that Harvey should have captained the side in South Africa. Johnson said Craig was the logical captain for the series against England. He added, however, that Craig had been the victim of a bad initial blunder by the Australian cricket authorities and that Lindwall should have captained the side in South Africa. There appeared to be many conflicting opinions.

What of the future for me? One thing I knew was that the next Test series against England would be tough. Peter May's team was all the time building a reputation as the finest in the world; their own media publicists were not backward in trumpeting this line. Providing I stayed fit, I would be the number one spinner for Ian Craig in Australia, and the way the matches had gone in South Africa there was a good chance I would be batting at number five, sometimes at four, depending on the circumstances. I loved the thought of it. Although Neil had a setback on the South African tour with his broken fingers and illness he would be vice-captain to Ian, but most of the conjecture at the end of this tour seemed to be whether Ian would hold his place as a batsman. Given proper fitness for both of us, I would be in the side with Alan Davidson and I would not be involved in any way with the running of the team. I had pushed any thoughts of captaincy right out of my mind: I was thoroughly enjoying myself as a player and was solely interested in that role. My whole career path had already changed because of Ivan James. Good advice is to assume nothing in this game!

The time between the return of the team from South Africa on the *Dominion Monarch* in April to the start of practice work-outs was not very long, but I had real confidence that the period between arriving home and the bowling of the first ball of the summer would be profitably spent. There's nothing like a losing series to dent your confidence: equally, a series triumph such as we had in South Africa does wonders to boost the way you look at the future. We weren't over-confident, but we now had an idea of how good we might be, bearing in mind this was very much a new-look side.

This was to be another chance for us to try to regain the Ashes, having lost them in 1953, which seemed not five years ago, but fifty. England, since the 1956 tour and Jim Laker's triumphs, had gone very well in the Test arena, playing series against South Africa, West Indies and New Zealand, fifteen Tests in all with nine wins, four draws and only two losses, both against South Africa. As we had the three-nil victory in the recent series, our confidence level was lifted by the fact that South Africa, with much the same team, had managed to draw their series against England in 1956–57, the season before we had gone there with Ian Craig as captain.

In the prelude to this 1958–59 season we had plenty of public-ity in Australia from cricket writers in England, most of it along the lines of what England would do to Australia and how good the England side actually was. There was one article which even said that a better idea than England playing Australia would be for England to play the World, thus making more of an entrancing spectacle for everyone. The point about that article was that it wasn't written in jest: they really meant it and believed every word of the sentiments noted!

One major thing happened to England's detriment, however. One of their finest cricketers, who I believed could easily be their trump card, had been dropped from the side for disciplinary reasons. Johnny Wardle of Yorkshire had troubles with the county and, having been told he was not to be retained by them for the next season, he criticised his employer's administration in a series of articles in the *Daily Mail*. Yorkshire had already told MCC he would be available to tour Australia, but they then dispensed with his services and, under the system operating in England at the time, he was automatically dropped by MCC from the seventeen invited to participate in the tour – very much master–servant. Jim Laker had been chosen, but withdrew, and later agreed to make the trip. It all sounded a bit of a dog's breakfast, if that isn't too harsh a term for cricket administration. Wardle, in the 1958 season in England, was Yorkshire's leading wicket-taker with 76. He was also the fourth Test cricketer in twelve months whose services were dispensed with by Yorkshire, at a time when they had a new captain, Ronnie Burnet, who was a very good strong character, a nice guy, no star as a first-class cricketer but almost certainly the no-nonsense type of amateur cricketer Yorkshire needed at a time when dressing-room squabbles were not unknown. Yorkshire only had to wait twelve months to find out what Burnet could do, because he captained them to winning the County Championship the following summer. They beat Sussex in an exciting encounter in their final game of the season by five wickets, after they had been set 215 to make in 105 minutes. Fred Trueman, Ray Illingworth and Doug Padgett were the stars of the season, and so too, definitely, was the captain, whose appointment had triggered the Wardle articles in the *Daily Mail* and his subsequent omission from the tour of Australia.

If those things were having some effect on the futures of various players in England, then there were other happenings, partly out of the public eye, partly in it, which were to have a marked effect on my own cricketing life, though I had absolutely no idea of this at the time.

The first was that in the previous season, 1956–57, Neil Harvey had captained Victoria very well, had topped the national batting averages with 836 runs at 104.50 and had finished second in the aggregates, although he had batted only ten times. He was in excellent form, then we all toured South Africa with the seasons coinciding.

Now Harv was back in Australia at the end of the South African tour and, like the rest of us, if not broke, then in an alarmingly impecunious state and faced with the prospect of receiving the grand total of £375 plus £50 expenses from the upcoming Test series against England. On a television show in Melbourne, when asked about his future, he said he was very unsettled as regards employment at that time and it had been necessary to think seriously about leaving Australia because of financial circumstances. There had been a possibility he might go to South Africa, the original home of his then wife, Iris. When the same television programme was shown in Sydney the next week, it underlined for a lot of people the problem facing Australia's cricketers at that time. Here was our best batsman thinking of going overseas because of financial difficulties directly associated with playing the game, despite playing it so well he was an automatic choice in every side since he had starred in Bradman's 1948 team ten years earlier.

If this were in any way embarrassing to the Australian Cricket Board, they managed successfully to conceal that state of mind and found no cause why players' remuneration should be increased from £75 a Test with £10 expenses.

It was almost twenty years later that Alan Barnes made his famous statement to say, if Rod Marsh thought remuneration in 1976 was too low, there were 50,000 others around Australia who would play for nothing. That quote was very well publicised. However, the same thing was often said to players in private many years ago, and it was deliberately emphasised as a way of making everyone toe the line.

Twenty years after that, in 1997, they were at it again in a different style but in the most disgraceful manner imaginable, when the Australian Cricket Board publicised details of players' earnings so as to put pressure on them and influence the manner in which they might then be perceived by the public.

The second thing to affect me was that the Melbourne television programme in 1958 brought a swift reaction from a good businessman, Joe Ryan, who ran John Dynon and Sons, high-class glassware manufacturers in Sydney. He was so upset at what he had seen and heard that he instantly phoned Neil and offered him a job with his firm and trained him to be a sales supervisor. Neil moved to Sydney in August 1958, not long before the arrival of the England team in Perth in early October. I was delighted Neil was to play with NSW, something which was likely to make our grip on the Sheffield Shield even more secure, as indeed it turned out.

The third thing to happen was that Ian Craig was diagnosed as having hepatitis.

The outcome of all this was that Neil Harvey had moved to Sydney, Ian Craig was ill, and the state selectors chose me to lead NSW in our Sheffield Shield match at the 'Gabba.

This was logical enough, although it was arguable that Neil should instantly be made captain of NSW over me, as the current state vice-captain to Craig, but it was all becoming very, very complicated.

As captain I made 29 and took 3–78 in the Queensland first innings, and on the last afternoon we were in with a shout of victory when they suddenly lost 4–18 and Lindwall and Walmsley had to defend desperately. I was able to set attacking fields and I was happy with the way the captaincy challenge had gone. This was only the second time I had captained NSW in a full match.

Ten days later we played Western Australia at the SCG and Ian came back to captain us for that match but made a duck. He didn't look well to me. The game seemed to be out of our reach on the final day when they were batting soundly but then I took 6–5 in 33 balls and we managed to scramble our way to an outright win with an hour to spare. I finished with 7–65 and it was a heartening start to the summer.

Ian was again captain a week later for the game against MCC, and although he was looking a little better it did seem as though he might have been trying to make a comeback too soon. Hepatitis was said in those days to be a very tough illness and very debilitating – it still is. He made another duck, caught at slip by Cowdrey off Tony Lock, Neil made 149 in a wonderful innings and Jim Burke 104.

I set myself to bowl well when we went out on to the field. Tony Lock had turned the ball a little and I reckoned this was a good chance to see if it were possible to gain some kind of an advantage over the batsmen I was likely to meet in the Test. At one stage I bowled five maiden overs and had the wickets of Graveney, Cowdrey and May, finishing with 5–48 from 28.4 overs, a performance which was a real boost in confidence.

There was no such confidence for Ian. He knew from the fact he was very weary during the game that he had tried to come back to big-time cricket too soon, and he notified the selectors that he didn't intend to play again during the season. It was a cruel blow for him. Taking the side to New Zealand and South Africa was one thing but to captain an Australian team in an Ashes battle is the ultimate and here it was, sheer bad luck, through illness, had deprived him of the chance.

The captaincy position was now that, with Ian out for the season, I was captain of NSW and Neil was vice-captain of the Australian team. Had we been about to leave for an overseas tour, there is not the slightest doubt Neil would have stepped into the position of captain of the touring team. In fact, he was about to lead an Australian XI against MCC at the SCG but it proved to be a disastrous match as a prelude to the First Test. Fred Trueman and a few others sometimes weren't over-caring of where they put their feet, and this time Fred gouged out two holes in the pitch at the Members' End during the Australian XI's first innings, after MCC had made 319.

It had no effect in that innings, but when Tony Lock bowled

into the footholes in the second innings, he took 6–29 from 16 overs. To go with their first innings of 128, the Australian XI were bowled out for 103. It wasn't the same as Laker bowling us out two years earlier in England, but it must have sent a shudder through the Australian selection committee.

The defeat wasn't in any way Neil's fault, but the next day, 26 November 1958, it was announced I had been made captain of the team for the First Test in Brisbane. It wasn't a case of being under-whelmed by the appointment, but there were a few little things that held me back from total celebration. First there was the fact that Harv had been overlooked again; then there was the background of information that gave me the knowledge that my appointment was regarded by some administrators as being forced on them by a series of accidents. From that moment I always looked with a wary eye on any beaming administrator who came up to me and said he knew I was the man for the job.

I was standing by the telex machine in the *Sun* sports depart-ment when the announcement came through, and I phoned Neil straight away. We had been good mates for the past five years and had already arranged that, whichever way the announcement went, we would lunch together at the Cricketers' Club and chat about what was looming as the most important match we had played together in many years. We talked very briefly about the fact that if Ian Craig had been fit and well, and had been in any sort of form, then he would have been captain, and that if Harv had stayed in Melbourne, as Victoria's captain and Australia's current vice-captain, equally there was no doubt he would have been captain after Ian pulled out of the season.

It could not have been otherwise and, even though I have been told since by cricket officials and media that I would still have been captain, what they say is untrue, sometimes deliberately so. They are merely saying it in hindsight and there was absolutely no way the selectors would have overlooked Neil had he been captain of Victoria. Why would they? Why choose ahead of the then Australian vice-captain and recently Victorian captain, someone who was only NSW captain because of Craig's illness? It would have lacked common sense and been very much in the too-hard basket. Trust me! That was my view then and I have had no cause, even for a moment, to change it since that time. Also my view is that Harv paid the cruel penalty solely because he was trying to do the right thing by his family and himself as regards some worthwhile form of employment and remuneration.

One really jarring note on being made captain came in some of the congratulations which were directly along the lines of how great it was to have a captain from NSW. I love NSW but that was a very parochial touch!

At the Cricketers' Club bar we had a drink and talked. Harv started it with, 'Mate, I'm with you,' and by recalling sitting on the balcony at Old Trafford in Laker's match, and what a lousy feeling it had been, bowled out by a fine bowler on a bad pitch. We had said then that 1958–59 would be our time.

The lunch wasn't in any sense a planning meeting, but rough ideas were laid down in the knowledge that Alan Davidson and I would be the main bowlers. One of Australia's big plus marks was that Ray Lindwall was in form, but would he make it back into the side? It seemed more likely it would be Davidson and Ian Meckiff to take the new ball, as had been the case in South Africa, and, I was hoping, with Ken Mackay as the third seam bowler. As the selectors had left Ray out of the side for South Africa it seemed unlikely at this stage they would change their line of thinking.

When the team was announced it was Benaud (c), Harvey (v-c), McDonald, Burke, O'Neill, Burge, Mackay, Davidson, Grout, Meckiff, Kline and Simpson, the latter being made twelfth man on the morning of the match.

I had a lot of good friends in the Australian side over the years, all of them different personalities. When I became captain, all of them needed to be treated in a slightly different fashion without moving away from the team concept. I was a team-mate of Colin McDonald's from the time we first toured England in 1953 through to the end of the 1961 tour of England and he was great. He kept us all on our toes, which is always a good thing, and he was one of the most courageous cricketers I saw. Send out

McDonald and Jim Burke to open the innings and you knew you had a good pair. When I became captain Neil was my vice-captain and Colin was the third selector. I couldn't have asked for better, nor for more support. There are many good things to remember in a lifetime of cricket; one for which I'm especially grateful is that I was a part of that trio. Once I had seen the team announcement I could make some plans and think about a few ideas concerning the game, and some not necessarily associated with the cricket.

As a side issue, I had heard on the grapevine Peter May had proffered the opinion in the nets that I might not cause much trouble to batsmen who played straight down the line, that I didn't spin the ball a great deal and that I had no worthwhile wrong'un. I was very cranky about this. One remark was said to have been 'he bowled me a Benaud' when a young practice net legspinner wasn't turning the ball. It had the effect of spurring me on to a considerable degree, on the basis that none of the England batsmen had seen me since Laker's series in England. I had changed my run-up, improved my delivery stride, I now had a flipper, I had been working on a wrong'un, I had broken records formerly held by Grimmett, O'Reilly, Wardle and S. F. Barnes, I had a spinning-finger remedy that was brilliant, and our opposition were merely inclined to consider it amusing. I might, to England, be the same old bowler, but to me I was a very different one! That was one of the reasons I was so keen to do well in the state match against MCC, hence the pleasure at taking 5–48 from 28.4 overs.

Whatever minimal pleasure might have been engendered for the Board at the thought of having me as captain would have been very much balanced by their worries. Apart from the reasons they may have believed noteworthy after the 1956 tour of England, there was the real worry that I was a journalist, and a hard-working one at that. Being on the Police Rounds beat with Noel Bailey, and against Bill Jenkings of the *Daily Mirror* and others, had given me a good grasp of how to file stories, what angles to take, and taught me to try hard to be constructive.

The Board had nothing in its fifty-three-year history to this time which indicated in any way they would be looking in a kindly, or even constructive, fashion at a captain of Australia who was also a journalist. They didn't look in kindly fashion at journalists anyway, and had a history of ensuring cricketers had no right to make comments to the media. Their brows knitted when anyone like Jack Fingleton tried to combine a career in cricket with one as a writer, which he was when chosen for the 1935–36 tour of South Africa and the 1938 tour to England. In Australia it was worrying to officialdom that a journalist should be permitted to walk over the imaginary white line at the doorway of the Australian dressing-room, and the same went for overseas tours.

I wanted to change that.

While we had been in South Africa we had a good rapport with the small Australian press contingent: Keith Butler was the AAP representative, R. S. Whitington was there, and Ray Robinson also. Now I was looking for some constructive team publicity from what was again a small press contingent, although in those days, wherever you went there was always a local press representative, and most newspapers would send their own men on tour inside Australia.

One of the reasons I was thinking of doing something to bring players and press closer together was that it would provide good coverage for the players. A second reason was that the game needed the media. We had gone through some ordinary times in Australian cricket during the 1950s, with the loss of the Ashes in 1953, the dirge-like over-rates of 1954–55, when a big part of England's tactical play revolved around making the batsman wait a long time for every ball, and then the Jim Laker series in 1956. In between times our successful tours of the West Indies and South Africa had been more low-key – much better than being beaten, but not the same as being on top of England.

At any rate, for better or worse, I said quietly to the Australian press that they would be welcome to come in for a drink at the end of the first day of the Brisbane Test, and there they were. Soon word spread around that it was possible to have a beer and a chat in the Australian dressing-room at the close of play, bearing in mind it would cease to be an invitation the instant anyone quoted a player, because that was against the Board's rules and against our contracts. What journalists could do, and did, was chat and listen and derive some useful background information for the future. We were happy and so were the journalists, and it did indeed produce beneficial publicity for the team. How it would have gone had we been beaten in every Test is another matter, but the players were mature enough to handle criticism in the media in the same way as they handled praise. Sadly in my view, it's not something which could be done in these modern times.

My second decision was that we would have a team meeting the evening before every Test started, not too protracted, although there was never a curfew while I was captain and every player knew he would be judged on what he did on the field. Anyone whose performance might be affected by what he had done the previous night was simply stupid, and with a tough series in front of us, I was confident everyone would concentrate. No curfew.

My pre-planning included a policy of hemming England in with close-in fieldsmen, making certain they were unable to get at us with the bat. When Peter May and Colin Cowdrey were at the crease, bowlers knew they faced a very tough task. The general feeling I had was that the England batsmen could be contained. Hem them in. We wanted our running between the wickets to be purposeful, even brilliant, I wanted them bustled. What I had seen of England indicated to me they shouldn't be able to match us in the field, not even come within a bull's roar of us in that department. It was my job to put into place the basic planning for the bowlers and the field-placings, and we discussed all these things at the team meeting. The other thing I wanted was enthusiasm throughout the team, and enjoyment. I reckoned a happy team, and an enthusiastic one which was supportive of good bowling, batting, fielding and brilliant catches, would do well.

I had watched the Australian XI match against MCC at the SCG a couple of weeks earlier, and I was determined, if possible, that no one would run down the line of the stumps, as had happened on the second day of that game, resulting in Tony Lock being close to unplayable in the Australian XI's second innings.

'Burkie and Colin,' I said, 'whichever one of you is at the non-striker's end, I want you to call the umpire's attention to Brian Statham or Peter Loader, whoever takes the new ball, and ask the umpire to keep them further out off the pitch. I don't give a stuff where their feet were, make the point first ball.'

I'm sure it was mystifying when it happened, because Brian had taken the first over and, as far as we knew, he had never before been spoken to by umpires in that regard. Burkie carried out his orders perfectly though, made a song and dance about it and it was picked up very quickly by the media. And what was more, we kept it going whenever there was the slightest hint of anyone running on the pitch, even to the extent that Jim Laker, when I was batting on the third day at the Vulture Street End, deliberately walked straight up the centre of the pitch. I watched this with pursed lips from the other end and caught his eye as he came nearer. I was opening my mouth to give him a burst when a sixth sense had me look down. He was wearing rubber-soled shoes . . . and a smile, by the time I lifted my eyes to meet his again. We said nothing.

Before a ball was bowled at the 'Gabba, England had a problem when Fred Trueman, their best bowler, had to pull out of the match with a bad bout of lumbago. Fred had also missed the game against Queensland. These days it would be classed as a stress fracture and there would be weeks of treatment, but years ago, if bowlers missed a game, they played the next one otherwise their place might be gone for good.

This opening Test was played on a pitch where you could hardly select the cut portion from the rest of the square. At the same time, because of the heat and the humidity, there was something there for the spinners all the time and spinners in fact took eleven of the wickets to fall.

The match itself was wonderful because we won, boring because it produced some of the slowest and worst cricket imaginable, with Trevor Bailey the star, if that's not a contradiction in terms. Five years earlier Trevor and Willie Watson had combined to frustrate us at Lord's, and now they frustrated the spectators.

The scores were Australia 186 and 147–2, England 134 and 198. Trevor batted 7 hours and 38 minutes for his 68 and he scored off 40 of the 426 balls he received. And he ran out Tom Graveney, with assistance from Neil Harvey who made a brilliant pick-up and throw.

Most of the play was dullsville for the paying spectators, and it was not at all what we had in mind for what I was hoping would be some form of cricket renaissance. It was best summed up at one stage during Trevor's innings by journalist Percy Millard who called to scorer George Duckworth, 'How long since Bailey has scored, George?'

'Twenty past two,' was the reply.

Ron Roberts's voice floated over the press box, 'Today or yesterday?'

The Second Test was a victory by eight wickets for Australia after Alan Davidson took 6–64 in the first innings, including Richardson, Watson and Graveney in his second over. Peter May made a brilliant 113 after I dropped him off my own bowling at 20. Accounts of the fielding lapse generally were along sympathetic lines that Benaud had missed a difficult diving chance. Although the photographs showed I was crouching in the end, it was only because I had tried to grab at the ball a second time as it was falling. It was an awful miss – I tried to take the gentle lob by pulling my elbows in to my waist, they hit my body and jolted the ball out of my hands. It was the easiest catch I missed in first-class cricket. I also had a sinking feeling that I might have cost Australia the match.

By the end of the first day England had only lost four wickets and had 173 on the board, with May and Cowdrey in charge. We took wickets with the second new ball and then Neil Harvey and Colin McDonald saw the team through to the close of play after Jimmy Burke had been bowled by a beauty from Brian Statham. Brian bowled well to take 7–57, including me for a duck, Peter Loader took the other three and then England were bowled out by Ian Meckiff and Alan Davidson in their second innings for only 87 and we made the necessary 39 for the loss of McDonald and Grout.

The Sydney Test finished in a dull draw, with England declaring their second innings closed at 287–7, and we were 54–2 off 25 overs when the game finished. Rain marred much of the game. The second day, in front of a crowd of 50,416, couldn't begin until after 4 p.m. and Ian Meckiff was able to bowl only three overs in the second innings because of a bruised heel. For modern-day followers, a summing-up of the statistics of the England second innings, when it is said Australia played defensively, is that Colin Cowdrey's century, to that point, was the slowest in eighty-two years of Ashes battles. In that innings Australia bowled 106 balls an hour and England scored 33 runs per 100 balls.

The Ashes were regained in Adelaide in the Fourth Test, where England again were at a disadvantage because of injuries: this time Godfrey Evans broke a finger and Tom Graveney kept wicket for the remainder of the match. The worst thing, however, from Peter May's point of view, was that Jim Laker was unable to play, which left England with Statham, Tyson, Trueman and Bailey as the bowlers, with Lock as the spinner. Laker had bowled more than fifty overs in the Test at the SCG and his finger was in bad shape, the corn cracked and the finger itself arthritic enough for him not to be able to straighten it. He had a net in Adelaide the day before the Test and told Peter May he would be unable to play. That evening we heard the team, with Laker included after May had persuaded him to hold off until the next morning. Supposedly this was a ploy so we Australians would not gain a psychological advantage in knowing England would take the field without him.

Australian journalists told me there was something funny going on, in the sense that Freddie Brown, the manager of the team, was on the surly side of diffident when answering the question 'Is Jim Laker fit to play?' His reply was 'He's in the twelve.'

On the first morning Freddie arrived at the press box which, in those days, was below the Australian dressing-room, and announced, 'Laker has come along and said his finger is no good and he can't play.' The general impression given by Freddie was that Jim didn't care. It was poor reward for a man who was one of the greatest bowlers and triers to play for England.

In the Adelaide match I made 46 and took nine wickets, Ray Lindwall made a comeback to the Australian side, and for me, it was a real thrill to captain him. He was a wonderful cricketer who had given me very good advice over the years, and it was a delight to see him take a wicket with his second ball. I made England follow on in this match, despite being met at the top of the stairs by Sir Donald, who pointed out, with a smile, it was the only way we could lose the match. I didn't feel as though we could lose, and on the final and sixth day, they began at 198–5 and we bowled them out for 270, then made the necessary runs with an hour to spare.

The last Test, at Melbourne, was awful for England. Some of the players were involved in a nasty car accident a couple of days prior to the game: Peter Loader had a cut arm, Brian Statham a badly bruised forearm and shoulder, and then Willie Watson badly strained a groin muscle the day before the match. Godfrey Evans and Arthur Milton were both still suffering from broken fingers, so it could hardly be said as a team they were in good physical shape. In addition, there had been heavy rain in Melbourne as a lead-up to the game, and when Sir Donald Bradman told me as I was going out to toss that Les Favell would be twelfth man, I decided, on the run so to speak, to put England in to bat if the coin came down the right way.

It was in this match that Lindwall passed Clarrie Grimmett's wicket-taking record for Australia, a reward for the man who was the finest fast bowler I had seen to that time. I ripped a side muscle in the match, trying to swing Jim Laker to leg, but finished with 64 and took five wickets. I was very happy, first of all with the regaining of the Ashes, and also with the fact this was the first time since I had started playing first-class cricket in 1948–49 I had been in an Australian team which had won a series against England. Ten years actually seemed like an eternity. Also, I had been able to debunk the pre-series statements that it was merely a matter of batsmen playing down the line to counteract my bowling.

The not-so-good part was that my batting hadn't been as success-ful as I had hoped following the tour of South Africa, something

I could partly ascribe to the fact that I was now captain and that I had determined to bat Davidson and me on either side of Ken Mackay when the occasion warranted. I didn't think the captaincy had affected my bowling, but dropping down the batting order did have an effect on my batting.

It was a wonderful summer, and the first thing Neil and I did in the dressing-room at Adelaide, after congratulating the opposition and then our own players, was to sit down and have a cold beer, gently clink glasses and murmur that it was better than Old Trafford 1956.

18

PAKISTAN, INDIA AND LEARNING ABOUT LIFE AND DIPLOMACY

CAPTAINING the first official team to India and Pakistan in 1959–60 was quite an experience, but we managed well and won both series against the odds. We achieved that without the hardly believable number of support staff which are part of every sporting team these days. Ten years after Partition all we had was Sam Loxton, formerly a 1948 Invincibles player and, eleven years later, manager of my team. We had Dr Ian McDonald, an expert in tropical ailments. We had Benaud as captain and we used our brains without bothering with today's compulsory bonding sessions. In 2011 cricket is still a game, but it is also a multi-faceted business.

One of the problems we faced in 1959 was that although the Pakistan cricket authorities told the Australian Board of Control that the matches would be played on turf, did they mean it? Woven into the equation was whether or not our Board would have the courage to pursue the matter with Pakistan if it suddenly became something in the too-hard basket. There were various answers to that, all of which added up to the fact that I should assume nothing, be careful, and think along the lines that if telex communication broke down or was delayed between the two Boards, then we would be flying blind. I was lucky no Board member had the slightest intention of going anywhere near Pakistan or India.

Most times there is a queue to be manager of a team to various areas; for India and Pakistan there was only the nomination of

Sam Loxton. Sam had moderate managerial credentials from the Board's point of view, in that he was perfectly forthright, calling a spade a bloody shovel if he wished. He had never been noted as being a great lover of traditional administration. He could be abrasive at times, particularly if he knew someone was trying to put something over him, he was known as a fine cricketer for the things he had done in Sheffield Shield, where the war zones of Victoria and NSW often met, he had been a member of Bradman's 1948 tour of England, and he was a great mate of Neil Harvey's. He was also a good organiser and he had toured India with that Commonwealth side in 1953–54 when Iverson had eventually gone as a replacement for Ramadhin. He knew the country well, and from the stories he told of that Commonwealth tour, he was aware of the nuances on a continent where various negotiations might be easy or extremely difficult.

I was now in a completely different area, because although I had captained Australia at home against England I had only toured with an Australian team under another captain, vice-captain and third selector, and with absolutely no position of responsibility or influence. This would be very different. It was only three years since we had visited Pakistan and India and played one Test at Dacca and three at Madras, Bombay and Calcutta.

Conditions would not have changed in that time, turf pitches would be roughly the same, although we couldn't be certain of the exact type of surface which would be provided in the various centres. It would be educational and there was a chance it would be a difficult tour, notably with possible medical problems, the types of pitches and any political overtones, about which we might know nothing in advance.

I was keen that we should have some medical assistance on the tour. The Pakistan and Indian doctors, pharmacists and general medical people would be very good and helpful on such a long tour, but my feeling was that we definitely needed a doctor travelling with us so he would be able to liaise with his local counterparts, and, more important, be instantly available at all times of the day or night, if needed. My unofficial recommendation to the

Board was that they should find out who was available and see what could be done. They did better than that. They went to Ian McDonald, who was the wicketkeeper for the Victorian Second XI when I was hit in Melbourne that day and who had played with distinction for Victoria before retiring to pursue his medical career, and persuaded him to take the job. It was something of a master-stroke, even to the extent that in a crisis we might have an extra player available. My biggest worry was hepatitis, something which these days is still a real problem in many countries; at that time it was the illness I feared might rip through the team. We struggled during the tour but, without McDonald, we wouldn't have made it.

With a turf pitch you are sometimes at the mercy of the groundsman, sometimes of the administrators, as we found out a couple of times during the tour. Matting pitches in Pakistan, though, were an entirely different matter, and on an unofficial basis, I constantly nagged the various Australian Board members I met to persuade them to ensure they had something in writing for me to take with me so that we would be playing on turf in the three matches in Pakistan. The Board insisted they were having trouble with those assurances, although they were continually told the games would not be on matting. That was almost all we could do.

On diplomatic matters I had written to Prime Minister Menzies, asking if the Department of External Affairs could let me have some detail of any known problems we might encounter during the tour, and also anything that was blowing in the wind. The reply allowed me to arrange a meeting with Peter Heydon, who had been Australian High Commissioner to India when we played there in 1956. He was now an Assistant Secretary in the Department of External Affairs, which was the department of Richard Casey, within a few months to become Lord Casey. While I was doing this, Sam Loxton had a stroke of inspiration and arranged for 4,000 cans of Foster's lager to be sent to the Australian High Commissioner of the day, Ray Gullick, who was then based in New Delhi. That sounds a lot of Foster's, but it worked out at two cans a man per day, often at the end of a long slog of six hours in the field. Sam's second most important job was to ensure, before a ball was bowled in any Test match, a bank receipt was placed in his hand signifying the local Cricket Association secretary had banked £6,500 (in Australian currency) and had listed it as a telegraphic transfer to the Australian Cricket Board.

Attached to the team was a media contingent which was minuscule when you compare it with the hustling, bustling press boxes of today. Michael Charlton was the Australian Broadcasting Commission's commentator who would also be doing other non-cricketing jobs during the tour, and Australian Associated Press sent Wally Parr as their man on the spot.

We were looking forward to the tour, although we were not quite certain what it would all entail, because this was the first time the Australian Cricket Board had sent a team on tour to the subcontinent. I reckoned, at that stage, we could have done no more by way of preparation. You hear of people beating their chests and intoning those slightly pretentious words, 'We are ready.' We, in fact, had absolutely no idea if we were ready, but we were available and had been chosen, so it was a case of let's get at it.

There had still been no telex messages concerning the type of pitch on which we would be playing by the time we arrived in Singapore, where we played a couple of one-day matches. We moved on to Dacca, where we were met by the local Pakistan officials and were given a very warm welcome. Fazal Mahmood was there to greet us, looking fit and happy, possibly with good reason, recalling the manner in which he had demolished us on matting three years earlier.

On our way to Pakistan we played a centenary match at the 'Gabba and I took a calculated gamble and every morning had the team practise on matting over closely mown outfield turf. I was particularly interested in the way Slasher Mackay bowled. Conditions weren't exactly the same, but on a pitch with canvas matting over short cut grass which was watered and rolled in the outfield it wasn't far away from what I remembered as the manner in which the surface had played in Karachi three years earlier. It would have been no use at all putting down a mat on an ordinary 'Gabba net pitch, as the under-surface would have been far too hard and the bounce of the ball would have been much higher than in Pakistan.

It's not often you can say in cricket that whatever planning you might have envisaged comes off, even to a certain degree. It did this time. When we left Dacca airport we asked to be taken to see the ground on the way to the hotel, and lo and very much behold, right in the centre of the most beautifully grassed square you have ever seen, was a cream dirt strip just waiting for a mat to be put on it. We were told there had been a problem in growing the grass on this particular section, there had been a problem with the water, there had been a problem with the roller, there had been a problem with the telex machine in sending a message to the Australian Board of Control to say the match would be on matting, problems abounded that day in Dacca. However, the fact that this came as no surprise to us was a plus-mark because we knew we had done all we could in Brisbane on matting with a soft surface underneath, and we were the only ones who knew this. Those who had decided the game was to be on matting might have believed we would be coming in cold, as had been the case in Karachi in 1956.

And I had Slasher. In Brisbane on the matting surface he was bowling the leg-cutter in a way which looked like a faster version of a leg-break but with his own method, which was merely by holding the seam upright and using his index and second fingers for the cutting action. He was cutting the ball more than I was spinning it. In the match itself in Dacca we did win the toss and we did put Pakistan in to bat, and we did bowl them out for 200, which wasn't a bad score. I finished with eight wickets for the match but the champion bowler was Mackay with match figures of 64–39–58–7. We bowled together most of the time in the match – I had 77–36–111–8 – but it was the pressure and accuracy of Mackay which undid them.

So, too, did Slasher's mate, Lindsay Kline, who was down at the ground every morning superintending the tightening of the matting. He was sent off in a taxi, or a second team bus, an hour before the rest of the team and his twelfth-man duties involved nothing to do with water, food, boot spikes or anything else like that. He was the tightener, the 'enforcer' of the mat, only that. Both lengthways and widthways, that mat was to be tight as a drum when we arrived at the ground, and so it was. Whether the hot sun then tightened it more I have no idea, but it was a perfectly fair surface and those of us on the tour will never forget stepping off the bus and hearing the ringing cries of 'Pull, you bastards, pull,' floating across the ground. Not politically correct, but effective!

We won in Dacca because of a number of things. Most important, Neil Harvey played one of the greatest innings of all time, making 96. He was several times physically ill on the ground, and was suffering from a bout of flash dysentery and half a dozen times had to leave the field, make some necessary adjustments and then go back out on slightly rubbery legs. No one had broken Ian McDonald's eating and drinking restrictions, but there were still problems and Harvey seemed to have most of them this day. It was a wonderful innings, a great win and a tough match.

So was the one in Lahore when Kline, back in his playing rather than rug-pulling role, bowled beautifully to take 7–75, Norm O'Neill hit a splendid century and we made it with a few minutes to spare after a one-a-minute run chase over the last two hours. Some blatant time-wasting didn't help, with Nasim-ul-Ghani and Haseeb Ahsan crossing from cover on one side of the ground to cover on the other, at walking pace, each time a single was made. Harvey, having played that innings in the First Test, now stepped away and deliberately allowed himself to be bowled so we could have two right-handers batting.

I played my part by going out to join Norm O'Neill and, on the way to the crease, diverting far enough to chat with Imtiaz Ahmed, the skipper, and set out for him, in very gentle but also descriptive fashion, what I thought about the tactics, which I said I knew were not being planned by him but were coming from the pavilion. He was the one instructed to fire the bullets.

These days, the diversion and the one-way conversation through a stump camera microphone would have brought a red card, a fine of the total match fee and a possible suspension for a month. Instead, things came back to a normal state and overs were bowled at a proper rate, though no faster than would usually have been the case.

In Karachi we played a draw, again on the matting, and this time in front of President Eisenhower, who was on a state visit to Pakistan. Sam and I took the opportunity to press with Pakistan President, Ayub Khan, the matter that no Test should again be played on matting. It was duly decreed after Sam had a final gentle go at him, working on the basis that continuing to play Tests on matting would hold Pakistan up to ridicule in the cricket world. Sam was brilliant and that was the last time a Test was played on the mat.

Between the Second and Third Tests three desperadoes or heroes, as you will, made the trip from Rawalpindi to Gilgit in Kashmir. Colin McDonald, Richie Benaud and, memory suggests, Ian McDonald, were picked up at the hotel and driven in an air force jeep to the airport. You need to realise Col was going through his slightly left-wing kick at the time, and part of this involved going to see what was happening in Gilgit, to see if there was an easy solution we could offer to the Kashmir problem between India and Pakistan; also to check how the people coped as regards accommodation, food, water and general living conditions, and if we three could do anything to improve it.

We also went back in time as regards transport. When we were at the airport, and were looking at the aeroplane scheduled to take us to the frontier, I said to the captain of the craft that the make of the plane reminded me of one in which I had travelled many years ago in Australia, ten years to be exact. He replied, 'Yes, how very observant, Mr Benaud, it is an Australian plane, a DC3, and we are indebted to you and your government for letting us have it. It had been used so much in Australia it was time to pension it off, your government passed it on to us, and here we are.'

We certainly were, and I was trying to catch Colin's eye, but he was studiously avoiding me. We walked over to the aircraft steps, climbed up them, and I knew instantly why he hadn't looked at me. It was because he had been told by the pilot there were no seats in the Australian 1950/Pakistan 1959 DC3 and he thought I might kill him – no seats, but thin rope nets to which we should cling en route.

Something worried me about the flight and I didn't properly work it out until we were about to board for the return trip. In Gilgit we had an interesting look around and a delightful potato and vegetable curry with rice for lunch.

'CC' was delighted. 'I knew you'd love it,' he said enthusiastically.

I said, 'Col, I've asked the pilot what the ceiling of a DC3 is and it's 20,000 feet. When I asked him about the radar on the plane on the way up he said there wasn't any. I've now asked him about the weather and he tells me thick fog is forecast. And we both know the peaks of all the mountains on the way up were 20,000 feet. How will the pilot be able to see the mountain peaks in the fog?'

'Don't worry about it,' Col said. 'The main thing is that we're doing the right thing and showing how much we appreciate what they've done for us.'

'I'll tell you something else,' I murmured grimly. 'I didn't pay much attention when he told me earlier because it was a perfectly clear sky and a beautiful day, but the pilot did say the weather forecast was so bad for later in the day they would never have taken off in normal circumstances. It was only because they knew how much we wanted to see Gilgit!'

On the way back the fog swirled around the windows, when, that is, the mountain peaks weren't appearing alongside them. CC, on landing safely, told me I should feel happy as I had gone through a character-building experience which would serve me well later in life.

To win that series in Pakistan was a triumph, though it may not seem so these days. It wasn't the fault of the Pakistan people that it was tough for a touring party because it was only ten years or so after partition and independence, with its good moments and some horrifying undertones. The fact that there was a tour at all said plenty for the diplomatic endeavours of those in Canberra, and we had kept to our side of the bargain to date, with our own form of diplomacy, and Australia's High Commissioner in Pakistan, Sir Roden Cutler, had been magnificent with his assistance and advice.

The team had performed brilliantly, Neil Harvey had played one of the best innings seen at Test level, Slasher Mackay had done what I wanted in the two Tests on the mat and we had used him only as a batsman on turf in Lahore. We had managed any problems with enough laughs at one another to keep us going, and our management team of Sam Loxton and Dr Ian McDonald had been resourceful, thoughtful and very, very efficient. Above all, they had kept us happy in the service!

My fingers had stood up wonderfully well on this tour to the rigours of having the seam rip across them in delivering the ball, thanks to Ivan James's finger remedy. However, I did have a shoulder problem which may possibly have been the start of similar troubles which were to bring to an end my career at Test level. On the first day in Karachi, I had slipped when throwing in from the boundary and damaged something in my right shoulder. It was the first such problem I had experienced and I needed injections before I was able to bowl on the second day. It wasn't a good omen.

The team had been very popular in Pakistan. A big crowd saw us off at the airport and when we arrived in New Delhi well over 10,000 people were there to welcome us, an extraordinary and heart-warming sight.

Our first Test against India was at Delhi and we won by an innings and 127, with Harvey making a brilliant 114. I picked up eight wickets for the match, Lindsay Kline four and Alan Davidson three, and the local players not only took plenty of stick from their supporters, but three of their bowlers were dropped for the Second Test.

At Kanpur they had a turf pitch on the ground for the first time, and India turned the First Test result around and thrashed us by 119 runs, a bowler new to us and picked out of the blue,

Jasu Patel, taking 14 wickets in the match. He played in other matches in the series but then never again played for India after that summer.

It was the first time Australia had been beaten in a Test in India. When we had lost on the last afternoon in Kanpur, I walked out on to the field and shook hands with Gulabrai Ramchand, their skipper, and all my players stood at the entrance to the playing field and clapped the Indian team into the dressing-room. The whole of our team went to their dressing-room and congratulated them. Then we watched as they were garlanded and fêted around the ground, cheered by thousands and hit by a few unripe guavas hurled or shanghaied by some of the happy students. There was not the slightest doubt within our team that we had been beaten by a better side and it was a matter now of organising ourselves for the next game.

We were helped in this by the article written and published in Kanpur by the Maharaj Kumar of Vizianagram, who had captained India in England in 1936, extolling the virtues of the Australians and saying what good sportsmen we were. He said as well, though perhaps a touch flamboyantly, that India's victory was 'in keeping with other great events of 1959: man's first rocket to the moon, Kruschev's visit to the United States and President Eisenhower's visit to India.' He added that the win was 'as incredible as the cow jumping over the moon. It was one of the most exhilarating moments in Indian history, parallel to the scene when, in 1947, India gained independence. The Australians,' he said, 'had been dragged from the ethereal heights of invincibility to the dust and din of defeat.' Never had he seen a team lose with better grace and spirit than the Australians.

As it turned out, however, in another article for the *Northern Indian Patrika*, a border newspaper, he had slated me and the Australian team for being the worst sportsmen imaginable. I would never have seen the article had not a good friend of mine, an Indian journalist, handed it to me. It takes a lot to have me in explosive mood but this was one of the days.

On the first day of the Test match in Bombay we had two little incidents, the first when Sam Loxton, our manager, came to me and said, 'Don't rush out for the toss. I haven't seen the receipt for the lodgement of the guarantee money yet. We might have a small problem.'

As Sam sat down alongside me, in bounced the Maharaj Kumar of Vizianagram, spreading around a 'hello' or two here and there. I put the two newspaper articles alongside each other on the table. I noted to him that in the one on the spot, in Kanpur, he had been full of praise for our sportsmanship, and in the other, up on the border, in the *Northern Indian Patrika*, he had been scathing about our sportsmanship and had said it would be better if we never came back to India. I added that we would need an explanation and an apology, before he would be welcome again in our dressing-room.

He blustered that some sub-editor had written the article and put his name to it and that I had besmirched his good name. There was plenty more bluster, as though he owned the dressing-room, which on reflection he probably did – ownership of the Cricket Club of India wouldn't be out of the question, and he might even have owned Bombay, which is now known as Mumbai.

We concluded with a compromise: he wasn't welcome in the Australian dressing-room until we received an apology, and he said he wouldn't come back into the dressing-room unless we all, as a team, apologised to him. My suggested compromise worked well!

Sam, after smiling at Karmarkar, the Indian Board secretary, and telling him it was a no pay-no play situation and 'Kar' would be the one who would have to explain that to the 70,000 present at the ground, was given the receipt for the telegraphic transfer and we started on time and played a draw. They were very busy at the ground in the Treasurer's office because a week before the game began every ticket had been sold for every day, a bonanza.

When we first saw the Bombay pitch we had reckoned there was a chance of no result. It looked an absolute belter and proved to be so. It was one of the easiest batting pitches I had seen since last I had played on the same ground three years earlier and the

On slow-motion film Jeff Thomson had the most perfect bowling action you could envisage. He was also the fastest bowler I ever saw other than Frank Tyson.

No one loved bowling fast and playing for Australia more than Dennis Lillee. When injury threatened to end his career he returned from four months in a back plaster to play again for his country and regain the Ashes.

If I wanted someone to bat for my life it would be Ian Chappell. He was a splendid batsman for Australia and a great captain.

Three of the greats of fast bowling. *Left to right*, Fred Trueman, Ray Lindwall and Dennis Lillee, the latter having formed a partnership with wicketkeeper Rod Marsh unequalled in Test history.

Daphne somehow secretly organised a *This is Your Life* appearance in 1976, but she has been forgiven thirty-four years later. Ted Dexter, on the left of picture, alongside him Ivan James, the spinning finger-remedy genius from Timaru, New Zealand, who saved my bowling career in 1957. My mother Rene and father Lou are on the right of the middle row, brother John back centre right.

A splendid team! BBC commentators watching a replay. Tom Graveney and Jim Laker on my right, Peter West in the front row with John Edrich, scorer Michael Fordham behind Peter and a youngster in front of me hoping that one day he might play for England.

for the captaincy; in Brisbane it was intense because the team, captained by Ray Lindwall, might make history.

Tension rose a little when Harv, who was anything but difficult to deal with on things like this, stormed back to his dressing-room after the refusal and, as he grabbed for his own pads, instructed Len Maddocks to do the same. He proceeded, with a certain amount of anger, to play one of the best innings I have seen in Sheffield Shield, making 209 and ensuring Victoria made us follow on. Not good news, but we managed, in the end, to escape with a draw and retained the Sheffield Shield by a point.

There were two things I wasn't to know about this summer and the following six months, the first of which was that dengue fever is quite a nasty ailment: suddenly I would start sweating and need to find my way to the nearest resting place. Secondly, that same dengue fever and its treatment of those days, with sulphanilamide, was, purely by accident, to be the saving of my spin-bowling career and the end of the McCool pain barrier.

We flew out to New Zealand two weeks later with Craig as captain and Harvey as vice-captain. The opening match was at Christchurch and I had all my normal cricketing gear plus a stock of the tablets I had been taking from the moment the dengue had been diagnosed back in November. In my wallet was a prescription written by Dr Jack Jeffery to purchase the last two batches of sulpha tablets. Our fourth match on the tour was at Timaru against the Combined Minor Associations. It was supposed to be a two-day game but the first day was totally washed out.

That evening, checking through my gear in the bedroom, I decided, for no particular reason, I would take some exercise and wander off to the chemist shop I had seen down the road and have him make up the next lot of sulpha tablets.

I was cranky and frustrated, my fingers had ripped open again a few days earlier bowling in Dunedin, and although I had cleaned them up a little they were painful. They were not necessarily a pretty sight when I handed the prescription over the counter to the chap who recognised me and asked how I was enjoying the tour. His name as it turned out was Ivan James, though at that moment he was to me another man in a white coat, this time dispensing medicines rather than decisions out in the centre of the ground.

'What's the matter with your fingers?' he asked.

'Aw, it's from the way they get ripped about from bowling, it's when the seam of the ball cuts through the skin.'

'What do you use on them?'

'I've tried everything – hardening them, softening, everything – and I've just got to live with it, I'm afraid.'

'I have something that might be a help. I've found it very beneficial for the treatment of leg ulcers for ex-servicemen, particularly if they are suffering the after-effects of being gassed.'

I said to him, 'I think I've tried everything, but I'll try anything new, anything at all. A fellow named Colin McCool once told me never to let a day go past without trying to find a remedy.'

He handed me the sulpha tablets, which I put in my pocket, and then gave me a small wide-mouthed bottle, plus a container with white powder and a piece of paper with his suggested remedy written on it. It said:

OILY CALAMINE LOTION BPC '54
BORACIC ACID POWDER

Rub the lotion into the wound and then dab off the oil which comes to the surface.

Rub in the boracic acid powder so that it forms a waxy filling in the wound.

Keep doing this as much as possible and definitely whenever there is a recurrence of the skin tearing. Make sure you keep the waxy substance filling the hole all the time.

He added that I should carry with me a piece of fine sandpaper so that before using the remedy I could sand off any bits of dead or torn skin.

I looked at this with a very wary eye, but as he had taken the trouble to ask me about my fingers and then make up his remedy and write out the details and instructions, I thanked him game drifted to a draw. On the other hand, the Madras pitch for the following Test, when we went out to look at it, was as hard as a block of concrete, but felt like a wide strip of sandpaper. We stood at one end for a very long time, trying to work out what was in the surface. Neil Harvey called me up to the other end and for a time neither of us could solve it, then I put my fingernail under a piece of whatever it was, lifted it out and said, 'It's sawdust.'

I went over to see the groundsman, smiled at him, shook hands and said, 'Nice pitch, congratulations. What an interesting idea to roll the sawdust in to bind the surface. Who told you to do that?' I was still smiling.

'Thank you for the compliment,' he said. 'The committee told me what to do and how to do it, and they will be very pleased you are so happy.'

Now, casting one eye at offspinner Jasu Patel who had become perfectly fit very quickly having missed the Bombay match, what we really needed was to win the toss and luckily we did. I said to the team I would settle for a first-innings total of 250 and I didn't care how long it took. Time wasn't important in this case because there was no way the game would go the full five days. I reckoned 250 would be plenty.

We were slow, but we did better than I hoped. Les Favell played the innings of his life on the first day, a century out of 183, and Slasher Mackay made a splendid 89 on the second day. The aim was to keep Patel at bay and he certainly spun the *balls* sharply. That plural is correct: a dozen balls were used during the match, with the sawdust surface ripping through the stitching, and in the dressing-room enclosure, with the umpires' agreement, we had sandpapered a box of new balls to remove the shine and threw another one out when the umpires called for it. We bowled India out for 149 and 138, won by an innings and 55 and the game took only three and a bit days. I finished with match figures of 8–86 from 67 overs, which gives an idea of what effect sawdust can have on a pitch, if rolled into the surface.

In the final Test of the series in Calcutta, we were depleted in playing personnel, with Gordon Rorke, Gavin Stevens, Lindsay

Kline and Ken Mackay ill. We were so short Mackay had to play, and I had a bout of neuritis in my left arm and a dislocated spinning finger from a knock sustained in Madras. A quick medical finger-pull by Ian McDonald did the trick, but why I should have had neuritis I have no idea, nor could Ian McDonald offer any explanation. In any case he was busy enough with people who were properly ill: he murmured, 'If it's only neuritis and a dislocation you're one of the lucky ones, just get on with it.' The match finished as a draw.

The four NSW members of the team played in the final Sheffield Shield match of the Australian season immediately on returning from India, outright points were vital for the final destination of the Shield. Bob Simpson was in the WA side and made 98 and 161, I took 6–74 in each WA innings and this was the seventh successive Sheffield Shield for NSW.

This had been quite a year – very busy, very successful – and we were looking now at the West Indians touring Australia from October to February. We thought it might be an interesting time, but no one had the slightest idea of what actually lay in store with the Caribbean team.

When I was away in Pakistan and India captaining the Australian team, I was still keeping an eye on what was happening with Cumberland. John was playing in the third-grade side as a quickish legspin bowler, under the captaincy of a good friend of mine, Alan Cramond, and the team were minor premiers, a fine achievement. As minor premiers, Cumberland had the advantage in the final against Gordon, who had to win the two-day match to be the Championship winners, the same system as applies in the Sheffield Shield final these days. The match was played over two Saturdays at Merrylands Oval and there was a standard rule that the side batting first could not close after 4.50 p.m. By mid-afternoon, with 270 on the board for a couple of wickets, Alan Cramond's tactics definitely hinged on being able to persuade Gordon to bat on past 4.50 p.m. Once the closure time had passed and Gordon sensed this was happening, they attempted to throw away their wickets, but the butter-fingered

Cumberland fieldsmen managed to keep them there until stumps when the total was well past 400.

The star batsman of the Gordon side was Tony Steele, a very good cricketer who later played for NSW and was the man who created the Adidas agency in Sydney, the one which produced the boots which so enraged the NSWCA and resulted in the John Benaud banning ten years later. A further irony was that it was Tony who took over the captaincy of the NSW side when JB was banned!

The second Saturday of the final arrived with some bad news: one of the Cumberland opening batsmen was unable to play because of illness, and therefore Alan Cramond's captaincy skill was tested even before a ball was bowled. He decided to promote John Benaud from number eleven to number one. He also gave him some instructions: 'Bat all day!' JB batted most of it, making 74 in what was, by a considerable margin, the slowest innings he played in any form of cricket, and Cumberland survived and won the Championship.

19

SHAPING A NEW CAREER, AND THE START OF THE THROWING BUSINESS

NINETEEN sixty was a watershed year for me. Whilst I was in India and Pakistan, a very good friend, Ron Roberts, sent me a message concerning a friend of his, George Greenfield, who was the head of a firm of literary agents, John Farquharson Ltd. Would I like to write a book, working title *World of Cricket*, embodying coaching sections and a variety of opinions on world cricket, and have it published around April 1961 before the start of the Australian tour of England; it was assumed I would be captaining that side. I agreed to it, especially after having undertaken the BBC Television course in England in 1956.

I was starting to consider my future, life after twelve years of cricket, so to speak. There was enjoyment to be had playing the game, more so if you were winning rather than losing, but there was absolutely no chance of any financial security. There were long absences from home, I had my wife and two children aged five and two who had to put up with being on their own, and it was time to start looking at media work, not just in Sydney, but on a larger scale. The book would be a start. A following offer arrived through George Greenfield to go to England in 1960 to cover the South African tour of that country for BBC Radio and a newspaper.

Ron Roberts himself decided to take another combined team, known as 'the Cavaliers', to Rhodesia and South Africa. He had already managed one such team to South Africa the previous summer. I informed the Australian Cricket Board of the Roberts tour and asked permission to go, and also informed the Board that, as part of my work as a journalist, I was going to England to cover the South African tour.

At the same time as we were in the middle of our tour of Pakistan and India, the England team set out on a tour of the West Indies. It was to turn out to be a significant event for a number of reasons, not least that it was something of a new-look England side. We had beaten them four-nil in Australia, they then returned the compliment to India, who toured England in 1959, by beating them five-nil.

In the series against India, and then in the Caribbean, only seven of the players who toured Australia were retained, and it was clear the England selectors were looking to the series against West Indies in 1959–60, and against South Africa in 1960, to build up for the Ashes battle in 1961. That had become the stated policy of the new England selection committee of Gubby Allen, Herbert Sutcliffe and Doug Insole, that they were embarking, in 1959, on a three-year plan 'so as to provide a side worthy of challenging Australia for the Ashes in 1961.' Some of those to disappear included Peter Richardson, Tom Graveney, Willie Watson, Arthur Milton, Trevor Bailey, Godfrey Evans, Jim Laker and Tony Lock.

Some never made it back, but Tom Graveney did, being recalled for the opening Test against Pakistan at Edgbaston in 1962. He made 97 and 153 in the Second Test and followed that with 37 and 114 before they dropped him again for the Fifth Test of the series. Probably 'rested' is a more appropriate word! In fact, from the time he was recalled, he played another thirty-one times for England, even captaining his country when Colin Cowdrey pulled out of the Headingley Test in 1968. Tom was an outstanding batsman, a good player of spin and pace and a very elegant stroke-maker. I was pleased he came back, because Australians always had a very high regard for his ability – we wouldn't have left him out even for one game, let alone for twenty-eight!

Visiting England in 1960 was a great opportunity for me to have a look at what they had to offer in their cricket resurgence, with an eye to the 1961 Australian tour. As it turned out, there were many other things happening, including a throwing controversy, and it was an educational five months working for the BBC, *News of the World* and the Sydney *Sun*.

As I arrived in England in 1960 I was saddened to hear Alec Skelding had passed away. He was a delightful chap and a very unorthodox umpire who had been a useful cricketer with Leicestershire. He was, to my eyes, an unusual figure when I first came across him, because he was the only umpire I had seen in England who wore white boots or shoes. These were worn in Australia by umpires, but in England it was brown brogues, or occasionally, in dry conditions, brown or navy suede. Umpires often wore brown felt hats as well.

Alec stood in some of our matches in 1953 and 1956, but the only time I played in a game when he was officiating was when we met Essex at Southend, in 1953, and he was very amusing as well as seeming a good umpire, and not solely because he gave Doug Insole out lbw to my topspinner. There was never a dull moment from a man who was highly respected by every cricketer who knew him and it was a treat to hear, 'And that, gentlemen, concludes the entertainment for the morning . . .'

By the time I was on my way to England, Peter May's side had returned with their first-ever victory in a Test series in the West Indies but there had been some contentious items on the agenda with time-wasting, throwing and short-pitched bowling heading the list. When May's side had been in Australia, in 1958–59, there had been many problems about bowling actions and dragging. That controversy had continued after the tour with the Imperial Cricket Conference, as it was in those days, stepping in to say they were working towards finding a proper definition of the throwing Law.

In Australia there had been several players under scrutiny. Ian Meckiff had been the one most mentioned, and I said at the time I had looked at Meckiff from different parts of the field and, like the umpires, was satisfied his action conformed with the laws formulated by MCC. I added that he had bowled in New Zealand, South

Africa and Australia and had never been called. The same question was asked in Pakistan and India and I gave the same answer.

That criticism of Australia's bowlers in 1958–59 was now followed by further criticism of the West Indian bowlers, of whom it was said there were at least six, two of them playing in the Tests, who had suspect actions. That was receiving considerable publicity, but so too was another matter which was important to me. In the Caribbean, from where May's team had just returned, there was a real push to have the West Indian captain, Gerry Alexander, removed and Frank Worrell made captain instead for the tour of Australia.

Sir Donald Bradman, who was to take over as Chairman of the Australian Board in late 1960, was working hard to come up with some form of agreement on the question of doubtful bowling actions, though he was careful to emphasise the difficulties in arriving at a definition. I was in England and, having summed up the mood and the general situation, started writing a series of articles to the effect that this, in my opinion, was for Australia the most important ICC meeting of all time.

I stressed that, instead of using the Board's representative in England, or it being a trip for a couple of ordinary administrators, the Australian Board must send Bradman and, as their second representative, Chairman Bill Dowling. The habit was that the Board's representative in England would attend ICC meetings and the various social engagements and then report back to the Board in writing about what had eventuated. This was going to be completely useless now because I could see there were tough discussions ahead. I hammered the point that it was essential Bradman appear as one of Australia's representatives, and as chairman, Dowling should accompany him. Bradman and Dowling duly arrived for the conference which began on 14 July.

In England, MCC had stated they would be providing full support for any umpires who might feel the need to 'call' bowlers with suspect actions. The problem was, would the definition stand up when they finally came up with a new wording? In the 1959

season in England there had been several bowlers no-balled for
throwing, including Tony Lock, who had worked on remodelling
his suspect bowling action after being shown some movie films
taken by Harry Cave in New Zealand at the conclusion of the tour
to Australia in 1958–59. The same kind of thing was being done
in Australia, where the word 'jerk' had also been removed from
the throwing definition.

In the history of Australian cricket there had been twenty-three
occasions when an Australian bowler had been called for throwing and that list had involved eighteen bowlers up to 1960.

Before Bradman and Dowling arrived in England there had been
some no-balling of South African Geoff Griffin. The first time this
happened he was merely called for dragging, by Paul Gibb standing in the match Derbyshire against the touring side. Griffin had
already been called for throwing in South Africa in February and
March 1959, when he was playing for Natal.

One of England's best umpires, Syd Buller, had officiated in
South Africa's opening game against Worcestershire when Griffin
didn't play. When the South Africans journeyed to Lord's in late
May to play MCC, two other good umpires, Frank Lee and John
Langridge, stood. Lee called Griffin once and then Langridge
called him twice for throwing, and once he was called simultane-
ously for both throwing and dragging. At a meeting at the end of
the match, the umpires said his basic action was OK but that he
threw the ball on the occasions he was called. When Griffin was
called eight times for throwing against Nottinghamshire, the team
management said he would be sent to Alf Gover's cricket school
for remedial treatment.

By the time Bradman and Dowling returned to Australia from
the London conference, and there had been much correspondence
between the two Boards, as well as other cricket Boards around the
world, considerable progress had been made. It had been made,
however, in a slightly odd fashion, with the compromise between
England and Australia being that during the first five weeks of the
Ashes tour, when I was likely to be captain, umpires would not
call, on the field of play, any bowler thought to be throwing, but

would complete a confidential report and submit it to Lord's and to the Australian team.

In addition to the decisions on throwing in 1960, the ICC brought four major issues under scrutiny:

1. *Time-wasting was criticised.* At last cricket administrators decided this aspect of play and captaincy was to the detriment of the game.
2. *Drag was under notice.* Umpires were trying to work off the front foot and one of the officials concerned in the Griffin throwing incidents, Syd Buller, an outstanding umpire, was to be a key man in that aspect of the game when we toured England in 1961.
3. *Pitches should not be damaged by bowlers in their follow-through* was another recommendation. Correct. We had already seen to our detriment in Australia, in 1958, what damage could be done, and we were about to see it very much to our advantage in 1961.
4. *Batsmen using their pads instead of their bat* came under fire, as should have been the case many years earlier. There was thought given to bringing in a Law that a batsman could be out lbw not playing a stroke, even if the ball pitched outside off stump.

This was a very important ICC meeting in 1960, and it did more for the game than had been done in the previous fifty-one years of the ICC's existence. I'm certain one of the main reasons for its success was that Australia, for the first time, had sent two top-class administrators and negotiators to England.

It was useful to have the Australian captain there keeping an eye on things as well, and I was able to steer Sir Donald and Bill Dowling in the right direction a few times, once in selfish mode when I persuaded them that, in addition to the bedrooms, for the first time an Australian team should have a team-room at the Waldorf Hotel in London, where we were to spend most of our time during the 1961 tour. They examined the room suggested by the hotel management, studied the proposition, agreed, and then persuaded the Board in Australia it should be done.

At this time I was also doing some work in the London office of John Fairfax Ltd, who published the *Sun* newspaper. It was a good time to be there, sub-editing and also writing my own stories back to Australia. It was the time of the Rome Olympics when Herb Elliott won the 1,500 metres, one of the finest sports performances I have seen from an Australian in any area.

It was a splendid year for Australia in other sports as well: Kel Nagle won the Open Championship at St Andrews by one shot from Arnold Palmer; Neale Fraser defeated Rod Laver in the Wimbledon singles final in four sets; and, although nothing to do with Australia, St Paddy won the Derby. Watching those three sports on television gave me an opportunity to listen to those incomparable television commentators: Henry Longhurst on golf, Dan Maskell, tennis, and Peter O'Sullevan, horseracing. They were even better than when I had heard them four years earlier!

Rothmans sponsored some televised one-day games which Frank Bough hosted on Sundays on the BBC and these were very well received. I played in some and took part in as many TV interviews as possible, enjoying the chance to become more familiar with the medium. When given the opportunity, I was very happy to be interviewed by Brian Johnston or Peter West on the BBC.

I thoroughly enjoyed my time with the *News of the World* as a feature writer on cricket, working with the regular cricket writer, seeking and filing my own stories and liaising with the sports editor, Frank Butler. Frank was my first of only a handful of sports editors there and I have been with the paper now for fifty years.

I had two weeks at the end of the summer to organise myself for Ron Roberts's tour of Rhodesia and Transvaal, and this was going to be excellent practice for the West Indies series in Australia. The Cavaliers team was not only a group of quality players, but good companions as well. Tom Graveney was my vice-captain, the others were Brian Statham and Fred Trueman, Alan Moss, Ken Barrington, Ray Illingworth, Geoff Pullar, Mike Smith, Norm O'Neill, Bob Simpson and Len Maddocks.

Our skills were good enough to win four of the games we

played and draw the other one, although we started with a hiccup in the opening three-day game, played at Salisbury, where David Lewis, the Rhodesian skipper, hit a brilliant 107 in their first innings of 241 and they then bowled us out for 155. Trueman and Statham were our opening bowlers and, as I was at pains to point out to them when we were walking on to the field at the start of the Rhodesian second innings, I hadn't come all this way to find myself chasing any more than 150 in our second innings.

Brian said nothing but gave a little nod, and Fred said, 'Bloody 'ell, soonshine . . . OK.'

Between them they removed Rhodesia for 52 in one of the most devastating spells of genuinely fast bowling I had seen in some years, and we won the match comfortably by six wickets. That was fun!

Something less than fun happened in the next game, on the same ground two days later, when I was bowling again to Lewis. He slightly lofted a straight drive and I instinctively shot out my right hand. He had hit it so well that the ball connected with the index finger, landed once and bounced into the sightscreen. That wasn't a pretty sight, nor was my index spinning finger because it was now slanted in two directions. There was no need for medical diagnosis because I knew it was broken, but the doctor wouldn't allow me simply to have it strapped and start exercising it as soon as possible and insisted it had to be put in plaster. I stayed on as captain and administrative manager of the Cavaliers, but there was no more cricket, and medical opinion was that the break was so bad I wouldn't be able to bowl again for around five weeks.

20

FRANK WORRELL, THE TIE AND SOME CHARACTER-BUILDING FOR EVERYONE

T HE Rhodesian doctor knew what he was talking about too, because I flew back to Sydney on 12 October and had to miss the first Sheffield Shield game against Queensland a week later. Ian Craig captained the side and Neil Harvey made a brilliant 135 in the first-innings win, while I was working back at the *Sun* newspaper in the sports department. Disappointing though it was not to be captaining NSW in this match, it did give me the opportunity to organise my reporting career, and when the NSWCA secretary, Alan Barnes, told me Frank Worrell was flying through Sydney on his way to Perth at the beginning of the West Indies tour, it was a good chance to welcome him and, at the same time, write a story.

The West Indian team arrived in Australia in bits and pieces and departed as heroes. Frank and I chatted at the airport and the media took photographs and noted the quotes they would use for their stories. This was to be the first time Test matches in Australia would be played over five days rather than six, with an hour added to each day, a sensible suggestion which had often been discarded by administrators because of warm weather and the chance to have six days of gate-takings rather than five.

Before Frank caught his plane connection for Perth we said farewell, and as he turned I called, 'I hope it's a great summer.'

He stopped and came back a few yards. 'We'll have a lot of fun anyway,' he said with a smile.

Neither of us had the slightest idea how true that would be, nor that there were to be various records established and broken, and that cricket in Australia was to undergo a significant and delightful change.

John Rutherford was captain of Western Australia in the game against West Indies captained by Frank three days later. They were friends because of the cricket they had played in the Lancashire League in England. Although he had led a Combined XI in Perth in 1958, this was the first and only time John captained WA in a first-class match and it ended very sadly despite WA beating the tourists. John made 0 and 4 in the game, and late on the final afternoon, as Western Australia were striving for their eventual victory, he suffered a stroke. He was helped from the field and never played first-class cricket again.

Only the medical people would know whether the stress of the afternoon, possible victory over the touring team, or the failure with the bat played a part in the stroke, but, by chance, it was Frank Worrell who had hit the ball Rutherford chased out towards the boundary. When John came back to where Frank was standing, the latter looked at him and asked how he was feeling, but there was no answer and he was rushed to hospital.

Rutherford was given minimal financial assistance with his health problems, although it's unfair totally to blame the Australian Board or the WACA for that. The education department, for whom Rutherford worked, politely declined, as a matter of policy, to provide a cent to assist him.

Just before the start of this 1960–61 season I played in a memorable game for 'Ruther' when he was given a benefit match by the Grimsby club in Yorkshire where he was the guest professional. It was the Sunday of the Old Trafford Test, and 'Pythagoras' Rutherford, so named by Miller in 1956, had already played a season with Rishton. Now, in 1960, he had the job of trying to make some money out of this game and, with his schoolmasterly thinking, he set out a few pages of graphs and the word 'publicity' was on top of all of them. Once he had me and a few others organised as players, he set about trying to talk West Indian fast bowler Roy Gilchrist into playing. He received a short sharp 'No' to that, so he went to Plan B which was to have the local newspaper editor do a full page story on the fact that he, Rutherford, had the measure of Gilchrist, had the feeling Gilchrist wasn't really very fast and that it was a pity Rutherford wasn't going to have the chance to show the people of Grimsby how to handle him. He sent 'Gilly' a copy of the article.

Gilly had quite a reputation in the Leagues for his treatment of opposition batsmen, sometimes in minor matters like bumpers and beamers. The letter and the enclosed article worked. Gilchrist sent a verbal message saying, among other things, that 'when he played in the match' he might 'separate Ruther's head from his body'.

With Rutherford's publicity machine in top gear, there was a full house on the day; you couldn't have crammed one more spectator into the ground and Rutherford made a packet! And he managed to keep his head attached to his body as well, despite receiving the full treatment.

There were some significant happenings in that match in Perth, apart from John Rutherford's problems. Graham McKenzie played his third game for the state and was carefully noted by Frank Worrell as a prospect for the future in international cricket. The West Indians set out to win the match when they had been set 487 for victory after the declaration. They made 393 with Garry Sobers hitting 119. McKenzie was a strapping young cricketer, over six feet tall and built like a brick wall, but a very good-looking brick wall. He was nicknamed 'Garth' after the handsome, husky, cartoon hero. Bowling at first change in the West Indian second innings, he dismissed Lashley, Hendriks and Ramadhin, and thoroughly impressed Worrell and Sobers during their 98-run partnership.

NSW beat Frank's side by an innings and 119 in three days at the SCG. Alan Davidson bowled magnificently in the first innings to take four wickets, I took 5–31 in the second innings, including Garry Sobers without scoring, and Frank tore a thigh muscle in the first innings and was severely hampered. Not everything was going well for the touring party at this stage, and the critics, of whom there were many, were seriously questioning their abilities – shades of South Africa eight years earlier. They had now been beaten by Western Australia, Victoria and NSW and drew their three other matches by the time the Test came along.

Not everything was going according to plan for me either. The broken finger had healed as far as the fracture was concerned, but despite the off-field exercises I was doing and incessant squeezing of a squash ball, a lot of bowling was producing stiffening of the joint. Then, in Melbourne, the opening day of the Sheffield Shield match was washed out and, after Victoria had put us in to bat, we were 162–4 at the close of play on the second day with Ian Craig, back from his injury, making 75. I was 15 not out.

I had some throat problems on the first day, and I spent the rest day, which was the Sunday, in bed, a doctor having been called. He said it was a very bad throat infection which seemed to be prevalent at the time, and cheerfully added that the antibiotics he had prescribed should do the trick within a week. I wasn't to play again in the game in progress at the MCG and there was a chance I would be all right for the Test starting in five days. This wasn't what I had in mind.

We arrived in Brisbane on 7 December late in the afternoon, practised on Thursday, 8 December, and Jack Ryder and Sir Donald Bradman didn't miss me with the fitness test despite my protests that I was feeling fine. However, their worries were only over the throat infection, they didn't know about the spinning finger which had taken a knock when batting in the game at the MCG.

It was a very tough fitness test and I thought for a moment I was going to fall over after I had bowled the first ball in the nets, but you needed to be careful with those selectors and avoid having them think for a moment you might not be completely upfront with them. At fielding practice I was in charge of hitting the short catches, and when we arrived back at Lennons Hotel, Davo, my number one bowler, the one on whom I'd based all my planning, said he thought he might have a fractured finger.

'Jeez, Davo, why can't you be more careful? How the bloody hell did you do that?' I exploded.

'*You* did it, mate, with that short catching fielding practice you say is so good for us.'

Two others – Colin McDonald (knee) and Ian Meckiff (ankle) – were struggling with fitness, and there was another matter of note. Already in the Australian season the campaign to have umpires call anyone with suspect bowling actions was gathering pace, and in the game between South Australia and Victoria in Adelaide, a month prior to the Test, South Australian umpire Colin Egar, from the bowler's end, had twice called Brian Quigley, also a South Australian, for throwing. Ian Meckiff, playing in the same match and said to possess a changed action, had been passed by both umpires in that Adelaide game, and there had seemed no doubt when we had played our match against Victoria that he looked a little different. Egar was about to stand in his first Test match in this game between Australia and West Indies at the 'Gabba.

The first televised cricket in Australia had been in 1958–59, when the final session of play in Tests could be shown, but this was the season when cricket was to be properly televised by the standards of that time. The Australian Cricket Board came to an agreement with the Australian Broadcasting Commission that Test and first-class matches could be shown on the 'box'. There had been not the slightest interest shown by any commercial television networks.

Our usual pre-Test team meeting was prefaced by a talk from Sir Donald Bradman, who, as Chairman of Selectors, had asked if it would be OK to come along and put a point or two to the players. This is commonplace these days, but I can assure you in 1960 it was very unusual. His talk was short and to the point. He said this could be a wonderful year of cricket and that this Australian team in 1960–61 could lead the way to one of the most attractive cricket series seen in Australia, but that it was totally up to the players, who, in the light of that, paid even closer attention to his next remark.

'The selectors will choose players they believe are playing good cricket, and they will look in kindly fashion on players who play aggressively and are clearly thinking about those who pay their money at the turnstiles. The selectors want you to be winners but not at the cost of making the game unattractive for the cricket follower.'

I can tell you it raised a few eyebrows in the room, and without exception, every player was impressed. Not least because several of us had been together through the 1950s, when we had witnessed a considerable amount of cricket which we wouldn't have wanted to pay our money to watch. This was the start of the 1960s, a chance perhaps for everyone?

In the Test match Sobers played a wonderful innings, fuelled a little by the newspaper article on the first morning which suggested he might have a few problems with my bowling. He had none. Take my word for that! He played an innings which I put into the top bracket of anything I have seen, an explosive exhibition of strokeplay and power which, in the context of the disappointing tour to that date, was magnificent.

Needing 233 to win on the final day, we were 92–6, and Davo and I, with the pads on, were having a cup of tea when Bradman came down to the dressing-room. He poured himself a cup and said how much he was enjoying the match, and then he asked, 'What are you going for, Richie, a win or a draw?'

I replied, 'We're going for a win, of course.'

All I received was a dry, 'I'm very pleased to hear it . . .'

Our policy after tea that afternoon was to try to rattle the West Indians with our running between the wickets and our selection of shots, carry the attack to them and see if they would crack. They did crack a little, but then so did we under the pressure. Although Joe Solomon's final throw to hit the stumps and run out Ian Meckiff created the tie and made history, our own effort was rather ordinary, with three wickets lost to run-outs in the last four to fall. If that were to happen to another side these days I would be very critical on television, as I was to Sir Donald when he expressed the view, 'This is the best thing which could possibly have happened for cricket.' Although I agreed with him, as captain I certainly would have preferred that we had played a little better and won. Bradman insisted I would change my mind as the years went on.

It had been a splendid match: some wonderful batting, brilliant bowling, and hour after hour where two teams were striving for the ascendancy rather than seeking to avoid it. There had been such tension in our dressing-room that players didn't remember where their gear was, some wanted to talk, some couldn't.

When the match was finished by that wonderful throw from Solomon, I walked on to the field to greet Worrell and we walked off with our arms around one another's shoulders. The 4,000 spectators came from all parts of the ground to cheer in front of the dressing-rooms and then, eventually, slowly drifted home.

In the dressing-rooms players mingled and drank what they wanted, beer or a soft drink, and the West Indians sang calypsos, in which we joined, though none of us had the ear for music they all possessed. Worrell was exhausted, so was I, and we sat quietly, saying little.

Sir Donald Bradman and the other selectors were enthralled by the match, as indeed they were by the summer and millions of television watchers and radio listeners were captivated by the sequence of events and the climax.

Not everyone felt precisely that way. The Australian Cricket Board at their next meeting passed a motion insisting that 'players should in future be out of the dressing-room within a few minutes of the end of a day's play in a Test match.' The Queensland Cricket Association had complained bitterly to the Board that the night the Tied Test finished, players had stayed in the dressing-rooms far too long. The Board agreed almost wholeheartedly, and eleven of the twelve of them around the rich-red mahogany table enthusiastically outvoted Bradman's solitary dissension! Apart from Bradman, there may have been someone else present who had been in a dressing-room as a first-class player, but they were thin on the ground. The remainder knew little of what happened on a first-class cricket field, and they knew nothing at all of the

camaraderie which existed between players and opponents. Nor, I
suspect, did they care overmuch.

The next two Tests went one to Australia and the other to West
Indies, each by wide margins, seven wickets and 222 runs respectively, and Davidson continued to perform like the champion he
was. We had come up with the tactics and special field-placings for
his bowling and they worked throughout the series. Unfortunately
he tore a hamstring and couldn't play in the drawn game in
Adelaide but took six wickets in the final Test. This gave him 33
wickets in three and a half Tests; his injury was a cruel blow, I can
tell you.

The last Test at the MCG was controversial and brilliant. After
I sent West Indies in to bat, we gained a first-innings lead, then
needed 258 to win and were 57–1 at the close of the second-last
evening. I had gone in as nightwatchman and was 1 not out. Bob
Simpson was 44 and I had sent him out with instructions to try to
hammer Wes Hall, saying I would take the blame if it didn't come
off. I reasoned if we could get them off balance at the start they
might be rattled. Nothing much rattled Frank Worrell though,
even if Simpson, in a wonderful blaze of hitting at the start, did
take 18 (4, 4, 4, 4, 2) from Wes's opening over. You can hardly
carry out a request in a style better than that.

Australia won the match by two wickets after West Indies had
been bowled out in their second innings for 321.

That match was almost fifty years ago, and it contained a side-
light I have never been able to explain. Eleven years earlier I had
met a family in Melbourne, Claude and Queenie Peck and their
son Graham, and in those days, with a rest day always on the
Sunday of the Sheffield Shield match or the Test, Jim Burke and
I saw a lot of them. They were a splendid couple and a delightful
family. Claude had been in the Second World War in Crete and
had gone through some very rough and tough times, and however
these things happen, had developed an ability to make predictions
through his dreams. He even won money for friends by dreaming
of certain racing colours going past the post.

Before the Second Test in this series against the West Indies,

Claude told a few of us in the dressing-room he had dreamt Frank Misson, making his debut, would take a wicket with his second ball. Frank was delighted to hear this, more so when he had Conrad Hunte caught at slip by Bob Simpson with his second ball. When it came to the end of the third day in this final Test, the Monday, I saw Claude in the dressing-room and we chatted about the day and the fact that it looked like being an exciting finish. West Indies at that stage were 126–2 and had a lead of 62.

Claude smiled and said, 'It'll be exciting, but don't worry, they'll make 321 and you'll win by one wicket . . . I dreamt it last night.'

The others in the group in the dressing-room chuckled and said, 'We'll remember that, Claude, but for the moment, have another beer.'

And they did remember it too, first when West Indies made precisely 321 and then, on the final day, when things were tight. In fact, we finished with 258–8, not the 258–9 he was talking about, but there is always the doubt that Wally Grout, given not out because the umpires didn't see the bail fall on to the ground, may have been out hit wicket at the start of Alf Valentine's twenty-second over. Eventually, after a tense period, Ken Mackay and Johnny Martin raced through for a bye to win the match.

I've never been able to come up with an explanation for all that, but people who know more about these things than I do insist that it is possible. It has never happened to me again, and although I won't say it was frightening, it was very strange.

Sir Donald instigated the Frank Worrell Trophy at the end of the series. Ernie McCormick, the former Australian fast bowler and a Melbourne jeweller, was chosen to design and make the trophy. Frank presented the trophy to me at the end of that final Test, the first such handing over and it was a wonderful occasion. Referring to his scalp, neck and body, Frank as well handed me his cap, tie and blazer as mementoes, bringing laughter from the 25,000 on the ground when he added there was no point in handing over anything to do with his legs, which were, to put it in modern parlance, well past their use-by date.

The finale to this was a sensational ticker-tape send-off for the West Indies through the streets of Melbourne.

Meanwhile the Australian Cricket Board were discussing, among other matters, the team to go to England in 1961 and also the management of the party. Syd Webb was to be manager, I knew that, and Les Truman was his assistant manager.

What I didn't know was that already there was disquiet about what might happen on the tour, and it was felt a strong assistant manager could be needed if there turned out to be a problem between me and the manager. What problem? At that stage I hadn't envisaged any problem with the manager. I knew Les Truman well, he was a genuine, quiet and self-effacing man who was secretary of the Western Australian Cricket Association and had been earmarked for this trip. I had no trouble with this, but at that stage, I didn't know Syd had been saying plenty about what was going to happen on the tour and how he would represent the Board, and how it was the Board's team and not the captain's. This would have gone down well in some quarters but it raised a couple of eyebrows on the Board, to the extent that Les Truman suddenly disappeared as prospective assistant manager. Perhaps 'disappeared' is the wrong term, because he came back as assistant manager on the 1968 tour of England; pushed sideways is a better description.

At the Board's cocktail party Bradman introduced me to the man who was to take Les's place. His name was Raymond Charles Steele and he was an outstanding character. Bradman was having a busy time in his first year as Chairman of the Board, and it was reassuring in 1960 and early 1961 to have him in charge, particularly because of the manner in which he had approached his first year. I reasoned it would be even better news if, in future years, more ex-players made it on to the Board and into the chairmanship.

The announcement of the Australian team to tour England came the day after the cocktail party when it had been announced Ray Steele would be assistant manager, and that morning I had breakfast with Bradman to discuss a few matters to do with the tour, but not the team itself. In Australia, captains do not have any official input into the selection of Test teams and touring parties, a system with which I am in complete agreement. I wanted it that way so the selectors could choose their sides without interference or pressure of any kind. After that, I could do with the team what I wished and I would always stand or fall by results.

All Don said to me at breakfast that day was they thought they had given me a good side and that we would have a lot of fun. I then went down to the Mornington races with Davidson, Harvey and a few others, and it was race-caller Bert Bryant who handed me a sheet of paper listing the touring party, moments after it had come down the line from his station studio. One of the most significant selections was that of Graham McKenzie, the nineteen-year-old from Western Australia who had so impressed Worrell and Sobers.

It had been an extraordinary summer, and between the end of the Fifth Test on 15 February and the next game in Launceston as the starter of the tour, I had my tonsils removed, rather a late operation aged thirty, and one that was correspondingly painful. After the excitement of the summer the matches in Tasmania were relaxing, so too was the ship trip to England on the *Himalaya*, at the end of which there was work to be done.

21

CAPTAIN OF AUSTRALIA
FOR AN ASHES BATTLE
IN ENGLAND – PAIN FIRST
AND THEN PLEASURE

I T promised to be great, it finished in splendid style, but in between, it was a grey time. There's nothing better than being on an Australian cricket tour of England: it's hard work but it is also the ultimate for an Australian cricketer and, for an Australian captain, even more so. We were fresh from the thrills and spills of the West Indies series, I had recovered from my operation, had promised Mrs McKenzie I would try to look after her very good-looking son and heir Graham, and I had also set out to come up with a tour policy, in conjunction with Neil Harvey and Colin McDonald. It was a very good chance to try to do some good for the game and for ourselves. The last time we had been to England was five years earlier when Ian Johnson was captain, and that tour could hardly be said to have been a rip-roaring success. A few officials in the old country, remembering 1956, may have found it difficult to believe I was about to return to England as captain.

Neil, Colin and I had our meeting a couple of days out of Fremantle, and the basis of it was that we wanted to come up with an official policy which we would produce at the press conference on arrival, and which we would try very hard to stick with. It was to cover policy about over-rates, walking, about winning and fear of losing, with a few other things thrown in as well. We decided we would try to play good cricket and enjoy ourselves. There was a careful distinction between that and what was being touted in England at the time as 'brighter cricket'. We intended to give every county side the chance to beat us if they were good enough, and if they did beat us it would be just too bad, or in their case just too good. We intended, if possible, to close our own innings on the opening afternoon of county games. When we reached discussion time, the players wanted to know what would happen if the opposition didn't play the same way. 'No matter,' was the answer, 'we'll keep at it.'

There were a lot of matches during the tour which showed the benefit of this thinking, and apart from anything else, it kept the team on its toes. One such game was against MCC at Lord's, during which we made two declarations, the second setting MCC 294 in four hours with around 72 overs available. *Wisden* described it as 'daring'.

The night before the last day, Walter Robins, who wasn't an England selector that summer, had come into our dressing-room to say how much he had enjoyed the match so far and I told him he should be there on the final day because we would provide a good finish. 'Robbie' seemed less than impressed, because his knowledge of the game told him that the amount of time available, and the risks of defeat entailed for Australia, didn't equate with a challenging last day.

When I saw him after the game was over and we had won with half an hour to spare, I asked him if he had enjoyed the day. 'I only arrived a short time ago,' he said glumly. 'I didn't believe you!'

I had awful trouble on this tour with my right shoulder. The injury happened in the Worcester game when I bowled a wrong'un to Tom Graveney and tore fibres off the supraspinatus tendon which runs across the top of the shoulder. Dr Brian Corrigan, a good mate of mine, saw me break down a second time at Edgbaston on the final day of the First Test and persuaded Syd Webb to allow me to go to Dr Alan Bass for treatment. Dr Bass was the team doctor at Arsenal Football Club and was pioneering new methods of treatment for this type of injury.

Later I read a full diagnosis: 'A terrible tear, very extensive, very unusual. The subscapularis was torn right down to the capsule that contains the shoulder and, at the start, he couldn't lift his arm above the shoulder without crying out in pain.' They were right about that! It was agony at first and then settled down merely into extreme pain. Dr Bass told me that if I missed the Lord's Test then possibly I would be fit to play at Headingley and certainly at Old Trafford . . . so I missed Lord's. That was heartbreaking.

There are many wonderful things about a tour of England, and for a captain the highlight is to lead the team at Lord's. I confirmed I wasn't a starter for the Test after we had practised the day before the match and were walking back to the dressing-rooms, and passed it on to the media through manager Syd Webb. Neil, as happened right through the tour, did a wonderful job in that Second Test, leading the side with imagination and verve. Although it was tight on the last day when we lost 4–19, he sent Peter Burge out with instructions to get stuck in and the game was won.

Then came the Headingley match, finished in three days on a rubbish pitch – not as bad as the one served up on the same ground in 1972 when 'fusarium' was said to have struck, but rubbish none the less.

At Old Trafford we were in strife for a long time, even though Bill Lawry hit his second century of the series, having already made one at Lord's. On the second-last evening, when we were in a certain amount of trouble, I went across to the Lancashire committee room for an after-match drink.

By chance Ray Lindwall was there, just the man I needed to talk to about the deep footmarks at the Warwick Road End. I asked him about the possibility of bowling around the wicket to the right-handers, recalling Tony Lock coming from a similar angle in Australia at the SCG in 1958, bowling left-arm over the wicket to the right-handers. Lindwall thought it might work but advised me not to stray off line, 'otherwise they'll kill you . . .'

One of the sidelines of the match was that Alan Bass came to Manchester, and in the intervals gave me the special physio treatment that was proving so successful to date.

The last day was a real thriller. We were under a lot of pressure because at several points England were clambering all over us. Each time we fought back, and it was one of the more exciting days of cricket in which I had been involved.

We had high hopes of setting England a target of something like 250, thinking at the start of play on the last day that we might add around 100 for the last four wickets. Those hopes disappeared almost immediately as we lost three wickets, but were rekindled by one of the most electrifying partnerships I had seen as a captain, with Davidson and Graham McKenzie adding 98 for the last wicket.

Ted Dexter flayed all our bowlers in a wonderful short innings, and he put England into a clear winning position. I went around the wicket to bowl into the footmarks, and soon after Dexter was dismissed, though not from a ball pitching in the rough. Brian Close was the danger, and I had him caught at backward square-leg near the umpire, having switched O'Neill to that position to replace the injured Slasher Mackay.

As was often the case in Australian cricket, Slasher did something which had an influence on the saving or the winning of a match. In the course of Dexter's batting savagery, we suffered a cruel blow when Mackay pulled a hamstring whilst turning quickly, possibly when he whipped around to see where Ted had hit him into the stand at the Warwick Road End. He told me about it between overs after Dexter's and May's dismissals and, with Brian Close trying to sweep almost everything, it seemed a good idea not to have Ken fielding near the square-leg umpire. He certainly wouldn't be moving fluently. I quietly swapped him with Norm O'Neill, who had been fielding at cover, and it was O'Neill who caught Close, although Brian has sworn on ten stacks of Bibles for the past forty-nine years that from the moment he walked on to the Old Trafford ground that afternoon, O'Neill was always the fieldsman near the umpire.

When we went off for tea, with John Murray and Ken Barrington the not-out batsmen, Mackay instantly had the physio, Arthur James, strapping his leg, and he came back out with us after the interval, though I had checked with him as to the state of the injury. 'It's fine,' he said, 'I won't let you down.' He never had done. I reckoned, when we walked out to the centre, that I might as well get what I could out of him before everything started to stiffen up so I gave him the first over, bowled from the Warwick Road End.

Ken Barrington knew, because the first few balls were only gentle medium pace, there was something wrong with Ken, but he didn't know what it was. The next ball was a yard faster and it darted back off the seam and had Kenny plumb lbw. I gave Slash another over and then said 'thanks' and he nodded but refused point blank to go off the field.

'I won't let you down,' he said again.

He never did let me down. The selectors knew what I thought about him, and I knew what they thought about him after he justified their faith in choosing him as Ron Archer's replacement to South Africa. In the 1962–63 series, having made Mackay twelfth man at the SCG in the Third Test match, they quite deliberately chose him in the twelve for the final Test in Sydney, knowing they were to make him drinks waiter on the morning of the match.

Some say selectors can be heartless at times, but the good ones I knew, like Bradman, Ryder and Seddon, had another dimension to them. They knew they were probably about to end Mackay's Test career and they cared. Ken had many friends in cricket and the three selectors already knew that two of his best friends, Neil Harvey and Alan Davidson, were retiring of their own volition after the 1963 match. They reckoned he deserved to be in the nominated twelve and that it would be nice for him to go out at the same time as Harvey and Davidson, rather than be in Perth playing in a Sheffield Shield game against Western Australia.

At the same time, they started Ken's replacement, Neil Hawke, on his 27-Test match and 91-Test wicket career. It was a brilliant yet somewhat controversial choice, and they did it so that if Hawke had a poor year in 1963–64, they could still take him to England, as he would have had one Test to his name on selection day in February 1964.

Ken Mackay carried the drinks out to us in his final Test and looked after us in the dressing-room, no less enthusiastic a cricketer than when he had started with Queensland seventeen years earlier.

At tea, it was 93 to win for England, five wickets to win for us and 85 minutes still to play. With twenty minutes to go, Alan Davidson knocked Brian Statham's off stump out of the ground and the Ashes were ours, the first time Australia had won a Test at Old Trafford since 1902.

There was plenty of jubilation in our dressing-room but I suspect England felt as though they had been sandbagged. It was a feeling that had come my way on many occasions playing against England over the years. Bowling around the wicket into the footmarks was something new in those days and it won a Test match.

From Australia's point of view, the tour had gone wonderfully well and *Wisden* summed it up in style.

> Adopting an almost carefree policy throughout their five months' stay in England, the twenty-third Australian team to visit this country returned home with their main object achieved. The tour was a personal triumph for Richie Benaud, possibly the most popular captain of any overseas team to come to Great Britain. As soon as he arrived Benaud emphasised he and his men wanted to play attractive cricket wherever they went and that they desired to keep the game moving by bowling as many overs as possible when they were in the field. Moreover, he stressed that, no matter what their opponents did, the Australians would not deviate from their policy of striving for the type of cricket which would please the onlookers.

This was what had been decided by Harvey, McDonald and me at that shipboard conference, so there was nothing unusual about how we went about it, although it did occasion some surprise in England, where they were desperately seeking a 'brighter cricket' answer to their own game.

A Special Inquiry Committee, set up at Lord's, had talked of a dynamic attitude hoped for in all cricket in 1961, and in what seemed to me a direct reference to Sir Donald Bradman and his pre-Tied Test talk to the Australian team on 8 December 1960, it was said selectors in England 'should be drastic in dealing with players whom they considered were not cooperating sufficiently in the suggested approach. Also, they should be sympathetic with those who did cooperate but were failing to do themselves justice.' Had they taken a tape recording of it, that could hardly have been closer to Bradman's 1960 speech and the Australian selectors' intentions!

Wisden then went on to say, 'The Australians' main assets were cheerfulness and boldness, particularly in times of adversity. They never deliberately set themselves to play for a draw.'

That was true and it all added up, in the end and despite the shoulder injury, to the happiest months of my cricketing life as a team member and captain. When we finished the tour and all the official duties, and said our reluctant farewells to friends, I was happy to step on to the ship taking us back to Australia. I slept for two days!

22

A WONDERFUL FOLLOW-UP

FROM the point of view of Australian cricket, what we had now was a wonderful summer devoted solely to domestic matches to follow up the Tied Test series and the retaining of the Ashes in England in such exciting circumstances. Prior to those victories we had wins against Pakistan and India and against England in Australia, so we had a real chance now of providing cricket which would captivate spectators throughout our own country. That was precisely what happened, and we had a season to stir those whose memories consisted mainly of the 'Golden Age', where attractive cricket and splendid competitive matches apparently took place every day.

There were many highlights, but notable for me was the game against Victoria at the MCG where my NSW players had every chance of backtracking on the vows to try to play attractive cricket and make 400 in a day, no matter what the position might be. Pace and spin did us easily and, when I walked out to join Grahame Thomas, I had a problem. I decided on the easy way out, I'd try 'the flog' as a solution. It worked. Our 255 for the seventh wicket took us only 176 minutes. After we had turned things around a little, we were having a chat mid-pitch and Grahame asked me if we were still going for the 400. I said we were, but when I was dismissed for 140, caught on the fence off Bob Cowper, it seemed 400 was out of reach, and so it proved . . . but only just! Johnny Martin, who throughout his career kept a record of the sixes he hit, tried for another off Cowper from what was the final ball of the day, was lbw and we had to be content with 398 instead of 404.

We had a very interesting preamble to the game at the SCG against South Australia. I persuaded my sports editor, Con Simons, to give the match more publicity than he had provided for any other Sheffield Shield game over the years. Con was very good. In fact, he said he would treat it as a Test match, providing I was able to file stories each day and obtain as many quotes as possible from players and NSW and SA officials. All this resulted in a good crowd of 6,500 for the opening day when we bowled out South Australia for 250 and then, at the close of play, we were 42–0. 'Let's get stuck into it and keep your eyes on that 400 in the day,' were the only instructions on the second day, the Saturday, and that's what we did, this time in front of 17,864 spectators who were so enthused they sounded more like a football crowd than staid cricket watchers.

There was some exhilarating cricket played, and in the next match against Victoria in Sydney Alan Davidson made a dashing 106. In the partnership with last man Doug Ford, 44 balls were bowled; Ford faced three of them, from one of which they ran a leg-bye. Davidson made the other 58 of their 59-run partnership. It was a wonderful effort.

In Perth the following week we were in all kinds of trouble at 38–6, on a pitch with some life, but not to the extent shown on the scoreboard. Fortunately Davidson was in such a rich vein of form by this stage that he hit another century, just as blistering an innings as against Victoria, this time making 108.

Despite WA facing only a small target the next morning, there was extraordinary confidence in our dressing-room, nothing false about it, only confidence that the job would be done. I set Davidson loose on them straight away, and as soon as Neil Harvey caught Shepherd off him with only three added, the game was as good as over. With 4–12 from seven overs on the final morning, Davo was simply superb. He finished with 7–31 to go with his 108, underlining what a magnificent cricketer he was at that time and had been for many years in Australian cricket.

That summer was one of the highlights of my cricketing life, as it was for those who paid their money at the turnstiles in Australia.

It was a delightful aftermath to my tour of England as captain and it was because of my players I was able to orchestrate such excitement on the field. NSW were just about unstoppable that summer, aggregating 64 points out of a possible 80 and always scoring so fast that we had the chance of bowling out the opposition twice.

I was happy enough with my own performances in 1961–62, heading the first-class wicket-takers and the averages with 47 at 17.97.

As soon as the season was over, I was on my way to New Zealand with Ron Roberts's international team and I managed to hold my form with bat and ball and also captaincy. Matches were played in Rhodesia, where the tour began in Bulawayo, then Dacca, as it was still known, in East Pakistan, followed by two games in New Zealand, two in Hong Kong and two in Bombay and Karachi.

Ron Roberts was a very good journalist and a fine cricketing man, and while he had organised several tours in his time, this was by far the most ambitious. The team covered more than 40,000 miles and twenty-five players took part, with some joining and others dropping off at different times. Before I joined the tour Ray Lindwall and Everton Weekes shared the captaincy, then I took over for the second half. Everton Weekes and Roy Marshall were the West Indian representatives, Neil Adcock and Roy McLean were the players from South Africa, and there were several from England including Tom Graveney and Harold 'Dusty' Rhodes, the fast bowler.

The Hong Kong match gave rise to the statement concerning the luck which often came my way as a captain, and the play on words of the old phrase about diamonds being a girl's best friend. In that game, a one-day affair, after fiddling about a bit, we suddenly needed to take the last three wickets in one over and they required only two runs for victory. Dusty Rhodes, as he walked past me, smiled and said, 'I'm going to enjoy this, Richie, let's see you get out of this one.'

I called up Neil Adcock and he took a hat-trick, two of which I caught at second slip. As we walked off the field laughing, Dusty came up shaking his head and saying ruefully, 'Skip, if you put your head into a bucket of slops you'd come up with a mouthful of diamonds.'

When we were in New Zealand, Doug Ford, from New South Wales, was our wicketkeeper, but Harold Stephenson of Somerset was due to rejoin the side for the Hong Kong games. Doug was well liked, and so he might continue the tour, we endeavoured to find a way to pay his air fares up to Hong Kong. The only way we could manage this was to back a winner at the races. Everyone in the team put in a tenner and we consulted the best judges of trotting in Auckland where the meeting was to be held.

They came up with what they said was a conveyance with good form, ability and was at a good enough price, 11–2, which would give us the £500 needed in those days for a return air ticket to Hong Kong. The fairy story would have been that it won and everyone had a splendid time in HK. In fact, it ran second by three long lengths, and all the good intentions disappeared into the bags of the satchel-swingers.

The final game of that tour was against the Pakistan Board XI team, which was very close to the side which toured England three weeks later. I went straight back to Australia after this and set myself to have a little rest and recreation, with England due to arrive in Australia in October 1962.

It looked from what happened in the series in England between Pakistan and England as though David Sheppard might well captain the team to Australia but, in fact, on 19 July came the announcement that Ted Dexter had the job and, a week later, that the Duke of Norfolk would be the manager of the team. This was an interesting appointment, which was said to have come about because of the inability of the MCC Committee to make a decision. The Duke apparently went home from the meeting at Lord's and, in conversation with the Duchess of Norfolk, she is said to have expressed the view that he should do it himself. I was on the sub-editor's desk in the Sydney *Sun* at the time the story came through, and it was my job to write the front-page story about Bernard Marmaduke Fitzalan Howard, the Sixteenth Duke of Norfolk, being appointed as manager.

At the start of the season I took the opportunity to go to Perth to cover the opening match of the MCC tour for the Sydney *Sun*. I travelled to Perth with Bob Gray, a good mate and my opposition cricket writer on the Sydney *Mirror*. We stayed at the John Barleycorn Hotel, and on the Wednesday night, we decided to have a look at Perth's nightspots which, in those days, were few in number. My, how time flies when you're having fun. We arrived back at the John Barleycorn at 4 a.m. in only reasonably good order, though I was certainly in better shape than Gray. That point was driven home to me when he went to sleep the instant his head hit the pillow and nothing I tried would wake him.

I adlibbed my story to the Sydney *Sun* and then picked up the phone and called Gray's *Daily Mirror*, gave his name and adlibbed a story for him to the copy-taker. His sports editor rang him later in the morning with profuse congratulations. My sports editor telephoned me after the first edition to say I'd made a bad start to the tour because Bob Gray had scooped me in the *Mirror* with a good story about Graham McKenzie. There wasn't much I could say other than, in future, I would try harder. Gray, when he awoke, thought it very amusing.

Unfortunately that was bigger news than much of the tour itself. It was a disappointing series, with two of the games played on the SCG when the whole square was almost devoid of grass. The pitches generally were of very ordinary quality. When NSW played MCC early in the tour the ball was turning at right-angles and the pitch was very slow. We hoped it would improve as the season advanced. I took 10 wickets in that match, 7–18 in the second innings, and the game was over in three days. It was OK for morale but not particularly reassuring as regards the pitch surfaces.

There were similar events in the Third Test when it was played early in the New Year. The game finished in three and a half days instead of five, again with an Australian eight-wicket victory but nothing to enthuse over as regards entertainment. This was a resounding margin, but we were actually fortunate: we needed 65 to win when light rain started to fall towards the end of the innings. Ted Dexter bowled three of the last six overs and had 27 taken from them, and we had the 65 needed for victory. The rain immediately became heavier and a storm hit the ground. It continued to rain for two days and no more play would have been possible. It was a lucky break; if England had delayed even by a few minutes, they would have escaped with a draw.

In the following Test we lost Alan Davidson in his fourth over when he tore a hamstring, and the attack without him wasn't capable of forcing a win, a forerunner of things to come in Australian cricket. This was the match where Ian McLachlan was made twelfth man for Australia and Norm O'Neill was given a reprieve by the selectors. Norm hit a brilliant 100 but McLachlan was never chosen again, although he did take a step forward into Australian politics and then became a highly-respected cricket administrator.

Twice during the 1962–63 summer Ian Meckiff was called for throwing, once in Adelaide on 12 January by Jack Kierse who was standing in the match with Colin Egar. Then Bill Priem called him at the Gabba on 5 March in the final game of the summer. Ian headed the first-class bowling figures for the summer with 58 wickets at 19.86, I was second with 55 at 25.76 and Graham McKenzie continued to be a star, with 51 for the season. In between those two calls on 12 January and 5 March I played two matches, one against South Australia in Sydney and the other the Fourth Test against England in Adelaide. In the game against SA, Gordon Rorke had let go a couple of deliveries which in my opinion looked unusual. He hadn't bowled much in either innings, just three overs in the first and four in the second.

Later in the dressing-room the NSW chairman of selectors, Dudley Seddon, said he wanted to know why Gordon hadn't bowled more. I had to admit that I thought there were one or two occasions when his delivery hadn't been completely legitimate. The answer I got was that the selectors would nominate the side and *they* would make sure the bowlers in the team were completely legitimate – my job was simply to captain, so would I remember that in future? I said to him that if I found in the New South Wales side in future any bowler I thought had in any way a suspect action, then I wouldn't bowl him at all, but to make my point I would open the batting with him and they could do what they liked about it.

A few days later the Test began in Adelaide and it was during this game Sir Donald Bradman had four of the five state captains to dinner at his home. Ken Mackay, Barry Shepherd, Bill Lawry and I were playing in the match, Les Favell at the time was playing a Sheffield Shield game in Brisbane. After dinner Sir Donald showed us some very interesting films he had gathered over the past couple of years concerning bowlers said to have suspect actions. At the end of the evening I said that, in future, I would not continue to bowl anyone called for throwing by an umpire, and I intended to go a step further, as I had done in Sydney a few days earlier, and not continue to bowl anyone in my team I considered to have a suspect action. I later also conveyed that to Les Favell, although I was hoping the throwing matters would fade away of their own accord.

The final Test at the SCG in that 1962–63 summer saw the retirement from Test cricket of Davidson, Harvey and Mackay. Ted Dexter set us 241 to make in four hours and what these days would be a minimum of 60 overs, but in a match which was no better entertainment than the others at the SCG that summer, the game petered out into a draw.

After that match, along with current players from England, New Zealand and West Indies, I captained a Ron Roberts team which played in South Africa, Rhodesia and also in India, the latter match to assist in raising money for the National Defence Fund. I couldn't recall any other time three national captains had played in the same side in a first-class match, but Ted Dexter, John Reid and I played together in the match at Salisbury.

In Port Elizabeth I had my first glimpse of Graeme Pollock, an exciting young talent and younger brother of Peter. Graeme made 209 not out against us. He looked outstanding. In fact, from what I saw of the South Africans on that short tour, they were likely to be a real force when they toured Australia six months later.

I returned to Australia in March and then flew to London for what was to be my first stint as a television commentator, having been asked by the BBC to cover the 1963 West Indies tour of England. It was an exciting prospect, seven years after I had taken the first encouraging and hopeful steps towards a career in television by spending my final three weeks of the 1956 tour on the BBC course.

I could not have asked for more than to make a debut in such a splendid summer. The cricket was excellent and it was priceless experience to watch and listen to and learn from commentators like Brian Johnston and Peter West.

It also gave me the opportunity once again to watch and listen from a distance to Longhurst, Maskell and O'Sullevan.

It was the year when, at Royal Lytham, Bob Charles became the only left-hander to win the Open Championship after a play-off with American Phil Rodgers, and Australian Fred Stolle went down in the Wimbledon men's singles final to American Chuck McKinley. Peter O'Sullevan called Relko to a splendid win in the English Derby. All three sounded just as good, or better, than had been the case seven years and three years earlier.

Towards the end of the summer I had my first taste of limited-overs cricket in England when I was one of the commentators at Lord's on the Knock-out Competition final. There was no sponsorship, and in fact it was a desperate throw by England's administrators to solve some of the financial problems affecting the game. These included plummeting attendances at county matches, decisions to be made in relation to the balance in styles of cricket, and the fact that the Rothmans limited-overs series had been so successful.

The fateful decision was made that there would be a knock-out competition, and the best and worst fears of everyone were realised. The best was that the game was fast and often exciting, attendances were good throughout the summer, and then the final was completely sold out. There were 23,000 present, but for some people, the worst aspect was that the crowd, though well behaved, was noisy and seemed to be enjoying themselves. The match itself was ordinary, from the point of view of being competitive, although the notable aspects were Ted Dexter's tactics, which were impeccable, and the fact that both Dexter and the Worcestershire skipper, Don Kenyon, gave plenty of work to the spinners.

One of the more dramatic Tests where I have been a commentator was the second of that series between England and the West Indies at Lord's, when Colin Cowdrey came out to bat with a broken arm but didn't have to face a ball. David Allen saw it through for England, for whom Brian Close played magnificently for 70 in the second innings, after Ted Dexter had flayed the West Indies for the same score in England's first attempt. This was the series when Fred Trueman was in such magnificent form with the ball. In the First Test at Edgbaston he had taken 5–75 and 7–44, and at Lord's he had 6–100 and 5–52.

Retirement years seldom go as planned, and this one was no exception. I had returned from England and the BBC Television work with high hopes for the future outside cricket, and the Australian selectors were aware of the fact that I would not be touring again. I did, however, want to play out the final season for both NSW and Australia. I was keen to do well in both areas and also be part of what I hoped was going to be an excellent summer for spectators around Australia.

Doug Walters, aged seventeen, joined Central Cumberland at the start of the season, having made his first-class debut against Queensland the previous summer, when he hit a brilliant half-century off Wes Hall and the other bowlers. Doug had been spotted by Jack Chegwyn on one of his country tours when they played a match near Dungog where Doug was born. Jack asked if I would look after him, and he came down to live at Wentworthville and was an immediate asset to the club, making 400 runs at better than 50 an innings. He was an asset also to Australia, a gifted young cricketer and a match-winner at every level.

The Australian selectors asked if I would travel to Perth to play against the South Africans in the Combined XI match and I was happy to do so. I had already talked the previous season to Sir Donald about the captaincy and we had agreed I would choose what I regarded as the right moment to step down, with Bob

Simpson certain to be the new captain. NSW, in a clear pointer, had announced him as vice-captain to me.

I flew to Perth with Bob for the Combined XI match and against South Africa he hit 246 in the second innings, so it could be said he was in decent form for the big matches ahead. I batted at number three and that day we put on 237 for the second wicket before I was out for 132.

As Clive Halse took the catch at mid-on, the loudspeaker system burst into the description of the horses jumping out of the barrier in the 1963 Melbourne Cup. Gatum Gatum, ridden by Jim Johnson, won it, and, as I had backed Ilqumuh which ran second, the long walk back to the pavilion added a little financial insult to the injury of being dismissed.

I had shown, though, that I was in reasonable form with the bat, something which continued through to the end of the summer, and I finished with 869 runs at 57.93, although my bowling figures were nowhere near as impressive, which was a fair indication that retirement might be, if not around the corner, then at least just down the road.

The last Test match in which I captained Australia, in Brisbane in 1963, was one of my more memorable, for a variety of reasons. First of all I had no idea it was to be the last time I would be captain, nor, for that matter, did anyone else. I was intending to captain both Australia and NSW right through to the end of the summer. After I won the toss at the 'Gabba in the opening Test against South Africa, we raced to 337–5 at the close of the first day, with Brian Booth making a brilliant 169. I gathered a quick 43 which took me to 2,013 runs in Tests and made me the first cricketer ever to do the Test double of 2,000 runs and 200 wickets. Seven years later Garry Sobers reached that mark, and he was followed by Ian Botham, Kapil Dev, Imran Khan and Richard Hadlee. As of 2010, nine more players have joined that group.

The sequence of events when we fielded in that First Test has been well chronicled: Ian Meckiff was called for throwing by Colin Egar in his first over, and in accordance with my stated policy I didn't bowl him again. It was a sad day for everyone:

Ian and his family; Col Egar, who was a good mate of Mecko's; spectators; and the players of both teams, who found it difficult to concentrate from then on.

Rain on the Monday of the game meant two things: no play, and Bill Lawry's practical joke following the publication in the media of details of police protection for the umpires Egar and Lou Rowan after Ian had been cheered from the field and the two umpires and the Australian captain booed from it. There were some lurid stories, one in the Melbourne *Sporting Globe* asking why Benaud hadn't bowled Meckiff from the other end.

Lawry, in one of his more elaborate jokes, set up Jock, the masseur, to front me with this pink *Globe* covering a gun. I was writing letters and he said, 'Richie, I'm a Meckiff fan.'

'Jock, I'm very busy at the moment,' I said.

He whipped away the newspaper, pointed the gun at me, said, 'You should have bowled him from the other end,' and then fired the gun. It wasn't quite a heart-stopper, but it was close for a moment or two until I realised it was a cap-gun!

Thirty years passed before the news was published that, on 12 September 1963, the Australian Cricket Board discussed Law 26 and Australia's attitude to it, and a motion was moved that the problem needed to be stamped out in Australia. At a meeting shortly after, Queensland delegate Clem Jones had placed on record in a minute that he objected to Meckiff's future selection for Australia.

If that Test match at the 'Gabba wasn't unusual enough, I went to play a grade match for Cumberland against Mosman at Mosman Oval. In trying to take a catch off Doug Walters' bowling at third slip early in the morning, I broke in three places the third finger of my bowling hand – my spinning finger. I looked down at my hand and said, 'Would you bloody well believe it?' I walked off the ground, drove myself to the hospital for confirmation of the break, phoned Dr Brian Corrigan and told him I wanted to play again as soon as possible – and started squeezing a squash ball 2,000 times a day.

This injury meant Bob Simpson skippered New South Wales

in the Christmas match in Melbourne against Victoria, making 135 in his debut innings as New South Wales captain. Then he captained Australia in the Second Test match against South Africa on the same ground a few days later. I went down and covered the match for various newspapers and it turned out to be a resounding victory for Australia, and Simpson.

In the course of the penultimate day of the match, when it looked certain barring another thunderstorm that Australia would win, I went round to the executive room of the VCA to have a word with Sir Donald Bradman. I told him I reckoned the way the game was going, this was the ideal time to step down. What better way for Simpson to start his captaincy career than with a victory? It would have been pointless if I had then come back to take over, particularly as I had announced I would not be available to go to England with the Australian side at the end of the season. The same applied to the NSW team which Bob captained for the remainder of the summer.

The Test series was squared one-all and I played my last Sheffield Shield match under Bob's captaincy in Adelaide, against South Australia, early in February 1964. It was one of the best games of cricket in which I ever took part, a real thriller with NSW winning by six runs with two minutes of play remaining. I made 76 and 120 not out and took five wickets. For me it was a delightful touch that my finale at this level should be between the two states who had played the day I watched my first Sheffield Shield match at the SCG twenty-four years earlier as a wide-eyed youngster.

The South Australian Cricket Association was kind enough to tender me a farewell at the ground immediately after this game, and it was a sad moment to reflect that it was the last time I would step on to a cricket ground in Australia as a player in a first-class match.

23

BRADMAN AND *WISDEN* AND TOURING, BUT NOT AS A PLAYER

Right from the time I saw my first proper limited-overs competition I loved the style of game. I have been accused over the years of being too supportive of the modern game and its players, and particularly of one-day cricket, a criticism I regard as nonsense. Cricket means only one thing to those who deeply and desperately hate the one-day game: that matches must be played over a long period, as has been the case since Test matches began.

It has been put to me by cricketing zealots that the only way to save the game is for those who care about cricket and its rich tradition to join in depriving others of the chance to watch the shortened version. This attitude is perfectly straightforward and patronising, suggesting that one group of people knows what is best for another group. Their belief is that, if most limited-overs matches were removed from the cricket calendar, the cricket-watching public would eventually abandon limited-overs cricket, restoring Test cricket to its sole dominant place in the game.

Well, I won't have a bar of that. I believe Test cricket is the best form of the game anyway, but I do add a rider: it needs to be good Test cricket. Since limited-overs cricket became part of the modern-day game, there has been a lot of good cricket at Test level and there have been many splendid one-day and day-night matches.

The argument is used to me that people will always remember a wonderful and close finish in a Test, whereas they will be pushed to talk at length about a pulsating finish in a limited-overs game. So what? When limited-overs matches came into vogue, no one claimed it was about to take the place of the Tied Test or the Old Trafford match when Australia beat England, nor, in modern times, the 1981 Test at Headingley, Botham's match, or the 2005 Edgbaston Test. I don't sit down in the evening with a glass of Chablis and start nattering about the day Viv Richards hit that wonderful century in Melbourne in the day-night game, nor the times there have been more than 50,000 spectators at the MCG for a limited-overs clash. But, and it is an important note, I haven't forgotten them.

We are living in a different era, a different world. It has been said to me that if God had meant us to be playing cricket at night he would originally have decreed cricket balls to be white. They *are* white, in fact, until those who run the game colour them red.

To some it was a crushing disappointment that Sir Donald Bradman should have given even the slightest hint of approval to limited-overs cricket when he wrote his thoughtful article in the 1986 edition of *Wisden*. Perhaps the disappointment is reflected in the fact that very few of the hardcore traditionalists quote from the article but often tell you the game isn't the same since Bradman stopped playing and Test matches began to be mixed up with what they call the one-day rubbish.

Sir Donald wrote that there was a stirring of emotions at the limited-overs game from those of a new and largely young audience, who yell and scream their support, and those dyed-in-the-wool lovers of Test cricket, who yearn for more peaceful, bygone days. He pointed out that, as with so many things, reconciliation between the factions is well-nigh impossible. And he added that, despite a deep feeling for the traditional form of cricket, his conviction was that we must accept we live in a new era.

He correctly noted the Achilles' heel of the limited-overs game, that a premium is placed on defensive bowling and negative and defensive field-placings, so one can be bored by countless singles being taken with no slips and five men on the boundary. He pointed out that the limited-overs contest has done something else: it has got rid of the unutterable bore who thinks occupancy of the crease and his own personal aggrandisement are all that matter. He commented on the lift in the standard of fielding, and that running-between-the-wickets has taken on a new dimension. Risks must be taken to maintain a run-rate.

As one might expect from Bradman, it was a perfectly balanced article and, more important, a constructive one. As a matter of interest, he suggested there would be no loss of face or pride if television were to be used to assist umpires in run-outs, stumpings or disputed catches, though it would not be possible to use the method in lbw appeals. All this he wrote as long ago as 1986. As has often been the case with Bradman, he was well in advance of others in their thinking on the game.

Favourite cricketers, favourite quotes. One of my more enjoyable moments came in the television commentary box more than twenty years ago. It was during a rain break at The Oval when we were showing some footage of the 1963 series, England against the West Indies, and Bob Willis, watching in the *Test Match Special* radio box, posed to Fred Trueman, tongue in cheek, the point that on the strength of what they had seen already, in taking all those wickets and ripping apart the West Indian batting line-up, Fred didn't seem to be all that fast.

That was the delicious moment for Fred to lean across and murmur, if that word can be used in connection with Fred, 'Black-and-white footage always slows you up!'

Nineteen sixty-four was an interesting year. The Australians toured England and Glamorgan beat them at Swansea. Any Australian would excuse the defeat because of the wonderful sound made by the massed Welsh choirs at every bar in the country. It was very impressive on and off the field.

Then, at Old Trafford, Bob Simpson made 311. If you are going to make your first Test century, and have waited a while to do it, you might as well go on with the job.

This tour was my first full-time stint as a journalist with an Australian team and I found it extremely interesting being on the road for a full six months. In those days the filing of copy was done either by telephone or by telex through Cable and Wireless, with no computers to facilitate sending of stories. As before, I was with the Sydney *Sun*, and Bob Gray was working for the Sydney *Daily Mirror*. We had some good battles, because although we were close friends we never once shared a story on any tour.

Gray and I often travelled together during that tour, though the Benaud-Gray caravan was no model for rally drivers. Bob, sensibly, has never driven any vehicle in his life, other than a golf cart backwards at the Paradise Island Golf Club in the Bahamas. The main problem with this was that he actually wished to go forward, but his snap decision, as to which was the correct way to point the direction lever while his foot was on the accelerator, turned out to be slightly astray. This was emphasised by the cart rocketing across the practice putting green, fortunately skirting the bunker.

He had a similar driving problem seventeen years later when Daphne and I, and Bob's wife Grace, were in Port Hacking in a small boat with an outboard motor, trying to make it to his cruiser *Pistasnute* which was moored fifty yards away to the left. He turned right instead of left, the boat rose high above the jetty, and we were all unceremoniously deposited in the water.

In 1964 in England it was a case of Gray navigating, Benaud driving, and this gave us a little scope for studying the fields for race meetings and keeping abreast of various 'good things' through that splendid publication *Timeform*.

Gray and I had a stroke of luck during that tour, in that we backed the Derby–Oaks double, Santa Claus and Homeward Bound. Keith Miller had already slung Gray and me the tip of Santa Claus for the Derby, to be run on 3 June, and a couple of days later, 'Flipper' Lewis told Miller that Homeward Bound must have a good chance in the Oaks but the proviso was that it must be soft going. At the time there had been very little rain in England in the lead-up to the major races, and the tracks, and training tracks as well, were bone hard. Gray and I decided to take the odds on offer about the double, which at that stage amounted to 7–1 and 25–1, with a point added to each because of the generosity in those days of the bookmakers with antepost doubles. It meant, in rough terms, Gray and I were to collect about £1,300 each if both steeds obliged.

We watched with interest when Santa Claus at evens thrashed a good field in the Irish Two Thousand Guineas on 16 May, beating Young Christopher by three long-looking lengths. He instantly shortened to 2–1 for the English Derby and finally started at 6–4. That was no surprise because of his effortless victory at the Curragh.

Ridden by Scobie Breasley, aged fifty, Santa Claus won the Epsom Derby after a few heart-stopping moments. Now all we needed was for Homeward Bound to swoop down the outside in the Oaks.

Gray and I were at the Trent Bridge Test during Derby and Oaks week, and as the race broadcaster Peter Bromley was calling the last two furlongs, we were on opposite sides of the Trent Bridge ground. We had already selfishly cheered the news that a cloudburst had hit Epsom an hour before the Oaks was due to be run.

With no play possible at Trent Bridge because of showers, I was climbing a ladder to do an in-vision piece for BBC and had to go up one-handed because I had a radio to my ear. On the other side Gray, half leaning out of the press box window, was oblivious to everything but the race and finding some decent reception from his own radio. When Bromley's voice rose several decibels, with the filly swooping on the leaders and winning with plenty in hand, Peter, with a slight touch of patriotism, cried, 'And it's Homeward Bound for England.'

'Pigsarse it is,' came the unbridled yell of joy from Bob at the press box window. 'It's Homeward Bound for Gray and Benaud.'

It wasn't that, in fact, but it was some useful spending money for the tour, and a little punting money as well, and the spectators standing on the ground in front of the press box were left shaking their heads about the strange behaviour and language of that chap wearing the bright check cashmere sports jacket and shouting at them.

On 10 July Gray and I set out from Leicester for Southampton for the game between Hampshire and Australia, having made some modest investments on a four-horse Yankee bet which finished with two horses, Nanda Devi and New Sovereign, trained by Johnson-Houghton and Elsey and running at Beverley and Chester. Racing by this stage was affecting our navigation, and we found ourselves on the A604 heading east instead of on the A1 going south. We knew the first two horses in our Yankee, one of them Althrey Don, had won at short prices and, just south of Cambridge, by now on the A10, we stopped at Trumpington, where a phone call to the bookmaker established that Nanda Devi had bolted in.

New Sovereign, a two-year-old bay filly and our final bet, was running in a maiden a few minutes later, and it must have been a sight for the good folk of Trumpington village to see these two Australians in the old red phone box outside the pub, holding one telephone receiver to two ears whilst cheering on the gallant steed to its splendid length and a half win over Star Money.

I was part-lessee with Ray Steele, Barry Jarman and Norman O'Neill of a horse called Pall-Mallann, which was coming along well, and we had high hopes of it winning a race at some stage in the summer. We had Ron Hutchinson ride it, Sid Dale was the trainer and eventually it saluted in a handicap, run whilst the Australians were playing Yorkshire at Bradford, on Saturday, 8 August.

On the morning of the match I was entrusted with the task of putting £200 on this conveyance with Messrs Ladbrokes, the genial offerers of odds of 5–1. It was difficult getting through to them on the telephone, and the time for the race was drawing very close when Denis Compton opened the door of the telephone booth and said, 'Put fifty on for me, will you?' At that moment Ladbrokes answered and I said I wanted to take the 5–1 and I'd have £200 on it thanks.

As it went past the post, and we were cheering it on, a slight chill ran up my spine as I suddenly realised I hadn't put Denis's money on. Pall-Mallann won, not with its head on its chest, but it beat Dinner Gong by three-quarters of a length, putting in a strong run to lead close to home. All that happened was that it cost me 250 big ones once I had paid the four winning bets to Steele, Jarman, O'Neill and 'Compo'. It was a little lesson in concentration – costly, but a good lesson.

After a tranquil Australian domestic season in 1964–65, Australia went to the West Indies to defend the Frank Worrell trophy, unsuccessfully as it turned out in Garry Sobers's first stint of captaincy. It was a fiery series: the West Indians played some splendid cricket, the Australians less so, and there was a touch of controversy as well, with some comments I made and photographs I took concerning Charlie Griffith's bowling action.

It was delightfully tropical in Trinidad on 18 May when I left there, and bitterly cold on arriving in England where, ten days later, coffee and soup were served instead of cold drinks in the First Test between England and New Zealand at Edgbaston. When South Africa arrived later, the weather was better, and so was the cricket, and Graeme Pollock in the Trent Bridge Test played one of the finest innings I have seen, hitting his 125 from 160 balls.

I also had the pleasure that year of commentating on another wonderful attacking century, this time from Geoffrey Boycott in the Gillette Cup final at Lord's where another capacity crowd was present. Two years later 'Boycs' was in trouble with the selectors after he made 246 in a Test against India. It was an odd business. At the close of play on the first day, England, having won the toss, were a very satisfactory 281–3 and, on the second day, they closed at 550–4. India had to follow on and then made 510 in their second innings, England batted again,

I laid down various conditions before I would finally accept the invitation. I stipulated that, except in members' stands at the various grounds, audiences must be allowed to mix freely and that bars, other than in the members' stand, must be open to all. I insisted on complete freedom to meet any non-white cricket officials I wished whilst in the country, and told the organisers of the tour I would be the sole selector of the International Wanderers team. I added a little rider as well: every time a South African opposition team walked on to the field, there were to be three non-white players included. The latter proviso could easily have been a problem, not for the obvious reason, but because everyone at the time was talking about selection on merit. The difference was that, even though on the surface there were no Basil D'Oliveiras hidden away ready to be selected on merit, I was interested to see if we might unearth one or two. There was an additional note that if the conditions weren't adhered to, we would all make our various ways home!

There were two occasions when I had to make it clear that these conditions would be invoked unless certain matters were attended to. They both took place in Port Elizabeth but were of completely different character and concerned both black and white. The first was on the morning of a one-day match, when one of the local black administrators came to see me to say he had been refused service at the bar at the back of the stand. I had an agreement with those running the tour that if anyone had trouble of this kind they would find me and let me have the details.

I went to look for the local officials in charge of the match, and together we went to find the chief of police who had created the problem. Built like a country barn, his opening remark was that he didn't care what I thought and he would continue doing exactly as he wished. However, after a short discussion during which I told him he could either be amenable or famous, he said he would reconsider and could definitely make the necessary arrangements.

I thanked him and mentioned he had instantly reduced to zero the chance of me and all my players catching the following day's plane out of Johannesburg for points east or west.

The same night, at a post-match reception at the ground, one of the white South African selectors, smarting bitterly under the defeat of the day, told the world that it was the last bloody time they would allow themselves to be forced into choosing three non-white players. In future it was going to be a test of strength. When the teams got to Johannesburg, South Africa would have their best possible team in the field and they would carve up bloody Lillee and stuff the rest of them, including me.

It only took moments to sort that out, with the same wording as the morning misunderstanding, but I waited until the right moment in Jo'burg to let Dennis know about it. He took 7–27 against the South African XI and gave the crowd a rare moment of cricketing joy with some of the finest fast bowling seen at the Wanderers. It would have been better had he been able to bowl out the little dark-haired batsman who showed enormous courage against him and refused to give an inch. This was Tieffie Barnes and he showed a rare brand of fight in combating Lillee and the other International Wanderers bowlers. I saw Tieffie again in 1994 when Channel 9 covered the Australian tour in South Africa. He looked very well and still plays a part in cricket in South Africa these days.

One of the best efforts on the tour came from left-arm spin bowler Baboo Ebrahim. The Wanderers were set 348 to make in the last innings of the Durban match and he bowled superbly as South Africa charged to victory by a margin of 122 runs.

Not the least interesting of the off-field confrontations was the meeting mentioned earlier with Prime Minister Vorster, Dr Piet Koornhof and Joe Pamensky in Parliament House, Cape Town, during our stay in that city. It would be an exaggeration to say, because of his general bonhomie and goodwill, Mr Vorster made a lasting impression on me, though he did deliver a speech, as though on the hustings, to let me know visitors to South Africa were expected to conform to the laws of the land. All I could do was reply that if I found any of my pre-tour conditions were not being adhered to, then I would remember his thoughts on the laws of his land and go home, and my players would go with me.

He heard it, but I doubt if it registered. It was an interesting experience to have someone talking at you, rather than to you, verbally poking you in the chest whilst never able to bring himself to catch your eye.

The Chappell brothers began to have an influence on Australian cricket in the late 1960s. Ian's batting against West Indies in 1968–69 stamped him as the best of the Australian players alongside Lawry and Walters, Bob Cowper having retired because of business commitments. When Ray Illingworth brought the MCC team to Australia in 1970–71, Ian's brother, Greg, made a splendid century on his Test debut at the WACA, and at the end of the series Ian was made captain of the Australian side after Lawry was dropped following the Adelaide Test. Ian was having lunch in a café when a phone call came from a journalist friend to tell him he was now captain of Australia and that Bill Lawry had been replaced by Ken Eastwood in the team.

Ian's initial reaction was to think of the circumstances and to say they would never get him as they had 'Phanto'. He meant it, too, and made certain that couldn't happen by announcing his own retirement as Australian captain in 1975.

Ian was one of the best five captains I have on my short list, the others being Keith Miller, who never captained Australia, Ray Illingworth and Mike Brearley of England, and Mark Taylor, who has done an outstanding job in modern times for Australia. Taylor remained a victim of the Australian Cricket Board's decision to separate the national captaincy between Tests and one-day matches.

Sir Donald Bradman resigned as an Australian selector at the end of that season, 1970–71, and the new selection committee was Phil Ridings, Neil Harvey and Sam Loxton. They chose the Australian team to tour England in 1972 when some outstanding cricket was played, other than on the Headingley pitch which was said to have been struck by fusarium blight the week prior to the match. Not that Australians were able to cast too many stones at overseas curators following the pitch-watering episode of 1954–55, and the one about to happen at the 'Gabba in 1974–75 when

Brisbane's Lord Mayor, Clem Jones, a frustrated curator-grounds-man, sacked the regular man at the 'Gabba ten days before the First Test and took over the job himself.

I had to call into the 'Gabba the afternoon before the game started, and there was Clem, on his hands and knees at the Vulture Street End, 'puddling' a small area of the pitch. It is apparently a well-known word, although not necessarily by groundsmen, for a method used in making watertight coverings for embankments, or lining ditches, canals, ponds or pools. I doubt if it has caught on with modern-day groundsmen since Clem's retirement!

In 1970 we had the Boots Business in NSW, one of the more extraordinary matters of cricket administration in the time I have been in the game; hilarious, too, in many ways. As it happened, I was in on it right from the start. I was passing through the executive room of the NSW Cricket Association, in the old Members' Stand at the SCG, when a New South Wales player dropped a catch at first slip. Two of those present in the room were NSW delegates to the Australian Cricket Board. Their considered opinion on the matter was, as they conveyed it to me, that the reason the catch had been dropped was because the fieldsman was wearing the new-style boots with the ripple-rubber heels.

These boots were very popular with the players who wore them, and they were widely regarded by sports-medicine experts as being ideal for cricket, because they put far less stress on players' knees and some muscles than conventional boots. They were unpopular with the administrators because they were different, something new. I pointed out that I'd actually worn them and thought they were good, but there was no response: they were too busy talking about the benefits of sturdy boots, made of leather and with solid uppers and spikes in the sole and heel.

The administrators actually banned the NSW team from wearing the boots, and did so the day prior to a match. My brother tried a new pair of the sturdy jobs, and found they blistered his feet. Because he then switched back to the 'spikes in the sole, ripple-heels', he was dropped from the captaincy of the NSW team and from the team for the Southern Tour. One of the team on that tour, John Rogers, wearing the regulation boots which didn't violate any NSWCA by-laws, fell when fielding a ball in the WA second innings, tore ligaments in his ankle and therefore was unable to play in the following game against South Australia at the Adelaide Oval. This little mishap was then highlighted by the fact that South Australia beat the newly shod NSW cricketers by 195 runs, with ten of the 'Sacas' wearing the boots which NSW players were precluded from wearing.

All this was a total nonsense, brought on by an overwhelming and overbearing urge by administrators to stamp their authority on players – nothing new about that in 1970, but it did lead to some interesting aspects in the game and its sidelines.

Syd Webb, QC, was a keen racing man as well as a cricket administrator and, as noted earlier, he had been my team manager in 1961. He was surprised, shocked, and maybe even appalled, when he found that Australian cricket teams touring England had been traditionally known by English cricket followers as Darling's team, Noble's team, Gregory's team, Armstrong's team, Collins's team, Woodfull's team and Bradman's team. That had continued after Bradman with Hassett and Johnson and it was hardly likely to change with Benaud, no matter what the legal stature of the manager or his position as an administrator in Australia. When the Board, or rather those with a feel for these things, sent Ray Steele as assistant manager in 1961, it turned out they knew more than I did. The phrase, 'it's the Board's team not the captain's' has a memorable ring to it to this day.

Syd and I finished up OK, but we had our moments during that 1961 tour, with his claim prior to the Second Test that the Board had instructed him to take over all media announcements. The ensuing 'gagging of the captain' provided a lot of amusement for many people, but not quite as much for me because I was having awful problems with my shoulder and was trying to get fit for the Lord's Test.

Nine years later, in 1970, Syd was Chairman of the NSWCA Executive, and along with Alan Barnes, Secretary of the NSWCA, he was having a 'boots' disciplinary meeting with my brother John. The meeting began with Syd telling JB in firm and decisive tones where he had gone wrong with the boots business. Unfortunately, in the course of making his various points about immaturity and other demerits, he twice called John 'Richie' instead of John. It was that sort of meeting: things didn't improve.

Shortly after this, and following an Australian Cricket Board meeting, Syd met up with racing writer Pat Farrell at Randwick races. I knew Pat well because he was turf editor of the *Daily Mirror*, the afternoon newspaper in Sydney. Syd chatted to him and told him that, at the recent Board meeting, 'he and the other NSW delegates had received unanimous backing from the other Board members for sacking John Benaud because of the boots business, and the fact that he wasn't any good as a captain anyway.'

Pat, a cricket devotee as well as a racing journalist, listened and made his shorthand notes in the settling pages of his racebook, but was actually far more concerned about backing a winner in the next race than listening to Syd go on and on about the Board. At any rate, he detailed the conversation and a few other racing matters in a column the next day and it did catch my attention. So much so that I immediately telephoned two of the Board members and put Farrell's column to them and asked for their reaction to Syd's remarks.

'Absolute nonsense,' was the reply. 'The Board wasn't in the slightest interested in parochial NSW business, it was nothing at all to do with us and it simply wasn't mentioned at all.'

I phoned Farrell, had him read out to me his shorthand notes from the racebook and then I wrote a column of my own, setting out various matters.

The following Tuesday, at the NSWCA delegates' meeting, those present were told no one had spoken to Farrell about cricket. Many have said to me there seemed no need to resign my life membership of the NSWCA because JB had been banned. Quite right: it would have been needless and it would also have been stupid. I resigned the membership because it had been said that Pat Farrell was a liar and had published something he knew to be false. The NSWCA accepted that this was so.

25

ASHES TO ASHES, DUST TO DUST, IF LILLEE DON'T GET YA, THOMMO MUST

ENGLAND had a splendid time at home against India and Pakistan in 1974 but it was very much a prelude to the MCC tour of Australia in 1974–75, a contest which was looking good because of the manner in which the Australians, under some brilliant captaincy from Ian Chappell, had beaten the West Indies in the Caribbean in 1973. My brother was in the Australian team on that latter tour but only played in the final Test because of injury to Keith Stackpole.

John had made it into the touring team in slightly bizarre fashion. He played in the First Test against Pakistan and made 24, then was out for 13 in the first innings of the Second Test in Melbourne.

On the third day of that match at the MCG it was announced Benaud had been dropped for the following Test in Sydney. Ian Chappell changed the batting order in the second innings in Melbourne, put JB in at three and he was 11 not out at the close of play. The next day he made 142, one of the best innings you will see, and was included in the touring party for the West Indies.

In JB's book *Matters of Choice*, written in 1997, the chapter called 'Chappelli' is compulsive reading.

John retired after that tour of the Caribbean and became editor of the John Fairfax-owned *Sun* newspaper in Sydney, having risen to the top job after starting as a copy-boy in the early 1960s; the newspaper is now only a memory since young 'Wokka' Fairfax decided to try to privatise the family business.

Ian Chappell's West Indian tour and its success, as well as problems, was taking our attention in the press box at Old Trafford early on the morning of 6 June 1974, the first day of the First Test between England and India. I was imbibing strong tea with John Thicknesse, the *Evening Standard* correspondent, a good writer with sound cricket knowledge and often forthright opinions which he managed to put into print.

The points at issue that day concerned Dennis Lillee and a chap called Jeff Thomson. Lillee had damaged his back in the West Indies in the opening game against Jamaica where his only wicket, late on the first day, was Michael Holding's. In the First Test, at Sabina Park, Lillee was about half rat-power, suffered severe back damage in the game against the Leeward Islands and didn't play again on the tour. There was no certainty he would ever play again. John Thicknesse wanted to know about Lillee, so I told him that until a week ago Dennis had been in a plaster cast from waist to shoulder. I added that Thomson, the other name he had mentioned, was possibly the fastest bowler I had seen since Tyson and Hall, but that he was all over the place.

Thomson at this stage had played in one Test and had been disappointing. During that match he seemed to have some trouble with putting down his left foot, and X-rays taken a week after the Test showed he had a broken bone sustained in a match the previous week. I did say I had seen Thomson bowl, and when they could get him off the beach and out of the surf, he looked a very good prospect.

'Thickers' scoffed at this and gave me something of a burst, and I did feel like offering an apology for having the temerity to suggest such a thing, but it turned out to be not all that wide of the mark. 'Thommo' was quite deceptive: what he did was, to put it in his own words, 'sort of shuffle up and go whang.' He 'whanged' faster than most!

As it happened, John Thicknesse had been commissioned to

write the foreword for *Wisden* 1976 on the MCC tour of Australia, and after the tour he was profuse in his praise of Thomson and of Lillee, the latter having managed to make a comeback. Thomson took 33 wickets at 17 apiece, Lillee 25 at 23 and Max Walker 23 at 29. They were irresistible. I was permitted to raise an eyebrow to Thickers at the end of the tour, not so much because of Lillee, whom we all knew might be a success if his badly damaged back had recovered, but because of Thomson.

My interest in Thommo was, initially, only second-hand. My brother had phoned me one morning in 1971 to say he had no doubt Thomson was the fastest bowler in Australia; he had seen him in a club match at Bankstown Oval and he had bowled with searing pace. Warren Saunders, an ex-NSW player, told me the same thing. Warren had his jaw broken by Thomson in a match at Hurstville Oval, and as soon as he could mumble a few words he was on the phone to tell state selector Neil Harvey that Thomson was the fastest bowler in the country.

In 1971–72 in Australia, when the players were jousting for selection in the 1972 team to tour England, Thomson was playing grade cricket with Bankstown-Canterbury, the club that would nurture all the Waugh brothers. Although he was the highest wicket-taker in the Sydney club competition, Thomson didn't gain a lot of publicity because he was so inaccurate; that, and his laid-back attitude, which occasionally had him and his mate Len Pascoe arrive at the ground after the scheduled starting time, each of them toting a surfboard and, possibly, a sun-bleached blonde companion.

With Pakistan arriving in Australia for the 1972–73 summer, and with the tour of the West Indies beckoning, there was much interest in the fast-bowling make-up of the Australian team. In October 1972 the NSW selectors chose Thomson for the Interstate Colts match against Queensland in Sydney, that game to be played at the SCG No. 2 because the No. 1 ground was still recovering from football. I had never seen Thommo bowl, so I went out to watch the first day when Queensland won the toss and batted. His figures the first day were 5–79 and he was very inaccurate, but boy, was he quick!

Two months later he was making his debut for Australia, against Pakistan in the match mentioned above, when my brother hit his 142; Thomson took 0–100 from 17 overs, and they found out later about the injury. He must have been in agony, because the break was so bad he could play no first-class cricket again that summer and it wasn't until the final game of the next Sheffield Shield season in 1973–74 that he enjoyed a sensational return and took 7–85 and 2–40 in 31 overs of blistering speed.

Perhaps John Thicknesse was right to scoff at my rating of Thomson in 1974: he was pretty well unheard of, especially in England. He had played only seven first-class matches, and no English cricketer looking forward to the tour of Australia had any idea of what he was about to do. Jeffrey Robert Thomson finished with 200 Test match wickets, a remarkable effort considering that only four years after his debut he suffered that awful injury to his bowling shoulder when colliding with Alan Turner at the Adelaide Oval, the pair of them trying to catch Zaheer Abbas off Thomson's bowling. He was a match-winner, and his partnership with Lillee goes down in Australian cricket history alongside Gregory and McDonald, and Lindwall and Miller.

26

LET THERE BE LIGHT

I T was Monday, 5 January 1998 when Shane Warne took his 300th wicket in Test cricket at the SCG, having started his career, almost to the day, six years earlier. This was a momentous occasion: a wonderful talent had been on show, and the ball with which he dismissed Jacques Kallis was worthy of the congratulations and the adulation which followed. It was especially pleasing to me that Warne should have achieved this milestone on the ground where I had played all my home cricket and, as a sideline, a ground which in the previous twelve months had improved immeasurably as regards pitch and outfield condition.

Pleased as I was for Warne, I was even more delighted by one other aspect of the game, which was that it had finished at 7.09 p.m. in conditions poor enough that the lights had been turned on by the umpires under the new playing condition passed by the International Cricket Council. Test cricket under lights – who would have believed it twenty years before that moment? Certainly not the Australian Cricket Board when they were at loggerheads with World Series Cricket. This was the ground where, at the beginning of Kerry Packer's WSC, there had been so much trouble with the installation of the lights. The Establishment, knowing they were a key ingredient, fought hard to stop them being put up, but WSC, with NSW State Government intervention, finally saw them installed.

On 28 November 1978, I was present at the inaugural match between Australia and the West Indies. I arrived at the ground two hours before the start of play scheduled for 2.15 p.m., anticipating, because reserved ticket sales had been outstanding, that there could be a problem with traffic, even over the couple of miles between Coogee where we live and Moore Park where the SCG is situated. By one o'clock, traffic jams were building up on all the roads leading to Moore Park and enquiries established that this was not due to any roadwork problems or accidents, but simply to hundreds of cars, all of them aiming for Moore Park and the SCG.

Nowadays there is a ceiling crowd figure of 40,000 at the SCG, but that didn't apply in 1978, and by the time we were moving towards the tea, or, as it became known in WSC, the dinner interval, there was a crowd of around 25,000 actually in the ground, thousands more were clamouring to be let in and traffic by now was really banking up on the feeder roads and the lights were beginning to take effect. Mr Packer arrived before the dinner interval and instead of the normal situation where ground authorities would close the gates for a sell-out crowd, he instructed they be opened to the public and we were estimating up in the television box that around 50,000 people were in the ground. The Hill was packed, the outer was packed, the Members' Stands were packed and it was one of the most wonderful sights I have seen.

The match itself was a low-scoring one. West Indies were slaughtered for only 128, Australia made the runs without any great difficulty, and seven hours after the first ball had been bowled, the winning run was hit.

The attraction of the day-night match, the excitement of the lights and the wonderful atmosphere combined to make it an evening I'll never forget, and after I had finished wrapping up the television commentary and the highlights, I walked around the back of the Noble Stand and into the Old Members, up the stairs and into the NSWCA Executive Room, where Daphne had already arrived.

I poured a couple of glasses of white Burgundy and we took them over to the corner where Kerry Packer was standing. The atmosphere was calm, even reflective.

'What did you think?' he said quietly to us.

We each raised our glass in a silent toast. The gesture covered

632 days of excitement and problems, strain and pleasure, and now a win as conclusive as that shortly before achieved by Australia.

We had first heard about World Series Cricket on 6 April 1977, a week after I had bumped into Kerry Packer at the Australian Golf Club where we were both members. He was in conversation with Mark McCormack, whom I had known for many years.

The ideas for World Series Cricket were put to me at a meeting at Australian Consolidated Press a week later; I said I found the concept extremely interesting, possibly exciting, that it ran along-side my ideas about Australian cricketers currently being paid far too little and having virtually no input into the game in Australia. I added to Mr Packer that I would go back and discuss the propo-sition with my wife and let him have an answer the next day. He reminded me that at the start of the discussion I had agreed the matter would be completely confidential and that was the way it must remain – no discussion with anyone, wife included. Daphne and I worked together in the consultancy business, so I told Kerry we would make the decision together and that I would come back to him the next day with the answer, which I did.

The answer was yes and we were looking forward to being part of it. I also gave him some notes which, in retrospect, turned out to be spot on for accuracy concerning the administrators who ran Australian cricket at that time, and listing Bradman, Steele and Parish as outstanding. As well, I mentioned the type of reaction which could be expected from the Australian Board and the type of letter which should be written to them to apprise them of what was happening.

As I was going out of the door Mr Packer's voice followed me: 'Excuse me, you haven't said what your fee will be . . .'

Although I knew Australian players at this time were financially treated poorly by the Australian Cricket Board, I hadn't actually realised the extent of their dissatisfaction. Apparently it had come to a head eight years earlier when Australia had toured India and South Africa, and although there was a profit to the Board of more than a quarter of a million dollars, the players received paltry amounts. They weren't alone. In England just prior to the start of World Series Cricket, a county player earned less than the average wage. West Indies cricketers were paid poorly, as were the stars from the subcontinent.

Between saying yes to the WSC proposal and the start of the next season there were many things to do, one of which was to cover the Australian cricket tour of England for the BBC and various newspapers and magazines whilst running our own sports consultancy. Daphne and I arrived in England in late April, stayed with the Morleys in Knightsbridge and kept a close eye on various happenings in the cricket world. We were very busy.

Much has been chronicled concerning the lead-up to the announcement of World Series Cricket, and it appears to have been a combined breaking story between journalists Peter McFarline and Alan Shiell. However, the first intimation I had that the story was to hit the streets was when the English sports writer Ian Wooldridge phoned me at the Morleys'. He said he was about to publish a big story in the London *Daily Mail* concerning a breakaway cricket movement, and did I have any information on it. I told him I'd ring him back as I was a bit busy at that moment. I didn't know about McFarline and Shiell then, and Wooldridge seemed to be the one with the story: the facts he had listed over the phone were substantially correct, although there were some minor omissions.

That 1977 summer in England revolved as much around the High Court as the cricket field. Justice Slade's judgement when handed down was not unexpected to me after I had listened to the background of other court cases. A precedent had been set twelve years earlier with the case of Florence Nagle, the would-be racehorse trainer, asking for the right to work; in 1963 there was the landmark George Eastham restraint-of-trade case; and, a year prior to that, a natural-justice verdict to do with decisions concerning the suspensions of players by sporting clubs. In the light of those matters it would have been unusual if the plaintiffs, Tony Greig, Mike Procter and John Snow, had not won their case against the defendants, the Test and County Cricket Board and Doug Insole. They do say, though, that you should assume nothing in legal matters.

A lot of people will tell you courtroom battles are boring, and I
suppose some might be, but not this one, with Robert Alexander
and Andrew Morritt as Counsel for the plaintiffs. It provided me
with some most interesting insights and every night I took home
the transcripts of the day and studied them. When I saw anything
that didn't seem to gel, I made a note and brought it up with
Robert Alexander and the instructing solicitors the next morning at the pre-court conference. Some were small matters, others
more important, and finally we even finished up with the exact
number of people present at the meeting in the Long Room at
Lord's, and which of them were visible and what they were doing.
Unfortunately, I had to leave before the Slade verdict was delivered in order to sort out with Lynton Taylor the matter of the
pitches and grounds in the various states in Australia.

Daphne had returned to Australia at this stage, and with
Barbara Loois, Irene Cave and others was setting up the complex
but small-staffed and very efficient WSC administration office
which turned out to be a vital part of the organisation's success.

That success was elusive in the first year of WSC, but as the
day-night matches gathered pace, and spectator numbers rose and
television ratings soared, things started to move very quickly.

David Hill was in charge of the cricket telecasts, which started
out as innovative and then kept on improving until these days they
have set the standards which others have copied, sometimes intro-
ducing new techniques with different camera lenses. World Series
Cricket did a great deal for the players and shaped a considerable
amount of the cricket we see today.

Coaching of the game has intensified, in general terms in a good
fashion, but sometimes along the lines of it becoming an industry.
New sponsors have realised, as a direct offshoot of WSC, that
cricket is a game with which they should be involved. The judgement in the WSC court case was a direct reflection on the fact
that monopolies were good neither for the game nor the players,
and the latter are much better off now that the old-style relationship has, to a certain extent, been changed. Players are no longer
precluded from pursuing a professional livelihood in a proper

fashion, a situation different from those employer–employee relationships in existence pre-1977. They are also flexing a few muscles, not without argument from administrators, but that is nothing new.

The best result from WSC came from the fact that if they are good enough, players are able to secure regular employment at higher standards of remuneration, and that the best players, the stars, are better off. Many players now, depending on their form and the choices of the selectors, will stay on longer in the game. Selection will always be the final arbiter, but there were many good players lost to the game before 1977 because they simply couldn't afford to keep playing.

27

FAVOURITE REFLECTIONS

THREE captains have offered good advice in different ways over recent years on matters about which I was aware but needed reminding. A. R. Lewis said to me that captaincy is two people, not one: the captain himself and his senior and most trusted follower. I related to that instantly with the happy circumstance of having Neil Harvey as my vice-captain.

Ian Chappell offered the thought that when a captain is involved in a decision about declaring his innings, he needs to remember the most important thing is to declare rather than close. To dangle a carrot in your declaration, so that, whilst giving yourself a good chance of winning, you also automatically open up the game for the opposition. He added that a closure was quite different, it meant you were closing one team, the opposition, out of the game.

There was one other thing Chappell said, and it is something Mark Taylor touched on as well in the aftermath of his batting problems and then his century at Edgbaston in 1997. Chappell said the most important thing he had discovered about himself, and about successful athletes, was that they are themselves and they don't try to be anything else. Discussing the innings he played in 1997 at Edgbaston, in his book *A Captain's Year*, Mark Taylor said his problem during the bad patch had been that he was going out there and trying to play like someone else, playing as others thought he should play, that he had tried every possible thing except batting like himself, something he had forgotten how to do. He then made a century.

An interesting addition which I liked concerned the fax Taylor had received from the Australian swimming champion Kieren

Perkins, which, apart from wishing him luck before the start of that Test, contained some excellent advice. A few weeks earlier Perkins had triumphed in the Olympic 1,500 metres freestyle final in Atlanta, against all the odds and predictions of the doom-sayers and the knockers. The message he sent Taylor was totally to ignore those people and beware of the FUD factor they create – Fear, Uncertainty, Doubt – and to remember, despite the hyperbole with which some people laud Talent, Genius and Education, nothing in the world can take the place of Persistence and Determination – a delightful and wonderfully accurate extension of 'do your best and never give up'.

There is no better example of the latter phrase than Headingley in 1981, where I was commentating for BBC and writing for the *News of the World* and Ian Botham won the game for England. I know it's a team game and Bob Willis took the second-innings wickets, and Mike Brearley captained the team with skill and panache, but this was Botham's match.

The England players sensibly checked out of their hotel on the fourth morning, which didn't mean they had totally given up, but they were looking realistically at the situation.

Australia had enforced the follow-on and were racing towards victory, Ladbrokes were offering 500–1 about England's chances, and Botham turned it all around with a remarkable 149*, with assistance from others, to the stage where Brearley and Willis exerted their own expertise.

Botham was magnificent, and Jim Laker shared my view that this was the finest Test on which we had worked. The climax, with Brearley marshalling his men, and Willis, 8–43, steaming in from the Kirkstall Lane End, was one of the more exciting events in Test cricket history. Botham's performance as an allrounder was superb – and all that after the England selectors, only two weeks earlier, had relieved him of the England captaincy and he had made a pair in the Lord's Test, trudging off the famous ground and through the Long Room in complete silence.

The same players were involved in another memorable commentary match two years later when England won a tight encounter at the MCG by three runs. Bob Willis was captain and he needed to break the last-wicket stand between Allan Border and Jeff Thomson, which already had added 37 by the end of the fourth day. There were 18,000 spectators present on the last day, with only the one wicket to fall and another 37 required for an Australian win. I was commentating when Willis turned to Botham for one last desperate attempt with Australia within four runs of victory.

Botham turned the trick with a ball Thomson parried to Tavare at slip and he knocked the ball up for Miller to take the catch. It was Botham's 100th Test wicket against Australia, to go with his 1,000-plus runs against the old enemy, something done previously only by Wilfred Rhodes. This was a gripping match and I have always counted myself as very lucky to have seen two games containing such excitement in the space of eighteen months.

The pleasure of commentating on outstanding players comes also with batsmen like Sachin Tendulkar, whom I saw make his first Test century at Old Trafford in 1990, and Mohammad Azharuddin, who hit 121 and 179 in the same series – sheer delight, and they both played brilliantly in Australia as well the following year when Warne made his Test debut.

I have commentated on few more exciting games of cricket than the one in Adelaide in the 1992–93 season when West Indies beat Australia by one run. Australia needed 186 to win, seven of their batsmen in the second innings totalled only 22 between them, Justin Langer on his debut made a second-innings 54, Mark Waugh 26 and then Tim May, batting with a broken finger, finished with 42 not out having destroyed the West Indian second innings with 6.5–3–9–5. With two needed for victory Craig McDermott was caught behind when a short-pitched delivery flicked his glove, a very good decision by umpire Darrell Hair, and the fighting 40-run partnership between McDermott and May was in vain.

The other two matches which have been memorable for me were ones where I *wasn't* commentating. They were the games at Sabina Park, Jamaica in 1995 and Port Elizabeth in March 1997. Daphne and I went to the Caribbean in late March of 1995 where

I delivered the Frank Worrell Memorial Address in Barbados during the First Test match. Mark Taylor was captaining the side in a four-match series and West Indies were close to unbeatable at the time, but on this occasion the lively pitch posed problems for them and the Australians won in three days. We then left for Sarasota in Florida, where I am the patron of the Sarasota International Cricket Club, a small but splendid organisation run by a Welshman, Laurence Parry. The club does things brilliantly and the members have a lot of fun.

From there we went to France, and as luck would have it, most sport was cancelled in the United Kingdom that week because of rain. At the same time the Australians were playing West Indies at Sabina Park in the fourth and final game of the series. Sky-TV, through TWI, decided to televise the whole of the Test from the West Indies and the coverage was brilliant from every point of view, with outstanding production. Richie Richardson made 100 for the Windies and Mark Waugh and Steve Waugh made 126 and 200 for Australia, then West Indies were bowled out for 213 in their second innings.

It was, by coincidence, around the time for a glass of wine with friends, and we were able to raise our glasses to Mark Taylor at the same moment as he lifted the Frank Worrell Trophy. It was almost thirty-four years since Frank had first handed it to me at the ceremony at the MCG hosted by Sir Donald Bradman with Michael Charlton as the master of ceremonies. It was a moving moment, being able to toast Australia and Taylor in a country which was at that time working hard to become an Associate Member of the ICC.

Almost two years later I was in Coogee when the Australian team, led by Taylor, were in South Africa. I was watching Foxtel pay-TV and the Australians were deep in trouble in the Test at Port Elizabeth. South Africa had a first-innings lead of 101 then they were bowled out for 168, with Jason Gillespie having match figures of 8–103.

The Australians still needed 270 to win, a daunting task in the fourth innings of a Test. Mark Waugh was seeing them through, and around midnight, at 258–5, I broke the rule of a lifetime about not moving when things are going well and of assuming nothing. I went to the refrigerator and poured a glass of wine in order to be ready for the celebrations. The next thing I knew Waugh was out, Warne also and Bevan. It was now 265–8 and I walked back to the fridge and placed the glass of Chardonnay on a shelf.

I doubt if Jason Gillespie will forget what happened next because he played one of the best innings of his life . . . and made 0 not out. He played a maiden from Jacques Kallis.

At the other end Ian Healy hit Hansie Cronje's third ball for six over square-leg and I retrieved my glass and raised it from afar. It was one of the more tense moments I have known, probably because I wasn't working.

It is very important to keep a clear head when you are working, and in that sense I have been very fortunate that, in working in the print media and television for fifty-odd years, I have been able to look on every match as being between two cricket teams, rather than, where it might be applicable, us and them. I believe one of the worst words a commentator can use is 'we', because there is no such thing in a contest where you are adding to the picture for the viewing public.

I thoroughly enjoyed the opportunity again to be in India and Pakistan for the 1996 World Cup and to watch the manner in which the Sri Lankans played on their way to becoming champions. They were very good, as were the Australians in England in 1997. Back in Australia in 1997–98, there was a splendid summer when the New Zealanders and South Africans toured.

The Australians came back well in England in 1997 after losing the opening Test at Edgbaston. It was a performance full of character, as was Mark Taylor's comeback. When, back in Australia, Judy Taylor, Mark's wife, backed her husband to make a century, part of that could be put down to hope rather than certainty, but I imagine it was a wonderful moment for all the family, as well as his many supporters.

It was slightly different for the Australian journalist across the other side of the ground at Edgbaston: he had taken the odds of

25–1 against Taylor reaching three figures and had a very large wager on it. As he also backed the Derby winner and collected thousands, it made small punters and fellow journalists like Gray and me sit up and take notice, as well as offering warm congratulations.

28

THE END OF AN AUSTRALIAN ERA

ALTHOUGH it was a good match, the final Test between Australia and Pakistan at the SCG in 1984 was notable for one other very significant fact: three of Australia's greatest cricketers retired from Test cricket at the same time. Greg Chappell, Dennis Lillee and Rod Marsh called it a day at the end of that match, some notable achievements to their names and in their careers. All three were great cricketers, as distinct from being merely very good.

I watched Greg Chappell hit a magnificent 182 to pass Bradman's highest aggregate for Australia in Tests, and, at the same time, become the first cricketer to score a century both on his debut and in his final Test innings. Greg Chappell was an outstanding batsman and no one could have played better than he did for his 131 in the Lord's Test of 1972 when the Australians were fighting back after the Ashes had been lost to Ray Illingworth's side in 1971. Among many wonderful innings I saw him play, that was my favourite. At The Oval in that series, while I was commentating for BBC Television, Greg (113) and Ian (131) provided the first instance of brothers hitting Test centuries in the same game, a performance which allowed the Australians to square the series.

During the 1984 Sydney Test I witnessed Lillee become the first cricketer to pass 350 Test wickets. He went on to 355, and by an extraordinary coincidence Marsh took the catch to give Lillee the 355th and his own 355th Test victim as wicketkeeper. The Marsh–Lillee combination captured 95 victims from 1971 to

1984, unchallenged by any other wicketkeeper-bowler pairing.

To lose three players of this quality at the one time was a real blow to Australian cricket, and although no one is irreplaceable, it did take a considerable time for proper reserves to be found, particularly as there were problems with Kim Hughes and the captaincy, from which he resigned in 1984. Spasmodically the Australians would provide some hope for the selectors, but the period up to the World Cup in India in 1987 was not good for Australia's players or cricket followers.

The World Cup win made a big difference, and then, when Allan Border sensibly exerted his authority as captain in 1989, the side became considerably tougher. He was a fine cricketer, hard but fair, sometimes uncompromising, but at the same time an entertainer, and he lifted the team on that 1989 tour after Mike Gatting's side had retained the Ashes in Australia in 1987.

The loss of the Ashes that year was not taken well by Australians because England, in a short period, had lost ten successive Test matches in 1984 and 1985–86 against West Indies when David Gower had been captain – two lots of 'blackwash', yet in 1985 and 1986–87 they had beaten the Australians in England and Australia.

When Border took the side to the UK in 1989 he was not prepared to be a nice guy and lose. He said so and laid his plans accordingly, successfully too. Part of the planning came in the opening Test at Headingley where the decision was made to open with Geoff Marsh and Mark Taylor and bat David Boon at three.

One of the bonuses of that tour was to have the Chairman of Selectors, Laurie Sawle, as team manager. Laurie had been instrumental in having Boon drop to number three four months earlier, in the final Test of the summer in Australia against West Indies, so that Taylor would open with Marsh. It was no surprise when Sawle stood out for the same thing the night before the Headingley Test. Taylor made 839 runs in the series and the right-hand/left-hand opening partnership was a real success.

Border captained Australia very well that summer and

throughout the remainder of his career. He was one of the finest Australian cricketers, and it was always a real pleasure to watch him play, and have the chance to be a commentator for matches in which he was taking part.

29

BEING THERE

T HE high point for writers and radio commentators comes in being there, capturing the moment and being able to describe it in word pictures for those not so fortunate. It is slightly different for me and for other television commentators. The ideal from my point of view is certainly to be on the spot, but the difference is that I want to have the expertise to add to whatever is on the screen. Viewers observe for themselves what has happened, to have the excitement of one instant wash over them as the audience, and then, if necessary, have the commentator add something which will be of value.

Working in television for so many years, I have been lucky to set the scene and watch many fine performances. I have also seen many new things, and I hope and expect to see many more before I finish. One such was the tournament in Sharjah in 1998 where I went to assist in the WorldTel television coverage, and it was a very interesting and exciting affair. I had never been to Sharjah before, had never seen a tournament played over a week on one ground and certainly had never before been involved in the rather strange hours needed to make it all work.

It was there I watched two of the greatest innings I have ever seen played in limited-overs cricket: Sachin Tendulkar was the batsman and he hit two centuries. The first, in which he guided, or blasted, India to the final, was a classic. So was the second century, for that matter, but the first, with him knowing that millions of viewers in India were sitting in front of television sets, willing him to succeed, was quite something.

I thought I had seen just about everything in cricket, but it is always unwise to think along those lines. The Australians led by Steve Waugh had played well and India not quite as well. India had to win the last game of the preliminary series against Australia and New Zealand to make the final; Australia's recent record against them was good and the Indian team led by Mohammad Azharuddin were wilting. There was only one man who could carry them through.

I have seen snow on the ground at Buxton, hail covering the whole of Lord's like a lovely cold, white blanket, sea-frets at Scarborough, ferocious rain and hail in Brisbane with the covers washed down to the fence at the Stanley Street End. Until this night I had never seen a desert sandstorm. Sharjah and Dubai are built on sand, and just outside the beautifully grassed areas, as is the case with Palm Springs, is desert.

There were 26,000 fervent Indian supporters in the ground that night, though the ceiling spectator figure is 20,000. When Tendulkar began demolishing the Australian bowlers with one of the most dynamic of batting performances, suddenly the sandstorm whipped in and players were forced to lie on the ground and crouch with their backs to the wind. No one could possibly play cricket. The worst aspect was that under the playing conditions India's scoring rate was just behind Australia's, and that would have kept them from the final, no matter what Tendulkar might have done.

Fortunately for everyone, the storm blew away and the game restarted. You wouldn't have thought Tendulkar had seen or felt it. He continued as though it had merely been a drinks break!

It was the most glorious exhibition of batting and ranks with two other innings I saw from Viv Richards over the years in limited-overs matches. There is, though, a cautionary end to the tale. The opinion was later expressed that Tendulkar's batting that night, then in the final, and what he had done in the Tests against Australia, had lifted him to a level not seen in the past fifty years. 'THE GREATEST SINCE BRADMAN', the headlines screamed.

Well, hang on a second, there have been some useful batsmen around over the years since The Don hung up his boots. I throw into the ring for starters the name of Garfield Sobers. I would follow him with Vivian Richards, and there are a few others in the background as well. Sachin is a wonderful cricketer, brilliant in the field, a superb batsman, and don't chuckle when I say it, a very good legspin bowler. I was extremely impressed with what I saw from him as a bowler when I watched the final Test between India and Australia in 1998 on television, then again in Sharjah.

When I started in television in 1963 fast bowling was in the ascendancy. Spinners were there, but not as the dominant force, and the West Indies, after their wonderful tour of Australia in 1960–61, were on their way up in world cricket. Their success under Frank Worrell continued under Garry Sobers and cricket's administrators viewed television with suspicion, believing it might keep people away from the turnstiles.

Over all those years in television there has been the usual ebb and flow of matches and tours, some wonderfully exciting, some less so, but all of them interesting. It often occasions surprise when, in answer to a question about commentating and whether or not I become bored, the answer is 'No.'

There have been very few days where I have gone home feeling disillusioned about a day's play. Something positive usually comes out of it, particularly if it involves a young player who suddenly has put up his hand and demanded that notice be taken of him, although some of these youngsters turn out to be shooting stars, fly-by-nighters.

Unfortunately, the public perception of a player's ability is often built up by what they read and hear in the media. If the player doesn't live up to all that hype, he is said to possess neither the skill nor the temperament required for the upper echelon of the game. What has happened is that the player has not lived up to the picture painted by someone who may have considerable or minimal knowledge of what goes on in the centre of a ground at international level, and has done the young player a disservice by painting him as a future champion, then knocking him down – the tall poppy syndrome.

From that point of view television is of vital importance,

because, other than being at the ground, it provides the only means for people to see for themselves, something newspapers and radio cannot do.

Cricket can be a lot of things to a lot of people as a sport, but never lose sight of the fact that luck plays a great part, and not merely on the field. Take Shane Warne as an example.

I first heard of Warne when he went to the West Indies in August 1990. Brian Taber, the coach, told me over lunch that he had seen an interesting young legspinner who had been at the Adelaide Academy, had experienced a few disciplinary problems but then had come through the Caribbean tour in excellent style. The report from tour manager Steve Bernard to the Australian selectors gave Warne a big wrap. It was Taber who with his knowledge of people had given Warne positions of responsibility on that youth tour and Warne had responded magnificently to the gesture.

Later in that Australian season he made his Sheffield Shield debut, against Western Australia in Melbourne, but didn't do much. I then went to England to cover the West Indies tour, and at the final Test at The Oval, Brendan McArdle, who played Sheffield Shield for Victoria, sent up a message to the commentary box asking if he and young Shane Warne could come up. Warne was playing with Accrington at the time, in the Lancashire League, and little snippets were reaching London that he was going OK.

We only had time for a short chat, but it was long enough for him, as a Victorian, to ask some advice on whether or not he should take a very good offer to move interstate. My advice to him was to stay with Victoria, purely because my old-fashioned instincts on the Sheffield Shield would not have allowed me to play other than for NSW, unless I had been forcibly moved by business to another state.

'Make a success of the important thing first, learn to bowl well before you start thinking about going anywhere,' I advised him.

My brother, who was a national selector at the time, was in charge of a team captained by Mark Taylor touring Zimbabwe, and Warne was included. He then made his Test debut against

India, took a belting from Ravi Shastri and Sachin Tendulkar but at the same time showed plenty of the attributes which were to take him to the top almost without an apprenticeship.

Towards the end of the summer Bill Lawry asked me if I would come to Melbourne for a special golf day he was arranging for the Victorian players and sponsors. It was a delightful day, almost as though Bill had specially turned on the Melbourne weather, and we had an excellent barbecue lunch, chatting with the sponsors and the cricketers.

When they announced the tee-times I walked with Shane across to the first tee, and in the course of the stroll he asked me if there was anything I could offer by way of advice. All I offered was that he should keep it simple and develop a fiercely spun leg-break as a stock ball. A ball which he could pitch perfectly at will, and which could therefore be used as both an attacking and a defensive weapon. I warned him it would take *four* years to do it properly. Like all champions he made a nonsense of such strictures and did it, 'on his ear', in *two*!

A month later Warne took 3–0 from 13 balls against Sri Lanka in the first Test in Colombo and the game was won by Border's team. It was an extraordinary victory. I was at Lord's at the time and the Texaco game between England and Pakistan was delayed by rain. The packed house was being kept up to date with the match in Colombo and there was continual high delight as the news came through that the Australians were being crushed, with Sri Lanka needing only 54 from 24 overs with eight wickets in hand. The final PA announcement was terse and to the point. 'Australia have won the Test in Colombo by 16 runs.' It was greeted with gloom, disbelief and muted applause.

Since that 3–0 Warne has done some wonderful things with the ball for Australia, none more so than dismissing Mike Gatting in 1993 at Old Trafford. It is rare for one ball to have such an effect on a Test series, particularly at the start of the five matches. Some have been so carried away by the delivery they say it spun a yard and was therefore unplayable. In fact, it spun about 14 inches and was almost unplayable. The real problem it posed for Gatting was that it moved as well, starting on middle and off and then swerving to a spot just outside leg stump before spinning back and hitting the off bail.

A dismissal I particularly enjoyed was the one with which he took the wicket of Shivnarine Chanderpaul at the SCG in 1996–97. The West Indians were right on target for a possible win or, at worst, a face-saving draw and Chanderpaul was batting beautifully. Immediately before lunch Warne bowled him a ball which did spin a yard. It was so wide that had it been a topspinner it would have been called wide, but instead, landing in the rough, it spun back and hit middle and off. It was close to the unplayable delivery and it snapped the West Indian resistance.

There have been others, stand-outs in Warne's career. Richie Richardson was one in Melbourne in the 1992–93 series in Australia when Warne dismissed him with a flipper which won the match, also Alec Stewart at the 'Gabba in 1994–95 when Shane had him with a slightly slower flipper which completely deceived the batsman. It was wonderful bowling.

Warne had Graham Gooch at Edgbaston in 1993 with a ball that pitched two feet wide of the leg stump, quite deliberately bowled at that spot, and whipped behind Gooch to hit leg stump. Gooch played Warne as well as anyone I have seen and he says the swerve Warne imparted to the ball was a big factor in the difficulty batsmen had in playing him, particularly as he had the ability to swerve the ball a lot, or a little. The other aspect Gooch talked about when I spoke to him some years ago was the difficulty in getting down the pitch to him because of the amount of side-spin he imparted to the ball.

There have been many theories about how best to play him, others on the matter of how he shouldn't be played. Above all he had control of that basic legspinner, the one that most of the time drifts towards the right-hander's pads and then spins from leg to off. The thing about Warne was that he would still have been difficult to play even if that had been the only ball in his armoury, but he had many others. Some he might not have possessed, but the batsman thought he had them, or at least couldn't be totally certain that he didn't have them. This in turn led to even more confusion and Warne did nothing to assist the opposition, nor should he have done.

If you want to be a good legspinner then concentrate on what Warne did and perfect that leg-break. That's not to say you will become as good as Warne, but you will improve and you could become a good bowler. What used to be a trickle of correspondence asking how to bowl leg-breaks became a flood when Warne began to captivate the watching audiences at the ground and the millions who watch on television. Even Warne, who was the best of his type to play the game and who did some things differently, adhered to many of the old-fashioned traits. Shane was an orthodox legspin bowler. He was, though, something else as well. He was an orthodox legspin bowler who combined a fiercely-spun leg-break with wonderful accuracy.

Comparisons are popular these days, and if you want to know how the respective merits of Warne and Benaud compare in regard to bowling, then you need look no further than one statistic. When Warne reached his 300th Test wicket he was playing in his 63rd Test, the same number I played in my whole career to take 248. Statistics sometimes lie, but definitely not this one: he is that much better than I was – and he went on to a total of 708 Test wickets. I had batting and fielding and captaincy to help me in any all-round ratings, but Warne is the best of his kind I've ever seen.

The earlier notes I have made about when I met Warne, and the other sidelights, lead me to emphasise that I am in the very good position of never having had anything to do with coaching him. The only times I offered him any advice were on the occasions when he asked, and fortunately he was so good that those occasions were rare. This stems from my determination when I retired never again to go into a dressing-room, on the basis that this area belongs to the players, which was exactly as I felt when I was playing. I have rarely departed from this, although one occasion was when Dennis Lillee broke my Australian Test wicket-taking record and I took a magnum of champagne in to him.

The night before the Lord's Test in 1997, Daphne and I had

a delightful meal with Shane and his parents, Brigitte and Keith, together with Allan Border and Austin Robertson, Shane's manager and a good friend. We walked around the corner from the Montcalm to Il Barbino, a small and delightful Italian restaurant, where I found it fascinating listening, and contributing a little, to a discussion between Warne and Border on various field-placings for batsmen and how Shane could improve on what had definitely been a below-par performance at Edgbaston. The Portuguese waiter at Il Barbino was one of the most avid followers of cricket in the United Kingdom, and was fascinated by the group and the shuffling of salt and pepper shakers and wine glasses to denote batsmen and fieldsmen.

On the occasions Shane did call to discuss a possible problem, or to check how he was bowling, I always tried to avoid a coaching answer in suggesting what, if anything, he should do. Instead I tried to pose him a question which would make him think about why the problem might exist. He has a sharp mind and he never missed coming up with the right answer to the few questions I posed. To me this approach is far preferable to providing a long, involved coaching answer. The important thing is that the player must be able to think and solve the problem for himself – there is no coach standing by your side in the centre of the ground if things aren't going right. The same arrangement existed between Dennis Lillee and me: I was always available to discuss a problem and be of assistance.

From the batsman's point of view, if you want to be able to play legspin well, then perfect your footwork. A leaden-footed batsman is manna from the cricket ground in the sky for a good over-the-wrist spinner, but you need good judgement as well. There have been many ideas floated about how best to play Warne and, as mentioned earlier, some of them have worked, some haven't. Poor footwork, however, means oblivion. One of the reasons Sachin Tendulkar has played so well against Warne and other bowlers is that his footwork is close to flawless.

The best players of slow bowling in my playing time were Neil Harvey and Arthur Morris. Being left-handers did them no harm against legspin bowling, but they were also wonderful players of offspin and any other type of spin. Harvey was brilliant against medium pace and fast bowling, his only detectable weakness was claimed to be that he was too attacking a player, that he didn't concentrate enough on grinding the opposition into the dust, and that he tried to score from many balls which could have been left alone. Precisely. Harvey was one of the greatest crowd-pleasers the cricket world has known.

It's my view that, in general terms of players I have seen since 1948, only batsmen like Harvey, Morris, or Sachin Tendulkar, Garry Sobers and Brian Lara, Mark Waugh and the Chappell brothers, Gooch and a few others would be equipped consistently to deal with a fully fit Warne. Others could do it on a piecemeal basis, and in fact have done so, and centuries were scored against him, some of them in attractive fashion but, to be able to do it consistently *and attractively*, is another thing.

I saw Harvey play some wonderful innings against spinners on pitches sometimes designed to favour spin, I felt the force of Garry Sobers's bat and brilliant skills, and I bowled against Ian Chappell in his early days. The others, Tendulkar, Lara, Mark Waugh, Gooch and Greg Chappell, I have watched, and they all had several angles to the fact they were fine players, but the most important was that their footwork, playing either back or forward or dancing down the pitch, was close to perfect.

There have been over-the-wrist spin bowlers who have turned the ball more than Warne – David Sincock for example, and Peter Philpott spun the ball a lot – but I have never seen anyone combine the amount of legspin achieved by Warne with such a degree of accuracy. It's not merely that he ran up and dropped it on the spot all the time: the spot varied with each batsman, but the result was the same, the ball dropped on the spot but it was the one worked out by Warne for each individual. That is the aim of every spin bowler who has walked on to a field, but very few have been able to achieve it.

Warne developed a number of variation balls, some for publicity, some for the more direct business of knocking batsmen over, and one of his skills seen in more recent times on spin-vision cameras and lenses was to vary the type of spin from side-spin to horizontal-spin, which is with the seam of the ball going towards the batsman in a flatter style.

On spin-vision cameras this delivery appears to be something *like* a leg-break; to the batsman it looks very much like one and it still drifts in the air from off to leg for the right-hander. However, it then skids straight on rather than spins as the leg-break does.

From all that I have read of the times around the late 1920s and early 1930s and from everything I have been told by those who knew him, Bradman was unique as a batsman and as a publicist for the game of cricket. This is no effort to compare Warne with him, but in Australia Warne had an extraordinary effect on the game of cricket. Warne was good for the game because he rejuvenated what was becoming a lost art, and most important he lifted the spirits of those who watch at the grounds and on television.

30

THE CLAW, AND OTHERS

ALAN Davidson, known generally as 'Davo', but also, because of his astonishing fielding, as 'the Claw', was a player with whom I almost grew up. We lived fifty miles from one another: he was at Lisarow near Gosford and I was at Parramatta, fifteen miles out of Sydney. He was a left-arm over-the-wrist spinner at Gosford High School, and I was a right-arm over-the-wrist spinner at Parramatta High. Alan and I used to work together in our practice sessions, although, because of the obvious differences in our bowling style, I would get through more physical work than he did. At the SCG we would be concentrating on bowling flat out in our own ways, and on accuracy. Somewhere along the line someone with a gift of foresight had turned Davo into a left-arm pace bowler who had a devastating inswinger and a ball which angled across towards the slip area. We were both hard hitters, 'dashing batsmen' was one term used about us when we were at school, and we both practised our fielding hour after spare hour until we were able to influence the selectors with that aspect of their team nomination.

We played together in the NSW team from 1949 onwards, with enough success to persuade the selectors there was some form of long-term investment to be made, but, as so often happens with this kind of thing, it wasn't until we were thrown in the deep end that we suddenly started to turn potential into reality. By the time that chance came along I had 73 Test wickets and Davidson had 16.

That tour of South Africa in 1957–58 was the turning point, and although statistics don't always tell the true story, they do in this case. From the moment we started as a double act in South Africa, and then bowled together over the five years to his retirement at the conclusion of the 1962–63 series, between us we took 333 Test wickets. He had a remarkable bowling average over that time, each of those 170 wickets cost him only 19.25 runs. At the other end I was far more liberal and conceded 25 runs per wicket, but the overall picture was one of being slightly on the niggardly side of things as regards offering runs to batsmen and taking wickets as well. Offered a choice, I suspect any legspinner would have felt as I did, and given anything for the opportunity to be at the end opposite to a bowler of Davidson's quality. Certainly, it made an enormous difference as captain to have him in my side.

I don't doubt, bowling my legspin at the other end, I was of some benefit to Davidson. I never had the slightest doubt that his left-arm pace bowling and skill was of immense benefit to me, and it showed over the six years of our combination. Not only was he a wicket-taker, but the pressure he applied with his accuracy allowed me great scope with tactics. Instead of having two spin bowlers on at the same time, I found opposition batsmen were keen to avoid facing Alan.

When he and I sat down to plan what methods he would use in the Tied Test series against the West Indies in 1960–61, it was a short and agreeable discussion: he wasn't to change his basic plan, but I wanted him to continue to keep the ball up to the bat in such a way that the West Indians would be drawn into the drive as their main stroke. Not much cutting and nothing on their pads. The cruel blow for us was that Alan damaged his hamstring in that Sydney Test, because he took 33 wickets in three and a half Tests when he was fit enough to be on the ground.

He will remain in Australia's history as one of the greatest cricketers ever to set foot on a ground for NSW and Australia.

Some of the matches I cover on television are perfectly straightforward, while some are more lighthearted. One such match was organised at the 'Gabba in 1993 for Allan Border, and Channel 9 used microphones on players and umpires as well as a camera in the umpires' hats. The latter concept was quickly shown to need more work, as a bobbing head doesn't provide a picture to compare with a camera placed in a motionless stump. Batsmen were able to talk to bowlers, commentators talked to both. When I was walking out to catch a taxi I was grabbed by a viewer who had been watching all this on television at the Cricketers' Club next door. He said how delighted I must be taking part in a day of such innovative television.

This was all very well, but I did have to explain gently to him that thirty-three years previously BBC Television had done all this at Lord's and Edgbaston in Lord's Taverners matches with Brian Johnston as link-man. Denis Compton and I had been 'miked-up' and gave a running commentary on what ball I would bowl to him, and he responded with what stroke he would play. In addition, we did the same thing without either being able to hear the other, though the television audience could hear both of us.

It shows that although there is a lot new in television, there is a lot that has been done before in the game of cricket, and much that needs to be explained. Similarly, it is 100 years since Charles Cowden Clarke edited a book which he called *Chronicles of Cricket*. It contained a fascinating, informative section on Nyren's *Cricketer's Guide* with splendid articles by Wm Lillywhite and W. Denison.

Often on television we will question whether the bowler really means what he is setting up superficially as a 'trap', or whether it is a bluff, or even a double bluff. Take, for example, the times where a bowler or a captain will set an extra man out at deep backward square-leg to go with the one already stationed at deep fine-leg for the hook. Is this to be the bumper which might be said to be the obvious follow-up, or is it to be the best outswinger the bowler can muster, the batsman having been conned into thinking the short-pitched ball is coming? Or the double-bluff, the bouncer, the batsman having twice tried to out-think the bowler and captain?

Commentators can make a living out of this kind of conversation. Watching your screen and hearing of the possibilities, you may think, as did the chap at the 'Gabba, that all this is new and brilliant and what a pity the old-timers couldn't have thought of that kind of thing.

In fact in Nyren's book published in 1888, he said, 'When it is difficult to part two batsmen, and either of them has a favourite hit, I have often succeeded in getting him out by opening the field where his hit is placed, at the same time hinting to the bowler to give him a different style of ball. This with the opening of the field has tempted him to plant his favourite hit, and in his anxiety to do so, has not infrequently committed an error fatal to him.'

Next time you hear the commentator setting up the play, just remember very little is new in this game.

Technology is constantly changing in television, so too production and direction. When I started on radio with the BBC in 1960 I had just a nodding acquaintance with TV, and when I started in television with the BBC in 1963 it was with black-and-white screens.

Television and cricket have been intertwined since 1938 when the England v Australia Test at Lord's was shown to the small number of people who had sets. The Oval Test when Len Hutton made 364 was also televised, after BBC officials pronounced themselves happy with all that had gone on at Lord's. It wasn't until 1950 that Tests in other regions were televised. A transmitter near Birmingham was needed before that could happen.

As far as I can see, there will be a steadily increasing amount of sport on television in years to come. One thing that should never change is that the commentators' task is to add to the picture put on the screen by the director.

The systems in England and Australia have been different over the years, with the BBC having just one producer-director in the production van, and, at Channel 9, a director in the van providing all the pictures for viewers plus, in the commentary box, the producer handling every aspect of organisation, massive or tiny, and at the same time creating the story for those who are watching.

These days the director's job is both simple and complicated:

simple because the end result is that the viewer sees just one picture, and complicated because the director may have more than a score of pictures on different screens from which he must choose quickly, correctly and, far more important, with a creative touch. Directors are the ones in charge of everything when I sit in the commentator's chair, and I have the greatest admiration for them because I know it is a job I would be unable to do successfully.

There is a fallacy in TV that the most important person is the commentator, something that could hardly be further from the truth. The commentator is important because he adds to what is on the screen in a fashion either quiet, noisy, subtle, dogmatic or generous. He recognises, or he should recognise, that he is in fact privileged to be invited into the living-rooms of the viewers around the world. It used to be around the nation, now we go further afield. This aspect of privilege is one thing never to be forgotten by a commentator. The *Oxford Dictionary* describes the word 'privilege' as 'a special advantage or benefit' and that is precisely what you are given when viewers invite you into their homes by pressing a switch.

31

THE BENAUD CONNECTION

I'M not too sure what, these days, Captain Jean Benaud would have thought of it all. The son of Joseph Benaud, a baker or pastry-cook and formerly a soldier, and Rose Blanche, domestic duties, he set out from La Rochelle in 1838, around fifty years after the French Revolution, and arrived in Sydney, according to the records, in 1840 on the *Ville de Bordeaux*. The ship carried what was classed as 'Black Oil', which more than likely was whale oil. In 1858 he married Caroline Powell, the daughter of a fellow mariner, on the mid-north coast of NSW. His arrival in Australia, as a widower, was in the year his future wife was born in Sydney, and when they married in Taree eighteen years later, he, as occasionally happens in life, appeared to have shed a few years, possibly for a better impression.

He was something of a character, but an influential one, in the Northern Rivers area and the mid-north coast of NSW, until his death in 1866. It was noted in later years that 'another splendid captain trading to the river in the early days of settlement was a Frenchman, Captain Benaud, of whom it was sometimes said that he carried too much sail in order to generate more and more speed. Captain Benaud's reply was courteous but to the point: "Ships were made to carry masts, masts were made to carry sails, and so the sails will go on."'

The Savilles and the Benauds are still prominent in the northern part of NSW, but the Benaud connection has made little impact on French life. There is, though, a delightful, quiet village called Benaud in France, near Clermont-Ferrand on the D229, and it takes only a short time to arrive and depart. It is a hamlet which doesn't appear in the French telephone system, but there are few other places where the back of a village sign is as close to the one you see when you enter a village. Despite the village name, there are no Benauds living in that area, though there are a few carrying the name in the south of the country.

Something I have always believed about cricket and about life is that the whole thing revolves around luck and skill, and the proportions are 90 per cent and 10 per cent in that order. The only proviso is that you don't attempt anything without having the 10 per cent.

I was lucky as well as being fortunate, and there is a difference. Some say I was far more luck than skill, but I doubt that is completely correct. I tried to make my own luck by throwing in a lot of hard work and I've found it a successful combination in both sport and business, so far anyway.

I wanted to be a Sheffield Shield cricketer for NSW and was one, I hoped to become an Australian cricketer and then toured England under Lindsay Hassett's captaincy thirteen years after I had first watched him play.

Bert Scotford was the catalyst for what came later at the *Sun* newspaper when I wanted to become a journalist and was lucky enough to meet Lindsay Clinch, Jack Tier, Noel Bailey and others who taught me a great deal about how to write and, without them knowing it, helped when I started in television.

Miller, Morris and Lindwall taught me a lot about cricket, and, more important, about life and friends, and that you are never missing when it's your shout at the bar. There have been many others, and if you have the privilege of knowing them but don't have the brains to learn from them, then it's your own fault.

Although there were injuries, disappointments and setbacks along the way, there was no shortage of the essential balancing ingredient of luck. Part of that has been to continue with cricket through different areas of the media; the game for me has been wonderfully varied, challenging and in many ways character-building. I'm no less enthusiastic about it now than when I was on the banks of the Murrumbidgee or in the fourth-grade team at

Parramatta High School. From the personal, business and cricket point of view, I'm hoping there are many more enjoyable years to come and, if they match the last forty-three with Daph, then I shall be very happy indeed.

Not so long ago cricket and the Benaud connection in France was gently strengthened when I was asked to become Patron of France Cricket, something I hoped might in a small way assist the game advancing in that country. Then, in June 1998, the ICC lifted France to Associate status in the cricket world, but such is the competitive nature of cricket these days they have again become an Affiliate cricket nation.

In addition, the French administrators have divided the country into six regions and have appointed Regional Development Officers to foster cricket in those areas. They have played in the European Indoor Championships and their Under-19 side is promising and they have Under-16 and Under-13 teams where youngsters are showing promise, but it is a competitive world.

Television will continue to play a big part in the development of cricket. During the Olympic Games in 2012 in the United Kingdom a match will be played between England and France to bring back memories of the first match between the countries played in Paris in 1900.

32

THE FREE-TO-AIR DEBATE

No matter what the film-makers might do with their modern-day angles and technology, and what new ideas the scriptwriters might come up with, there is nothing stranger than real life, with its highs and lows and, best of all, surprises.

In 1999 Chris Broad, the former England opening batsman, father of Stuart presently playing for England and himself now an elite Test match referee, wrote a book, with the assistance of Daniel Waddell, an experienced freelance journalist who has a fine reputation as a writer. The book was named *And Welcome to the Highlights: 61 Years of BBC Television Cricket*. The BBC, in a brilliant decision, gave the two authors unfettered access to all existing files, cupboards, books and memos; they could look at what they liked and use it in any way they wished. It was, and is, a splendid publication because of the writing skills of the co-authors and the fact that they had a real feel for the game of cricket and the history of British television. It wasn't until I read those pages that I knew that Peter Dimmock, the Head of Television Outside Broadcasts, and Bryan Cowgill, Head of Sport, had discussed me as a potential television commentator during 1962 when Pakistan toured England, and the discussion came up again early in 1963. In 1961 I had captained Australia when we retained the Ashes in exciting circumstances at Old Trafford, and it was a great thrill when George Greenfield of John Farquharson, our Literary Agents, asked if I would be prepared to come to England to act as a television summariser for the 1963 summer when England would be playing West Indies captained by Frank Worrell. In 1960–61 Frank and I had captained West Indies and Australia in the Tied Test series and I was still playing for Australia at the time of this request. In 1960 I had worked for BBC Radio when the South Africans toured England. Robert Hudson was the cricket producer at that time.

One of the most interesting items in *And Welcome to the Highlights* is on page 31 and it shows the dismissal of Bradman at The Oval in 1948. There have been many arguments over the years about whether the bowler, Eric Hollies, was bowling over or around the wicket in the dismissal. One of the reasons for argument was that at the time only three cameras were used by the BBC and the familiar footage of the dismissal showed Hollies in a close-up, bowling around the wicket, which he often did, and then there is a vicious cut to Bradman being bowled. However, on page 31 of the book, Bradman's dismissal is shown with the bails falling and Arthur Morris standing in the non-striker's area at the bowler's end of the pitch; and Hollies is not visible at all. We do know though that, as Bradman was walking off with a duck against his name in his last innings, he was being accorded his second standing ovation in a matter of a few minutes. Hollies is said to have walked over to the fieldsman at mid-off, Jack Young, the Middlesex left-arm spinner, and said, 'Best bloody ball I've bowled all season and they're clapping *him*.'

One of the more extraordinary aspects of the Bradman dismissal was that Hollies had received the invitation to play for England but told the Warwickshire secretary, Les Deakins, that he intended to decline. He made the point that the rubber had already been decided and, with Warwickshire high in the Championship table, he would rather play in the two vital games against Hampshire and Middlesex. Eventually he was persuaded to play at The Oval and, with one ball bowled from over the wicket, wrote himself into cricket history.

Hollies had made his Test debut against West Indies at Kensington Oval, Barbados, in January 1935 with Bob Wyatt as his captain and in a match where rain had turned the pitch into a 'sticky' and batting was a hazardous business. West Indies won

Colin Ingleby-Mackenzie, President of MCC in 1998, and John Barclay, President in 2010. Barclay captained Sussex with distinction, Colin was skipper of Hampshire in 1961 when they won the Championship and we beat them at Southampton in the tour match. It meant we had to fill in a bit of time before catching the bus; what better way to do it than accept Ingleby's invitation to talk captaincy tactics over a bottle of Dom Pérignon at the hotel down the road?

Michael Atherton has sensibly made the transition from player, and being captain of his country, to working on television as a commentator and writing for newspapers and media outlets. And it's been a pleasure to watch him on the field, listen to him on Sky and read his prose. The formula is well thought out.

The greatest legspinner of all time. Shane Warne had a great bowling action and gave the ball a real rip. When he began in Test cricket it was with 1-150 and his learning curve began at Colombo (SSC), Sri Lanka, on 22 August 1992 when Allan Border brilliantly caught P.A. de Silva off Craig McDermott. Border instantly brought Warne on and he took 3-0 in two overs and Australia won by 16 runs.

Mark Taylor with a model of the urn after retaining the Ashes in 1997. After a poor start to the England tour he then hit a great century at Edgbaston. It was a wonderful comeback and I was never more pleased for any century-maker. Taylor is currently on the Cricket Australia Board and is one of the five best captains I have ever seen.

Waugh and Waugh. What a combination, though different in style and method. Steve Waugh (*r*) was as tough as they come; Mark (*l*) was one of the great and graceful cricketers to play for Australia.

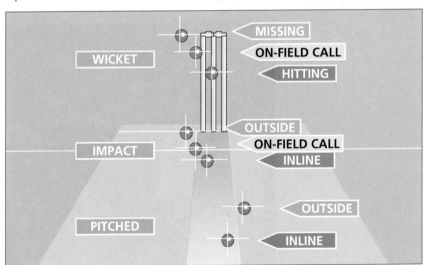

The referrals system is still very much a work in progress. It will stay that way until the ultra-rich ICC pay the fees to have the system operating successfully in all Test matches around the world. To expect television networks to do their job for them is just pie in the sky.

The green boxes show the third umpire he must report the ball as having missed the stumps, impacted outside the line or pitched outside the line, as the case may be. The red boxes show the third umpire he must report the ball as having hit the stumps, struck in line or pitched in line, as the case may be. The orange boxes mean the third umpire should report that he does not have a high degree of confidence so the original on-field decision remains.

Modern cricket is different. It is exciting and varied and it attracts people paying their entrance money at the gates and those who watch on television. It also produces new methods. Here are four batsmen with exciting variations to their strokeplay.

Tillakaratne Dilshan of Sri Lanka has invented the scoop shot where he extends the bat down the pitch and scoops the ball over his helmet and over the head of the wicketkeeper. In this innings in 2009 he made 57 off 28 balls against New Zealand in a T20 match. Make certain you are wearing the helmet!

In August 2008 Kevin Pietersen again produced switch-hitting, changing from being a right-hander to a sweeping left-hander. MCC and their Laws committee's reaction was brilliant; it amounted to 'go for it ...' He made 94 in this innings against South Africa.

Left Far more orthodox, but still innovative, was Adam Gilchrist against Pakistan at the SCG in 2005, straight-driving for six in making a brilliant 113.

Below Michael Hussey, in the T20 World Cup, only made 17* for Australia in this final at Kensington Oval, Barbados. England won the final with 18 balls to spare. In the semi-final though Hussey had won the match for Australia over Pakistan by hitting 60 off 24 balls faced.

Michael Vaughan, a high-class captain who led England to victory in the Ashes battle in 2005, was also a fine opening and high-order batsman.

Three great cricketers and one who is looking better every time I watch him bowl, whether I am at the ground or watching on television. (*Above*) Sachin Tendulkar, playing a typically aggressive stroke, has been a great player for many years. I watched him make his first Test century at Old Trafford in August 1990. It was a wonderful experience for me.

What a superb action shot of Andrew Flintoff bowling in the first Ashes Test at Lord's in 2005.

And the one striving to become a better bowler when he is already a very good one. Graeme Swann, the England offspinner, will learn more about cricket on the Ashes tour of Australia in 2010; he spins the ball and drifts it beautifully in the air away from the right-handers. He has also posed many problems for left-handed batsmen and quite likes bowling to them. Which is more than I did!

1977, staged to commemorate 100 years of Test match cricket. The first Test had been played 15–19 March 1877. Both games resulted in a victory for Australia by 45 runs. In 1977 the ABC televised the game and, under a separate arrangement, Channel 0-10 Brisbane also provided a commercial coverage. Ron Archer, the former outstanding Australian allrounder, was the Chief Executive Officer for that network; he was just as good at television as he had been at cricket.

Before working on that Centenary Test, I also covered three matches in Adelaide for Channel 0-10. These were South Australia v Victoria (Victoria won by an innings and 123 runs), then South Australia v Queensland (match tied) and South Australia v New South Wales (match drawn). In those three matches the late David Hookes, the brilliant left-hand batsman, hit five centuries: 163, 185, 105, 135 and 156. This extraordinary and delightful scoring earned Hookes a place in the Australian team for the Centenary Test, where he made 17 and 56 and had that wonderful tussle with Tony Greig. Dennis Lillee confirmed his place as Australia's greatest fast bowler with 11 wickets in the match and Derek Randall made 174 in England's second innings. It was the first commentary I had done in a Test match in Australia, fourteen years after I had started my long stint with BBC Television in the United Kingdom. To this point I had covered for the BBC three Ashes series in England, 1964, 1968 and 1972, all on free-to-air, as was the type of coverage in Australia with Channel 0-10.

That précis is a lead-up to the fact that in the United Kingdom in 2010 there was a move to return Ashes matches in England to free-to-air television.

In those early days I worked only on free-to-air television and that remains the case. I have never worked on pay-television, neither Sky in the United Kingdom nor Foxtel in Australia.

In England I have worked for the BBC and Channel 4 and in 2009 I worked on each Saturday of the Test matches on the splendid Channel 5 highlights, which went to air at 7.15 p.m., hosted by Mark Nicholas and produced and directed by

Gary Franses. In Australia, I have only worked for Channel 9 free-to-air television, starting with World Series cricket for the Nine Network in 1977 and going through to the present day with Test matches, 50-overs-a-side one-day Internationals and Twenty20 games.

Channel 9 is the free-to-air television company which buys the rights from Cricket Australia. There is then an arrangement whereby Foxtel cover the Sheffield Shield, the domestic one-day matches and the KFC Big Bash Twenty20 competition. They also have the TV rights to the Champions' League and other sports events. Foxtel production is good, their directors know what they are doing and do it well, and their commentators adjust very well to the different types of cricket they put to air.

It should be understood that in Australia, although free-to-air television companies buy the rights to sports events such as the Ashes in England, they are not compelled to put the events to air. That in time to come could change to 'Use it or Lose it'. The Ashes coverage in 2005 (Channel 4) and 2009 (Sky), and the Wimbledon coverage in both years (BBC), had been bought by Channel 9 for Australian showing, but this posed problems for the Channel 9 programming. They decided to bring in the tennis, as they were quite entitled to do, and they sought another free-to-air station to screen the five Tests, as they were also entitled to do. They did this through SBS in Australia, a multicultural network, and SBS had excellent rating figures that provided them with a very pleasant surprise.

The move to take Ashes coverage in the United Kingdom away from Sky and give/sell it to a free-to-air network came from what is known as 'The Davies Review', but it is something that will be decided by the Secretary of State for Culture, Olympics, Media and Sport. Test cricket in the UK was delisted in 1998 and, when the question of cricket rights last came up, the BBC and Channel 4 showed minimal interest from the programming point of view, and even less interest in outlaying money. The idea put forward now is that all Ashes series played in England should be free-to-air; other cricket, if I have read it correctly, can be shown by any network if they buy the rights. Unless there is something I have missed, that seems to be an extraordinary suggestion.

There is a direct correlation between English and Australian cricket in that the first British people who came to Australia started playing cricket in Sydney and the first reference to cricket in Australia is to the playing of matches in Sydney in 1803. In Australia we have developed a great competition called the Sheffield Shield and from the matches played in that competition we choose our Test teams. A similar system exists in England, with counties not states, and has done for a much longer time than the Australian programming style.

If either country were to lose the financial benefits that come from different styles of television coverage, the game wouldn't end, because cricket is always evolving in some way, but it would be badly affected.

Most important in Australia is how Cricket Australia funds grass-roots cricket; that is the area from which young cricketers arrive to play in various grades with club sides until they reach Sheffield Shield and then Tests. In Australia at any one time you might have around seventy players taking part in various inter-state competitions. There are of course many other participants in the Australian cricket structure, though not as many first-class players as in England.

In England on any day you might have more than 210 taking part in matches associated with the eighteen counties. But each county has a system whereby it is impossible to miss a talented player and that system is very much grass-roots, entailing work with schools, clubs and the funding of every possible opportunity to spot young cricketers for the future.

That is one aspect. There is also the funding of the club game, where people are able to play cricket and, just as important, to enjoy the company of the players of their own club and, more so, mix with the players of other clubs. Getting to know other people is part of cricket; village cricketers may need less funding but they are an unsung lot who form the framework and lifeblood of cricket.

In Australia, then, I work on free-to-air television, watch television and purchase pay-TV so that I am able to see every form of cricket and record matches I am unable to watch live. It is part of my enjoyment of watching and learning. My experience in England tells me that targeting only Ashes matches over a six-week period every four years in a new-style contract will be fraught with danger for the game of cricket in England, as well as saying, in effect, that countries other than England and Australia don't matter a stuff.

It is quite beyond me why administrators and Members of Parliament would be thinking in this fashion. The next television deal will be signed in 2013 and I assume will run to 2017. Who on earth has the slightest idea what television will be like in 2017? Between now and then there will be analogue changing to digital, which has already started, and there will be developments in technology that will be mind-boggling in their capacity to change the manner in which we watch, what we watch and how all that appears on the various types of receiving machines we will have when the time arrives. My feeling is, if the proposed matters concerning free-to-air Ashes become law, the county system in England will be dramatically changed, and changed for ever to the detriment of the sport.

Bear in mind also the recent piracy of sports telecasts on the internet. Cricket Australia is just one of a number of sporting organisations around the world losing millions of dollars because it is possible to watch live cricket broadcasts illegally without paying for them. I imagine governments from different countries will need to pass legislation to stop this, if, that is, they are able to do so under restraint-of-trade regulations. That could be one of the most important events in sport but it depends entirely on careful negotiation between sport and government.

Those who are determined to take cricket, tennis and other sports away from pay-TV in the United Kingdom need to explain what they are going to do to protect those sports from financial failure. Perhaps the government making the decision will provide all the lost finance; perhaps though that is not considered to be part of their brief. In July 2010, the new coalition government announced they would be deferring any decision on matters raised in the Davies Report until 2013. My view is they should scrap it.

33

THE GREATEST SERIES

G REAT matches have been part of Test cricket since the first game was played between Australia and England in 1877. There have been wonderful Test series as well, though not necessarily between the two founding countries. The Tied Test series of 1960–61 between Australia and the West Indies was the classic in this regard; each team constantly attacked and the crowd of 90,800 at the MCG on the second day of the final Test still stands as the record attendance for any day of cricket. If that is ever to be broken it will almost certainly be on the same ground.

For twenty-four years I was of the opinion that the best series I had ever watched as a commentator was the one played in England in 1981 where there was drama and pathos, joy and disappointment and a great deal of skill from the players. Ian Botham had a little earlier captained England against the West Indies in the Caribbean and he led England at home in this 1981 series but only for two of the five Tests. In 1980 and early 1981 he had played sixteen innings against the West Indies in home and away series, making only 242 runs at 15 per innings, so it seemed likely the cares of captaincy and the defeats were having a severe effect on his form. Then when the Australians, led by Kim Hughes, arrived in the summer, Botham was captain for the opening two Tests, the first won by Australia at Trent Bridge and the second drawn at Lord's. In the course of the latter Botham made a pair and was advised by the Chairman of Selectors, Alec Bedser, that he would be relieved of the captaincy; some said it was by mutual agreement. The decision turned out to be to Australia's detriment because Mike Brearley was reappointed England captain and he revolutionised the team, gave them a purpose in life, and in cricket, and won the series in the most extraordinary fashion. It also resurrected Botham's career; he made 50 and 149 not out and took 6–95 and 1–14 at Headingley, with England winning by 18 runs after Kim Hughes had enforced the follow-on. Then came 5–11 from 14 overs at Edgbaston, five wickets and 118 at Old Trafford and 10 wickets in the final Test at The Oval. Some comeback, some series! It was almost a quarter of a century before I saw anything to match it and then it came with even more drama than had been the case in 1981.

Prior to the Ashes series in 2005, England, Australia and Bangladesh played a limited-overs series sponsored by NatWest and the matches almost went according to the best-laid plans. England and Australia played in the final; the scores were tied with England 196–9 at the end of 50 overs after they had bowled out the Australians for the same figure in their 49th over. An inkling that it wasn't going to be just any boring old summer came in the fact that at one point England's innings stood at 33–5 and then there was a splendid partnership between Paul Collingwood and Geraint Jones and the match finished with a misfield by Brett Lee that allowed the scores to be levelled. That was on 2 July at Lord's, the match played in front of a crowd of 25,000. Nineteen days later, with anticipation at an unprecedented height, the two teams prepared for the opening Test of the five-match series. Ricky Ponting was the captain, the selectors had chosen a strong touring party and Lord's looked a picture. Despite Australia not having been beaten at the Home of Cricket since 1934, there was strong anticipation that this was to be a stirring series, with England having a real chance of providing an upset. In fact, it turned out to be one of the most desperate four days of modern-day English cricket, Australia winning by a massive margin of 239 runs.

This was a shuddering start for England, their hopes had been high and there was no doubt their selectors had chosen an outstanding team to do battle. Michael Vaughan was captain and his accompanying line-up for that opening game was Marcus

Trescothick, Andrew Strauss, Ian Bell, Kevin Pietersen, Andrew Flintoff, Geraint Jones (wk), Ashley Giles, Matthew Hoggard, Steve Harmison and Simon Jones.

The first-day crowd for this opening Test in 2005 numbered 30,601, which was the highest attendance figure at the ground in sixty years, dating back to the time at the end of the Second World War when England played Australia, not in a Test match but in a three-day game between England and Australia to celebrate the conclusion of the war. In the Australian Services squad there were two repatriated prisoners of war, R. G. (Graham) Williams and D. K. (Keith) Carmody. Williams had been shot down during the Libyan campaign and spent four years in a German prison camp teaching Braille to the blinded prisoners and also to Germans blinded by the war. There was also Lindsay Hassett, captaining the Services' team, and Keith Miller, batting high in the order and bowling occasionally but described by *Wisden* 1946 as 'the fastest bowler in the country'. In that game at Lord's he bowled only nine overs in each innings, his first victim was Bill Edrich. Miller had never bowled in a Sheffield Shield match and the first time he rolled his arm over in Australia was in the Bradman's XI v McCabe's XI charity match in 1941; his victim was South Australian Ken Ridings, the catcher was wicketkeeper Don Tallon. It would be a good story to say that was the start of a great partnership between 'Nugget' and 'Deafy' Tallon, but that didn't begin until five years after he had bowled for that Services' team in England.

Thirteen years ago I asked Nugget about those Victory Tests and he said the matches were fun, but sad as well because of those unable to be there. He told me about Graham Williams and the fact that his story had been in the newspapers of the time and also on radio programmes. Williams had been the opening bowler for South Australia before enlisting and he was tall and broad-shouldered at the time. After the prison camp he was still tall, but there was nothing broad-shouldered about him; he was gaunt. When Albert Cheetham was caught by Hammond off Wright for a duck Williams came down the steps and on to the Lord's ground to join

Miller in the centre. Miller said he would never forget the moment Graham set foot on the ground; the thirty thousand spectators rose and clapped softly until the moment he reached the pitch. The only sound was that soft unbroken applause. Miller said it was the most touching thing he had ever seen or heard, almost orchestral in its sound and feeling. 'And whenever I think of it, tears still come to my eyes.'

The two teams taking part in that Lord's match and the other Victory Tests provide a Roll of Honour scoreboard for ever in the history of cricket.

England

L. Hutton c Sismey b Williams	1	b Pepper	21
Flt.-Sgt. C. Washbrook st Sismey b Ellis	28	lbw b Pepper	32
Capt. J.D. Robertson lbw b Ellis	53	c Sismey b Cheetham	84
W.R. Hammond b Williams	29	lbw b Ellis	33
Sqn.-Ldr. L.E.G. Ames c Price b Cheetham	57	b Ellis	7
Sqn.-Ldr. W.J. Edrich b Miller	45	c Workman b Price	50
Sqn.-Ldr. R.W.V. Robins b Cheetham	5	c Hassett b Pepper	33
Lt.-Col. J.W.A. Stephenson c Sismey b Price	31	b Price	1
Lt.-Col. S.C. Griffith c Sismey b Cheetham	9	not out	4
Lt. D.V.P. Wright b Price	0	run out	1
A.R. Gover not out	0	st Sismey b Pepper	1
b 1, lb 6, w 1, nb 1	9	b 18, lb 8, nb 1	27
	267		294

Australian Services

Flt.-Sgt. J.A. Workman b Gover	1		
Capt. R.S. Whitington c Griffith b Wright	36	lbw b Stephenson	0
W/O A.L. Hassett b Stephenson	77	c Hammond b Gover	37
Sqn.-Ldr. S.G. Sismey c Wright b Edrich	37		
P/O K.R. Miller c Ames b Stephenson	105	run out	1
F/O R.M. Stanford st Griffith b Stephenson	49		
Sgt. C.G. Pepper c Griffith b Stephenson	40	not out	54
Capt. A.G. Cheetham c Hammond b Wright	0	run out	0
W/O R.G. Williams c Griffith b Wright	53		
Sgt. C.R. Price c Robertson b Stephenson	35	not out	10
F/O R.S. Ellis not out	1		
b 9, lb 10, nb 2	21	b 4, lb 1	5
	455	Four wkts.dec	107

Australian Services Bowling

	O	M	R	W	O	M	R	W
Cheetham	13.1	1	49	3	17	2	44	1
Williams	19	2	56	2	21	7	47	0
Pepper	19	2	59	0	32.4	7	80	4
Ellis	31	8	59	2	17	3	33	2
Miller	9	2	11	1	9	1	23	0
Price	9	1	24	2	19	3	40	2

England Bowling

	O	M	R	W	O	M	R	W
Gover	25	3	90	1	11.4	1	51	1
Stephenson	36	4	116	5	11	0	51	1
Edrich	17	2	61	1				
Wright	37.3	9	122	3				
Robins	10	0	45	0				

In 2005 there was great anticipation in the crowd at Lord's and around the country. There was even more when England bowled out the Australians for only 190, having at one stage had them 87–5. Justin Langer top-scored with 40 and there was a little flurry of strokeplay from Simon Katich, Adam Gilchrist and Shane Warne to take the total past the 100-mark, but then Steve Harmison ripped through the bottom half of the order. Glenn McGrath bowled superbly to take the first five England wickets and when the fifth, Flintoff, went, the England score was only 21.

With England bowled out for 155 the Australian lead might only have been a small 35 but it was the psychological blow that was the most painful for the England team and their supporters.

The Australians then made 384 and only three England batsmen reached double figures, McGrath again doing well with 4–29 and Shane Warne 4–64. What made it a great deal worse for England was that after an opening stand of 80 between Trescothick and Strauss, Pietersen was the only other batsman to reach double figures. In fact, on his debut he top-scored in both innings, quite a feat from someone who instantly looked completely comfortable at Test level. Thirty-three years earlier I had watched the other Test where an England batsman had top-scored in each innings on his Test debut. This was in the 1972 Ashes match at Old Trafford, the first of the series, and the player was Tony Greig who, like

Pietersen, was born in South Africa. England won that Old Trafford match by 89 runs and it prefaced the Lord's Test which became known as 'Massie's Match' because of Bob Massie taking 8–84 and 8–53 in a total of 59.7 overs. It was also the match where Greg Chappell played one of the greatest innings I have ever seen, 131 in Australia's first innings. This brought to a close the longest period Australia had not beaten England, in all eleven matches to that time, from Manchester 1968 to 26 June 1972. An interesting personal achievement came out of that opening Lord's Test in that Glenn McGrath was named Man of the Match. It was the third time he had been Man of the Match in an Ashes Test at Lord's, in 1997, 2001 and now in 2005.

In 2005 the Australians could hardly have been happier as the Second Test approached. A wonderful victory at Lord's, an England team well and truly set back on their heels in that opening Test and an Edgbaston pitch which, although it looked batsman-friendly, always promised to have enough in it to provide a real possibility of a contest and a result. That was the situation forty-five minutes before the first ball was due to be bowled and, at that point, Ricky Ponting was about to move to the dressing-room, from the fielding practice area, to don his blazer and baggy green and think about walking to the centre with Michael Vaughan. It was at that moment, with his Australian team tossing balls to one another, that one of those balls was knocked away by a player. It went near Glenn McGrath, who stepped on it as he was taking a catch.

In stepping on it, he twisted his ankle.

In those two seconds Australia turned from being favourites to do well, perhaps even to win, to being on the wrong side of luck, and there is nothing worse than having luck run against you. There was no one to blame, though there should always be someone on the lookout for potential accidents of that kind. But, basically, it was just one of those things. McGrath couldn't play, Jason Gillespie had beaten Michael Kasprowicz for a place in the original XI, now both were in the starting line-up and McGrath was in the pavilion, fuming, but unavailable for the match.

It seems that Ponting had intended to bowl first. There was some moisture under the surface of the pitch and McGrath was the man most likely to be able to take advantage of it. I can only tell you what I said at the time in the Channel 4 commentary box: 'Punter has to bat, it's thrown everything out of gear but he has to bat if McGrath is a no-chancer.'

Instead, he sent England in, which had always been his tactic; they had batted poorly at Lord's against high-class bowling. Most of that high-class bowling had come from McGrath and Warne, though Brett Lee had bowled many good overs. Now Lee had with him Gillespie and Kasprowicz. As a captain, I didn't mind putting the opposition in to bat; I did it three times in Test matches and Australia won all three. There were good reasons. In 1959 against England, in the final Test in Melbourne, and in 1961 against West Indies in the Fifth and last Test in the Tied Test series, also in Melbourne, we had gone through some wet days leading up to the match. In both Melbourne games the pitches were well grassed and green – and I had Alan Davidson, both times fully fit, though on each occasion he had been forced to recover from hamstring problems and pass a fitness test. When the time came he was completely fit and performed magnificently. The third time was against Pakistan in 1959 in what was then called Dacca on that tour when, despite all the promises from Pakistan that we would play on three turf pitches, we found ourselves wearing rubber-soled shoes for the match.

England at Edgbaston in 2005 might well have thought all their birthdays had come at once; certainly Michael Vaughan did well not to change the expression on his face when he heard the words indicating that Australia would be in the field. Trescothick and Strauss played some delightful strokes against the Australian pace attack, putting on 112 in very quick time; in fact, the whole of the first day was played at great speed. The second new ball was due when the England innings ended at 407 with just four balls still to be bowled to complete the first 80 overs and have the umpires taking their new red cherry out of its cellophane packet. It was exhilarating stuff. Ian Bell and Geraint

Jones were the only two not to reach double figures and there were some alarming bowling figures from the Australian attack. Lee went for 111 from 17 overs at six an over, Kasprowicz was five an over, Gillespie four and the fourth bowler used, Shane Warne, took four wickets, but even the champion legspinner was five an over.

There was no stopping the England batsmen. When Australia batted, the frenetic pace continued, with still no recourse to a second new ball, Australia making their 308 from only 76 overs. I asked the question in the Channel 4 commentary box: 'What on earth is happening in these modern times? There was a time when a captain would take the new ball when the 200-run mark had been reached. Out there today we would be able to have a new ball at 40 overs under the old system. Can you believe it?' The Australians went at it as though it was a limited-overs match and, under the same type comparison, the new ball could have been taken at 50 overs. The pitch was good for batting, though it was clear there would be some turn for the spin bowlers as the game went on and there may also have been some deterioration in the surface. And, as always, there would be the bowlers' footmarks for Shane Warne to use, also Ashley Giles.

It was evident on the second evening of the game that we could still be in for some excitement because Andrew Strauss half-shouldered arms to a legspinner from Warne and the ball spun a yard and crashed into his leg stump. Then Trescothick, nightwatchman Hoggard and Vaughan all fell to Brett Lee and England suddenly were 31–4 and the Australians were back in with a chance. Now, though, Flintoff appeared in all his majesty. At the other end was number eleven Simon Jones who played a passive part, but what a starring role it actually was. Flintoff hit four sixes and the last-wicket pair put on 51 frenetic runs to leave the Australians with the task of making 282 to win. England then bowled so well and Australia, unable to match their brilliance and expertise, faced the embarrassing situation of the home side claiming the extra half-hour so a result might be reached in three days. Three days? That was one of the more extraordinary happenings I had seen in a Test match, or series, in good conditions. The umpires had sought a result on the third evening with 1,037 runs made and 37 wickets having fallen.

Michael Clarke went with the score at 175 and, when stumps were drawn at the same score on the third day, Warne, Lee and Kasprowicz were all that stood between England and a famous victory, Jason Gillespie having been sent in as a nightwatchman the previous evening. Now there's a rarity, Jason going in at eight instead of ten. Bear in mind though that only six months after this Edgbaston Test Gillespie made a double century against Bangladesh as nightwatchman.

On the fourth morning at Edgbaston Warne's foot slipped and he trod on his stumps having made 42 and then Lee and Kasprowicz still needed 62 for victory. They made all but two of those runs in one of the most exciting sessions of cricket I have seen.

To add to the extraordinary excitement, Kasprowicz was the last man given out and the technology we had then showed he wasn't out. Umpire Billy Bowden made the decision after Steve Harmison, bowling from the Pavilion End, had dug one into the pitch; the ball reared at Kasprowicz and brushed a glove, going into the air for Geraint Jones to run from the wicketkeeping spot and dive and take the catch. In these days of technology and referrals it is possible that, because it was such a flurry of bat, gloves and whatever else came into the equation, the third umpire, when referred to by his colleague at the bowler's end, would have said Kasprowicz's gloved hand was not on the bat at the crucial time and therefore the batsman was not out. That would have been a pity and I will always be pleased that no referral system was available that day. Kasprowicz, having seen the replays, said all the right things, including, 'If I had been bowling and not been given that decision, I would have been real dirty . . .' It is correct that in the commentary box, when we were watching the replays as most of the players were leaving the field, we were able to see that the batsman's hand was not on the handle when struck by the ball. Billy Bowden could not have seen that and the batsman at the non-striker's end, Brett Lee, didn't see it either. In the immediate aftermath he had sunk to his knees in disappointment, as indeed had Kasprowicz.

It had been something of a weird Test match, with McGrath's injury, Ponting winning the toss and not batting with his one-nil lead in the series, the hectic run-making, the spirited bowling, the wonderful striking of the ball and the splendid bowling from Andrew Flintoff. The Lord's Test had produced its own brand of excitement, Edgbaston produced something different, but we were not to know then of the slightly bizarre things that would happen at Old Trafford and Trent Bridge.

So far two Test matches played in the five-match series, a strong victory to Australia in the opening encounter, a pulsating four days in the second and now, here we were at Old Trafford about to start the second part of back-to-back Test matches. I suppose it was something of a respite for the players, and certainly for the commentators, that Edgbaston had only lasted four days, finishing on 7 August, so there was an extra day's 'relaxation' before the Old Trafford game began on 11 August.

I toured England as a player three times, 1953 under Lindsay Hassett, 1956 under Ian Johnson and then I captained the team in 1961. For me, Old Trafford was something of a mixed bag. I didn't play on the ground in any match in 1953, but was twelfth man in the Third Test of that series and Australia's score in our second innings was 35–8. Fortunately we ran out of time but Alec Bedser, Jim Laker and Johnny Wardle gave us some heart-stopping moments on that final day after heavy rain and an uncovered pitch had posed problems. 1956 was Jim Laker's match, also played on an uncovered pitch, but one that, according to Bert Flack the groundsman in a television interview, had been specially shaved the day before the Test began on the instructions of senior English administrator Gubby Allen. Bert said he had told Gubby the pitch would disintegrate if he carried out the instruction but sensibly, in the light of continued employment, he obeyed orders and then immediately covered the pitch to keep it from prying eyes. Rain turned the surface from a dusty bowl to a soft one. Jim took 19 wickets and Tony Lock one, in the main because

Australian right-hand batsmen are far more comfortable leaving the ball going away towards the slips from the left-arm spinner than they are playing the ball turning in to them from outside the off stump.

Five years later we were hoping for revenge, but there were problems. I had torn fibres and a muscle in my right shoulder in the opening match of that tour at Worcester in bowling a wrong'un to Tom Graveney. I hadn't been able to play in the Lord's Test, the place above all others where you want to lead your team on to the field. Neil Harvey was captain there and did a wonderful job, winning the game on a pitch which, when examined later by experts, was found to have a 'ridge' at the Nursery End. More credit then to Bill Lawry, who made a great century.

We lost at Headingley, Fred Trueman taking 11 wickets in the match, two of them me without a run against my name. After Fred had bowled us out in the second innings he came into our dressing-room for a convivial beer at the close of play and told me not to worry too much about having been bowled. 'It would have knocked over even a decent batsman,' he declared. It brought the house down!

When we played at Old Trafford in 1961 we were in all kinds of trouble for much of the game. Bill Lawry had made a magnificent 74 and 102 and then Alan Davidson, 77, and Graham McKenzie, 32, added 98 for the last wicket and allowed us to set England 256 to win after we had lost three for nought in 15 balls earlier in the day. This was the match where I talked to Ray Lindwall in the Lancashire committee room the night before the last day, asking whether it might be worthwhile to bowl around the wicket to the right-hand batsmen because there were great areas of bowlers' footmarks at the Warwick Road End. They had been made principally by Fred Trueman and Jack Flavell and the idea I put to Ray was that they could provide a lot of awkward bounce. When the time came, and Ted Dexter was belting hell out of us in one of the best short innings I have ever seen, I went around the wicket and had him caught behind by Wally Grout. Trying to keep two overs ahead of the play, I told my vice-captain, Neil Harvey, we had no chance of drawing the match; it would be either won or lost. I then called for drinks on a cold Old Trafford afternoon, not because I was thirsty but to tell the players, as a group, rather than by a dramatic dash to each of them. I asked them to produce the greatest fielding of their lives. They did!

No such problems for Ricky Ponting in 2005 as he moved towards the Old Trafford Test; all he needed was to leave the hotel early to be sure of being able to get into the ground. That applied to all of us. Daphne and I were staying with Bernard and Shirley Lawton at Chapel-en-le-Frith which, in the usual course of events, is a one-hour drive from Chapel to parking the car in the ground. It was an eleven o'clock start and I like to be at the ground two hours before the start on a normal day. This wasn't going to be a normal day. So I left Chapel at 7 a.m., arrived at Old Trafford and tried to find a way through the crowds six deep in the streets waiting to buy their tickets for the day. It was chaos, but wonderful chaos. On the final day of the match, with all the excitement bubbling, around 12,000 spectators were turned away and the gates were closed and locked because 22,000 were already in the ground.

The last moments of the match involved Brett Lee and Glenn McGrath battling to achieve a draw. And that, after Ricky Ponting had played the innings of his life to make 156 and then tickled Harmison to Jones for a caught behind. Simon Jones had bowled magnificently in the first innings to take 6–53 and, with his brilliant control of reverse swing, he was a real threat again on the last afternoon. But, and it was a very big but, he had a niggling injury, severe cramp which might also have been a hamstring problem, and through my binoculars I watched him at mid-on give a shake of his head to Vaughan and then there was the quietest and least noticeable change of personnel. Stephen Peters came on to the field and Jones quickly walked off and the Australians and the crowd didn't realise; Vaughan had done it very subtly so as not to let Ponting know he was a bowler down. In the Channel 4 commentary box I said to Mark Nicholas that Jones was gone and we mentioned it in passing to the seven and a half million viewers watching at the time.

England carried all the statistical honours of the match. The two captains were brilliant, Vaughan leading the way with 166, Ponting replying with 156. Vaughan declared at 280–6, McGrath fought through second-innings pain to take 5–115, one of them Pietersen for a duck. Warne was unable to take a second-innings wicket but then made 34 at a critical time but was out to Flintoff . . . and then Ponting was gone.

Glenn McGrath has often said he is, or was then, the best number eleven in the world and he had played more than 100 Test matches. None of his innings and none of the runs he had made were as important as what he was about to do at Old Trafford on 15 August 2005. He was walking out to join Brett Lee and there were 24 balls to survive. For both of them, not just McGrath. McGrath had been advised to bat out of his crease to lessen the chance of an lbw and he did that. What his team-mates hadn't said was that when the ball had been played or had gone through to the 'keeper, he should go back into his crease. The 'keeper's throw missed. Lee and McGrath survived, the Australian balcony erupted with joy and laughter; how on earth did the pair survive 24 balls for a draw? When the last ball was bowled McGrath had become the highest-scoring number eleven in the history of Test cricket. He had made 556 runs in 111 Tests. It was one of the great moments and we were about to go to Trent Bridge with the series still squared at one–one.

England named an unchanged team for the fourth successive Test, a move full of confidence and also fully justified; Australia on the other hand were again without their batting hero of Old Trafford, Glenn McGrath. Not because of any lingering problems from his foot injury at Edgbaston but this time because of a strain in his bowling elbow. Ponting and his co-selectors chose Shaun Tait, a young fast bowler from Adelaide who had impressed many opposing batsmen by the pace at which the ball approached them. Michael Kasprowicz was recalled to the team and Jason Gillespie, who had been struggling with his form throughout the tour, was omitted from the final XI.

Sitting in the commentary box on the first morning of the game,

I wondered what the cricketing gods had in mind for us this time. Some were of the opinion that we had run out of time for drama, that there had been enough extraordinary cricket to last for several years and those spectators at the ground, and the millions watching on television, would have to settle for something far more mundane. In fact, it finished up with grown people leaving the television set on while they went and hid behind a sofa; some I know even went to bed and pulled the covers over their heads, still with the television set on so they could hear what was happening, but fearful of watching it. The ones who told me about doing that were a mixture: a few ladies, mostly men, some of whom could buy and sell parts of Nottinghamshire or London, big businessmen who quailed at the thought of bringing bad luck to England by looking at the screen.

The first hush came with the toss after Vaughan and Ponting had joined Aleem Dar, Steve Bucknor and match referee Ranjan Madugalle in the centre of the ground. Ponting called incorrectly. It was a good toss to win for Vaughan because the pitch looked a belter, a thought emphasised by the manner in which Andrew Strauss and Marcus Trescothick batted in the opening session, Strauss being out in unlucky fashion sweeping Warne and having the ball balloon off his right boot to Matthew Hayden at slip. Rain caused a delay in the second session of play and when things got going again Tait claimed his first Test wicket when he bowled Trescothick and had Ian Bell caught at the wicket playing at a very fast delivery in slightly offbeat fashion. This was Adam Gilchrist's 300th Test match dismissal and then the Australian captain produced one of the gambles of the year when he brought himself on to bowl and had Michael Vaughan also caught by Gilchrist. In an Ashes series that so far had produced hardly believable results and incidents, nothing was stranger than the Australian captain dismissing his opposite number. Andrew Flintoff soon put that right with a blistering century from only 121 balls and, with Geraint Jones making a splendid 85, it looked as though England would finish their first innings around the 500-mark, and in quick time as well. In fact they finished at 477, Shane Warne taking the last three to finish with 4–102. The Australians really used just four bowlers; it only increases to five if you count Ponting, which would err on the side of generosity despite his success.

For Australia, what followed was little short of disaster, Hayden, Ponting and Martyn making 9 between them, the latter pair lbw and shown by TV replays to be decidedly unlucky. There was some resistance from Michael Clarke, Simon Katich and Adam Gilchrist, and once again Brett Lee, with 47 and top score, was fighting to keep his team in the game with bat as well as ball, but it was to no avail and Michael Vaughan was able to have one of his most pleasurable moments in cricket when he told Ricky Ponting Australia would follow on.

That had last happened in Pakistan seventeen years earlier when Javed Miandad had hit a double century against Allan Border's team and Pakistan won the match by an innings and 188 runs. It was not a statistic over which Ponting would like to linger but the Australians this time, at their second attempt, got away to a better start, with Langer and Hayden posting a half-century stand before the reverse swing started to take effect, as had been the case in the first innings when Simon Jones bowled superbly to take 5–44 from 14.1 overs. England's reverse swing was in the hands of Troy Cooley, an Australian who played for Tasmania, who was, and is, widely recognised as the authority on swinging the ball in so-called reverse fashion. The necessary requirement as well is that the pupil, the bowler, is a good learner and when Cooley was first doing the job for Australia the bowlers were very good. Cooley, in the normal course of negotiations with Cricket Australia, asked for a pay rise but, for whatever bone-headed reason, that was declined by the Australian administrators. England heard about this and snapped him up. Very sensible too and the reversing of the ball by the English bowlers in that 2005 series was a key factor in victory. The Australian administrators didn't make the same mistake again. Cooley was approached and agreed to rejoin the Australian team and, in the 2009 series in Australia against Pakistan, it was evident he was making a difference. He has also worked well with the Australian Academy.

In their second innings, following on, Australia really needed around 420 to be able to set a feasible challenge of around 150–160. The pitch was still good but there was plenty of spin to be had out of the footmarks for Warne. In the end Australia could only set a target of 129 for England but there were still a few twists and turns to come for the nervous spectators at the ground and watching from behind their sofas, or with the covers over their heads. It began with Warne. Thirty-two runs had come from the first five overs in the England second innings, so now the task was less than a hundred with all wickets in hand. Almost. Warne ran in off his few paces and in the space of a couple of overs and 25 runs had sent back to the pavilion Trescothick caught by Ponting, Vaughan, with the first ball Warne bowled him, and then Strauss caught by Michael Clarke at leg slip from a viciously spun leg-break. Then Pietersen and Flintoff calmed nerves with a 46-run partnership, but Lee had Pietersen caught by Gilchrist and produced the most wonderful reverse-swinging inswinger to remove Flintoff and now, at 116–7, it was to be left to Ashley Giles, Matthew Hoggard, Steve Harmison and Simon Jones. The last three wickets had gone for 13 runs and another 13 were still needed; Ashley Giles was waiting in the centre when Hoggard arrived.

It is said that Hoggard asked what the bowlers were doing as he had found it difficult to watch the television screen in the dressing-room, the same difficulty television-watchers throughout the country were having even though the pictures were beautifully coloured and the commentary restrained. Giles is said to have chuckled and reassured his new batting partner. 'Binga's bowling very fast and reversing it all over the place, Warnie's turning it square!' Small comfort, but it might have been just what Hoggard needed rather than a whispered admonishment to 'do your best'. That's what Matthew was going to do anyway – he had sometimes been used as a nightwatchman because of his common-sense approach – and, when Lee slightly overpitched a reverse-swinging inswinger, Hoggard smashed it through the cover area. Giles took the risk in the next over of playing Warne to midwicket, hitting against the spin, and it showed a touch of genius and bravery because he got away with it.

From what I have been told, the players were drained at the end of the game, and for a considerable time thereafter, and I'm not at all surprised. In the commentary box we couldn't afford to be drained; it was another of those matches where less commentary is actually more, definitely a case of merely adding to the picture on the screen, providing information and letting the viewer enjoy it all in slightly nervous fashion. On the last day at Old Trafford Channel 4 had seven and a half million viewers; on this final day at Trent Bridge almost eight and a half million viewers watched, providing some of the biggest audiences in the history of cricket television. Total TV viewing was said to have increased from 14 million in 2001 to 22 million in 2005. A great credit to Channel 4.

There were four centuries in the final Test at The Oval: Andrew Strauss 129, Kevin Pietersen 158, Justin Langer 105 and Matthew Hayden 138. Before any of those centuries were completed one of the biggest crowd roars of the summer came when the coin had hit the ground at the toss. Mark Nicholas, the Channel 4 presenter, had turned to Michael Vaughan and not to Ricky Ponting, so England had won the toss. It was a good one to win. Paul Collingwood had been brought into the final XI in place of the injured Simon Jones. The England batting had been strengthened, but Collingwood could also bowl medium pace and Harmison, Flintoff, Giles and Hoggard were there.

Unusual happenings – the Australian batsmen, Langer and Hayden, accepted an offer of bad light from umpires Bowden and Koertzen on the second afternoon and they did it again on the third afternoon. Very strange tactics when you consider Australia needed every available minute if they were to win the game.

Wonderful cricket – Kevin Pietersen's 158, coming in at 67–3 after Glenn McGrath had produced two great deliveries to dismiss Vaughan, caught at the wicket by Gilchrist, and then Ian Bell, caught at slip by Warne. The hat-trick ball was another beauty. Pietersen the new batsman was a flurry of gloves, bat and body and the Australian appeals could just about have been heard at Lord's. Umpire Bowden considered it for a moment and then slowly shook his head. Great decision. The ball had flicked Pietersen's shoulder but had missed his glove by the tiniest of margins. Lee then bowled a great outswinger to Pietersen and the ball flew to Warne at slip as a regulation chance, though what was regulation in this series? It was simply a missed catch. Warne then dismissed Trescothick and Flintoff and suddenly the Australians were in with a chance, 133 in arrears, five wickets needed and 70 overs still to be bowled. Then came some of the greatest batting I have seen in a Test match; it wasn't the runs Pietersen made, it was the way he attacked the Australian bowlers and took the game out of their reach. At lunch, however, when he walked off with Paul Collingwood, it would have been to a gloomy and anxious England dressing-room. Anything could be about to happen: they might be bowled out and Australia, in a hungry run chase, could win, the series would be squared two–two and despair would be the word of the day and the month and the rest of the year.

Pietersen needed some guidance and the man who had to come up with the game plan was the captain, Michael Vaughan, who had a wonderful series; an inspiring five matches and now he had to find the right words to inspire Pietersen. He also had to take into account that Lee and Warne were bowling beautifully; he needed to use his imagination to lift his batsman. He didn't sit down with Pietersen, which would have been too formal, something like a speech. Instead, he said, 'Get out there after lunch and express yourself, and stop messing around.'

David Graveney, the Chairman of the England selection committee, found it a bit much; he went to the car park and sat in his car, listening rather than watching. Pietersen, well, he just went out and expressed himself by taking 35 off Brett Lee's first three overs after lunch. For England it was the perfect finish and when Langer and Hayden opened the Australian innings in fading light the umpires quickly removed the bails and the Ashes were back with England. Glenn McGrath bowled Pietersen for 158; it was the last ball I called on British television after 42 years with the BBC and then Channel 4. Shane Warne took 12 wickets in the match and 40 in the series, a magnificent performance even for the greatest legspinner ever to play the game.

34

TWENTY20

SEVERAL times over the last decade or so I have been asked to describe Twenty20 cricket. The main reason for the question is that people know the game began in the United Kingdom and that I worked there in the northern summers for almost fifty years. My reply is generally perfectly simple. The game is part of the evolution of cricket over the years and it could be argued that this form of the game might well be older than Test and first-class matches, though younger than the 50-overs-a-side matches which, in Australia, could loosely be said to have started in 1970–71 when Australia played England in the inaugural one-day International match. This happened because the Third Test scheduled in Melbourne over the New Year had been abandoned on the third day because of heavy rain and a conference between Australian Cricket Board members and the MCC team manager David Clark, plus two other English cricket administrators, Sir Cyril Hawker and Gubby Allen, decided to play a limited-overs fixture. There was a slight problem because they forgot to tell England's captain Ray Illingworth about it, possibly because they knew he was unlikely to be in favour because of the very heavy workload on his players. It was a match played with 40 eight-ball overs for each team, roughly the equivalent of the 50-overs-a-side matches played these days, as it works out as 53.2 six-ball overs. All countries now play their games in six balls to the over, of course – another little piece of evolution in cricket.

Australia won the match by five wickets, bowling out England for 190 from 39.4 overs and then making the required runs from 34.6 overs. The two top scorers were John Edrich (82) and Ian

Chappell (60), with Edrich the first Man of the Match in limited-
overs Internationals. In 1972 the Prudential Insurance Company
sponsored a three-match series, 55 six-ball overs maximum each
side, between England and Australia. Brian Close was made
England captain, Ian Chappell was by now captain of Australia
in Test matches and one-day games. There were big crowds at
all three games and, with the series one–one, the third match at
Edgbaston saw England win by two wickets in an exciting finish,
with Tony Greig and John Snow the unbeaten batsmen. The games
were played under similar playing conditions as in the modern
times, though there were no restrictions on field-placings and a
bowler had a maximum of 11 overs. Three years later the first
limited-overs World Cup was played in England. The matches
were 60 overs a side, the participating teams were West Indies and
Australia, who met in the final, India, Pakistan, Sri Lanka, New
Zealand, East Africa and England. Fortunately the final was on
the longest day of the year, 21 June 1975. The match, played at
Lord's, didn't finish until 8.42 p.m. and the West Indian captain
Clive Lloyd hit a magnificent 102 from 85 balls after the first
three West Indian wickets had fallen for 50 in 15 overs. It was an
historic day in the evolution of cricket.

It is incorrect, however, to think that Twenty20 is a totally
recent innovation. It has been officially played since 2003 and
there were unofficial matches played in this shortened version of
the game as far back as 1999. It really got under way because of
English cricket losing one of its long-term sponsors, a tobacco
company, who sponsored the Benson & Hedges Cup for twenty-
six years up to 1998. They then signed another contract and the
cricket authorities and the company went on together to 2002,
but then it came to an end. In 2001, the marketing manager of the
ECB addressed a meeting of the county chairmen and persuaded
them to try the new format as a replacement. The playing time of
a match was to be something like three and a half hours and the
players of both teams would be on the ground, one team in the
field and the batting side, after some experimenting, housed in a
form of dugout, though later we have had teams seated on chairs.

The aim was twofold: it was a chance for spectators to be closer to the players, and the players themselves needed to be on the ground so the batsmen could move quickly to the centre when a wicket fell.

The game has taken off globally and one very important aspect is that in many countries the domestic cricket format has changed; certainly there are Tests and 50-overs-a-side games, some of them played as day-night fixtures, and then there is also T20. In the eight leading cricket nations, together with Bangladesh and Zimbabwe, plus Canada, Kenya and the USA, a wide variety of competitions have been established.

Australia	KFC Twenty20 Big Bash
England	Twenty20 Cup
India	DLF Indian Premier League, Indian Inter-State T20 Championship and Indian Cricket League
New Zealand	HRV Cup
Pakistan	Pakistan Super League and RBS Twenty-20 Cup
South Africa	Standard Bank Pro 20 Series
Sri Lanka	Inter-Provincial Twenty20
West Indies	Stanford 20/20
Bangladesh	Dhaka Premier League T20, National Cricket League T20, Port City Cricket League (PCL)
Zimbabwe	Metropolitan Bank Twenty20
Canada	Scotiabank National T20 Championship
Kenya	National Elite League Twenty20
USA	Pro Cricket, American Premier League and NYPD Cricket League

In Australia the first game of T20 was played at the WACA in Perth between Western Australia and Victoria in January 2005; the crowd was 20,000. There were other large crowds; at the 'Gabba in 2007 Queensland and NSW played in front of a crowd of 27,000, and the previous year 38,000 spectators watched Australia play South Africa. Just to show nothing ever really goes to plan in cricket, on 1 February 2008 Australia met India in a T20 at the MCG and it was predicted that the record crowd for the ground, established in the Tied Test series in 1961, would be comfortably beaten. That crowd was 90,800, and in recent years new stands have been built at the ground and 100,000 can be accommodated there. The record still stands, however. The problem was that India batted first and were bowled out for only 74 and the Australians coasted to 75–1 in 11.2 overs. Once the potential spectators could hear what was happening, they made for their homes and their television sets and the crowd was only 84,041. The fact that it was a one-off game might well have been the reason for the big crowd, but if the ground record at the MCG is to be broken it will be Twenty20 that will do it and I want to be there when it happens.

Going back to the questions I am asked when describing T20 cricket, I always say something along the following lines: a Twenty20 match can legitimately be compared to a certain situation in an Ashes Test. Imagine that, with England holding the Ashes, the five-match series stands at two–two. On the final day in the match at The Oval, England have been bowled out in the afternoon to leave Australia with 170 to make to win the series and therefore regain the Ashes. The umpires decide they have 20 overs in which to make the runs. It is a perfectly normal situation in Twenty20 but quite different from, say, the Tied Test at the 'Gabba where Australia, in the last session of play, had two hours in which to make the required runs to win. Then it was a matter of the fielding side giving as few overs as possible, unless the state of the game changed and they needed to bowl as many as possible. That often could become complicated but nowadays in a Test match the overs are carefully calculated and the umpires would have specified the requirements to the team chasing the victory. The figure of 170 is what I have worked out as a par score from watching the KFC Big Bash matches in Australia and other T20 matches, where the cricket has been excellent, the excitement outstanding and the crowds hardly believable.

I am writing this watching the Queensland v Western Australia match at the 'Gabba on Saturday, 16 January 2010. The ground is packed with the third highest crowd of the summer with this new competition. We have had 35,000 at Homebush in Sydney, 43,000 at the Melbourne Cricket Ground and other turnouts of more than 20,000. Channel 9 are always undertaking good research into attendances as well as rating of people who are watching the matches on television. In 2009, our research showed clearly that for Test matches the crowds are made up of adults who take their children to the matches, but the position is completely reversed in Twenty20. It is the young people who run the show and the organising of personnel to travel to the cricket grounds. It is the young ones who persuade the parents to take them, so for this type of game the level of youth present is far higher than any other, including the 50-overs-a-side Internationals.

Five years ago I wrote that any type of cricket able to bring to the grounds thousands of spectators and have hundreds of thousands, even millions, watching around the world on television, must be good for the game. There was no shortage of people blasting me for saying and writing that. Most of it was along the lines of 'how could you possibly say anything like that when you have been brought up in the traditional form of the game?' The answer is that while I have certainly been brought up in the traditional form of the game, I have seen it evolve in many different directions in the past seventy years.

I name that time span because it covers the years I started primary school cricket at Burnside, North Parramatta, then went on to Parramatta High School in wartime, from 1942 to 1946. I played one-afternoon cricket from fourth grade and, following that, when two-day cricket resumed, I was selected in third grade, second grade and then chosen in first grade, where I played in the Central Cumberland First XI with my father during my last year at high school. That was a great thrill and it was certainly part of traditional cricket. Then into the NSW Colts' coaching class and practice afternoons, Tuesdays and Thursdays, the NSW Sheffield Shield team in 1948, debut in the Australian team against West Indies at the SCG, in 1952, a tour of England in 1953 and 1956 – all that was traditional and there was no other way of playing the game.

It was also unheard of for a cricketer captaining his country, Australia, to fly overseas, in this case to the United Kingdom, to write for a newspaper and work in radio or television. This was the first deviation I had from traditional things to do with cricket and it involved working for the BBC. Tradition is wonderful and I'm all for it, but never forget the evolution of the game which began all those years ago in the south of England in the Kent and Sussex areas. And never forget Dr Grace's words about Alfred Mynn and how astonished the latter would have been had he still been around when Grace was in his splendour.

On 1 February 2010 I received an email from Cricket Australia giving the information that the Australian selectors had nominated a thirteen-man squad for the KFC Twenty20 International against Pakistan at the MCG on Friday, 5 February. Nothing too unusual about that except that the selectors, chaired by Andrew Hilditch, said they had chosen the squad taking into account the performances of players in International Twenty20 matches and the KFC Twenty20 Big Bash and also the balance of the side so as to be able to implement match plans and tactics for Twenty20 cricket going into the World Cup. 'On this occasion there are significant changes between the one-day and the Twenty20 side as we look at several players who could play a key role in our World Twenty20 campaign,' Hilditch said.

Certainly it showed the difference in selecting cricket teams in the year 2010 compared with the time I began playing Sheffield Shield cricket in 1948. Then there were three selectors, Sir Donald Bradman, Jack Ryder and Dudley (Snow) Seddon, and Australian cricket didn't need more than three because there were only four states contesting the Sheffield Shield: Queensland, New South Wales, Victoria and South Australia. Western Australia had just been admitted on a restricted basis in 1947–48; they played four matches in the season and they actually 'won' the Shield in that summer. The matches they played coincided with Test matches against India and Bradman, Ryder and Seddon were busy choosing the touring party to go to England for an Ashes series. That team was unbeaten and later was to be nicknamed 'The Invincibles'. In the Western Australian matches, because the Tests were played at the same time, the opposition wasn't at full strength but, irrespective of that, they still played very well under the gifted leadership of Keith Carmody. They could hardly have made a better start to their Sheffield Shield future than to beat South Australia by an innings and 124 runs at the WACA in November 1947.

Nowadays the Australian selectors face the task of choosing Test teams with regular overseas tours taking place, teams to play in 50-overs-a-side fixtures, and Twenty20 teams adept at changing their game and their methods to fit in with the style of contest they face. In a fourteen-man Test squad named by the selectors these days, often only half of those players will be in the 50-overs-a-side squad and different players again will be in the Twenty20 squad.

A very good example was in the email I have mentioned above, in that Michael Hussey didn't appear in the list of players. Yet, the previous evening in a 50-overs match at the WACA against Pakistan, Hussey had held together the Australian batting and ensured Australia completed a clean sweep of the five-match series. Michael Hussey's brother, David, *was* in the Twenty20 squad; he is a specialist of the type Andrew Hilditch was alluding to and it was a good example of the way selectors have to think in these modern times.

In the evolution of cricket, the selectors have had to keep up as well, and it is a non-stop business for them. Twenty20 has certainly changed the lives of many people and I couldn't be more pleased. Although there are many who scoff at the game in its shortened varieties, some kind of one-day cricket has always been played right from the time England took the game to other countries. In Australia, for example, when cricket began being played in the early 1800s, there were many one-day matches, though no night cricket, even if some of the matches might be finished in the twilight. More than 140 years ago, when *Wisden* first came on to the bookshelves, it contained many examples of one-day matches at Lord's, although matches played to a certain number of overs were thin on the ground.

Twenty20 has already done a great deal for cricket, most notably producing crowds beyond anyone's imagination in places as diverse as Lord's and Melbourne. Yet there is a feeling in many quarters that there is little skill attached to this form of the game. My belief is to the contrary: there is a great amount of skill in all forms of the game. I have seen extraordinary fielding and catching, and batting which has to be innovative otherwise the match is lost and the prize is gone. There are those who say the winning of a cricket match should not be paramount but I regard that as a load of nonsense. The only thing you can't do in a limited-overs match is play a draw. Rained out perhaps, but that is bad luck. You could play a tie and then have the excitement of a Super Over decider. You will also see some extraordinary strokes – reverse sweeps, innovative flicks and the Dilscoop among others – and now there are some delightful players who occasionally use those shots in the longer forms of the game.

The real key to the popularity of the Twenty20 lies in its entertainment. From the first ball bowled or received, the aim of the players has to be entertainment, even though they may not realise they are doing that. They look at it simply as the winning of the match and I love it. I will listen carefully to those who don't like it, but then I will go and switch on my television set and get ready for the day or the evening. Spectators have realised that when they pay their money at the turnstiles they could be in for an exciting time. That though is not guaranteed – they could also be in for a fizzer.

One thing I can guarantee: cricket will never be quite the same again and that is no bad thing. The proviso is that the 40-over match, 20 for each team, becomes part of the framework of international and domestic cricket, alongside the 50-over competitions and the Test matches.

T20 is one of the greatest things ever to happen in the game of cricket. There have been few more exciting finishes to a cricket match in the past 133 years than the Australian victory in the semi-final of the T20 World Cup in the Caribbean in 2010.

Never lose sight of the fact that it also has made the task of Australia's selectors, and other selection committees around the cricket world, one of the most challenging the game of cricket has known.

35

RICKY PONTING: THE MOST EXTRAORDINARY CAPTAINCY

T HE most important thing about being a Test cricket captain is that you make your own decisions. There is a very good reason for this: you are the one who takes the blame if it all goes wrong. There may be seventeen players in a touring squad and twelve in a home Test team, with one left out on the morning of the match, but it is your thinking and your decisions that are responded to by the players. Sometimes all is sweetness and light, sometimes you feel as though nothing you touch will turn to gold. But in making your decisions you take the blame and the credit, depending on how the game finishes.

I first saw Ricky Ponting play in a Test match on 8 December 1995 at the WACA ground in Perth. I watched him from the commentary box as he made a delightful 96 before being given out lbw to Chaminda Vaas. It was one of those decisions that in these modern days of technology and referrals would have been known as a 'howler'. I had earlier watched him in a limited-overs match Channel 9 covered and had heard a great deal about him from Ian Chappell and Rod Marsh after Ian had assisted young players at the Board of Control's Academy in Adelaide, where Marsh was in charge. Chappell had a very high opinion of the young Ponting and there seemed no doubt he was destined to be an outstanding batsman for Australia. Six years before his Test debut, his uncle, Greg Campbell, had toured England with Allan Border's team in 1989, when he played in the opening Test match at Headingley but took only one wicket. Australia had gone into that First Test without a spinner; they changed their team for the Second Test at Lord's, bringing in legspinner Trevor Hohns, who played throughout the remainder of the series. Australia used only twelve players in the summer. When he returned to Australia Campbell turned in some good performances, but recurring injuries to his knees and wrist hampered him and he played no more first-class cricket after 1992. Cricket was in the family; having an uncle who had played for Australia would have done Ponting no harm at all and gave him something to match.

He played first-class cricket in the Sheffield Shield in the 1992–93 season in Australia, making his debut for Tasmania against South Australia in Adelaide. It was a tough start because South Australia won by 215 runs. Ponting made 56 and 4 and in the opposition was Tim Nielsen, later to be Australia's coach when Ponting was captain. Nielsen made 109 in South Australia's first innings. Playing for Tasmania at that time was Troy Cooley, who bowled at considerable pace but also had some trouble with the front-foot Law and was called many times for no-balling.

The Australian system works well for captains. The latter group are very fortunate to be so honoured, though my own experience was a sad introduction after Ian Craig contracted hepatitis in 1958 and was unable to play during the summer where he had been listed to be captain. Australia has had only twenty-three Test captains since the end of the Second World War. Don Bradman continued as captain in the first series after the war, then Bill Brown, Lindsay Hassett, Arthur Morris, Ian Johnson, Ray Lindwall, Ian Craig, Richie Benaud, Neil Harvey, Bob Simpson, Brian Booth, Bill Lawry, Barry Jarman, Ian Chappell, Greg Chappell, Graham Yallop, Kim Hughes, Allan Border, Mark Taylor, Steve Waugh, Adam Gilchrist, Ricky Ponting, and Michael Clarke. Interspersed in that group were captains who led the national team when World Series Cricket was played in the 1977–79 period; others, like Neil Harvey in 1961, took over because of injury to the appointed skippers.

Ponting first captained Australia on a short tour to Sri Lanka in 2003–04. In what turned out to be something of a rough and tough series, Australia inflicted the first ever whitewash on Sri Lanka at home. Before the Tests, Ponting led Australia to a three–two victory in the 50-overs-a-side competition. It was an unusual tour. Australia's three victories in the one-day competition came by 84 runs, five wickets and then 40 runs, Sri Lanka's two wins were by one run and three wickets. In the four games he played Ponting made 58, 69, 63 and 67. Adam Gilchrist skippered the team in the final game when Ponting was ill. Under Ponting's leadership Australia won the three Tests by 197 runs, 27 runs and 121 runs. It would be difficult to think of a better way to begin a captaincy career, particularly as in the Tests his batting didn't suffer from the responsibility of leadership. He made 21 and 28, 10 and 27 and 92 and 20. In the Third and final Test, Michael Kasprowicz had Sri Lankan batsman Herath lbw to win the game with eight balls remaining. There were some who complained that this wasn't a great Australian team and the final result wasn't a true reflection of the play. My view, from a considerable distance, was that it was a performance full of merit, not least from a young cricketer captaining his country for the first time and in conditions that weren't totally in favour of a visiting team.

It may be when historians closely study Ricky Ponting's career they will come up with the answer that his term of captaincy was one of the most extraordinary in the history of the Australian game. Shortly after the clean sweep against Sri Lanka, he led Australia in England when England regained the Ashes for the first time in eighteen years. In 2006 it was back to Australia, where West Indies and South Africa were touring and it was another quite remarkable summer. Six Tests were played, three against each country. Australia beat West Indies three–nil and South Africa two–nil, with the Perth Test an exciting draw. Again there was some brilliant cricket played by the teams taking part and wonderful entertainment for those paying their money at the turnstiles and watching on television.

In 2006–07 Ponting led Australia against England in Australia, won the First Test at the 'Gabba, then somehow conjured up a win in the Adelaide Test, after England had won the toss and made

551–6 (dec) and Australia had replied with 513, Ponting making 142 and Michael Clarke 124. In another exciting finish, Australia made the required runs for victory, losing only four wickets. Then the Tests in Perth, Melbourne and Sydney were comprehensively won by Australia for a five–nil victory in the series, about the most emphatic answer one could possibly give to having lost the Ashes in 2005. Now though there was a problem, because it was clear that at some stage Ponting would lose three of the greatest cricketers ever to play the game. Shane Warne, Glenn McGrath and Adam Gilchrist were about to choose their time to leave the Test match arena and I sat back one afternoon at Coogee and wondered how Ponting was going to manage the transition. The answer was that there was nothing he could do about it; a dozen high-class players had already retired or been left out of the team in the past fifteen months, but there was nothing he could do, other than his best. And use his brain as well as his cricket talents.

When Ponting had made his Test debut in Perth against Sri Lanka in 1995, Shane Warne was in the team, so was Glenn McGrath, but it was another four years before Adam Gilchrist made it into the Test side. He had been turning in some splendid performances for Western Australia but Ian Healy, having been chosen to tour Pakistan in 1988–89 and then England in 1989 when the Ashes were regained, was clearly the number one wicketkeeper, a point he underlined by his performances behind the stumps and with the bat in 1993, which was Shane Warne's first tour of England. Healy kept very well to Warne on that tour, and to the end of his Test career he continued as a top-class wicketkeeper, though his batting did fall away by his own high standards.

Adam Gilchrist made his Test debut in the 1999–2000 series against Pakistan in Australia in the opening game in Brisbane, not necessarily what Queensland cricket followers wanted to see, but right from the start in that Test, and the following one in Hobart, Gilchrist's work was outstanding and he suddenly became one of the real stars of Australian cricket. Gilchrist played his last Test for Australia in the match starting on 24 January 2008 against India, McGrath's last Test was in 2007 and Warne's final appearance was in 2007 at the end of the Ashes series in Australia. When McGrath and Warne bowed out in that Sydney Test, McGrath took six wickets, Warne made 71 and, as a sideline, Gilchrist made 62. The phrase is sometimes over-used but it certainly was 'the end of an era', even if Gilchrist did play on for a short time before complete retirement from Australian cricket, with Brad Haddin coming into the wicketkeeping position for the May 2008 tour of the West Indies. It was a new-look team for Australia and therefore Ponting had plenty of thinking to do. Australia won the series two–nil with one drawn but Australia suddenly were a work in progress.

It was similar to the end of the 1962–63 and 1983–84 summers in Australia when we lost three great cricketers. The first time was when Neil Harvey, Alan Davidson and Ken Mackay retired at the conclusion of the final Test against England and then, in 1984, Greg Chappell, Dennis Lillee and Rodney Marsh all retired from Test cricket, but Marsh did continue to play some one-day matches with the national team. Davidson was a great allrounder, a fast left-arm bowler with wonderful control, magnificent fielder and, batting down the list, a destroyer of bowlers. I used Mackay as a bowling allrounder, a style quite different from when he played Sheffield Shield for Queensland. Losing players of that quality makes life very difficult for a captain.

When Ponting lost Warne, Gilchrist and McGrath, they didn't all leave him at the same time but the effect was similar to the two occasions mentioned above. There were other issues to contemplate as well, none more important than the change in media approach. A captain always has to be available for print media conferences at the close of play. In recent years television networks expect a captain to provide something different for the viewers, not simply a 'grab' from a television opportunity where three or four interviewers are looking for something they are able to label 'exclusive', even if that term is not necessarily accurate. Ponting did it well; he was always affable and helpful.

Twenty20 was a very important issue. The KFC Big Bash in Australia – that is, T20 games played between the six states – was starting to draw big crowds. New South Wales found a young left-hand batsman who went on to play T20 for Australia without having played a first-class match. David Warner very quickly established a record playing a domestic T20 for NSW against Tasmania when he hit 50 off just 18 balls, wonderful to watch. The domestic T20 matches were pretty much packed out on the smaller grounds around Australia and in Sydney the games were played at Homebush Stadium rather than the SCG. In the light of this, Australia's cricket administrators started to talk publicly about changing the structure of programming so that more T20 matches could be accommodated. Cricket Australia's CEO, James Sutherland, was quoted as saying an expanded Big Bash would eventually force a reduction elsewhere in the domestic calendar. 'We don't see in the short term, the next couple of years, any major compromises but, having said that, if the success of the Big Bash grows it may well create such noise and such demand that there will be some sort of further expansion,' Sutherland said. 'Our long-term planning has a way to go but I would see the time come where the KFC Big Bash has its own summer time window so we can have our Test and one-day players available for interstate T20 duties. What we have always said about T20 is that it is a new way to bring people to the game. One-day cricket has done that in the past, it has broadened the spectrum of cricket fans over the past two or three decades. We make no secret of the fact that we want cricket to be more popular to potential cricket fans. These days people are increasingly "time poor" and T20 provides us with the opportunity to create a revenue stream from a league-type competition that in the past has been denied to the game of cricket.'

Ponting is a great fan of the KFC Big Bash, though in 2009 he retired from Twenty20 competitions to concentrate on Tests and 50-overs-a-side Internationals and the World Cup that goes with that format. In early 2010 he replied very quietly and calmly to what was being proposed and made the point that Australia's first-class programming must not be affected because it is the finest structure in the cricket world.

'I'd hate to see in Australia the day where we start playing more

T20 cricket at the expense of Sheffield Shield cricket. One thing I think we have over other nations is the great strength of our domestic cricket,' Ponting said. 'It has developed and brought on a number of very good players during the course of the past 100 years of Australian cricket. Let's hope there is some way an expanded competition and a full roster of Sheffield Shield games can work in together; that would be the ideal.' Ponting added that to him it seemed unrealistic to carve a window in the crowded international programme to accommodate an expanded T20. 'The IPL in India can't get that, even with the money they are throwing around.'

Ponting also said he envisaged real problems if administrators tried to squeeze T20 competitions into the Australian summer by playing Sheffield Shield matches in places like Darwin or Cairns, or anywhere else in the Top-End. 'Those young guys are not going to get the chance to play at the SCG, the MCG, those sorts of venues, or play at the 'Gabba early season when the pitch is green. Those are the things that have made Australian Test players as good as they are because they've learned to adapt to different conditions; in the same conditions you encounter when you play Test matches.'

Ponting added, 'I'm sure they'll find some way around it. I'm not sure exactly what it's going to be because all the talk is just about making the Big Bash bigger. I'm supportive of that because it's been a great tournament this year. However, I don't want it to interfere with young up-and-coming Test players who need the right opportunities and experience to play good hard, solid Sheffield Shield cricket. That's what's made all of us guys what we are today, the fact that we've been brought up in a really hard, tough first-class cricket system, and I'd hate to see the day when that's ever changed or compromised.'

I was delighted to hear what Ponting had said because in my view the situation could not have been better expressed. I've always felt the Australian system of strong cricket in country areas, city clubs with a good competition with the next step to the Sheffield Shield competition, is the best in the cricket world.

I have been an observer of the game over the past sixty-two years and Ponting gets full marks from me. Like all captains he has made decisions that have backfired and future captains will do the same thing. I think Ponting has done a splendid job in the time he has been in charge of the team, not just with his on-the-field captaincy, but also with his thinking and willingness to speak up, in constructive fashion, about the game itself.

It is not common for cricket captains to step down but then continue to play under the new captain. On the other hand, there have been quite a few occasions when a captain is removed by the selection committee, who consider the team would play better under a new captain, and yet the 'old' captain is such a good cricketer that he is needed as a player. Ricky Ponting loves cricket, loves playing and it was his decision to step down, and then it was his decision to make himself available for selection in the Australian team. Certainly, in Australia, Ponting and Benaud are the only two I am able to find who have done that and the wording in each case was the same.

Earlier in this book I related how I spoke with Sir Donald Bradman at the SCG and told him I would be working in the media from April 1964 and wouldn't be available for the tour of England. Our arrangement was that I would tell him when it was 'time' and I added, after meeting with him on the last day of the Test at the MCG, that I was 'available for Australia in any capacity'.

Bob Simpson and I never had the slightest problem; he was a good captain and he never needed advice, though on a couple of occasions he asked something about one of his players. For my part, the only thing I suggested was that I field away from the slip and gully cordon, where he was certain to be at first slip. Being a working journalist, I was aware that if we were in the same area and were chatting, it would be assumed I was offering advice. It was a good decision and it also gave me the chance to do something I hadn't done in years – test my throwing arm from the boundary.

When Ponting and Clarke announced they would be playing together in an Australian Test team, many people in England professed bewilderment that this should happen. Perhaps it went smoothly because of the essential differences in the structure of cricket in the two countries.

36

LOOKING AFTER THE GAME

THE Australian Board of Control for International Cricket was formed on 6 May 1905. There were four members and two Member States, Victoria and New South Wales. The four men who formed the Board were E. E. Bean and L. A. Adamson from Melbourne and A. W. Green and W. McElhone from Sydney. Queensland joined later in 1905, South Australia joined in 1906–07, Tasmania in 1907–08 and Western Australia in 1914–15. It was a turbulent time, with changes made in the game and the Board of Control taking over all aspects of touring. Then, in 1912, six of the most prominent Australian cricketers declined to tour England for a triangular series between England, South Africa and Australia. Those six players were Warwick Armstrong, Hanson Carter, Albert Cotter, Clem Hill, Vernon Ransford and Victor Trumper. In 1909 the great Australian allrounder and captain M. A. Noble played his last Test match and, having made clear his feelings about Mr McElhone, on 13 January 1910, he completely severed connection with all forms of cricket. Two years later he didn't miss the members of the Board when on 29 February 1912 he began a published letter to the *Sydney Morning Herald* with the words: 'I say that the Board of Control has acted unjustly and dishonestly and has violated its own constitution . . .'

The First World War meant that between 22 August 1912 and 17 December 1920 Australia played no Test cricket and, when it did resume, the Australian captain was Warwick Armstrong, one of the Big Six who had refused to tour England for that triangular tournament. Another in the group, Vernon Ransford, became Secretary of the Melbourne Cricket Club in 1939. He was a very quiet and popular administrator who saw the MCG through the 1956 Olympics and passed away in 1957. It has been said that in 1938, when nominations were called for the position of MCG Secretary, the two applicants were Vernon Ransford and Don Bradman. There were occasions between the formation of the Australian Cricket Board of Control and modern times when relations between players and administrators could be frosty, and players certainly needed to know their place, which was a considerable distance below administrators. There were other arguments in the 1990s, when it seemed the old bad times would return, but somehow those problems were sorted out, in the main because of the outstanding work done by Mark Taylor, captain of the Test team at that time.

One hundred and five years after the formation of the Board of Control there are excellent relations between Cricket Australia and the players represented by the Australian Cricketers' Association. They will argue, sometimes vehemently, on matters to do with Memorandums of Understanding and other aspects but, in my view as an observer, things could hardly be better between those on the field and those managing matters off it. Any arguments are constructive and for the good of the game.

Like administration, cricket has changed a great deal and now, with T20, 50-overs-a-side Internationals and Test cricket, administrators need to be right up with the pace, or even a couple of overs ahead of the play, in the scheduling and programming of all forms of cricket matches.

The Chief Executive of Cricket Australia is James Sutherland and he first joined cricket administration in the late 1990s. He didn't arrive there without credentials. For a start he had qualified as a chartered accountant and had a degree in commerce. You may wonder what on earth that has to do with cricket, but it is a requirement in these days of high-powered negotiations that those participating know what they are talking about. Sutherland had other advantages; he had spent five years as an executive of Carlton Football Club in Melbourne, a tough job in itself, where dealing with players who are household names is a twenty-four-hour task.

People in Victorian and Australian cricket circles were looking for someone new and capable in an administrative position
and Sutherland's name was mentioned. Malcolm Speed was then
head of Cricket Australia and he may have thought a bit of assistance wouldn't go amiss. Sutherland was young but at the same
time experienced. He had one other priceless advantage: he was a
cricketer. He had played for Melbourne University and Melbourne
Cricket Club and he was also an assistant state coach. Nothing
too dramatic about that, but it was unlikely to be a handicap,
nor was the fact that he had spent five years with Ernst & Young
learning the ropes of business consultancy and accountancy. In his
short cricket career he played four Sheffield Shield matches and
nine one-dayers. His debut was in 1992 against NSW at the SCG
and he took the wickets of Mark Taylor and Steve Waugh before
rain washed out the match.

In February 2010 Sutherland was interviewed in the *Weekend
Australian Financial Review* by journalist Damon Kitney and it
was an interview that should be widely read by those who have
an interest in the programming of cricket in Australia in years to
come.

As he has done on many occasions, Sutherland said Cricket
Australia's vision was wanting cricket to be Australia's favourite sport. He pointed out that one aspect of this vision was that
Cricket Australia operates as a not-for-profit entity with 26 per
cent of its revenue going to the players and the balance going in
distributions or dividends to the state Cricket Associations around
Australia, all six of them. That money then goes to keep the State
Associations running smoothly and to grass-roots cricket, which
is so important for young people around Australia.

One of the important requirements for a cricket administrator,
or observer, is to be constructive. A point Sutherland made in this
interview was that one-day cricket can be scheduled to make it
more significant. He said that at the moment there are ten one-
day Internationals played in an Australian summer, and he could
foresee it would not change to less than two lots of three games,
head-to-head.

His immediate priority is expanding the Big Bash T20 matches into an eight-team national competition that is city-based, rather than state-based. The new teams would have different identities from the six current interstate teams and there would also be two new teams.

He added that this would continue the strong patriotism around the Australian team but administrators and players would be able to bring a brand new dimension into cricket that other sports currently enjoy. He said, 'So we have the best of both worlds.'

It all added up to one of the best-written articles I have seen on this aspect of cricket and, as well, Sutherland's thoughts were very constructive.

Sutherland's remarks and those I have quoted on the same matters by Ricky Ponting, for me, provide the perfect combination for Australian cricket.

The formation of the game has changed dramatically in the past ten years, but one continuing influence is the International Cricket Council, an administrative body which started in 1912 and has continued with mixed success for almost a century. It would certainly be better if one could say 'continual' success but that would be an enormous exaggeration.

It was first formed as the Imperial Cricket Conference and the first meeting of that august body took place at Lord's in 1909. The ICC proposed the 1912 triangular contest between England Australia and South Africa that happened to coincide with problems between administrators and players in Australia. While the relationship between the two organisations in Australia has changed for the better, there has also been a change in the ICC, and not just because of the name-change to the International Cricket Council. Attitudes have changed as well, but not all their programming and scheduling of international cricket around the world has been of benefit to the game of cricket and its participants. With more countries and more types of matches to consider, there is no doubt the task facing modern administrators can be difficult. Sometimes, though, that difficulty is compounded by extraordinary thinking and decisions on the planning of all kinds of cricket.

Not least of the strange sequences to take place in recent times has been the introduction and advancing of various aspects of an umpiring referral system or, more appropriately, perhaps that should be 'systems' because they haven't just had one go at it but several. There may be various reasons nothing really good has come from it, but the most likely explanation is that it hasn't been properly thought through.

On the day prior to the Brisbane Test between Australia and the West Indies at the 'Gabba in November 2009, David Richardson of the ICC gave a talk to Channel 9 producers, directors, commentators and many others. It was a briefing given by Mr Richardson and the Hawk-Eye company, the organisation behind the device which predicts the path of the ball after it leaves the bowler's hand and what it will do after hitting the pitch. It is part of the new technology of the game of cricket and needs to be given a trial over an extended period. Hopefully though the trials will be successful and not raise the hackles overmuch. At the meeting we were able to ask questions and we received answers, though, as with all technology, it was clear there was still an element of trial and error.

In the course of that conference between the ICC, Hawk-Eye and Channel 9 personnel, plus a few who thought they'd like to be a part of a new whiz-bang procedure, we were given an eight-page information pamphlet. It consisted of:

Why are we persisting with the use of technology?
– Majority of players in favour
– Majority of umpires in favour
– Better player behaviour
– Fewer incorrect decisions

Decision Referral System (DRS) reduces the number of incorrect decisions?
– Over the 11 Tests covered in the trial series there were 37 possible umpire errors

- 30 errors were corrected
- CD% went from 91.7% to 97.6% (2.4% of replays inconclusive or umpires still made incorrect decisions)

Why players and not umpires initiate the process?
- Umpires will be safe rather than sorry
- Too many delays
- Do not want to de-skill the umpires
- Shift responsibility to players
- 3rd umpire: no practical way of ensuring reviews for not-out decisions

What was learnt from the trials?
- Players need to be better at judging whether to review
- Umpires need tighter protocol; for lbws
- An understanding that the aim is to correct the clear mistakes (the 'shockers')
- 3rd umpire technology to be upgraded

Aim of DRS?
- To eliminate clear mistakes
- Technology will not provide conclusive answers in all cases

DRS involves
- <u>Umpire Review</u>
  Lines decisions, clean catches + bump balls
  (This is the same as before)
- <u>Player Review</u>
  Any other decision concerning whether batsman dismissed

Player Review
- Any decision taken by the on-field umpires concerning whether the batsman is dismissed. No other decisions made by umpires (such as wides, leg-byes etc) are eligible for a player review. **It is not a referral system** because the final decision remains with the on-field umpire – the decision is reviewed by, not referred to, the third umpire.

Who can ask for a player review?
- Only the dismissed batsman in an 'out' decision, or the fielding captain, or acting captain, in a 'not out' decision.

Then what happens?
– The on-field umpire will initiate contact with the third umpire and a full exchange of factual information should then take place between the third umpire and his on-field colleague to establish if there is any reason why the original decision should be changed.

High degree of confidence
– If the third umpire, having reviewed the available technology, cannot answer a particular question posed by the on-field umpire with **a high degree of confidence** then he should report it to be **inconclusive**.

Remember – DRS is designed to eliminate obvious errors. If the replays are inconclusive, the on-field umpire's original decision, whether **out** or **not out**, will stand.

PITCHED – if the technology shows that the **centre** of the ball pitched outside the leg stump then the decision will be **not out**.

IMPACT – If the technology shows that the **centre** of the ball was between wicket and wicket at the point of impact then it's **out** (all other factors being in place of course). If the technology shows that **no part** of the ball was between wicket and wicket at the point of impact (and the batsman was playing a stroke) then it's **not out**. Otherwise, the on-field umpire's original decision should not be changed.

WICKETS – if the technology shows that the centre of the ball would have hit the stumps within an area demarcated by a line drawn below the lower edge of the bails and down the middle of the outer stumps then it's **out** (subject to the proviso below and all other factors being in place of course). If the technology shows no part of the ball would have made contact with any part of the stumps or bails then it's **not out**. Otherwise, the on-field umpire's original decision stands.

Proviso: if the point of impact is greater than 250 cm from the stumps, the third umpire will inform his on-field colleague of this exact distance, the approximate distance from the point of pitching to the point of impact and where the ball is predicted to hit the stumps. The on-field umpire will then apply the normal principles concerning levels of certainty in making his final decision.

Number of Reviews
Each team is allowed to make **two** unsuccessful player review requests per innings.

If the original decision of **out** is upheld, but for a different method of dismissal than the on-field umpire originally intended, then the review will **still** be regarded as being **unsuccessful**.

The Technology
The following technology may be used by the third umpire (where available):
- Slow-motion replays
- Super slow-motion replays
- Ultra-motion replays
- Stump microphone sound (at normal speed and slow-motion)
- Approved ball tracking technology
- Pitch mat generated by the ball-tracking technology
- Hot Spot footage
- Any other form of technology that meets the required standards of accuracy and efficiency

The referral system is still very much a long work in progress at the time I am writing this paragraph. There has been a great deal said about it by a number of people, including players, captains, ex-players, ex-captains and a wide variety of media people, some of whom have played cricket, others who have not played but have watched a myriad of matches.

As might be expected, Ricky Ponting has a sensible approach, sharing my view that the trialling of the system should have taken place in one-day or T20 matches before being used in the Test arena. At the time he was talking about the Australia v West Indies Second Test of the series in 2009 and he noted that the game just completed at the Adelaide Oval had been marred by inconsistency and then the departure of Mark Benson. There had been media speculation that Benson had returned to the UK because of the decision review system, which Benson categorically denied. In fact, he had been unwell at the start of the match and was to undergo a series of medical assessments. At the time he had not resigned as an elite panel umpire.

Ponting met with the umpires and stressed he was supportive of the system itself and felt that in the end it would have a good impact on the game. He talked with the umpires in Adelaide concerning additional technology which might be used, but stressed again that once the system was trialled comprehensively it would be for the good of the game. He said, 'We're all still coming to terms with it and the more we play with it the more we'll appreciate it.'

Ponting received backing from match referee Chris Broad in Adelaide, with the ICC representative saying the system itself needed reviewing. 'The use of technology is long overdue and this is the start of the process, but any new tool that comes into the game of cricket takes a while for everyone to understand the way forward,' Broad said.

The referral system remains a hazard. Those in favour of it, or even in love with it, as seems to be the case with the ICC, will regard this as sacrilege. By far the worst thing that has happened recently is that the on-field umpire refers to the third umpire the question of whether a bowler bowled a no-ball. What weak umpiring. The front-foot Law is the worst Law ever introduced to cricket, but for vacillating umpires to say they can't make a decision without help from the third umpire's lounge is beyond belief. If umpires have to make this embarrassing call, they have a real problem in remaining on the elite panel of umpires, and the referral system itself has an even bigger problem.

One of the very best articles I read on the use of referrals was written by Peter Willey. He was a man dedicated to doing the best job he could as the person responsible for making the decisions. He was also dedicated to his family and the ICC decreed that, being an Englishman, he could never again umpire a Test match in England when England were taking part. You may wonder at the last few words, but in 2010 Willey could have umpired a Test in England because Australia were playing Pakistan in 'the old country'. Cricket wonders will never cease.

It is one of the quaint things about cricket these days that an umpire like Simon Taufel, recognised as being the best in cricket, is unable to umpire in Test matches where the Australians are playing. When they brought in the concept of 'neutral' umpires I found the idea amusing, even though it was also insulting to umpires like Taufel, suggesting, as it did, that they would be biased towards their own country. When I played and captained, the two best umpires I knew were Syd Buller from England and Colin Egar from Australia. Buller started with Yorkshire as a youngster then moved to Worcestershire, where he played for eleven years and was county coach for four years before becoming an umpire. I first saw him in 1956 when he officiated at Trent Bridge in the First Test and at Headingley in the third game of the series. Then, when I first worked for BBC Radio in 1960 when the South Africans toured England, Syd Buller stood in the Second Test at Lord's. Geoff Griffin, the South African pace bowler, was called eleven times for illegal bowling by Frank Lee, the umpire standing at square-leg. In a match arranged after the early finish to the Test, Buller called Griffin for the same offence. The bizarre follow-up to this was that Lee then umpired the following Test at Trent Bridge with Charlie Elliott; Buller was objected to by the South Africans and so didn't stand in the final Test at The Oval. Quaint, bizarre, stupid, take your pick.

Fortunately Buller umpired in 1961 when I captained the Australian side to England and we formed a very high opinion of him, Charlie Elliott, John Langridge, Eddie Phillipson and Frank Lee throughout the five-match series.

Two of those umpires, Buller and Phillipson, umpired in the first match of the tour against Worcestershire and they came to me with a very sensible and interesting piece of information before the start of play on the opening day. This was to the effect they had received advice that the English authorities intended to bring in a front-foot no-ball Law as an experiment. They told me the umpires had met and that in all the Test matches, and in other games where the Australians were taking part, they would be working off the back foot, trying to ensure the bowler's front foot landed somewhere on the batting crease. They would advise the bowlers when they were going a bit too far but would only no-ball a bowler for a blatant over-stepping.

A common-sense approach, which unfortunately in life these days, is not all that common.

There was only one no-ball bowled in the five Test matches; that was by Fred Trueman in the opening Test at Edgbaston. In all on that tour, with the common sense applied by the umpires, we played thirty-seven matches, one against the Club Cricket Conference, two against Ireland, one against Scotland and one against Minor Counties. There were thirty-two first-class matches including the five Tests. In all those thirty-seven matches there were fifty-three no-balls bowled during the whole six-month-long tour. And then they brought in the worst Law of cricket ever produced, the front-foot Law. A statistic of some consequence is that from 1876–77 until 1968–69 in Test cricket fewer than 5,000 no-balls were bowled. Between 1969–70 and 2010 there were more than 30,000 no-balls bowled.

Peter Willey suggested there may come a time when television technicians responsible for providing the pictures for referrals will need to be 'neutral', as is the case with the umpires. He also said that increased use of technology has posed problems for umpires because they have lost the art of being able to make run-out judgements. The reason for that, he argues, is that the umpires never have to bother because run-outs are now always referred. In his wide-ranging article in *Wisden Cricket Monthly* he suggested it would be a good idea to increase the number of Test match officials and have them standing in only one Test in each series. There is certainly merit in that, as it would make certain that if an umpire had an 'ordinary' match, he didn't then have to back up again the next week. Willey added that the more technology is brought into the umpiring part of the game, the more umpires will relate simply to referrals rather than their own split-second judgement.

There are many umpires who will definitely agree with Willey, which brings me back to the ridiculous situation of the best umpires not being able to stand in Test matches in their own country. Why for heaven's sake can't that be overturned now that the ICC have decided to use technology in this fashion and to this extent, where referrals are the norm and the fielding and batting teams are allowed to choose their moments to object to a decision? The ICC Committee will have to make up their minds: is technology the only answer to umpiring problems and, in fact, are those problems being magnified in order that technology can take over?

Somehow the two items should be intertwined so we have the best umpires standing plus the technology to back them up.

37

NEVER BET ON ANYTHING THAT CAN TALK

PEOPLE who know of my interest in horseracing often ask if I bet on cricket and the answer is always 'No!' With my good friend Jack Bannister, the former Warwickshire fast bowler and horseracing devotee, I have a little competition which we call the 'Nap of the Day' where each of us will nominate a horse from any of the meetings held on a Saturday in England. Loser is up for a champagne dinner at the end of the English cricket season, and we have been remarkably even in winning and losing over the years. I have a bet at Royal Ascot in June every year, particularly if there are some Australian horses like Choisir, Takeover Target and Miss Andretti in the fields. Like most Australians I have a bet on the Melbourne Cup each year and might have a couple of other bets during the twelve months. I have always been more interested in studying the form in *Racing Post* and, before that, in the old *Sporting Life* and the *Sydney Morning Herald* 'Form' supplement on Fridays and Saturdays, and working out what I think will win. Jack and I have one six-month competition involving Flat racing in England and the second in the jump racing season and events taking place on artificial surfaces. I have had a policy over the years of never betting on anything that can talk, hence the decision never to put any money on cricket.

It was probably no more than justice that the one time I tried to deviate from that policy, twenty-nine years ago, I was unable to get any money on. It was during the Headingley Test of 1981 when things were going awfully awry for the England team.

England were in such trouble that the genial satchel-swingers, Ladbrokes, offered 500–1 about England's chances of victory. In the commentary box with Ted Dexter before the day began, and with the brightly glowing 500–1 on the scoreboard, we discussed the virtues or otherwise of each of us putting ten pounds on England to win. Neither of us expected that victory to happen but, in a two-horse race with one an odds-on favourite and the other 500–1 against, one simply *had* to have a bet. We both put two fivers in an envelope and I was entrusted with the job of placing the bet when Godfrey Evans came to the commentary box before the start of play, as he had done without fail for the past fourteen years as the representative for Ladbrokes. Ron Pollard was his boss and between them they worked out the odds available.

That day at Headingley, however, both Godfrey and Ron, having posted the 500–1 and 'knowing' Australia were certain to win, were on their way down the motorway when the first ball was bowled. What happened at Leeds though was that Ian Botham went berserk with the bat, with the able assistance of Graham Dilley, who made 56, and Chris Old, who hit a quick 29. From the time Botham came to the crease another 251 runs were added and the Australians were thoroughly rattled. It was a wonderful batting performance which began as a bit of fun for the spectators and ended with Bob Willis taking 8 wickets as part of a staggering recovery, one of the greatest in Test match history. Ted and I were philosophical about it, but it did underline for me the perils of betting on human beings!

Almost twenty years later there was the Hansie Cronje affair and betting on cricket became commonplace, with illegal book-makers on the subcontinent and elsewhere playing a part in some unusual deals involving the corruption of players. For me, there was one hero in the latter problems, an Indian Joint-Commissioner of Police, K. K. Paul, who was based in Delhi. He had received information from one of his detectives, Detective Ishwar Singh Redhu, that he had heard some recorded conversations and thought they should be investigated. The recordings had been made in connection with possible extortion in the Indian business world, but as both policemen were interested in cricket it seemed unusual to them that some of the conversations on the mobile phones sounded so odd. At the time all this happened, and after Cronje had been charged with being involved in the match-fixing of cricket, I wrote a twenty-paragraph article for the *News of the World* in the United Kingdom. The first paragraph said, 'This is the greatest crisis in the history of cricket.'

It remains so, despite the work done by Lord Condon, who headed up ICC's Anti-Corruption and Security Unit. In 2009 Lord Condon said forcefully that no one should ever believe they have beaten the cancer of corruption in cricket.

One of K. K. Paul's many sensible observations was that in modern times the easiest way for those wanting to bet on cricket, or persuade players to be part of their organisations, was to use spread betting. The 500–1 story involved straightforward betting where a bookmaker offers odds and a punter accepts. Spread betting, however, with its many variations, widens the scope for playing around and in recent times there are many more betting markets available.

One of those is betting exchanges such as Betfair, which is not only in the United Kingdom but in other countries as well. Lay betting, or betting on something to lose rather than win, is an innovative thing for the punter, though the racing officials keep, or try to keep, a weather eye on proceedings. The punter is able to play the part of the bookmaker. If you 'lay' a horse and it loses, then you will have won your money.

If you are setting out to win money by betting on something to get beaten you need to have the right information. In Australia, and other countries, Betfair is a big business and it operates in many sports as well as cricket, and one of the key points of its operation is that there exists within the company a 'customer integrity system' whereby the betting organisation will work with the various sports authorities to alert them to any unusual activity as regards betting.

Betfair and other exchanges have alerted authorities in

football, tennis and other sports when there have been some 'suspicious' betting patterns. These may be where a seemingly unbeatable football team is backed to lose or a tennis player is meeting an opponent ranked 200 places lower. If the latter is heavily backed to win, it might ring some alarm bells. In Australia in early 2010, Racing Victoria received an alert from Betfair that there had been what might be regarded as unusual betting activity in horse races over a period of several months. Betfair's Hugh Taggart pointed out that they monitor their betting operation seven days a week and, when they think it necessary, they will provide information to any relevant sports authority. It is my belief that cricket authorities need the same type of connection with betting exchanges to make certain they are ahead of the game.

A person for whom I have a great deal of respect is Tim May, former Australian spin bowler and a fine cricketer, who recently said in *Wisden Cricket Monthly*, 'Twenty20 is just ripe for corruption. The shorter the game, the more influence each particular incident can have. So I think it opens up a great deal of opportunities for illegal bookmakers to try to corrupt players into providing various different outcomes in the game, if not the result itself. Cricket needs to be very, very careful.'

Ominous words but, as is usually the case with the Chief Executive of FICA, sound common sense! A combination of spread betting as noted by K. K. Paul and Twenty20 as mentioned by Tim May could possibly result in serious problems, and it is a matter which definitely needs to be addressed. It would obviously be a more difficult problem with illegal bookmakers, rather than those working in the public area with sports authorities.

Tim May and David Morgan, the latter at the time President of the ICC, agreed that it certainly needed addressing, Morgan adding that it may well be 'the fixing of matches has been stopped but we need to take a close look at some of the betting patterns in T20 matches. The Anti-Corruption Unit, which the ICC set up, has been very successful and I am convinced there is no evidence that matches are being fixed. But, with so many competitions now coming in, intricacies about how many wides are being bowled in an over, and the like, are tailor-made for the gambler. I realise there is no room for any complacency.'

Wise and cautionary words from the outgoing President.

David did a great job as President of the ICC, but even he could not have imagined how accurate his worries might be, regarding not only T20 but also other aspects of cricket. In a very short space of time Test cricket became the target for those who have no regard for the game itself, only for the chance to make money out of it – not with genuine and honest match payments from their governing authority, but by trying to destroy the game with the new-style spot-fixing, rather than old-style match-fixing.

That is sad enough; sadder still was the death of the Chairman of the Croydon Athletic Football Club in early October 2010, found with a gun in his hand in the garage of his home. As Chairman of Croydon Athletic, he had been appalled that his beloved club had been dragged into the Pakistan spot-fixing stories. Inquests and coronial inquiries are still pending, but it is one of the worst things I have known connected with cricket.

38

PLAYERS PRESENT AND FUTURE

W HEN I first walked on to the Sydney Cricket Ground on 31 December 1948 it was as an eighteen-year-old allrounder, or rather that was the manner in which I was described. I was also carrying an umbrella because, although it was only raining lightly, it continued to rain all day to ensure there would be no play on the opening day against Queensland. An 'allrounder' was a slight exaggeration because the reason I had been chosen in the team was that I was a young batsman who could bowl some legspin. In fact, in the early matches of the 1948–49 season, I had headed the batting averages for my club, Central Cumberland, but had taken only 1–178 with the ball in first-grade club cricket. The legspin bowler in the New South Wales team at this time was Fred Johnston, a very good bowler and team man and a great help to young cricketers.

There was only one reason I replaced Fred in the NSW team and that was because English cricket authorities had decided, in the interests of so-called 'brighter cricket', that the fielding side should be allowed a new ball after 40 eight-ball overs had been bowled with the one in use. In England, because the Law specified six-ball overs, the fielding side was allowed the new ball after 55 overs. In 1947, the Law regarding the new ball had been that it could be taken after 200 runs had been made off a ball. When England's cricket authorities came to the decision to change the taking of the new ball for the 1948 Ashes summer they contacted the Australian Board of Control and the Australian captain, Don Bradman, to see if they would agree. The Board said they needed to have a meeting, Bradman said instantly, 'Do it now,' and he persuaded the Board to send a cable immediately and to make sure it was written into the playing conditions for the tour. It was done. Bradman knew the bowlers he had, and although as a selector he had two others alongside him and all three made certain spin bowling was well catered for, the Australian pace attack took full advantage of the new playing condition.

Bradman had at his disposal Ray Lindwall, Keith Miller, Bill Johnston, Ernie Toshack and Sam Loxton. Three of them were allrounders and Johnston and Toshack were good pace bowlers without any real pretensions to batting. The slow bowlers were legspinners Colin McCool and Doug Ring, the offspinner was Ian Johnson. It was rare for Bradman not to call for the second new ball after the 55 overs.

This then was the position when I was chosen in the NSW team and Fred Johnston was left out. With the 40-over experimental Law in use in Australia, I was there to bowl overs number 38 and 40, or a few more if the captain thought it a good idea. In England they realised their mistake and the following summer changed the figure from 55 overs to 65 overs and then, for the Australian tour of England in 1956, it was changed again to 200 runs or 75 overs, whichever the fielding captain preferred. Not before time either!

My debut therefore was one that depended on the playing conditions at a particular time. Because cricket continually evolves, the nature of players' careers changes too, and in these very modern times it is quite possible that some cricketers may not be able to play in a Test match, or even in a Sheffield Shield game, but their careers might entirely be in the shorter versions of the game.

I believe a top-class cricketer should be able to play any form of cricket, though since the Australian cricket selectors decided around ten years ago that they would choose players specifically for a role in each type of cricket, they have gone for specialists. There was a time when the selectors would choose a Test squad and just replace a few players; Australia had a very good record in that time. Adam Gilchrist was an outstanding player in the period from 1996 to 2008; Mark Waugh was a wonderful player in both forms of the game, so too his brother Steve. The best I ever saw though in limited-overs was Michael Bevan. He played some Test matches for Australia but with moderate success, with the bowlers testing him around off stump, a tactic Bevan was unable to counter. Bevan played limited-overs cricket for ten years, making his debut in 1994 and playing through until February 2004. Tactically he was magnificent with the bat, out-thinking the bowlers for much of the time and refusing to be unbalanced by the pace of the game. Almost always he set his own pace and there has never been a limited-overs cricketer better than Bevan at reading the game.

There were many matches which seemed lost and then were won because of Bevan's skill and tactical nous. Of those there were two which have always stood out in my mind: the World Cup match against England at Port Elizabeth in 2003, and the match at the Sydney Cricket Ground when Australia defeated the West Indies in 1996.

The great thing about Bevan's innings on New Year's Day 1996 was that it was produced against all the odds. In a match reduced to 43 overs because of rain, West Indies, led by Courtney Walsh, scrambled their way to 172–9, with Carl Hooper making a brilliant 93 off 96 balls, but there were only three double-figure scores in the WI innings. When Bevan walked out to bat at number six Australia had lost 4–32 and then suddenly it was 6–38. A small resurgence came from Ian Healy, but Bevan then found Paul Reiffel staying with him until the score had reached 157. Shane Warne, the new batsman, was run out going for a fourth run and now it was Glenn McGrath coming through the gate.

This final over had so far been dot ball, Reiffel's dismissal by Phil Simmons and Warne's run-out, and still four runs were needed to win the match, Bevan at the non-striker's end, McGrath facing. There were fielders everywhere inside the circle, but McGrath calmly pushed the ball between two of them for a single to give Bevan the strike with two balls remaining. Next ball was a dot ball to Bevan, a beautiful yorker right in the blockhole, so the last ball had to go to the boundary for a win.

It took Walsh a considerable time to set his field and Bevan just as long to decide where he was going to hit the ball. Walsh had as many as he was allowed on the legside boundary and the problem was if Harper bowled another good yorker it would be very difficult to hit it between the fielders. There was nothing wrong with the ball Harper bowled, but Bevan had picked his mark and out-thought the opposition. As Harper's arm came over Bevan gave himself room for the shot and smashed the ball straight down the ground to the sightscreen at the Paddington End and the game was won by one wicket with no balls remaining.

It was one of the great innings in the history of limited-overs cricket.

In Port Elizabeth in 2003 England had to beat Australia to go to the next stage of the World Cup and they were well on the way to a big score when Andy Bichel took an astonishing 7–20 from his ten permitted overs. Bichel then came to the crease when Australia had lost 8–135 and shared a great 73-run partnership with Bevan, the latter hitting the winning runs with two balls to spare.

I was lucky enough to watch both matches from the commentary box. They provided some of the most exciting cricket I have seen and extraordinarily Bevan wasn't Man of the Match in either game: Paul Reiffel and Andy Bichel received the awards.

In future years there will be many cricketers who are better known for their limited-overs cricket than their Test cricket, but that will be because they haven't been able to make it into the longer and more traditional form of the game.

39

THE FUTURE OF THE ONE-DAY GAME

I MAY have seen more Twenty20 cricket than most people because I was around when the first proper game was played in England in 2003. It was a match at Chester-le-Street between Durham and Nottinghamshire and it finished in a win for the host team; the margin was 'five balls remaining'. I saw excerpts of it on television. Three days later I was at Trent Bridge for Nottinghamshire to host Lancashire. It was something different. Trent Bridge had laid on the entertainment, some dancing girls, who seemed to be having a hell of a time, as did the people who had paid their money at the gate. The ground holds, or held at that time, 15,000 spectators; there were 16,000 in attendance that evening.

They had come out of their offices at five o'clock, bought a packet of sandwiches, a few cans of beer for their mates, stepped on to the bus they had specially organised with a non-drinking driver and been driven to the parking area at the football ground next to the cricket ground. They watched the match, which was a very lively one, cheered their local heroes, returned to their bus and they were back in their villages or towns half an hour after the conclusion of the game. It was a daytime match put on for the people, on the basis that the hours of twilight in the United Kingdom offer the opportunity to have spectators come to the ground to watch 40 overs of quick-fire cricket after they have finished work.

It was regarded then as *not* being what you would call 'proper cricket', in the same way as when one-day cricket began in England in 1963. That was sneered at by some administrators who said rather wearily that they supposed they had better put it on but not many people would bother going to see it. That soon changed after an action-packed competition brought in big crowds, engendering great enthusiasm, and 25,000 spectators crammed into Lord's for the final between Sussex and Worcestershire. *Wisden* said of the first year:

The new Knock-out competition aroused enormous interest. Very large crowds, especially in the later rounds, flocked to the matches and 25,000 spectators watched the final at Lord's where Sussex narrowly defeated Worcestershire by 14 runs in a thoroughly exciting match. It says much for this type of cricket that tremendous feeling was stirred up among the spectators as well as the cricketers with numerous ties being decided in the closest fashion. At Lord's, supporters wore favours and banners were also in evidence, the whole scene resembling an Association Football Cup Final more than the game of cricket and many thousands invaded the pitch at the finish to cheer Dexter, the Sussex captain, as he received a Gillette Trophy from the M.C.C. President, Lord Nugent.

Sussex emphasised their superiority in the one-day game when they beat the West Indies by four wickets in a Challenge match at Hove on September 12.

There were two points which invite criticism. Firstly, the majority of counties were loath to include even one slow bowler in their sides and relied mainly on pace and secondly the placing of the entire field around the boundary to prevent rapid scoring – Dexter used this tactic in the Final – became fairly common. The success of the spinners at Lord's may have exploded the first theory.

There is no doubt that provided the Competition is conducted wisely it will attract great support in the future and benefit the game accordingly.

Since then, the one-day format has indeed attracted great support and benefited the game, yet recently there has sometimes been a campaign, mostly by the print media, to denigrate 50-overs-a-side Internationals and have them removed from the international cricket programme. This will best be countered by having, for the most part, good exciting matches for spectators at the ground or watching on television. Unfortunately, the problems associated with the 2007 World Cup in the Caribbean provided those critical of the 50-over game with plenty of ammunition. The tournament in the West Indies was an appalling piece of mismanagement by the ICC and their officials, and the Caribbean islands were done a complete disservice. I quailed when I saw the prices for admission tickets, and a listing of food and drink prices inside the grounds, which can simply be put down to monetary greed. It was done on the basis that it was a World Cup and that people would be desperate to get a seat and would pay anything for the 'privilege'. Only when the local organisers showed a little common sense and dropped the prices did reasonable crowds turn up. As it was, there was more than US$30 million in ticket revenue. The fact that many could not pay the prices of admission, and were not permitted to take their own food and drink into the ground, meant that a great deal of the wonderful Caribbean flavour of cricket was lost, not only at the grounds but also on television.

When the 2011 World Cup got under way it turned out to be a good event. It is difficult to use the word 'great' because of the length of the whole tournament and the fact that some teams had an inordinate amount of time between matches. The overall length of the event is to do with the televising of the matches for an extraordinary amount of money; that money being shared between all the participants, we assume. There is no sensible reasoning, though, behind such long gaps between matches; it was simply poor programming. Even so, it was much better than the 2007 World Cup in the Caribbean. The ICC had learned from the crass errors there and the event was well organised by India and Sri Lanka in particular, who fought out a well-contested final, with India coming out on top.

Not long afterwards the ICC announced that for the next World Cup, to be played in Australia and New Zealand, there had been a change of plans. Any inept organisation can change plans when the whim takes them and panic has become part of the so-called planning. Their idea was to have only the eight full Test teams and another two, Zimbabwe and Bangladesh, to make up ten teams.

That's a load of rubbish. This is the way it *should* happen:

• The 2015 World Cup will consist of ten teams.
• The eight proper Test nations are automatically in the World Cup. Those countries are Australia, England, India, New Zealand, Pakistan, South Africa, Sri Lanka and West Indies.
• The other two places will be decided by a competition involving Bangladesh and Zimbabwe joining with the top four Associate countries in a six-team round-robin competition. The top two at the conclusion of that competition will join the eight teams already automatically participating.

This method gives the Associate countries their chance to prove they are good enough to be there and it also provides Zimbabwe and Bangladesh with the opportunity to show they are considerably better than the cricket world believes.

Because cricket needs to evolve, there are always reasons for trying out new rules and playing conditions and making certain they are trialled before being utilised in the competition proper. The one-day format for international matches has undergone several changes in recent years, including the introduction of Powerplays. The following briefly lists some of the important aspects of the game as it was being played in Australia in January 2010.

Format 50-overs-a-side, both day and day/night Internationals

• 1st Powerplay
  10 overs   overs 1–10
• 2nd Powerplay
  5 overs   (batting or fielding side, whichever asks first)
• 3rd Powerplay
  5 overs   (batting or fielding side, the other team)

- For the first Powerplay only two fieldsmen can be outside the restricted area.
- For the second and third Powerplays only three fieldsmen can be outside the restricted area.
- In a non-Powerplay part of the innings, no more than five fieldsmen can be outside the restricted area.
- There can never be more than five fieldsmen on the legside at the instant of delivery.
- Once nominated, Powerplays cannot be reversed.
- Should either team choose not to exercise their Powerplay, the Powerplay overs will automatically commence at the latest point in the innings; viz, at the start of the 46th over.
- Batsmen asking for a Powerplay have until the umpire at the bowler's end reaches the stumps.
- The fielding captain can nominate a Powerplay at any time prior to the commencement of the over.
- The umpire standing at the bowler's end shall determine which side first made the request.

I have read a number of articles written by cricketers, ex-cricketers and journalists concerning playing conditions that might be improved a little, and have talked with some television commentators who have a keen eye for things that might or might not work, including, from Channel 9, Ian Chappell, Mark Taylor, Tony Greig and Mark Nicholas. In other areas, representatives of the print media and pay-television have noted some interesting ideas. I've added a few thoughts of my own to those of Peter Roebuck, Damien Fleming and Derek Pringle.

Fifteen suggestions to consider the future of 50-overs-a-side Internationals

Powerplays

1. The batting Powerplay must be taken before the 40th over.
2. The batting or fielding Powerplay can only be taken after the 20th over.

3. Batting and fielding Powerplays must be taken between the 20th and 40th overs.
4. Maintain the Powerplay provisions for the entire innings.

Field-settings
5. Four men to be inside the restricted fielding area during the final five overs.
6. With the reverse sweep/switch hitting being used, allow six fielders on the legside.

Bowlers
7. Five bowlers to bowl a minimum of five overs each.
8. A maximum of 12 overs for any bowler.
9. A new ball to be used at both ends at the start of the innings, as in 1992 World Cup.

Other ideas
10. If you lose the toss and later both teams want the same Powerplays, the team losing the toss has preference.
11. Time for an innings 3 hours, not 3½ hours, and to be strictly enforced.
12. Curators to produce hard pitches, and provide bowlers with some assistance. No featherbeds.
13. Boundaries to be as large as possible for great running between the wickets.
14. There must be home and away colours as in baseball. Grey with red markings could be the away uniform.
15. ICC matches to be trialled using 4 x 25 overs format, rather than 2 x 50 overs.

There are fifteen options above, some relating to the same aspect of the game, but they have already inspired some lively debate. It is a very good idea that changes might be considered to maintain the importance of the 50-over game.

40

TOO MUCH OF A
GOOD THING . . . ?

I N Australia in the 2009–10 season a lot of cricket was played. Two teams visited Australia; first of all West Indies, under the captaincy of Chris Gayle, played three Tests, the first of those at the 'Gabba in late November, and that turned out to be a calamity for the Caribbean team who had been sent to Australia without any kind of proper preparation. What on earth were the West Indies Cricket Board thinking about? Were they thinking at all? The team arrived in Brisbane a week before the Test, practised at Allan Border Field but had no practice at the 'Gabba itself. They were mown down by the Australian bowlers, who could hardly believe their luck once Ricky Ponting's team had declared at 480–8. The Australian bowlers dismissed West Indies for 228 and 187 and they were lucky to make that many. The one bright spot for them, although they were made to follow on, was that Adrian Barath made a second-innings century and he looked a very good young player, only nineteen years of age. Unfortunately he was injured and unable to play in the Third Test in Perth, the last of the series.

There's no doubt it was a busy Australian summer. Six Tests in all, against West Indies and Pakistan, and Australia won five, with the Adelaide Test against the West Indies being drawn. Pakistan had plenty of problems at the time, being unable to host teams in their own country and restricted to using places like Dubai for some home games.

When the Pakistan team captained by Mohammad Yousuf began the Boxing Day Test against Australia in Melbourne, it was to a background of disharmony from their own country, where captaincy was high on the discussion list and goodwill thin on the ground. The Australians won the First Test of the three-match series by 170 runs and they won the Third in Hobart by 231 runs. In between, at the Sydney Cricket Ground, there was one of the most extraordinary games of cricket I have ever watched from the commentary box, where Ricky Ponting won the toss and decided to bat on a well-grassed pitch which was likely to have a bit of life in it for the pace bowlers. It is a ground where the preferred option is not to bat last because the ball has always turned for the spinners on the final day, and that has been happening since the first Sheffield Shield match I watched there in 1940.

Australia made 127, Pakistan gained a lead of 206 and then, on the second last day, the Australians looked to be gone and forgotten when, after being 217-3, they lost five wickets for 40, with Michael Hussey having to look to Peter Siddle and Dougie Bollinger to stay with him. Mind you, Hussey was lucky to be there at all as Kamran Akmal had dropped him three times during the early part of his innings and there was a fourth marginal fumble as well. Hussey and Siddle added 123 in their stand for the eighth wicket but the tactics from Mohammad Yousuf were unfathomable. He kept the field back for Hussey, which was understandable in part, but he also didn't attack Siddle. It was one of the most mysterious passages of play I have seen. In the end, Siddle was dismissed by Mohammad Asif and Pakistan were set or, more to the point with their awful tactics, had set themselves the task of making 176 to win and they never really looked like doing it. It was one of the most shambolic pieces of captaincy and thinking imaginable.

The Pakistan Cricket Board threw their own wobbly in the aftermath of a disastrous tour in which Pakistan won nothing but did raise a few eyebrows here and there with their lack of skill and tactical expertise. PCB Chairman Ijaz Butt demanded an investigation by a six-man committee into the circumstances surrounding the tour, more particularly the stunning loss to Australia in the SCG Test. Some players were fined the equivalent of A$70,000 (£40,000) and the full report and recommendations distributed by the Pakistan Cricket Board in March 2010 are set out below. Perhaps more interesting is what is *not* included in the report concerning exactly why the players were banned and fined.

RECOMMENDATIONS

After careful and detailed analysis of the events, the personal accounts of the team management and players and examination of records, videos and statistics, the unanimous recommendations of the Committee were as follows:

1. Mohammad Yousuf and Younis Khan, keeping in view their infighting which resulted in bringing down the whole team, their attitude has a trickledown effect which is a bad influence for the whole team and should not be part of national team in any format.
2. For the shameful act of Shahid Khan Afridi, which has brought the game and country into disrepute, he be fined Rupees Three Million (US$35,000). A warning be issued to him by the Chairman PCB and he be put on probation for six months, during which his conduct be strictly monitored.
3. Kamran Akmal be fined Rupees Three Million (US$35,000). A warning be issued to him by the Chairman PCB and he be put on probation for six months, during which his conduct be strictly monitored.
4. Umar Akmal be fined Rupees Two Million (US$23,400). A warning be issued to him by the Chairman PCB and he be put on probation for six months, during which his conduct be strictly monitored.
5. Rana Naved-ul-Hasan and Shoaib Malik be fined Rupees Two Million (US$23,400). They should not be part of national team in any format for a period of one year.

Recommendations of the Inquiry Committee have been accepted by PCB in totality.

The recommendations of the Committee will go a long way to arrest the continuing decline in Pakistan cricket and improve the state of cricket in Pakistan. It is a landmark exercise which is an outcome of labour and hard work of the members of the Committee.

Ricky Ponting's team followed their three-nil victory against Pakistan in the Test series by beating them five-nil in the one-day series and then won four–nil against the West Indies, with one match at the SCG washed out. By the evening of Tuesday, 23 February 2010, at the Sydney Cricket Ground, Ponting was a very pleased cricket captain. So he should have been, with Australia having just won both T20 matches against the West Indies to provide a clean sweep for the whole season, and he had every right as well to be a tired captain. By the end of the summer, when he was preparing to fly to New Zealand for another series of 50-overs-a-side matches and two Tests, he expressed some cogent views about how much cricket should be played in a season.

Competition and having a genuine contest are vital aspects of a good cricket series, whether it is in the long version of the game or in one of the two shorter formats. The fact is that there were very few competitive matches during that Australian summer. There was also a financial crisis in Australia, as well as around the world, and when financial times are tough potential spectators will have a careful look at what they are spending and what they get in return.

Ponting was quoted in *The Australian* newspaper, in a very good interview with Malcolm Conn and Peter Lalor, as noting cricket fans will not have the money to support domestic T20 matches and the 50-overs-a-side Internationals as well. 'It was no surprise to me,' he said, when asked about smaller crowds at the grounds. He went further: 'People have only a certain amount of money to spend on entertainment. If you play as many games as Australia have this year, and you wish to take your family along, you are probably looking at $150–$200 a day.' Ponting sensibly pointed out that it's not just the ticket prices but also the cost of things such as food and drinks purchased inside the ground.

'People are starting to prioritise which games they go to. If you have the option to sit at home and watch the game on television, it's a no-brainer what you are going to do.'

It was an excellent article and its content is something to which the cricket authorities, not just in Australia but in England as well, should pay careful attention.

The quantity of cricket also seems to be having an effect on the players themselves. Early 2010 saw England's captain resting from the tour of Bangladesh, Australia's captain no longer playing and captaining Australia at T20, and some players saying they are intending to cut back on their activities. Is it a question of 'burn-out' or is it just something that goes with the territory? Or possibly with the money?

Injuries are the biggest problem, though, even if it is a matter of 'possible' injuries. A player prone to injury needs to think about the fact that his cricket career is definitely a job. Two players instantly come to mind, Andrew Flintoff and Shaun Tait; Flintoff is a wonderful all-round cricketer whose knees eventually gave way. Tait, with his great pace and hard bowling action, sensibly decided he could only keep going in the shorter form of the game where his overs were limited to a small number. For those two cricketers the sensible thing was what they eventually did: play cricket but in such a way that they don't break down again.

It is always sad to see a great player injured and unable to play a full part in matches where he is representing his country at the highest level. Andrew Flintoff fought hard and at times bowled magnificently, but it was tough going. Even with his batting he was restricted, in fielding certainly so, and he retired from all forms of the game in 2010. In July 2008 in England, in the Third Test against South Africa, he took his 200th Test match wicket to become only the fifteenth player in 132 years of Test cricket to achieve the 'double' of 2,000 runs and 200 wickets. There were times when his concentration faded a little, but against Australia in 2005, in the Ashes battle in England, he was simply magnificent.

At the 2010 Allan Border Medal evening at Crown Towers in Melbourne Brett Lee came over to the Cricket Australia table to say hello to Daphne and me. He was out of the game through injury at the time and hoping for a faster recovery than the medicos were predicting. I put it to him that with his brilliant command of both forms of swing, orthodox and reverse, it might be an idea to concentrate on the shorter form of the game. A day or so later Brad McNamara, the Channel 9 producer, mentioned to me that Neil Maxwell, Brett's manager, had phoned to say that Brett would almost certainly be retiring from Test cricket and would I be prepared to offer a couple of quotes about him as a cricketer. I was happy to do that, though unhappy it was in circumstances when he was leaving a part of cricket that he loved.

I said, 'I hope Brett is able to play for Australia in limited-overs Internationals. He is a master of orthodox and reverse swing, so important in the shorter form of the game, and no one has been more proud to represent his country in Test cricket. He and Glenn McGrath formed a splendid partnership with the new ball in both forms of the game from 1999 to 2007 and being one of only nine Australian pace bowlers to take 200 Test wickets is a great achievement.'

I know more about injuries than most as I suffered with them right from the time of my debut in first-class cricket through to the end of my career, when I was having considerable trouble with my bowling shoulder. I had sustained that injury bowling in the first match of the 1961 tour of England on 2 May at Worcester. It wasn't until the game against Middlesex at Lord's on 25 July that I felt the treatment I had been having was working well. That treatment was devised by Brian Corrigan, an Australian sports medicine specialist who was at University College Hospital in London for several years and who had formed a very high opinion of the Arsenal Football Club team doctor, Alan Bass. Brian was an expert in sports injuries and I certainly wasn't the only Australian sportsman and athlete he was able to get back on to a sporting field. In that Middlesex game I bowled 50 overs and took 4–38 and 5–32 and suffered no ill effects, so I reckoned I had half a chance in the Fourth Test taking place two days later.

One of the things about being injured is that most of the time you don't want to stop playing. Brett Lee has been like that, suffering an injury but wanting to be part of the action out in the centre of the ground and in the dressing-room. He has had a fractured foot and a bad arm injury and he wasn't the only one in the 2009–10 season to have a setback.

Lee's captain, Ricky Ponting, finished up having a great season. It was significant though, when reflecting on the summer, that Ponting said he probably should not have played the first two Tests against Pakistan after being hit just above the left elbow during the Perth Test by West Indian fast bowler Kemar Roach. It was a very good delivery, tucking Ponting up as he played his stroke, and it was obvious for some time that he was in real trouble. The bowlers knew they had in front of them a batsman with a problem. In fact, Ponting explained that problem in a very good article he wrote under his own name in *The Australian* newspaper on Monday 22 February and pointed out that because he could no longer play his shots off the front foot he was therefore focusing far more on his back-foot strokes.

'As soon as you get those things out of kilter, it makes batting difficult,' he said. 'It was probably to my detriment as much as anyone else's that I kept playing the way I did.'

That's often the way sportspeople think, that it will be all right on the night, or the day as the case may be. Ponting explained it well when he said, 'As captain, that's what you feel you have to do. You want to be out there and you want to be leading the team.'

One of the notable stories from late 2009 was the success of Australian allrounder Shane Watson. A place couldn't be found for him in the Cardiff or Lord's Test matches that year but, when the selectors left out opening batsman Phillip Hughes, Watson came in to bat in an unaccustomed position, at the top of the order.

Watson had been a splendid cricketer for a considerable time but injury always seemed likely to cut his career short. Back problems, hamstring problems, everything was going wrong but, with a changed method of treatment, he became fitter for cricket than he had ever been in his life and played magnificently as an allrounder. He kept that form going until the end of the season in February 2010.

At the Allan Border dinner, when he was named Border Medallist of the Year, he paid a special tribute to Mr Victor Popov, a sports physiotherapist from Queensland. Mr Popov was an Olympic Team physiotherapist at the Atlanta Olympic Games and when the Olympics were held in Sydney. He is also the head physiotherapist at the Brisbane Lions AFL club and has worked with professional cycling teams in France.

Decision-making can be the most important aspect of recovery. Brian Corrigan and Alan Bass reorganised my treatment in 1961 and it worked. Shane Watson chose wisely with Victor Popov in 2008 to reorganise his future and it had a remarkable effect on his career and on Australian cricket.

The Watson–Popov combination had another triumph in 2011 when Watson was again named the Border Medallist of the Year after another outstanding summer. He achieved this even though he was a member of an Australian side which lost an Ashes battle against Andrew Strauss's vibrant team, the first Ashes defeat for Australia in Australia since 1986–87.

41
SCORERS AND STATISTICS

CRICKET people around the world seek all kinds of information. It might be to do with players or administrators, anything that will improve their knowledge and love of cricket. Among those helping them in that quest are the scorer and the statistician – sometimes separate people, sometimes one person will do both jobs. I have said over the years that they always have been and always will be vital to the game of cricket, from the backyard to the Test match arena.

Bill Frindall was one of the finest and sadly he passed away on 30 January 2009, having contracted legionnaires' disease in Dubai whilst participating in a Lord's Taverners cricket tour in the area. He loved playing cricket and being a scorer and statistician for the game.

Bill constructed his outstanding 'Frindall's Method' of linear scoring having seen the method used by Bill Ferguson, the Australian who travelled with many cricket teams in his wonderful career. Bill Ferguson also created his own innings diagrams, as overleaf:

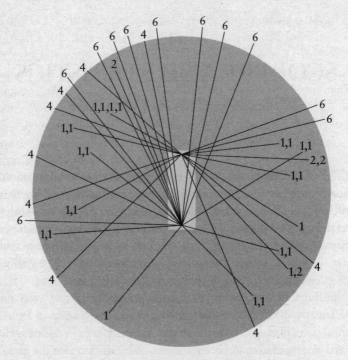

R. Benaud. Australia v T.N. Pearce's XI at Scarborough Festival 9th September to 11th September 1953. Score of 135 runs in 110 minutes, made up of eleven 6's, nine 4's, four 2's, and twenty-five singles.

Presented to Richie Benaud by Bill Ferguson on 12 September 1953

The scorebook I used as a youngster when scoring unofficially was the small *Unrivalled Pocket Cricket Scoring Book*. When scoring for the Cumberland Second XI, I had the larger version of the *Unrivalled*, the one used in Club, Sheffield Shield and Test matches in the early days in Australia. It was a great compliment from there to be asked in 2000 and 2004 to write the forewords to Tom Smith's *New Cricket Umpiring and Scoring*, the internationally recognised and definitive guide to the interpretation and application of the Laws of cricket and of scoring.

In the television commentary boxes these days a sophisticated system is used to keep a record of every ball bowled. For Channel 9 in Australia Max Kruger is an excellent scorer-statistician. For Channel 4, and more recently for Channel 5 in the United Kingdom, Jo King does an outstanding job; Malcolm Ashton has been around a long time, a splendid scorer, statistician and a good bloke. Irving Rosenwater was a brilliant cricket historian, as well as a scorer and statistician, and Wendy Wimbush, apart from doing an extraordinary amount of work for the Cricket Writers' Club, splendidly handled the scoring in media centres around the UK. Before his untimely death, Bill Frindall, as well as working for BBC Radio, produced and printed records of every Test match played and every statistic known to the game. He was preceded at the BBC by Arthur Wrigley, Roy Webber and Jack Price.

ENGLAND v AUSTRALIA 2nd Test at Lords, London

A sample of the linear method used by Bill Frindall at Lord's 1975

All of the modern scorers use the same basic system which allows the whole match to be replayed. I have always thought this to be one of the best scoring methods I have seen in any sport and I was even more intrigued some years ago to learn how it came about, back in the 19th century, long before Bill Ferguson.

The information came my way because during a BBC telecast at Headingley in early August 1994, in the course of the England v

South Africa Test, we showed a youngster sitting in the crowd. He was avidly watching the cricket and keeping, in very neat fashion, his own scorebook of the match. I remarked that I had done the same as this lad when I was his age and I hoped he might one day go on to be a good cricketer and enjoy the game as much as I have done.

A week later I received a letter from Ken Pendlington enclosing a newspaper cutting dated 16 January 1914 noting the death of his grandfather. The story it told was that Mr John Atkinson Pendlington, a great lover of cricket, when reviewing on a winter's evening the important contests as reported by Lillywhite and *Wisden*, thought it should be possible to devise a scorebook to record the result of every ball bowled in a match. He soon had it worked out and took the score at Scarborough in Lord Londesbrough's match against the Australians in 1893 (Mr C. I. Thornton's XI). This record showed, for all time, the number of balls each batsman received from each bowler, and what runs he made from them. It caused much amusement and pleasure to Dr W. G. Grace, who was watching the match at Scarborough and was presented with the authentic document.

John Atkinson Pendlington was born in South Shields in 1861 and he and his son played for Benwell in the Northumberland League. He was noted as a Shakespearean scholar and a good conversationalist and he founded the Tyneside Supply Company, which later became the British Electrical and Manufacturing Company of Newcastle and London. When once asked his religion he is said to have answered, 'I am neither heterodox nor orthodox, but just a paradox.'

42

THE FASCINATION
OF THE ASHES

Ashes Test matches are unique. The manner in which the phrase was first coined sets the whole thing apart from other Test matches, even those with names of players or ex-players attached to them. The rather romantic story of Ivo Bligh, later Lord Darnley, and Janet, Lady Clarke, who burned a bail and placed the bail's ashes in an urn, adds a happy touch to the events of the early 1880s. The occasion was a cricket match played at Rupertswood outside Melbourne on Christmas Eve 1882. Ivo Bligh and his touring team had met Sir William and Lady Clarke, the owners of Rupertswood, while voyaging back to Australia after the Australian team had won a cricket match at The Oval. The term 'Ashes' came into being when it was part of an obituary notice in the London *Sporting Times* which lamented the fact that the death of English cricket had been witnessed and that the 'ashes' would be taken to Australia. Ivo Bligh was the captain of the England team which toured Australia in 1882–83 and he was quoted as saying he intended to bring the Ashes back to England. Miss Florence Morphy, the music teacher to the Clarke children, was at the Christmas Eve match with other ladies when Lady Clarke handed the terracotta urn, as a present, to Ivo Bligh. Bligh and Florence Morphy were later married and she became the Countess of Darnley when Bligh was elevated to the peerage.

It was Fred Spofforth, 'The Demon', who took 7–46 and 7–44 at Kennington Oval in the 30th match of the Australian tour of England, played on 28 and 29 August 1882. This was the game that led to the first mention of the Ashes and it has been remembered down the years for Spofforth's inspirational exhortation of 'this thing can be done' when the Australians had set England 85 to win and then won the match by 7 runs.

Ever since then, the never-ending battle for possession of the Ashes has fascinated cricket followers in both hemispheres – and recent series have been no exception. It has been a splendid time for Anglo-Australian cricket. The 2005 series in the UK, when Michael Vaughan captained England to victory against Ricky Ponting's team, was the best and most exciting I have seen. The series there in 2009 was also great to watch, though one's nerves were less stretched. Ponting was captain again, but this time Andrew Strauss was his counterpart. The First Test at Cardiff was drawn, England won at Lord's, Edgbaston was drawn and Australia had a comprehensive victory by an innings at Headingley. The final Test at The Oval was a clear-cut victory for England, with Jonathan Trott making a century on his Test debut.

In Australia, in 2006–07, it was a five-nil whitewash for Ricky Ponting's team and it was the series for which Andrew Flintoff had been appointed captain; Andrew Strauss was in the team but not as captain. It all went wrong for England as over-confidence led them to take their eye off the ball and Australia swamped them. Australia won the opening Test at the 'Gabba and then England fought back in the Second Test in Adelaide, winning the toss and amassing 551–6. After Australia had fought back with 513, Shane Warne bowled superbly in England's second innings to take 4–49 off 32 overs and Australia comfortably made 168–4 for victory.

That five-nil series win was a real drubbing but, because of their 2009 exploits, it was England who held the Ashes when they arrived in Australia in November 2010. It was clear, with Andrew Strauss as captain and Andy Flower as coach, there would be no relaxing this time. That's exactly the way it should be in the oldest cricketing contest of all.

43
THE KEY TO SPIN BOWLING

S PIN bowling is one of the great challenges in the game of cricket. Do it well and it can be a marvellous experience, have a setback or two along the way and it can also be a miserable one. Legspin bowling, because of the nature of the delivery, is often thought to be the most difficult to bowl, but one needs to be careful in an assessment of that kind because offspinners, or as they are sometimes termed 'orthodox spinners', can have just as much trouble in getting their delivery right. You also need a great deal of luck. Both types of bowler I have mentioned need to have good temperament, skill, strong fingers and an ability to turn the ball. At the same time, you can have a spin bowler who doesn't turn the ball at all. One such was Jack Hill, the quickish over-the-wrist spinner from Victoria who toured England in 1953 and West Indies in 1955. Jack was nicknamed 'Snarler' and he certainly gave the batsmen little respite, nor did he give them the comfort of thinking they could actually bat. I have always regarded him as one of the unlucky bowlers around Australia, though I suppose any spinner who makes two overseas tours with an Australian team can regard himself as being fortunate, because there are so many who don't quite make it at the right time.

Jack was around when England were dominant in world cricket. In 1953, when Jack and I toured under Lindsay Hassett's captaincy, England, captained by Len Hutton, regained the Ashes. In 1954–55 in Australia, again under Hutton's captaincy, they retained them. In 1956 they retained them again. When we toured West Indies in 1955 Jack played just the one Test at Barbados, but he headed the bowling figures for all matches in the tour. In Australia, in 1955–56, when the selectors were considering the team to tour England in 1956, Jack, in the Australian season, took 25 wickets at a cost of 23 apiece but couldn't beat Jack Wilson of South Australia for a place in the team. Jack Hill was an extremely accurate bowler, skidded off the pitch and woe betide anyone who tried to play the pull shot against him.

During the 2009–10 summer in Australia, his name came up in various discussions I was having with other commentators about the requirements needed to be a successful spin bowler. Accuracy was one requirement but one that kept recurring was patience. There was a story doing the rounds that the Australian selectors had called Nathan Hauritz in for a 'chat' and reminded him that, as an Australian spin bowler, he might be expected to have a hand in bowling out the opposition on the last day, or the fourth innings of a Test. Hauritz had been around for a while, he had toured England and he had improved his bowling on the tour by studying the methods of the English spin bowlers, particularly Graeme Swann, whom I regard as a very talented spinner. One of the things Swann is able to do is curve the ball away from a right-hand batsman and then spin it back at him from outside the off stump. He is also a real danger to left-handers because he possesses a very good topspinner which is cleverly disguised. Hauritz was sensible enough to study video-tape of Swann bowling in the Test matches and his own bowling improved, not dramatically, but steadily. That improvement continued in Australia and I was pleased to see it because I always have a lot of time for cricketers who try hard and work at their game.

One person who constantly tried to help Hauritz was his captain Ricky Ponting. Ponting knew that rebuilding the team after the loss of Warne, McGrath and Gilchrist was likely to be tough. That it would require patience. Not everyone was prepared to allow him that luxury. Ponting knew what was likely to happen to the Australian team after the match against West Indies in Barbados in June 2008. Australia had won the Test but West Indies had made 387 in defeat in the fourth innings of the match. He knew the future was likely to be a hard grind and that the team would be a work in progress for some time. Preferably a short time but that wasn't guaranteed.

I kept looking at the patience aspect when I was watching the Australian bowlers work hard and do their best. Ponting knew that in the various media outlets patience wasn't high on the list. He had Mitchell Johnson who had lost form in England and was having trouble with his bowling action and delivery stride, but had a great deal of ability to balance all that. Ben Hilfenhaus is a good swing bowler but suddenly he was injured and out of the calculations, remaining so for the rest of the 2009–10 season. Peter Siddle is a Victorian pace bowler who never fails to give 100 per cent to his captain but he has also developed stress fractures of the back. Doug Bollinger suddenly appeared when he was sent to Perth to play for New South Wales and picked up eight wickets. He then made the Test side and, despite being a left-arm pace bowler, as is the case with Johnson, was a completely different style of bowler. Brett Lee suffered an arm injury, as happened to Stuart Clark; the latter became available but the selectors decided to go with Bollinger. Inspired choice.

There were a number of spin bowlers around the country and Hauritz was given the nod. In Melbourne, where the Australian side played Pakistan in the opening Test of the three-match series, Ricky Ponting produced some of the finest captaincy I have seen in my time in the game as a player or media man. He made two declarations in the match, the first at an unlikely time in the first innings where the Australians were well on top. Then, in the second Australian innings, he declared again, with a carefully calculated move that gave both teams the chance to win the match, or Pakistan to save it if needed.

How many times do you see captains do that kind of thing in these modern times? He received double reward for his thinking. Australia won the match and Hauritz picked up his first five-wicket haul.

In the commentary box Shane Warne had been talking to me

about patience in bowling and how important this was and how difficult it was for some bowlers to appreciate the importance. Some observers of the game, and those who went to the grounds when Warne was bowling, might be of the opinion that he didn't show all that much patience in that he was always 'at' the batsmen, hustling them, using mind games which sometimes involved saying nothing at all. Warne was the greatest legspin bowler the world has ever seen and, as he took over 700 Test wickets in his career, in my view, not only was he a great wicket-taker but he was also a patient bowler. After our conversation I wondered how best to convey the aspect of patience to the people who wrote to me asking for advice on legspin bowling and how to go about it. In the two pages (yes, only two and shown later in this book) I send to aspiring young bowlers who write to me, I have a short paragraph to deal with the subject; it is only thirty-eight words in length.

Shane talked with Nathan Hauritz on the final morning of the 2009 Boxing Day Test and whatever he said certainly worked for the offspinner and he turned in a splendid performance. No matter how long you are in this game there is always something more you can learn; that's why cricket is such a great game.

It is also a dangerous game and one that can produce despair, as Hauritz found at Bellerive Oval in Hobart towards the end of the 50-overs-a-side series against England in 2011 when he threw himself at the ball in a bid to save runs. He dislocated his shoulder, a fracture was feared at first, and he was then unavailable for the World Cup.

After I'd listened to Shane Warne in Melbourne in that 2009 Boxing Day Test, I went back to Crown Towers and looked up four bowlers in Ric Finlay's *Tastats* records. Ric provides the best statistical detail in cricket; his data comes through to my computer, and to many other computer owners who subscribe to the service, and it is invaluable.

This night in Melbourne, thinking about patience, I settled down to look at the records of Grimmett, O'Reilly, Benaud and Warne. They are noted in order of debut in Test cricket.

Name	Debut Test No.	Date	Tests	Wickets	Strike Rate	Balls Bowled	Debut Figs	Overs per wicket
		v Eng SCG					5–45 &	
C.V. Grimmett	162	Feb 1925	37	216	67.19	14,513	6–37	11
		v SA Adelaide					2–74 &	
W.J. O'Reilly	215	Jan 1932	27	144	69.61	10,024	2–81	12
		v WI SCG						
R. Benaud	347	Jan 1952	63	248	77.05	19,108	1–14	13
		v India SCG						
S.K. Warne	1,181	Jan 1992	145	708	57.49	40,704	1–150	9

What better evidence could anyone have that patience is a requirement; that the greatest legspin bowler ever to step on to a cricket field took a wicket every nine overs? In a day's play Shane could bowl 27 overs and take 3–75 and his strike-rate would stay at a wicket every nine overs. That's why young legspinners, or for that matter young spin bowlers of any type, need to rethink their method and bear in mind that spin is vital, ability is essential, method is very important, protection of spinning fingers is a must, but patience, to complete your bowling career in Test cricket, may well be the key factor. Only one wicket every nine overs!

To no one could this apply more than Steven Smith, the Australian allrounder who has moved from Sheffield Shield cricket and into the Australian Test team. He was chosen for the World Cup T20 in the Caribbean in April 2010 and then was drafted into the Australian ODI squad for the England tour. It was a wonderful day for him when he made his Test debut against Pakistan – not only playing for Australia for the first time, but at Lord's, in a team that won by 150 runs. It was also useful experience for him to face Danish Kaneria, a talented legspinner. Kaneria trapped him lbw in both innings; Smith though was quick to learn and when Ponting gave him his opportunity with the ball in the second innings he took 3–51 from 21 very good overs. His victims were opening batsman Imran Farhat, Kamran Akmal and allrounder Umar Gul. Smith is an accomplished batsman in all three forms of the game and one of the best fielders I have seen. He will find legspinning a fascinating part of his Test cricket career and also the most difficult. As a promising young legspinner, he should never forget Shane Warne's strike-rate, only one wicket every nine overs.

44

KEEPING IT SIMPLE

Over-rates

THERE was a time when cricketers did the simple things. They tried to bowl as fast as possible, move the ball off the seam as far as they could, spin it like a whirling top and, at the same time, bowl with such impeccable length and direction that the opposition batsman was rendered strokeless. The batsman, on the other hand, was always trying to play strokes for the entertainment of the crowd, whether at the ground or watching in the comfort of a living room. He was constantly trying to outsmart the bowler and the opposing captain. Played in that fashion, there was a good chance the matches would be well attended and the contest appreciated.

In these modern times, something guaranteed to drive away those who pay their money at the gate is the poor over-rates, which seem to be the rule rather than the exception at Test match level. No day's play ends at the appointed time.

When the home authorities produce their official programmes for a Test, say at Lord's or the Sydney Cricket Ground, that programme is bought by the paying spectator for something like five pounds, or ten dollars. It says: Hours of play: 11 a.m. to 6 p.m. Lunch interval: 1 p.m. to 1.40 p.m. Tea interval: 3.40 p.m. to 4 p.m. (If for any reason there are changes to the scheduled hours of play, details will be announced over the PA system.) However, that word 'scheduled' is the beginning of the massive problem that ends up with spectators being ripped off.

It is clearly understood that weather and bad light can have an effect on how much cricket is seen by the spectator. No worries about that. But the over-rates are so appalling that the game never finishes at its proper time of 6 p.m. It has developed in such a way that spectators – if, that is, they wish to see a whole day's play – sometimes arrive home an hour later than should have been the case.

There is a simple solution and it involves the use of the Spirit of Cricket Preamble to the Laws of Cricket. It reads:

1. There are two Laws which place the responsibility for the team's conduct firmly on the captain.

Responsibility of captains
The captains are responsible at all times for ensuring that play is conducted within the Spirit of the Game as well as within the Laws.

Only 44 words but some of the most important ever written about the game of cricket. What to do about a slow over-rate in a Test match? Suspend the captain responsible for one Test, with a two-match suspension for a repeat offence. That *should* make it clear that the nonsense must be stopped. If not, go to three!

My belief is that we are past the time when time-wasters can laugh at the paying spectator; instead they should be brought to account.

Double-bouncers

One of the great things about cricket is that it continues to evolve; cricketers are constantly trying to come up with something new to provide problems for the opposition. Generally, though not always, it is the bowler endeavouring to find a way to trouble the batsman, as he feels he is the poor downtrodden one on the field and that all the Laws of the game have been created and altered to favour the batsman.

In June 2010 the Warwickshire County Cricket Club in England, through their bowling coach Graeme Welch, came up with a style of pace bowling that involved the ball bouncing twice before reaching the batsman. (Perfectly valid according to the Laws of Cricket, Law 24.6.) I thought this was innovative and interesting and read the story with great anticipation. Then the ECB issued a directive to county clubs, coaches and umpires, saying, 'The practice of bowling a ball that bounces twice should be disallowed with immediate effect. It is considered inappropriate for the image and spirit of our game.'

Hello?

There happen to be quite a number of things in cricket which are inappropriate for the image and spirit of the game. The story I read said nothing about the ECB having conducted a series of trials, in match circumstances, to assess the situation precisely. In any case, batsmen over the years, apart from Bodyline, have always found some way to counter bowlers' thinking. Might the batsmen not have worked out what to do with this double-bouncing ball and belted hell out of it? That would have put a stop to it in far better fashion than a heavy-handed ban without cricket followers even seeing it in action.

In contrast, I was pleased to see that the response of MCC, the custodian of the Laws of Cricket, again showed a common-sense approach to the game. Keith Bradshaw, their chief executive, said, 'We don't think it is against the Spirit of Cricket or contrary to the Laws.'

Good on him and good on MCC.

They had shown the same common sense when Kevin Pietersen first played the switch-hit. In the face of complaints that he was dragging the game of cricket into the chamber of horrors, MCC deemed it legal because it showed expertise and no one should bother trying it unless they had a considerable amount of batting skill. By restating Law 36.3, they also underlined what comprises the offside of the wicket. This is determined by the striker's stance at the moment the ball comes into play for that delivery. The ball comes into play when the bowler starts his run-up or, if he has no run-up, his delivery action. Pietersen, because he makes a study of batting, was able to perform his shot successfully, and now it is up to the bowlers and the fielding captains to find a successful counter.

Some of the ideas introduced to cricket will be successful after being trialled extensively, some will be trialled and given a dismissive wave of the hand. Others will be looked at and set aside for the moment but, because they have some merit, may well make a comeback. When we were sports consultants to World Series Cricket in 1977, it was said to me, 'Benaud, if God had meant cricket to be played at night he wouldn't have made cricket balls red.' The remark, I suppose, has some ecclesiastical merit, but that falls away in the light of what has happened over those thirty-three years.

Polishing off the time-wasters

Time-wasting is generally attributed to the fielding side, yet there have been occasions when I have been watching a match when the batting side is culpable. For the fielding team it is a relatively simple matter of more conferences between captain and bowler, more and more field changes that involve moving a fielder two yards to the left and then a ball later, after another conference between captain and bowler, moving him back to precisely the same spot. For the batting team it is a matter of the batsman not being ready when the bowler turns and starts his run-up.

These days, with a specified number of overs to be bowled rather than a set finishing time, it can only really be a factor towards the end of a day or an innings when there seems to be a worsening of the light. The batting side may be in trouble trying to avoid a follow-on or they may be hanging on grimly on the final day. The umpires have met in the centre, have had a look at the dark clouds but so far haven't used their light meters. The batsmen are well up with the pace and, with no chance of winning the match, they suddenly see the chance of saving it by using up time in this way.

The umpires should be on the alert for this and they are entitled to make their feelings quite clear to the two batsmen. Law 42.10 plainly states that in normal circumstances the striker should be ready to take strike when the bowler is ready to start his run-up. It goes on to say that the umpire can warn the batsman for wasting time, giving a first and final warning, which will apply throughout the innings. Each incoming batsman will be told of the situation and the warning. If time is again wasted by a batsman, five penalty runs are awarded to the fielding side.

It is important to understand that this is a *team* offence, not just an offence by one batsman. What is definitely required is that umpires are on the lookout for captains, bowlers and batsmen who are simply making fools of them, also the administrators of the game. It's way past time to put a stop to that nonsense.

One thing I am hoping to see from the administrators is a move to allow only the bowler to polish the ball. The ICC could, if they were to get their collective brains into gear, stop any form of ball-tampering in one short sentence.

Playing condition: Allow only the bowler to polish the ball.

At the end of each over the ball should be given to the umpire to make sure nothing untoward has been done to it. The umpire then gives the ball to the new bowler, who has precisely six deliveries to work on it legally. The remainder of the fielding team are banned from doing anything with it. What could be simpler? Just think of the ridiculous posturing and polishing that goes on at the moment. The ball is tossed by the 'keeper to gully, who works fiercely on it before throwing it to cover, who polishes and then sends it to mid-off, who polishes madly, sometimes going through contortions liable to produce torn muscles or, at best, considerable pain.

It is often said about cricket that it is a simple game, only made difficult by people. This would be a simple playing condition and it would work well.

Split captaincy

As someone who was not originally destined to captain Australia but eventually did so through mischance, as well as the illness of others, I was always enthralled by the tasks facing the captain of any international team. And that was when only Test matches were played. I started by captaining the Central Cumberland club in Sydney; I was shortlisted to lead the New South Wales Sheffield Shield team but played under Ian Craig in that side, as well as when he was made captain of the Australian team to go to New Zealand early in 1957 and later in the same year to South Africa. Neil Harvey was vice-captain on both those tours and he decided to move from Melbourne to Sydney in early 1958. It was at that time Ian contracted hepatitis and, curiously, I was made captain of Australia.

In those far-flung days we played only first-class cricket (with NSW) and then represented Australia at Test match level. The Australian Board of Control, as it was so aptly named then, made certain you didn't get too full of yourself by paying the players a match allowance on the basis of being an amateur. We did, though, have a great deal of fun, exactly as the more professional players of today have fun.

Captaincy now is a different business. It's not just a case of being skipper of the team in a season comprising eight first-class Sheffield Shield matches and five Tests. A captain in Australia might have the pleasurable job of leading his country in Tests, 50-overs matches and T20 games, and his state in Sheffield Shield games and one-dayers when he is available. If, that is, he is able to fit it all in with his family commitments. We are, however, seeing more and more instances where questions are being asked about captains in different countries and all captains are being forced into making decisions.

The Australians' situation was, as noted earlier, that Ponting decided to step down and play under the new captain, as I had stepped down 47 years earlier. On both occasions the Australian team needed to be rebuilt. Back in 1963 Neil Harvey, Alan Davidson and Ken Mackay had retired at the conclusion of the final Test against England at the SCG, while Ponting, in modern times, had lost three great players in Gilchrist, McGrath and Warne. A captain's task is hard enough without having to work with a number of players new to Test cricket.

Daniel Vettori has retired from the captaincy, having done a

wonderful job for New Zealand over the years, a splendid cricketer and an outstanding tactician. There are problems in Sri
Lanka, not least because of former captain Hashan Tillakaratne's
claims of match-fixing many years ago. India, who won the World
Cup, seem stable, with M. S. Dhoni's captaincy keeping him a
couple of overs ahead of the play, and Tendulkar's enduring skill.
Keeping two overs ahead of the play was a tactic taught to me by
Keith Miller and it remains one of the best pieces of advice I ever
received. Graeme Smith is stepping down from some areas of the
national captaincy in South Africa, Pakistan is an unknown quantity from day to day and it is unnerving to see West Indies trying
to work out their problems as well as win a match or two.

In England, Andrew Strauss, after the Ashes triumph in Australia,
needed to decide in which form or forms of the game he would
continue to lead England. It was clear Andy Flower would have
liked to have Strauss captaining in the 50-overs-a-side format, but
Strauss did the sensible thing, with the next World Cup not until
2015, and decided to concentrate on Test cricket. I admire him
for that decision and the chance it provided for Alastair Cook to
lead England in the shorter version of the game, and also for him
to look ahead to the possibility of Test captaincy, plus the more
remote possibility of leading in that 2015 World Cup. Cook is
fortunate Andy Flower has signed a new contract with England;
Flower will work closely with Hugh Morris, the England managing director, and it seems a good solution. The captaincy of the
England T20 squad is another matter. Paul Collingwood, if fit,
would certainly have held that role; he and his team brought
England their first-ever global trophy when they triumphed in the
World T20 in 2010. I would assume the coach and the selectors
talked to Collingwood and explained why he was being axed.
But then, we all know what 'assumption' produces in life! Stuart
Broad will be the T20 captain of England and, although he is a
fine all-round cricketer, he will find it an exacting task.

Could I do the three jobs? Of course I could, but for how long
at the speed at which cricket is played these days? I fear it would
be a short time frame.

45

A SAD FAREWELL

W E were lucky to have them. Mum and Dad were as good as you could have as parents and they looked after JB and me and made certain we understood that there was no more important aspect of life than people. Mum passed away in October 2008 and we gave her a good send-off: seventy people at the crematorium where Dad had been farewelled in 1994, aged eighty-nine. Although Mum didn't drink alcohol, there were many glasses raised to her at the Mean Fiddler, all by people who hadn't reached her age.

She was 104 when she left us. The last five years of her life were spent at an aged care facility at Greystanes, not far from North Parramatta where she and Dad had spent fifty-eight very happy years. She went there when she realised she had forgotten how to use the microwave and she felt it was time to be looked after.

She had her 100th birthday at the care facility surrounded by relatives and friends and looking at a signed photograph from Her Majesty the Queen wishing her a happy birthday. She was in excellent shape until a bad fall incapacitated her and a few months later it was a merciful release. She was a splendid lady.

Lou had been a schoolteacher through the depression years in Australia; he was a fine cricketer and person and we said goodbye and thanks to him sixteen years ago. He was one of the best and it says so where he rests these days alongside Rene.

Two captains listed to lead England and Australia in the Ashes battle of 2010-11 in Australia. Andrew Strauss, shown here hitting a boundary on his way to 161 at Lord's in 2009, has the task of retaining the Ashes on Australian pitches and in Australian conditions. Not easy, but he is certainly capable of doing it. Ricky Ponting is still on a 'work in progress' with the Australian side and the beating they received at the hands of Pakistan at Headingley in 2010 will have given England a great boost. Cricket captaincy is one of the more difficult tasks in sport. They both know that to be the case. I certainly found it to be so!

One of the great photographs. Ricky Ponting at the SCG in 2010 in pensive mode on the final day after he had batted first and Australia had been bowled out cheaply by Pakistan. Ponting never gave up and he inspired his team to victory, one of the finest pieces of captaincy I have ever seen.

pitch to wicketkeeper Adam Gilchrist and the Australians had won. Shane Warne had turned in a wonderful spell of spin bowling, removing Herschelle Gibbs with a magnificent leg-break and then taking the wickets of Kirsten, Cronje and Kallis. The final against Pakistan three days later was an anticlimax, with Wasim Akram deciding to bat on a green-top on winning the toss and seeing his side bowled out for 132 in just 39 of the 50 available overs, and Australia made the required runs for victory in 20 overs.

Eleven days later England played the first Test match of the summer against New Zealand and won well. It was the start of the Channel 4 coverage and, despite the 'grey-haired old fogeys' bit, I eventually made it into the Channel 4 team, whose work was widely praised. The commentary team and Sunset + Vine worked on the First Test at Edgbaston, but the coverage there was by satellite and cable; the first of the free-to-air matches was at Lord's on 22 July. The commentary box and the production was the same as usual and the Channel 4 administrators wisely took advice from Channel 9 in Australia and used the experienced services of Sunset + Vine's Chief Sports Producer, Gary Franses, and Channel 9's Director, Rob Sheerlock, who is the best with whom I have ever worked. Channel 4 continued to cover Test cricket in England until the end of the 2005 Ashes series and since then television cricket in the UK has been controlled by Sky, a pay-TV company requiring a subscription fee. It was a big change from free-to-air, but it was one welcomed by the ECB, who received more money for the TV rights than they had ever dreamed about.

In Australia, after I finished playing Test cricket in 1964, I occasionally did a little television commentary on a limited-overs competition as part of a sports consultancy contract with the Australian Board of Control. That work was done with the Australian Broadcasting Commission and, because it was part of our sports consultancy contract, I received no payment, nor did I ask for any. In 1976–77 the season consisted of Sheffield Shield matches and the Centenary Test match at the MCG 12–17 March the four-match rubber two–one, with victories at Port of Spain, Trinidad, and Sabina Park, Jamaica; in the latter match the great George Headley made 270 not out.

The Broad/Waddell book contains many other interesting features and gives a very good rundown on how sports television began in the United Kingdom and where it stood at the turn of the century when the rights to cricket were lost by the BBC.

There may be others who have been involved in the televising of cricket longer than I have, but their numbers would be thin on the ground. I worked with the BBC from 1963 until 1999, when Channel 4 took over in a fanfare of word pictures of how they were about to change Test match cricket coverage for ever. The first thing they said was that they intended to remove from the commentary box those three grey-haired old fogeys who had dozed away over the years. The following Sunday, in the *News of the World*, I was able to write that I had seen their statement and gathered they were referring to David Gower and Tony Lewis, but who could possibly be the third person mentioned?

There were some wonderful matches in the 1999 World Cup, which was the last thing I covered for the BBC, notably the game in early June between Pakistan and South Africa before a capacity crowd of 15,000 at Trent Bridge where South Africa won by three wickets, Lance Klusener and Mark Boucher adding 45 in the eighth-wicket partnership. Then there was the Australia v South Africa semi-final at Edgbaston where the two teams were tied on 213, South Africa batting last. It was a bizarre finish with Allan Donald and Klusener together. The Australian captain, Steve Waugh, knew that a tie would be enough and then, in the extraordinary mix-up of Donald dropping his bat and then hesitating for the run, the Australians kept their heads and South Africa collectively lost theirs. Eventually Donald was trying to make it to the striker's end, but Mark Waugh, skirting around from mid-on, flicked the ball to the bowler Damien Fleming who, instead of throwing it to the other end, merely rolled it down the losing four wickets before winning. It was not the most exciting of matches to watch, but it certainly wasn't the most boring. However, Boycott was dropped. He was more than likely the victim of people wanting to be seen by the public to be making an example of someone, to try to produce what passed in those days for brighter cricket.

24

WORRELL AT FORTY-TWO
LEAVES A LEGACY

FRANK Worrell, in every sense of the word one of the greatest cricketers the world has known, died on 13 March 1967 aged forty-two, two days after Barbados attained independence, and the Rest of the World team, captained by Bill Lawry, finished their game against Barbados, a match organised as part of the celebrations. Apart from being a great cricketer, he was a wonderful leader of men, and few in the history of cricket have had a better influence on the game and on other people.

On Boxing Day of the same year, S. F. Barnes passed away while the Australia v India Test was being played at the Adelaide Oval. He was said by some of those who played with him, against him, and others who watched him, to be the greatest bowler who ever lived.

My first marriage came to an end early in this same year. My wife and I had been separated for over two years, and I was divorced for desertion. It wasn't the first time couples involved in sport and business had broken up, and I doubt it will be the last. Long separations are always a problem, though it appears to be easier these days when rules and regulations are relaxed to a great extent. That certainly wasn't the case in the 1950s and early 1960s.

Later in 1967 Daphne and I were married, and not long ago we celebrated forty years of being together at home and in business. Daph started with the BBC in the mid-1950s, then worked for E. W. Swanton, which is a good grounding for anyone. She has been personal assistant to several international cricket team managers over the years. Somehow she manages to unravel the chaos I produce, though I imagine it is no easy task.

Nineteen sixty-eight proved to be a momentous year, and not just because it was the year Bob and Grace Gray were married in London and Daphne and I were appointed official caterers to the event. Gray had been best man for me when Daph and I were married the previous summer. The Grays' wedding ceremony was held at St James's, Spanish Place, on Sunday afternoon, the rest day of the Lord's Test, and the reception was at Bob's flat near St John's Wood.

The Benauds decided not to try to outdo Fortnum & Mason, and instead provided smoked salmon sandwiches and a bath-tub full of crushed ice, champagne, Foster's and soft drink. The assembled guests included all the members of the Australian team playing at Lord's at the time, bar the skipper, Bill Lawry, who was spending the day with fellow pigeon fanciers.

The early-afternoon reception was timed so the players were all able to have an early night prior to play resuming at Lord's on the Monday. This was very important because Australia were one-nil in the series at that stage, having turned in an outstanding performance at Old Trafford to win the opening Test by 159 runs. In the rain-marred first three days at Lord's, England had moved to 351–7, and that was when they declared on the Monday morning, at which point the Australians were bowled out for 78. I am able to say, hand on heart, that the festivities the previous day, particularly the catering, had nothing to do with it, and Bill Lawry, who hadn't attended the nuptials, was the only batsman to make a duck. Eventually, with more rain delaying play, the match finished as a draw.

The Test series that year was squared and the Ashes retained by Australia, despite England winning at The Oval in the final game. This was an unusual and very good finish: it was a damp game and spectators were called into action on the last afternoon to assist in drying the ground so the England bowlers could have their chance at the Australian batsmen – along the lines of human super-soppers! It worked too. The ground, which might not have been ready for play in time for a result, was improved by the volunteers to the extent that England had time to win in what was an exciting end to the summer.

I was lucky to be part of the BBC TV commentary team for that Test, witnessing one of the great fighting innings, Basil D'Oliveira's 158 after he was called into the side as a replacement for Roger Prideaux who had done well in the previous Test at Headingley but now had severe bronchitis. Dolly knew that if he were to have any chance of gaining selection for the tour to South Africa, he must make runs in this game, a sort of last chance. He was assisted by some poor catching from Australia, lapses which drove Lawry to distraction.

Despite the innings, Basil was not immediately chosen in the MCC team but was included when Tom Cartwright was injured and failed a fitness test. This led the South African Prime Minister, John Vorster, to announce that the MCC team would not be welcome because it had now been selected with political aims. Vorster's language in that announcement was described as 'crude and boorish', so I was interested to meet him in Cape Town, with Joe Pamensky and Dr Piet Koornhof, when I was manager of the International Wanderers side which toured South Africa eight years later.

In 1975 I was approached, at the conclusion of the World Cup and the four Tests between England and Australia in England, to see if I would be prepared to play in or take part in a private tour of South Africa. Playing was out of the question because of a bad back and a determination to retire completely from that side of the game, and I had always sworn, having been a player and seen what troubles and stress they cause managers, that I would never, under any circumstances, become a manager, so I sensibly declined the offer. However, with two distinct areas of pressure being applied to me, I began to have second thoughts. One pressure group was constantly telling me South Africa were doing *all* the right things, which was rubbish; the other group told me only critical things about the country. I decided to have a look for myself and make up my own mind.

46

THE LONG AND SHORT OF IT

ICC World Twenty20

THE 2010 World Twenty20 in the Caribbean was one of the more extraordinary cricket competitions I have witnessed. I watched it on television and it was, for the most part, riveting. There were a few slow-moving matches, but it had a splendid start, good middle matches and a great ending when England came from nowhere to beat Australia in the final.

The Hussey brothers, David and Michael, born in Morley, Western Australia, have become important members of the Australian limited-overs teams. David, the younger, moved to Victoria to play his cricket; Michael stayed in Perth. To Michael Hussey goes the accolade for playing the heroic match-winning innings that enabled Australia to reach that final against Paul Collingwood's team when victory looked to be impossible.

One of the stars of the Australian team led by Michael Clarke was Cameron White, captain of Victoria in the Australian domestic competition and Clarke's deputy in the Caribbean. White is a magnificent striker of the ball and he played brilliantly throughout these games, with 85 from 49 balls his finest effort. In the semi-final against Pakistan he slammed five sixes in five overs to give the Australians a glimmer of hope. In the first innings, Pakistan, who had been low-key for much of the competition, had suddenly unleashed everything at the Australians and set them a target of 192 to win – quite a difficult task if you consider 170 a par target. Pakistan then bowled and fielded well and the Australians were gone for all money when Michael Hussey walked to the centre of the St Lucia ground.

Even Hussey, splendid thinker of the game that he is, later said he felt it couldn't be done but was going to have a go anyway. Chances looked slim when Steve Smith was stumped off Ajmal in the 17th over and Mitchell Johnson walked out. By the end of that over 34 were needed from 12 balls. Hussey proceeded to take 16 from the 19th over, but victory was still improbable. Johnson was on strike at the beginning of the final over and common sense said he had to push the first ball so they could scamper through for a single and give Hussey the strike. He somehow managed to do this, and Hussey was left with five balls to face with 17 needed. In fact, he hit 22 – 6, 6, 4, 6 – and the Australians had won with one ball to spare.

Both Pakistan and Australia knew the winners would meet up with England in the final, Paul Collingwood's team having disposed of Sri Lanka with the greatest of confidence in the first semi-final when chasing a target of only 129. England fielded brilliantly in that match and their bowlers were in great form, four of them conceding 24 or less from their individual bowling spells.

In the final England were far too good for Australia; they outplayed them in every department, which was no mean feat considering the psychological boost Australia had from their win over Pakistan.

I thought it was a wonderful competition with a lot of excitement and was pleased common sense had prevailed with ticket pricing and permission for the local cricket followers to bring food and drink into the ground, in keeping with tradition in the Caribbean until the ICC made such a botch of things in the 50-overs-a-side World Cup in 2007.

The 2010–11 Ashes
Rarely has there been a better-prepared cricket team at international level than the one Andrew Strauss captained to retain the Ashes in 2010–11 in Australia. It wasn't just an overnight plan but one which began in the English summer when England beat both Bangladesh and Pakistan and were interested onlookers in the 'spot-fixing' claims which came out of the Lord's Test match

when the *News of the World* published a story on Sunday, 29 August 2010. The story alleged that three Pakistan players were involved in the activities – Mohammad Amir, Mohammad Asif and the captain Salman Butt – and, after an ICC inquiry handled by Michael Beloff, QC, they were subsequently banned from playing cricket. All slightly unnerving for England, because it took attention away from the manner in which Strauss's team had won two Tests against Bangladesh and three of the four against Pakistan. The three Pakistan cricketers later lodged an appeal in Switzerland with the Court of Arbitration for Sport and the judgment is awaited with great interest in the world of cricket.

When England's team was named for the tour of Australia there were no real surprises and Andrew Strauss and the England coach Andy Flower were very happy with the final list. Alastair Cook would have been relieved to see his name in the squad because he had been through a tough period at the top of the batting line-up. A century against Pakistan in the loss at The Oval would have given the selectors a boost as well, because they knew he was a splendid batsman, just going through a 'rough trot' during the controversial summer, a time when he was assisted a great deal by Graham Gooch, formerly an outstanding opening batsman for England. Gooch also assists Essex, where Cook plays, and the whole scenario had a good feel to it, something that was made to look an understatement when Cook went on to enjoy such a wonderful tour of Australia.

One of the great decisions made by Strauss, Flower, Gooch and the relevant administrators was to move right away from the tactical methods of 2006–07, when Australia won the series five-nil. In 2010–11 Cricket Australia asked if there was anything Strauss and Flower wanted, and there was surprise when the answer was that they wished to play three lead-up matches on three of the grounds where Tests were to be played. In the end, that wasn't totally possible because of the Australian domestic programme, but they did play on two of the Test grounds, Perth and Adelaide, and, instead of the 'Gabba, they were given a match against Australia A at Bellerive Oval in Hobart. England and Australia were scheduled to play a 50-overs-a-side match on that ground on 21 January 2011, so it was almost what England wanted. Those three matches were very beneficial for Strauss's team; there were declarations in the games, but the hard practice gave England a good start to their tour and had them in form before the First Test began.

In the lead-up match at Perth, Andrew Strauss made the most of a good pitch and finished with 120 not out. His opening partner at that stage, Alastair Cook, made only 5 and 9 and looked a little on the rusty side from what I saw sitting in Sydney and watching television. All that changed in the Adelaide match when, on a typically good Adelaide pitch, Cook made 32 and 111 not out and the game ended in a draw. But Strauss would have been very happy with many aspects of his team's performance, not least that they were sharp in the field. In the match against Australia A at Bellerive in Hobart, England won by ten wickets despite a courageous century from skipper Cameron White, but what was most encouraging for Strauss and Flower was that the two pace bowlers, Tremlett (4–54 and 3–67) and Bresnan (2–65 and 4–86), showed they were coming to terms with the requirements of bowling well on Australian pitches. After the conclusion of that Hobart match, England had four days' practice before the opening Test at the 'Gabba in Brisbane, and they made the most of batting and bowling in the nets at a ground where over the years not all had gone well for England.

The pitch looked to be typical of Brisbane, a touch of green in the surface, which was hard-topped, though it had the usual amount of moisture, with the temperature likely to be between 25 and 30 degrees throughout the game. It was a very good-looking pitch and Strauss had no hesitation in batting first when he called correctly. Now his job was to walk out with Cook and try still to be there at lunch on the first day. That didn't work out as planned. Ben Hilfenhaus was given the new ball and when Strauss tried to square-cut the third delivery he hit it hard and straight at Mike Hussey in the gully and the fielder took a good catch right in front of his eyes.

Australian cricket followers had mixed views about Hussey's selection in the opening Test match. His age and form were the favourite 'knocking' topics, but he had been a favourite player for many years and he was in reasonable form coming into the game. He is an athletic cricketer and in this England first innings he showed that, even though years were advancing, they hadn't yet caught up with him. He certainly carried that into his batting when Australia were 143–5 in reply to England's 260. He was joined by Brad Haddin and the pair added 307 for the sixth wicket. This underlined to everybody that Haddin is a splendid wicketkeeper-batsman and Hussey is still a good player with a wide range of strokes and fierce determination to carry him through the tough times. It showed one other thing. This was a really good batting pitch, and after three days, with England resuming their second innings at 19–0, Australia needed to bowl very well if they were to take a lead in the series. In England's first innings Cook had made 67 in more than four hours; he now batted throughout the second innings for an unbeaten 235. Strauss was stumped off Marcus North after making 110 and Jonathan Trott partnered Cook for six hours, with the England innings declared at 517–1. The Australians used six bowlers and the scorecard at the end of the match demonstrated the determination of the England team and the manner in which they would go about avoiding defeat.

For Ricky Ponting and his team it was a chastening experience. There was a good bowling performance from Peter Siddle in the England first innings when he took a hat-trick and had 6–54 from 16 overs, but that was followed by 0–90 from 24 overs in the second and the Australian attack looked threadbare by the time the umpires finally removed the bails. I was impressed by the manner in which Steve Finn bowled in his first Ashes match for England. He took 6–125 from 33.4 overs, and though he is short in experience he did well on a pitch where other bowlers were gasping. It came as a great surprise to me when he was left out of the side after the Perth Test, the reason given that he was too expensive. In one way I can understand the thinking, because young bowlers with little experience are often expensive and, if that goes against the tactics of the team, they are certainly expendable. I shall be very surprised, though, if Finn does not come back to the England team. He is only twenty-two years old, has ability and is a tall lad. What he needs is a good bowling adviser so he retains his bowling action and knows where he wants the ball to hit the pitch every time he brings his arm over. I know about that from being advised by Bill O'Reilly in 1953 on the precise manner in which I should change my bowling style. He added that it would take me four years to make it work and he was right, 1953–57. As it happened, the bowler who replaced Finn later in the series was Tim Bresnan, the bustling Yorkshire allrounder who came in for the Melbourne and Sydney Test matches and took six wickets at the MCG and five at the SCG. This was good selection from Strauss, Flower and the others on the committee.

The Second Test in Adelaide, played in excellent conditions, was a great surprise to Australian cricket followers, though the word 'great' in this instance means 'big' rather than 'enjoyable'. No complaints from the Australian team when they won the toss, because to do that on the Adelaide Oval is a very handy flip of the coin. The problem was that they didn't take advantage of the slice of good fortune and they made only 245 in their first innings; once again it was Hussey (93) and Haddin (56) who saved them from complete collapse. That didn't look likely when the Australians were three down with only two runs on the board and Ponting, Katich and Clarke already back in the dressing-room, Katich the victim of an appallingly stupid run-out. James Anderson bowled superbly, using swing, reverse swing and movement off the seam to confuse the batsmen; it was a classic display of pace bowling. Australia, having squandered the benefit of batting first, then took a real hammering from the England batsmen. Pietersen hit a brilliant 227 from only 308 balls faced, Cook was in form again with 148, and Trott (78) and Bell (68*) allowed Andrew Strauss to declare at 620–5.

The Australian bowling was very ordinary. Doug Bollinger had come into the team to replace Hilfenhaus, while Mitchell Johnson was left out on the morning of the match, the reason seemingly, having taken 0–66 and 0–104 in Brisbane, that his confidence was shattered. I'm not at all surprised! Ryan Harris came into the team in his place and was Australia's best bowler, with 2–84 from 29 overs. Australia's second innings was marginally better than their first attempt; they made 304, to provide England with victory by an innings and 71 runs. At one stage, with Michael Clarke and Michael Hussey sharing a partnership of 104, there was a chance of the match being saved, but Kevin Pietersen, bowling offspin, did the job for Strauss, having Clarke brilliantly caught by Cook at leg gully. A good bumper from Steve Finn then accounted for Hussey and, with Graeme Swann claiming Doherty and Siddle to complete a five-wicket haul, Strauss and his team were able to celebrate a splendid victory. Now England, one-nil in the series, were very much on top in the battle for the Ashes, with Perth, Melbourne and Sydney still remaining as venues and Australia needing to win two of those matches.

One of the best qualities of cricket is its unpredictability. No one could have envisaged what happened at the WACA ground in Perth, where the Third Test began nine days after the caning in Adelaide. At the end of four days of extraordinary cricket, Australia had squared the series and were able to look forward with confidence to the final two encounters at the MCG and the SCG.

Mitchell Johnson is a very important part of the Australian bowling attack. Bowling left-arm at considerable pace, he is very much a confidence player, as evidenced by his omission from the previous Test in Adelaide. He is also a useful left-hand batsman, a hard hitter and someone who, in form, can change the course of a cricket match at any level. After Ponting won the toss at Perth and decided to bat, not everything went as planned. Ponting and Hughes were out early, followed by Michael Clarke, Shane Watson and Steve Smith, and they were five wickets down with only 69 on the board before Hussey and Haddin again saved the day with 61 and 53 respectively. But Johnson was the real batting star for the Australians, making a brilliant 62 from only 93 balls.   He then proceeded to take 6–38 and the secret was that he suddenly began to swing the ball in to the right-handers. It was the first time he had done this during the summer and he is certainly not the easiest player to coach in the art of swing. Ryan Harris bowled consistently well and was rewarded with figures of 3–59 and 6–47, and the 267-run margin for Australia, with England bowled out in their second innings for only 123, was a wake-up call for Andrew Strauss and his touring party.

Australia's hopes of regaining the Ashes lasted only a short time in the Fourth Test at the MCG. Andrew Strauss won the toss and put Australia in to bat on a pitch which had a greenish tinge on top and there was certainly some moisture below the surface. It was likely to be a tough first session for the Australians and so it proved. England bowled superbly, James Anderson again leading the way by dismissing Clarke, Hussey, Smith and Johnson, while Chris Tremlett got rid of Watson and Ponting in an inspired early spell. Tim Bresnan, brought in to replace Finn, took two wickets and the Australians, all out for 98, were never in the hunt. England amassed 513, with Trott making 168 not out, wicketkeeper Matt Prior a dashing 85 to add to his six catches in the Australian innings and Alastair Cook (82), sharing an opening stand of 159 with his captain. In the Australian second innings Bresnan's 4–50 gave him six wickets for the match and made it a fun Ashes debut for him.

As had been the case in the four earlier matches in the series, the final Test in Sydney showed Australia's batting, bowling and fielding to be inadequate, even shambolic at times. With scores of 280 and 281 during 190 overs of the match, the Australian batting continued to limp along as it had done throughout the summer, whereas England had only the one real stumble in Perth. In the other four Tests they dominated the Australian bowling to the extent that there were team innings of 517–1, 620–5, 513 and 644, which suggests firstly that the batting was outstanding and secondly that the Australian bowlers chosen by the selectors weren't able to lift their game at any stage during four of the five Tests. Strauss and Flower out-thought the Australians, and although the latter were certainly in a rebuilding stage, the time has come when selectors and administrators in Australia need to regroup. They need to do it quickly and with particular accent on programming, so that the basis of Australian cricket, the Sheffield Shield, is again used as the benchmark. At the time of writing, April 2011, the Sheffield Shield often seems merely to be of nuisance value to those running the game. The cricketers are there and are willing; administrators and selectors need to utilise them.

ICC World Cup 2011

The Ashes series finished on Friday, 7 January 2011 and the 50-overs-a-side series between Australia and England began on Sunday, 16 January. The seven-match contest ended in Perth on Sunday, 6 February, with Australia, led by Michael Clarke, winning 6–1. The following evening, the prestigious Allan Border Medal function was held at Crown Towers in Melbourne and the Australian team left for India a few days later to take part in the World Cup.

The Australians were beaten by India at Ahmedabad in the second quarter-final of the World Cup. Ricky Ponting made a very good 104, with Shane Watson, Brad Haddin and David Hussey contributing well. The score of 260 was all right but never likely to put too much pressure on the Indian batsmen. So it proved, with Tendulkar, Gambhir and Yuvraj Singh the stars in India's five-wicket win.

England did no better than Australia in the tournament. They too went out at the quarter-final stage, being beaten by Sri Lanka in a match in which Sri Lanka made 231–0 against an England total of 229–6, even though England had won the toss and had first use of a very good batting surface. For Sri Lanka, Upul Tharanga made 102 and Tillakaratne Dilshan 108. England's best moment came in the 21st match of the event when they played South Africa. Andrew Strauss's team were bowled out for only 171 but, astonishingly, when South Africa had belted their way to 124–3 in 31 overs, the rest of the batsmen collapsed to be all out for 165, with Stuart Broad taking 4–15 in 6.4 overs and James

Anderson 2–16 from 6 overs. It was said to be a 'choke' and that would seem to be an accurate assessment.

India were worthy winners of the final, beating Sri Lanka in a high-class contest at Mumbai after Sri Lanka's Mahela Jayawardene had hit a brilliant unbeaten 103 from only 88 balls and the tailenders, Nuwan Kulasekara and Thisara Perera, had profited from the batting Powerplay to lift the team to 274–6. The pitch was good but this was an imposing target and India were away to a poor start when the brilliant Virender Sehwag was lbw to Lasith Malinga second ball of the run chase. When Sachin Tendulkar was out for 18, also to Malinga, India needed strong leadership and a lot of skill. They found that from their captain M. S. Dhoni, with a willing partner in Gautam Gambhir. They reached their target with ten balls to spare; a brilliant effort and wonderful to watch on television.

There were many heroes in the Indian team, but the one carried from the field to rapturous applause was Sachin Tendulkar. It has been a privilege to watch him from the time I was in the TV commentary position at Old Trafford in 1990, when he became the second youngest cricketer to hit a Test century, to the times I now watch him on the television screen. A great sportsman in every sense of the word.

Appendix I
THE TEAM

A FEW years ago I set out to be a selector for the team I would like to represent me on the field. I paid a great deal of attention to those players I believed had a beneficial effect on the game of cricket, who stood out as champions and were outstanding in their own eras. In addition, I wanted them to have had an influence on cricket itself. I chose three teams, as selectors do when they need to know who will be the twenty-two back-up players in case of injury or loss of form. I decided to choose a twelfth man and a manager as well. Only one of my final choices, Sachin Tendulkar, is still playing.

The Team

1	J. B. Hobbs
2	S. M. Gavaskar
3	D. G. Bradman
4	I. V. A. Richards
5	S. R. Tendulkar
6	G. St. A. Sobers
7	Imran Khan
8	A. C. Gilchrist
9	S. K. Warne
10	D. K. Lillee
11	S. F. Barnes
12th man	K. R. Miller
Manager	F. M. M. Worrell

First of all, the last two names: Keith Miller and Frank Worrell. Miller, with Arthur Morris and Ray Lindwall, was a great mentor to me and a wonderful cricketer so, as you might imagine, I was seeking any way I could to have him in the top eleven players. Miller was the greatest allrounder I played with or against, but you have to remember the timeframe is that Miller retired from cricket in 1956, just two years after Garry Sobers had made his debut against England in the Caribbean. I played against Garry in the 1955 Australian tour of the West Indies and then in the Tied Test series in Australia in 1960–61. He was a marvellous cricketer who was able to do just about anything on the cricket field and to do it in high-class fashion.

For me it was rather freakish good fortune that not only did I play with Miller and against Sobers but I also worked in the commentary box when four great allrounders were in action on the field: Imran Khan, Richard Hadlee, Ian Botham and Kapil Dev. To see any of them would have been splendid, to be lucky enough to watch and talk about all of them was extraordinary luck.

Frank Worrell remains the best person I have ever seen in man-management. In these modern times man-management of a West Indian cricket team is an enormous task. Frank was the first black West Indian cricketer to be allowed to captain a team away from the Caribbean and he was one of the reasons the face of cricket in Australia, and perhaps in other parts of the world, changed for ever because of that Tied Test series. No one but Worrell, and I mean no one, could have done it for the West Indies. He remains one of the outstanding people I met and was the finest captain I played against. I hope he continues to be revered in the West Indies as well. His passing was a great sadness for those who knew him and admired him for all he had done for West Indies cricket and the people of the West Indies. We can only guess at what might have been his future contributions to the game and to people had his life not been cut short by illness, aged forty-two, in 1967.

The players I have listed above form a very strong combination from every point of view; the bowling strength is a splendid mixture of pace, spin and attacking intent. I have met all the team members, even Sydney Francis Barnes, said to be the world's leading bowler of his time. There also seems no doubt that he was at times an awkward character but certainly very straightforward. Having batted against the late Alec Bedser with his devastating leg-cutter, I can imagine the difficulty of facing Barnes, who gripped the ball between the first and third fingers of a very large and strong right hand, and then spun it at pace.

On 23 May 1953, when Australia played the Minor Counties at Stoke-on-Trent, I opened the batting with Colin McDonald and S. F. Barnes bowled the first ball, not of the match but prior to the match. It was a wonderful sight. Barnes was dressed immaculately in his suit and tie; he removed his jacket, but not his tie or braces, took several paces and bowled the ball with a lovely high action on a good length, fractionally outside off stump. He was eighty years and one month old at the time. He passed away fourteen years later and the remarkable thing about him was that everyone who played with him or against him, or observed him from outside the playing area, and who talked to me about him, said categorically that he was the greatest bowler. Certainly the Australians who played against him were of that opinion. At the MCG on 30 December 1911, aged thirty-eight, he took 5–6 from 11 overs in the opening session of play and England won the Test by eight wickets.

I like the look of the batting order. Jack Hobbs and Sunil Gavaskar make a wonderful opening pair and Don Bradman, Viv Richards and Sachin Tendulkar will do a job for the captain before Garry Sobers and Imran Khan look after the middle order. Adam Gilchrist revolutionised the position of wicketkeeper and number seven batsman in Test cricket, but I can only get him in at eight, and then Shane Warne and Dennis Lillee will be a wonderful sight with the ball.

One thing of which you can be certain is that everyone looking at those names will instantly be able to come up with their own better eleven players; that's one of the joys of selecting!

Appendix II
LEGSPIN COACHING

CRICKET is a straightforward game, and everything to do with it should be kept as simple as possible, therefore I have written only two pages on the subject of bowling, particularly legspin bowling. I believe the advice is good and uncomplicated. It could be extended into 200 pages or even a book, but that would mean the youngster wanting to learn to be a legspinner would be wasting a couple of hours of valuable practice time.

For over-the-wrist spin, grip the ball so that the seam runs across the first joint of the index finger and the first joint of the third finger. For the leg-break, and the overspinner or topspinner, the ball is spun off the third finger. The wrist is cocked, but *definitely not* stiffly cocked, which would prevent flexibility and, in delivery, would give you the feeling the ball was simply falling out of your fingers. In delivering the ball, you look at the spot on the pitch on which you want the ball to land, your bowling hand starts level with your face and then describes what could loosely be termed an anti-clockwise circle to the point of delivery.

The position of the bowling hand dictates in which direction the ball will spin.

At the moment of delivery the positioning of the hand is as follows: *Leg-break*: in delivery, the back of the hand is facing your face. (The ball will spin out with the seam rotating in an anti-clockwise direction towards slip.) *Overspinner or topspinner*: in delivery, the back of the hand is facing the sky and then the batsman. (The ball will spin out with the seam rotating in an anti-clockwise direction and towards the batsman.) *Wrong'un*: in delivery, the back of the hand is first facing the sky and then the ground. (The ball will spin out with the seam rotating in an anti-clockwise direction towards fine-leg.) You should be side-on to the batsman and looking over your front shoulder as you deliver the ball. A good guide for a right-hand bowler is that *in delivery stride to a right-hand batsman, your front arm should be in line with fine-leg so you are, in effect, looking 'outside' that front arm.* In 'following through' your bowling hand will finish up going past your front thigh.

This means, if you have done it correctly, your body, at the finish, will have pivoted and rotated anti-clockwise. This 'pivot' is of *great* importance. If you bowl a ball that is too short, you can be almost certain it happened because you were chest-on to the batsman, rather than side-on, and you dragged the ball down into the pitch.

When you are bowling in a net, make a white shoe-cleaner mark the size of a large coin on what seems to you to be a good length: that is, with the ball landing where, if you were batting against a legspinner, *you* would *not* like it to pitch. In your net practice, make sure you bowl against the tail-enders as well as the top-class batsmen. The position of your arm in delivery is of the utmost importance. *Think of looking at a clock face.* Look at the area from nine o'clock to midnight. Nine o'clock is 'round arm', *ten o'clock to eleven o'clock is the perfect position,* between eleven o'clock and midnight is potentially very dangerous, past that perpendicular point is completely useless.

At Scarborough (UK), at the conclusion of the 1953 tour, I had dinner with Bill O'Reilly. It was the evening of Thursday, 9 September, the night before the Australians beat T. N. Pearce's XI by two wickets after three wonderful days of cricket. I distinguished myself with the bat but not the ball, and the latter was the purpose of the dinner. Throughout the tour Bill was unhappy with my bowling and he could see that I was just as unhappy. Over the two hours he listed six things for me to do if I were to become a good bowler. He added that it would take me four years to get it right, and he was correct, 1953 to 1957. In 1957, by using O'Reilly's advice during the Australian tour of South Africa, I took more first-class wickets in that season than any other bowler had done before or since. If O'Reilly *bolstered* my career, a Timaru (NZ) chemist, Ivan James, *saved* my career by dispensing the mixture that completely cured the problem I had with my spinning fingers being ripped to pieces by the stitches on the ball. Below are O'Reilly's six points from 1953.

1. **Plan:** don't bowl six different balls in an over in a desperate bid to claim a wicket so the captain won't take you off. Develop the ability to land a hard-spun leg-break on the *chosen* spot on the pitch, ball after ball.

2. **Patience:** bowling is a tough game and you will need to work on a batsman with your stock ball, sometimes for several overs, before executing your plan. It may not work the first time or even the second.

   If you take a wicket on average every 9 overs in Test cricket, you will have a better strike-rate than any of Warne, O'Reilly, Grimmett and Benaud. If you take a wicket on average every seven overs, you could have the best strike-rate of any modern-day Test bowler, fast or slow.

3. **Concentration:** this must be 100 per cent when you are running in to bowl. The spot on the pitch where you want the ball to land (judged by looking from the *middle* stump at the bowling end to the *middle* stump at the batting end) should be the most important thing in your mind from the moment you turn at your bowling mark. Clarrie Grimmett was the first to use and advise this.

   If someone offered you $10,000 if you could bowl a ball and hit an object 19 paces away, in trying to win the money, would you, as you were bowling, look at the wicketkeeper, the stumps or a batsman's feet?

4. **Economy:** this game is a war between you and the batsmen.

   Is there some very good reason you want to allow him more than two runs an over, thus possibly giving your captain the idea you should be taken off?

5. **Attitude:** calm, purposeful aggression and a clear mind are needed, plus a steely resolve that no batsman will get the better of you over a long period of time. Always remember as well that cricket is a game to be enjoyed and that you are responsible at all times for ensuring play is conducted within the Spirit of the game, as well as within the Laws.

   In other walks of life you will want to be mentally strong and on top of the opposition. Is there some particular reason why, within the Spirit of the game, this should not be the case in your battle with the batsmen?

6. **Practice:** all practice should be undertaken with a purpose.

   You think hard before doing most other important things in life, why should you allow cricket practice to be dull and boring?

Good luck, and enjoy your cricket.

Appendix III
MY LIFE SO FAR

Name: Richard (Richie) Benaud
Born: 6 October 1930
Wife and date of marriage: Daphne, 26 July 1967
Family links with cricket: Lou Benaud, my father, a legspin bowler, was an outstanding country cricketer. He was a schoolteacher who, in 1937, was transferred to Sydney. When I made my debut in Central Cumberland's First XI in 1946, he had already been in the team for nine years. My brother John played for NSW and Australia, was an Australian selector from 1988 to 1993 and also was chairman of the NSW selection committee.
Education: Parramatta High School.
Career outside media: With Daphne as Benaud and Associates Pty Ltd, International Sports Consultants.
Relaxations: Golf, horseracing, reading and the occasional glass of Montrachet or Lynch-Bages.
Broadcasting: BBC Radio 1960. BBC Television 1963–99. Channel 9 Television 1977–. Channel 4 Television 1999–2005. Channel 5 Television Test match highlights 2009.
Newspapers: Journalist with *The Sun* (Sydney newspaper) 1956–1969. *News of the World* 1960–. Freelance journalist 1969–.
Books: *Way of Cricket* (1961); *A Tale of Two Tests* (1962); *Spin me a Spinner* (1963); *The New Champions* (1965); *Willow Patterns* (1969); *Benaud on Reflection* (1984); *The Appeal of Cricket* (1995); *Anything but . . . an Autobiography* (1998); *My Spin on Cricket* (2005); *Over But Not Out: My Life So Far* (2010).
As a player: Played for NSW (1948–64) and Australia (1952–64). The first cricketer (1963) to complete the double of 2,000 runs

and 200 wickets in Test cricket. The first Australian (1961) to complete the double of 2,000 runs and 200 wickets in Sheffield Shield cricket. One of ten Australian cricketers to have scored 10,000 runs and taken 500 wickets in first-class cricket.

Overseas tours: Australia to England 1953, 1956, 1961 (captain), West Indies 1955, Pakistan and India 1956, 1959–60 (captain), South Africa (1957–58).

Extras: Captain of Australia 1958–63 (28 Tests). Awarded the OBE 1962. One of *Wisden*'s Five Cricketers of the Year 1962. In excess of 500 Test matches as a player, watcher and commentator.

Appendix IV
TEST CRICKET AND SHEFFIELD SHIELD DOUBLES

Test Cricket Double
Allrounders who have achieved the Test Cricket double of 2,000 runs and 200 wickets. Asterisk denotes still playing at 1 May 2011.

	Name	Test No	Date
1.	Richie Benaud	548	December 1963
2.	Garry Sobers	685	April 1971
3.	Ian Botham	911	November 1981
4.	Kapil Dev	952	March 1983
5.	Imran Khan	973	December 1983
6.	Richard Hadlee	1013	September 1985
7.	Wasim Akram	1406	March 1998
8.	Shaun Pollock	1544	April 2001
9.	Shane Warne	1593	March 2002
10.	Chris Cairns	1689	March 2004
11.	Chaminda Vaas	1719	October 2004
12.	Daniel Vettori	1798*	April 2006
13.	Jacques Kallis	1800*	April 2006
14.	Anil Kumble	1808	June 2006
15.	Andrew Flintoff	1883	July 2008
16.	Harbhajan Singh	1988	January 2011

Sheffield Shield Double

Allrounders who have achieved the Sheffield Shield double of 2,000 runs and 200 wickets.

	Name	SS Match No.	Date
1.	Richie Benaud	598	December 1961
2.	Alan Davidson	607	February 1962
3.	Johnny Martin	662	January 1965
4.	Terry Jenner	855	November 1974
5.	Ray Bright	1119	February 1985
6.	Peter Sleep	1226	November 1988
7.	Ken MacLeay	1277	March 1990
8.	Greg Matthews	1323	December 1991
9.	Tony Dodemaide	1340	February 1992
10.	Brendon Julian	1498	March 1997
11.	Tom Moody	1560	March 1999
12.	Shaun Young	1618	March 2001
13.	Andy Bichel	1754	November 2005
14.	Ashley Noffke	1820	November 2007
15.	Damien Wright	1849	November 2008

Appendix V

SOMETHING FOR ADMINISTRATORS TO PONDER

Is Twenty20 Cricket splendid entertainment?

1. If more than 20,000 spectators attend matches consisting of only 40 overs and enjoy themselves, then that is wonderful for cricket.

2. Twenty20 techniques will be to the benefit of Test cricket, as has been the case with 50-overs-a-side limited-overs cricket. However, not all Test cricketers will be good at T20 level.

3. Winning the Twenty20 World cup every four years and the 50-overs-a-side World Cup every four years should be the ambition of every cricketer unable to play Test cricket.

An interesting statistic on no-balls in Test cricket

Between 1876–77 and 1968–69 there were fewer than 5,000 no-balls in Test cricket under the back-foot Law.

Between 1969–70 and 2010 there were more than 30,000 no-balls in Test cricket under the front-foot Law.

Is there any common sense associated with England's invention of the front-foot Law?

The white, green, pink, yellow, orange and any other coloured ball

Limited-overs cricket and the World Cup have brought untold riches to administration and worthwhile increases in income to players. Is there a reason relatively little money has been spent on producing a proper white ball? Is it merely laziness, couldn't care less, can't be bothered, or because the easy way out is to use two balls an innings? What investigation has been completed on the composition of the white football used in the 2010 soccer World Cup played in South Africa?

Appendix VI
THE SPIRIT OF CRICKET

Finally, a gentle reminder concerning the Spirit of Cricket.

The Laws of Cricket have been around a long time. They are occasionally changed, most times for the better, occasionally not so.

When Ted Dexter and Colin Cowdrey started talking about a Preamble to the Laws of Cricket, to be named The Preamble – The Spirit of Cricket, their determination was to keep it as simple as possible. That is one reason the Preamble is fewer than 500 words.

Although the whole of the Preamble is important, I have always said that the most important aspects come in Paragraph 1 and Paragraph 6.

Paragraph 1 reads:

Responsibility of captains
The captains are responsible at all times for ensuring that play is conducted within the Spirit of the Game as well as within the Laws.

Paragraph 6 reads:

Violence
There is no place for any act of violence on the field of play.

In my view, if there is any form of violence on the field of play or the laying of a hand by one player on another, the player or players responsible for this should be fined double their relevant match fee and suspended for four matches in the same type of match in which the offence occurred. The captains of the suspended players should be suspended for two matches in the same type of match in which the offence occurred.

INDEX